RAY BROWN

Popular Music History
Series Editor: Alyn Shipton, Royal Academy of Music, London.

This series publishes books that extend the field of popular music studies, examine the lives and careers of key musicians, interrogate histories of genres, focus on previously neglected forms, or engage in the formative history of popular music styles.

Published

An Unholy Row:
Jazz in Britain and its Audience, 1945–1960
  Dave Gelly

Being Prez: The Life and Music of Lester Young
  Dave Gelly

Bill Russell and the New Orleans Jazz Revival
  Ray Smith and Mike Pointon

Chasin' the Bird:
The Life and Legacy of Charlie Parker
  Brian Priestley

Desperado: An Autobiography
  Tomasz Stanko with Rafał Księżyk,
  translated by Halina Maria Boniszewska

Eberhard Weber: A German Jazz Story
  Eberhard Weber, translated by Heidi Kirk

Formation: Building a Personal Canon, Part 1
  Brad Mehldau

Handful of Keys:
Conversations with Thirty Jazz Pianists
  Alyn Shipton

Hear My Train A Comin':
The Songs of Jimi Hendrix
  Kevin Le Gendre

Hidden Man: My Many Musical Lives
  John Altman

Ivor Cutler: A Life Outside the Sitting Room
  Bruce Lindsay

Jazz Me Blues:
The Autobiography of Chris Barber
  Chris Barber with Alyn Shipton

Jazz Visions: Lennie Tristano and His Legacy
  Peter Ind

Kansas City Jazz: A Little Evil Will Do You Good
  Con Chapman

Keith Jarrett: A Biography
  Wolfgang Sandner, translated by Chris Jarrett

Komeda: A Private Life in Jazz
  Magdalena Grzebalkowska,
  translated by Halina Boniszwska

Lee Morgan: His Life, Music and Culture
  Tom Perchard

Lionel Richie: Hello
  Sharon Davis

Long Agos and Worlds Apart:
The Definitive Small Faces Biography
  Sean Egan

Mosaics: The Life and Works of Graham Collier
  Duncan Heining

Mr P.C.: The Life and Music of Paul Chambers
  Rob Palmer

Out of the Long Dark: The Life of Ian Carr
  Alyn Shipton

Rufus Wainwright
  Katherine Williams

Scouse Pop
  Paul Skillen

Soul Unsung:
Reflections on the Band in Black Popular Music
  Kevin Le Gendre

The Godfather of British Jazz:
The Life and Music of Stan Tracey
  Clark Tracey

The History of European Jazz:
The Music, Musicians and Audience in Context
  Edited by Francesco Martinelli

The Last Miles: The Music of Miles Davis, 1980–1991
  George Cole

The Long Shadow of the Little Giant (second edition):
The Life, Work and Legacy of Tubby Hayes
  Simon Spillett

The Ultimate Guide to Great Reggae: The Complete Story of Reggae Told through its Greatest Songs, Famous and Forgotten
  Michael Garnice

This is Bop:
Jon Hendricks and the Art of Vocal Jazz
  Peter Jones

This is Hip: The Life of Mark Murphy
  Peter Jones

Trad Dads, Dirty Boppers and Free Fusioneers:
A History of British Jazz, 1960–1975
  Duncan Heining

Two Bold Singermen and the English Folk Revival: The Lives, Song Traditions and Legacies of Sam Larner and Harry Cox
  Bruce Lindsay

Vinyl Ventures:
My Fifty Years at Rounder Records
  Bill Nowlin

Ray Brown
His Life and Music

Jay Sweet

SHEFFIELD UK   BRISTOL CT

Published by Equinox Publishing Ltd.

UK: Office 415, The Workstation, 15 Paternoster Row, Sheffield, South Yorkshire S1 2BX
USA: ISD, 70 Enterprise Drive, Bristol, CT 06010
www.equinoxpub.com

First published 2025

© Jay Sweet 2025

All rights reserved. No part of this publication may be reproduced or transmitted in any form or by any means, electronic or mechanical, including photocopying, recording or any information storage or retrieval system, without prior permission in writing from the publishers.

British Library Cataloguing-in-Publication Data
A catalogue record for this book is available from the British Library.
ISBN-13   978 1 80050 535 3 (hardback)
            978 1 80050 536 0 (ePDF)
            978 1 80050 603 9 (ePub)

Library of Congress Cataloging-in-Publication Data
Names: Sweet, Jay, author.
Title: Ray Brown : his life and music / Jay Sweet.
Description: Sheffield, South Yorkshire ; Bristol, CT : Equinox Publishing Ltd, 2025. | Series: Popular music history | Includes bibliographical references and index. | Summary: "Ray Brown: His Life and Music is the first full-length biography of Ray Brown, one of the most outstanding practitioners of bass playing in jazz music"-- Provided by publisher.
Identifiers: LCCN 2024017066 (print) | LCCN 2024017067 (ebook) | ISBN 9781800505353 (hardback) | ISBN 9781800505360 (pdf) | ISBN 9781800506039 (epub)
Subjects: LCSH: Brown, Ray, 1926-2002. | Double bassists--United States--Biography. | Jazz musicians--United States--Biography. | Jazz--History and criticism.
Classification: LCC ML418.B76 S84 2024 (print) | LCC ML418.B76 (ebook) | DDC 787.5/165092 [B]--dc23/eng/20240416
LC record available at https://lccn.loc.gov/2024017066
LC ebook record available at https://lccn.loc.gov/2024017067

Typeset by Witchwood Production House Ltd

Contents

Preface vii
Foreword ix

1. The Steel City and the Aluminum Bass
1926–1944 1
2. Working the Territory
1944–1945 13
3. Dizzy, Bird, and Bop
1945–1946 18
4. The Dizzy Gillespie Big Band
1946 27
5. "The New Star"
1947 34
6. Fitzgerald, Granz, and Peterson
1947–1949 41
7. Time Changes: Fitzgerald to Peterson
1950 54
8. The Oscar Peterson Duo and Early Trio
1950–1952 63
9. Navigating the Changes: Transitions
1953 73
10. The Studio Recordings of the First Classic Oscar Peterson Trio
1954–1958 80
11. The JATP Tours and Records
1954–1958 89
12. The Classic Oscar Peterson Trio with Singers
1954–1958 101
13. The Session Recordings of the Classic Oscar Peterson Trio
1954–1958 106
14. Sideman Sessions without Peterson
1955–1958 120
15. Bass Hits! *This Is Ray Brown* and the Poll Winners
1956–1958 127
16. The Second Classic Oscar Peterson Trio (Part 1)
1959–1961 135
17. The Second Classic Oscar Peterson Trio (Part 2)
1962–1965 148

18	Solo and Sideman Sessions 1959–1965	157
19	Commercial Studio Efforts 1966–1969	165
20	Jazz Efforts 1966–1969	172
21	Sessions 1970–1974	182
22	The L.A. Four 1974–1983	195
23	Sideman Sessions 1975–1979	206
24	*Brown's Bag*: Albums Listing Ray Brown as a Leader 1975–1979	216
25	Milt Jackson, Dizzy Gillespie, Monty Alexander, and Notable Sideman Sessions 1980–1984	221
26	The Ray Brown Trio with Gene Harris and Further Leadership 1980–1991	230
27	Sideman Sessions 1985–1989	235
28	Sessions 1990–1994	239
29	Green and Brown: The Ray Brown Trio 1991–2002	243
30	*Some of My Best Friends* and Final Sideman Sessions 1994–2002	252
31	SuperBass 1991–2000	260
32	Coda: Remembering Ray Brown	267

Select Bibliography 278
Notes 280
Index 288

Preface

Writing this book was the most taxing project of my professional career. It was undoubtedly a labor of love: love for the music and the talents of the man who made it. However, writing a biography on a subject such as Ray Brown presents several issues. For one, the work is so extensive that it is difficult to decide what to include and what to leave out. Additionally, unlike many legendary figures in jazz – such as Billie Holiday, Charlie Parker, Django Reinhardt, and Bix Beiderbecke – the Ray Brown story is not a tragic one and does not fit into a film-like storytelling arc. Ray Brown's career and life were well organized and as steady as the bass lines he delivered. The interest in his story and character lies not in reports of abandonment, addiction, abuse, personal tragedy, or untimely death. In fact, much of his uniqueness lay in his ability to avoid the evils that faced a working jazz musician from his era, surrounded as he was by many who struggled with drug abuse and chaos. That is not to say his life story or the man himself was boring. He was not. Ray Brown was charismatic and authoritative. His ability to maintain control and his incredible skill placed him among the world's most influential musicians and most fascinating people.

After much thought, I landed on a few central themes to tie the Ray Brown story together. The first is Brown's development as a bassist and musician. This book describes that development and discusses how his skills and inventiveness on the instrument rank him as one of the most impactful and celebrated bassists of all time. A second central theme concerns how Brown's playing and his choices combined to keep him at the forefront throughout jazz's most creative periods, with the skills and foresight to remain relevant and navigate successfully through the jazz's many subgenres, including swing, bebop, cool jazz, hard bop, Latin jazz, third stream music, and soul. Ray Brown became one of his generation's most sought-after bassists by being versatile. This led to connections to the music's biggest stars, including Louis Armstrong, Duke Ellington, Count Basie, Billie Holiday, Ella Fitzgerald, Lester Young, Coleman Hawkins, Dizzy Gillespie, Charlie Parker, Oscar Peterson, and many more. The stellar list extends beyond jazz: Brown's bass can be heard on hundreds of films, commercial works, and pop records. With well over 2,000 recordings to his name, it is a challenge to find a significant artist that Ray Brown did not record with, especially within jazz. Outside of his work as an accompanying bass player, Brown was also an astute and successful businessman and educator who managed careers, supported young talent, and organized recording sessions and festivals. This book explores Brown's relationships with many of the most famed figures he helped support. It also explores Ray Brown's transitions from sideman to leader and how he handled his many shifting roles and made a success of them.

With a figure as accomplished as Ray Brown, there are difficult choices to make with regard to the depth of discussion about each recording and achievement. I have chosen to emphasize and analyze those recordings I consider particularly impactful – culturally or musically. I also prioritize those many recordings in which Ray Brown served as a leader or co-leader.

I hope this book will encourage more people to take an interest in a man who truly helped elevate the role of the bassist in jazz and a figure who supported many of the essential musicians of the better part of the twentieth century.

Acknowledgments

I want to thank my family and friends for their continued support. Dr. Lewis Porter for his incredible guidance, mentorship, and wisdom; my colleagues at Monmouth University; Sanford Josephson, Renee Coppola, and R.J. Ponce; my entire staff at Sweet Music Academy; and the many fantastic musicians who spent time speaking with me about Ray Brown. A special thank you to Alyn Shipton, who instantly believed in this project and challenged me to be a stronger writer and researcher. Thanks also to Dean Bargh for patient editing and overall production.

Foreword

> People forget how beautiful the bass is in its own register. It's gorgeous if you just give it a chance and listen to it, and let the people hear the bass in its own backyard. Don't take it out of its backyard! You don't have to play it high. Play it down low and let the bass be itself. It's a gorgeous instrument, but I think even some bass players are afraid to trust the bass in its own environment.

Ray Brown spoke those words when I was talking to him, for a radio documentary in 1996, about his most recent work. Yet he could have been referring to any point in his long and illustrious career as one of the premier bassists in jazz history. Whether he was a member of a band, accompanying the jousting soloists on Jazz at the Philharmonic, leading his own groups, directing a studio session, or playing in an intimate chamber setting, his love for his instrument and absolute trust in what it could offer the listener never wavered.

In this book, Jay Sweet takes us through the highs and lows of Ray Brown's life, but also gives us the most detailed study yet of his remarkable recorded legacy. There are other jazz bassists who have recorded more – notably Ron Carter – but none have worked in quite such a variety of styles and genres within the music as Ray Brown; yet he always remained identifiably himself. Over the years, I got to know Ray well, working with him on broadcasts and recordings, and being privileged to be in the studio with him for some of his sessions as a leader. However, Jay's book has opened my eyes and ears to large tracts of his work with which I was unfamiliar, and this has been a most welcome voyage of discovery.

One facet of Ray's character and musical personality that emerges strongly was that he always liked working with a variety of other musicians at his very high level. "Most musicians know each other," he told me.

> Somehow we manage to meet and usually we try to play together somewhere – so you get to play with almost everybody after a while, sooner or later, in one fashion or another. It might be a jam session, a record date, or on a job, in a big band or in a small group, but it means I've played with pretty much everyone in the music business. I guess I got there by virtue of age – if you live long enough, you just get there anyway!

This mixture of the matter-of-fact and the wryly humorous is characteristic of Ray, and Jay Sweet has captured this well in his writing.

Ray Brown also mentored the careers of many younger musicians. These were often players of his own instrument, notably John Clayton and Christian McBride, but also others from across the jazz spectrum, including numerous pianists such as Benny Green, Dado Moroni, and Geoff Keezer. One of his great enthusiasms was the pianist and singer Diana Krall, and, just as she was starting out, he took me to hear her at one of her very first gigs in New York. He told me then that his interest in younger players was because of his own experience getting started, first in Pittsburgh – where he would sneak into the all-night jam sessions at the Black union as a teenager and be welcomed up to the stand – and then in New York, where he was taken under the wing of Dizzy Gillespie. He always valued that encouragement, and never forgot how important it was.

So, join Jay Sweet on this voyage of discovery through Ray Brown's career, and bear in mind something Ray told me when we were discussing his friend and fellow bass player Oscar Pettiford. I asked if Pettiford had favored a particular action for the bass or a special type of string. "No," said Ray,

> It didn't matter how he set up his bass, he got that same sound on any bass he picked up. When you get where you're going as a musician, you have a sound in your ear, and that's the sound you will always get when you pick up an instrument. You don't hear anything else but that sound. That is yours. So that's how, if you happen to hear a record, you know at once who is playing.

And, as ever with Ray Brown, what he was saying about Oscar Pettiford was every bit as true of himself. That sound, and the consummate musicianship that came with it, is what made Ray truly special.

Alyn Shipton
Series Editor, Popular Music Studies

1 The Steel City and the Aluminum Bass
1926–1944

Raymond Mathews Brown, the world's most consummate bass player, was born in Pittsburgh, Pennsylvania, on October 13, 1926. At the time of his birth, Ray Brown's parents, Clifton and Margaret, lived at 2618 Emma Street. Ray was the youngest of three children, which include his sister Marguerite and his brother Clifton Jr. It appears from the details of a 1920 census report that Brown's house was either a two-family home or that the Browns shared the home with a man named Samuel F. Betto and his family. Census reports show that both Brown and Betto were born in Florida, both men's mothers also grew up in Florida, and their fathers grew up in Alabama. Brown and Betto are only three years apart and had young children by 1920. It is also interesting to note that the Browns and the Bettos are the only two Black families listed on the 1920 census living on Emma Street. It seems reasonable to assume that Samuel Betto and Clifton Brown may have known each other before moving into the same residence.

There has been some confusion over the years about Clifton Brown's occupation. In the 1920 census, Clifton is listed as a "tester" in the steel industry. A 1926 city directory listing shows him as a "lab" worker but without providing a company name. A social security document reveals him to be listed from 1927 through 1931 as a "janitor" for the Stevenson Foster Company, a printing business located at 421 7th Ave in downtown Pittsburgh and the same company he worked for in 1936. In a 1930 census report, Brown identifies himself as an "office building porter." In an interview, Ray Brown's wife Cecilia stated, "His father worked in the buildings downtown. I don't know if it was janitorial. It was something like that, and his mother was a homemaker." But Ray himself would often tell interviewers that his father had been a "chef."[1]

While it is certainly possible that Clifton Brown worked two different jobs, no documentation has yet emerged to confirm that he was indeed a career chef. Of course, he might have worked as a chef on occasion or on a date later than 1936. Regardless of the details, the important thing to note is that neither Ray Brown's father nor his close relatives made their living as musicians.

Ray Brown's hard-nosed, blue-collar attitude may well be attributable to his upbringing in Pittsburgh, a city that has always been associated with progress and hard work – which may also help to explain why so many prominent jazz musicians have emerged from this industrial city. This list includes legends like Earl Hines, Roy Eldridge, Billy Strayhorn, Art Blakey, Billy Eckstine, Ahmad Jamal, Henry Mancini, Mary Lou Williams, and Stanley Turrentine. Brown consistently referenced these greats throughout his career and was seemingly honored to be counted among their number.

Located west of the Allegheny Mountains, Pittsburgh is known for its many natural resources and accessibility by river, resulting in a strong association with growth and development. By the 1800s, ironworkers had begun to seek their fortune in Pittsburgh, and as early as 1875 many African Americans had been recruited from the south to work in the mills, a recruitment drive brought about by a union strike by white employees which nearly destroyed Pittsburgh's iron industry. The new Black inhabitants were frequently met with violent hostility by the striking workers. In the middle of the nineteenth century, Andrew Carnegie's Carnegie Steel Company was a symbol of the rise of big business in the Industrial Revolution and dominated Pittsburgh's growing economy. Unskilled laborers remained in high demand and a typical working week consisted of twelve-hour shifts, seven days a week. Labor shortages caused first by World War I and then by another major strike in 1919 gave Black inhabitants an opportunity to secure better jobs with solid wages: the number of Black employees in Pittsburgh increased from 2,500 to 14,610 in less than five years. But when the Great Depression threatened to devastate the steel industry, it was the Black steelworkers who were often the first to be laid off. But with the growing demands for production during World War II, Pittsburgh's steel industry made a triumphant comeback, and the increased demand for labor brought 10,595 Black newcomers to the city. By 1950, Black workers represented 6.5% of the city's workforce.[2]

It is unclear why Ray Brown's father decided to move to Pittsburgh from Florida. Most accounts place Clifton in the category of "unskilled worker," so may have moved to Pittsburgh to secure a better future for himself and his family. While there may be some uncertainty about Clifton's profession, his love for music remains in no doubt. Although neither of Ray Brown's parents was a musician, both adored the sounds of the famous African American big bands and jazz soloists of the time. Music played a considerable role in the Brown household. In a 1993 interview for *Cadence*, Ray Brown recalls his earliest musical memories:

> My parents loved music. In those days, for entertainment, they used to give parties, and my father . . . his favorite piano player, was Fats Waller. That's all I had to relate to. He loved Fats Waller; God bless him. And there was a guy in the neighborhood who used to play the piano badly, but he looked like Fats Waller. He was a big fat guy. He was a truck driver or somethin', but he played parties and sang, put on a hat just like Fats Waller wore and tails, you know. And I used to remember my folks sayin' "After you have a couple of drinks, he sounds better." But he would play

for these parties, and he would sing . . . he sounded a little bit like Fats Waller. You know, "Your Feet's Too Big" and all that kind of thing . . . My mother liked Jimmie Lunceford's Orchestra. She not only liked the way they sounded, but she liked the way they dressed, the way they looked. That was probably the best-dressed orchestra in the business, the Lunceford orchestra. And so, the family was into music. We used to sit around the kitchen table at night and listen to Louis Armstrong on the radio, and we listened to Benny Goodman after he got the sextet with Count Basie and Charlie Christian. So the core was there, I think. And I remember my father said, "I found another piano player I like too." It was Art Tatum. He was right on the track, dead set, couldn't have been any better.[3]

Clifton's affection for jazz piano may have prompted him to provide piano lessons for Ray and his sister Marguerite. Ray Brown's piano studies began around the time he was eight years old. Although he never fully explored his potential as a pianist, he would continue to play the instrument throughout his life. In a 1996 radio interview with Ted Panken, Brown talked about his early piano lessons, which began at ten:

I had piano teachers. The first one was kind of uppity. She would pass me in the street . . . I'd be playing marbles, and she'd stop the car and pick me up and say, "All right, let's go." I had to go home and wash up and come in there [for a lesson]. She'd inspect my nails. She was very proper . . . I told my mother I didn't like that piano teacher. So my mother said, "Well, what do you want to do?" I said, "Well, there's a couple of ladies . . . There's a lady named Ruby Young I want to study with." Ruby Young had her own band. There were two bands in Pittsburgh at that time led by women. One was Gertrude Long and Her Nighthawks, and Ruby Young and her band . . . So Ruby was teaching lessons. I took my first lesson with Ruby Young, and after the lesson, I said, "Can you play some jazz for me?" – She just sat up and played some stride and everything, and then I was very happy. This is what I wanted to do, and this is what I wanted to hear.[4]

When Ray entered Herron Hill Junior High School in 1937, he decided to switch from the piano. His first instrument of choice was the trombone, but basic practicalities got in the way, as Brown recalls: "The school didn't provide one, and my folks couldn't afford one."[5] This meant that if he was to enter the Junior High School orchestra it would be as a pianist. But the orchestra had a surplus of capable pianists, and Brown grew tired of waiting in line to play only one or two songs. Surveying his options, he noticed that the orchestra needed bass players and that the school had an extra bass that was not being used. He recalls:

There were twenty-five pianists in the orchestra, and I was sitting around doing nothing. They had room for three bassists and only had two, so I picked up the bass and started messing with it. The next thing I knew, I was playing in the orchestra. I started bringing it home, copying things off records. I listened to everybody: Armstrong, Basie, Lunceford, Ellington, and Benny Goodman.[6]

Ray had no formal training on the bass and learned mainly from records, progressing quickly. He remembers the instrument he played at Hill Junior High: "It was an aluminum bass. Guys would throw snowballs at it. My buddies would help me carry it home." As his interest grew, he sought out every opportunity to hear new music, and Pittsburgh was undoubtedly able to accommodate his growing need. During Brown's youth, Pittsburgh had two great jazz centers, the Stanley Theater and the Roosevelt Theater. The city also boasted one of the most vital Black music unions and a surplus of beer gardens with jukeboxes that played the latest jazz recordings. Brown recalls:

> We had two theaters in Pittsburgh, one downtown. The Stanley Theater, where all the big-time shows came, like Dorsey, Basie, Ellington, Charlie Barnet, you know. When you got fairly big, you went to the downtown theater. And if you were smaller, like Benny Carter and Fats Waller, Claude Hopkins, Don Redman . . . all of those guys played at the black theater. It was great. It was the Roosevelt. There were shows every week, you know, ten cents.[7]

Brown also remembers having been moved by church music, but the church music that moved him did not come from his family's own house of worship:

> I grew up in a house where everybody went to church on Sunday. My mother cleaned house every Sunday morning. If you came in at eight-ten, at eight-thirty, you left for church. Drunk, sober, or whatever, you left. And it was sort of high-falootin' for those days, black church. When the music started getting a little bit good, if the people started moving a little bit, they would say, oh no, no, no, no, we don't want to sound like the heathens, you know, and they would keep everything sort of imitating the white churches. So I'd be selling newspapers, and I'd go by these little [makeshift churches] – there'd be a little store that closed, and they got soap or something on the window so you can't see through. And there would be twenty, twenty-five people in there, and it would be a piano and a couple of tambourines, and they would be stomping. I mean, I could not leave. I'd just stand out there in the snow and listen. I mean the time and the feeling. You can't buy this. Anyone who wants to play jazz music should experience that because this is the essence . . . and it makes you feel good and makes you move and does a lot of things to you. This is what the race is all about. This is our contribution. This was it. There's something magnificent. and I didn't get that in our church.[8]

Although the young Ray Brown loved music and often went out of his way to discover new sounds, he was not yet sold on music as a possible career choice. As a youth, he was conscious of racial discrimination and had pride in

Ray Brown as a young student.
Photo from High School Yearbook

Pittsburgh's Black community's advancements. In fact, racial discrimination nearly turned him off to music at an early age. Brown explains:

> I wanted to be a fireman because we had in Pittsburgh . . . about three blocks from where I lived, they had the first and only all-Black fire company. That's a visual image for a kid. I went to see the symphony orchestra, which we had to go to see once a month in school, and there were no Blacks; we didn't even have a black janitor over there. So I'm sayin', to see these Black guys riding this truck, we used to just follow them all over the place. They were like heroes. But then I went to the theater and saw the live bands; then I was nailed.[9]

By the time Ray entered Schenley High School in 1940, he was utterly enthralled with the bass and jazz music. With its unique history, it seems as though Brown couldn't have asked for a better center for culture and education than Schenley High. Erected in 1916, it became the first school in the United States to cost over one million dollars to construct. Centrally located in Pittsburgh's Oakland section, it was surrounded by the University of Pittsburgh, Carnegie Mellon University, Carlow University, and Robert Morris University. The university district also housed the Carnegie Museum of Art and Natural History, Carnegie Music Hall, the Carnegie Library, and the Phipps Conservatory. With its Indiana limestone construction, Schenley High School was considered the showplace of the citizens of Pittsburgh. The school even housed a three-manual Skinner pipe organ. From the outset, Schenley's student body derived from various racial, social, ethnic, and economic backgrounds, drawn from Pittsburgh's four major communities: Oakland, Hill District, Bloomfield, and Lawrenceville. By the time Ray Brown was enrolled in 1940, the school was housing 3,012 students.[10]

At Schenley High, Ray was able to join the school's Symphonic Orchestra and further develop his skills in a classroom setting. He also continued to take note of the music he heard on the streets and on recordings. While

Ray Brown with his High School Orchestra. Ray is on the far left, second row from the top.
Photo from High School Yearbook

he enjoyed many of the day's popular swing bands, it was Jimmy Blanton's playing with Duke Ellington's Orchestra that most impressed the young Ray.

Considered the father of modern bass playing, Jimmy Blanton took the upright bass to new heights of experimentation and changed people's attitudes to the bass and its role in a jazz context. Before Blanton, bassists were generally just timekeepers and rarely given extended solo spots. But Blanton emancipated the bass from this stereotype, and his rhythmic and melodic innovations were crucial to the development of Ray Brown's bass playing.

Born in Tennessee in 1918, Jimmy Blanton first started playing a three-string bass in groups led by his mother, who played piano. After attending Tennessee State for a short time, Blanton moved to St. Louis, where he frequently worked with riverboat bands such as that of Fate Marable or the Jeter-Pillars Orchestra. In the autumn of 1939, Blanton got his big break when Duke Ellington discovered him – by this time, Ellington was already renowned as one of the most successful and innovative swing big-band leaders. Ellington hired Blanton for his group as soon as he'd heard the young bassist. At that point, Ellington had been using two bassists: Billy Taylor and Hayes Alvis. Blanton served as a replacement for Alvis, and Taylor, who was likely intimidated by Blanton's prowess, left soon thereafter. Around this time, Ellington also added tenor saxophonist Ben Webster and master arranger Billy Strayhorn. With Blanton, Webster, and Strayhorn, Duke Ellington entered one of his most creative and critically acclaimed periods, which lasted from 1939 to 1941, and in which Jimmy Blanton was often allowed to showcase his talents. Ellington would frequently write specifically for Blanton: on compositions like "Koko," "Jack the Bear," "Concerto for Cootie," "Chloe," and "Sepia Panorama," Blanton is prominently featured and can be heard stating melodies and playing counter-lines.

As well as delivering fine solo work, Blanton also had a unique approach to time. While bassists of his generation would tend to cut their note values short after their initial attack, Blanton held his for their full values. In doing so, he created a whole new approach to walking bass lines. His technique helped propel the band rhythmically, and his rich tone can be heard clearly on many of Ellington's finest recordings. In October 1940, Ellington helped secure Jimmy Blanton's reputation by featuring the bassist on four duet numbers, including the popular ballad "Body and Soul," in which Blanton was given ample opportunity to solo. These duet recordings became personal favorites of Ray Brown, and he studied them carefully as if they were classical etudes. Much later, Brown later got the chance to recreate Blanton's masterworks with Duke Ellington on the 1973 Pablo Records release *This One's for Blanton!*

After a battle with congenital tuberculosis, Jimmy Blanton died tragically in 1942 at the age of only twenty-three. Although his time had been short, Blanton opened the door for future generations of bass players like Oscar Pettiford, Charles Mingus, . . . and of course Ray Brown.

It is imperative for all young jazz musicians to have a figure to emulate. Before musicians can find their distinctive voice, they must first imitate, simulate, and then restructure their influencers' works to create their own distinct sound and approach. It's common to see developing performers form an attachment to a central figure early on, whom they worship as a musical hero. For Ray Brown, Jimmy Blanton became that central figure. If he hadn't studied Jimmy Blanton's recordings so rigorously, Ray would never have been able to create the signature approach and personal style that we recognize today.

Ray Brown's first exposure to Blanton came from listening to records with an older local bassist named Carl "The Crusher" Pruitt. Brown now began to take notice of the great Ellington bassist. In an article for *Jazz Educators Journal*, Brown explains:

> There was this jukebox at the beer garden in town: and the way it was built, the bass notes really boomed out. I mean, you could really hear the slap bass and the short-note lines bassists were playing at the time. All of a sudden, I heard "Things Ain't What They Used to Be" coming out of the jukebox, with these long, flowing, walking bass lines underneath. I found myself listening through every note the bassist was playing on the tune. It was Jimmy Blanton with Duke Ellington. He didn't play like any other bassist before him or at that time. There were long notes in his bass lines. He was a huge influence on me.[11]

On one occasion, Brown even got the opportunity to see his idol:

> I saw him . . . he played a one-nighter. You couldn't hear him very well . . . no amplification, but the records were tremendous, completely revolutionized the whole thing. Just nothing like that went on. His sound and

> his time, his concept of how to play a note. I used to stand there until the very last note, and that's what playin' the bass is to me . . . havin' great time and great notes. You just can't beat that.[12]

Jimmy Blanton was undoubtedly the creator of modern jazz bass playing – and incredibly gifted for his time – but Ray Brown would eventually surpass Blanton's technicality on the bass.

While still in high school, Brown continued to develop at a high level and began to play local gigs with area musicians. He even formed a band with pianist Walter Harper, one of his classmates and a close friend. Brown also joined and hung out at Pittsburgh's Black Music Union, known as the "Musicians' Club." The club was known for its marathon jam sessions, and it was not uncommon to see local heroes like Stanley Turrentine, Art Blakey, Ahmad Jamal, and Joe Harris participating in these celebrated jams. Often nationally known acts would come to the jam sessions to check out the local talent as they moved through Pittsburgh. At the club, Brown could showcase his abilities, and local musicians began to notice.

Soon older musicians began approaching the young bassist about doing some gigs. Brown remembers:

> As a teenager in Pittsburgh, I delivered newspapers, and one of my customers had a band in town that worked a lot. Some of his sidemen were regularly getting drunk by the last set of his gigs and weren't making very good music by the end of the night. So he decided to hire a couple of younger guys like me. One day he said to me, "Come on, we're going to join the Moose Lodge." And I thought, "What for?" But soon, we were gigging in Elks Clubs across Pittsburgh for good money. More money than my father was making in those days. I didn't own a bass, so I always took the school bass home for gigs. My director thought I was practicing a lot until one day; he saw a picture of me in the paper with that bass on a gig! Then he said I couldn't do that anymore, and my father bought me my first bass at a pawn shop for $40.[13]

This account suggests that Brown soon realized that music could be financially lucrative as well as personally rewarding. He quickly became aware that performing music was only one part of becoming a professional. Even as a teen, Brown studied the business side of music with as much dedication as he devoted to learning his instrument. He recognized the importance of developing and maintaining contacts and taking advantage of opportunities presented by chance or else actively pursuing them. Ray Brown quickly understood his worth and value as a focused and talented young musician. Although his recall of the amounts he was paid varies from interview to interview, Brown often talked about how impressed he was to be making money by playing music, and (as in the quote above) he would compare his early income to that of his father. In a newspaper interview, Ray recalled, "My father wasn't making but sixteen bucks a week. I was making six bucks on weekends – eight bucks sometimes."[14]

There is no question that Ray Brown's Pittsburgh upbringing and the many talented musicians situated in that city shaped his career. In interviews, Brown sometimes mentioned names of local bandleaders he worked with although he rarely elaborated. Two musicians who worked with Ray Brown in Pittsburgh were Walt Harper and Cecile Brooks Sr. In interviews, both men offered a further glimpse into Brown's teenage development, the bands he worked with, and the inspired Pittsburgh music scene of the early 1940s. Pianist, recording artist, and club owner Walt Harper had fond memories of Brown. He explains:

> We were in school together, high school. Ray was very astute. He was always smart. He wasn't athletic. He was always with his bass and taking lessons; Ray was a genius even here. His father and mother kept him very close to them . . . He had to be home at certain times at night. They were pretty strict with him. He had a brother who was an accountant. He was a very smart guy who died before Ray, and he had a sister. She just recently passed away.

Harper later discusses an early group he had with Brown:

> Our earliest group started as R&B, and then we ended up in jazz. Ray and I formed the band in High School, and I went on and kept the group up until now . . . At one time, we had a trombone and tenor and then trumpet and tenor . . . We did popular material of the time. Ray was always good. I'll tell you what, we were in school, and I used to write little figurations for him, and Carl Pruitt came up to rehearsal once and said, "Nobody could play that." So, Ray played it for him, and Carl brought the whole Benny Goodman Band up to hear him play, and that was the first time we knew he was a genius.[15]

Cecile Brooks Sr. was one of Pittsburgh's most celebrated drummers. He also had fond memories of Ray Brown; he explains:

> He went to school with my sister. He's a little older than I am. They dated in high school. With Ray, I was an up-and-coming young drummer. We played together around here in the early forties and fifties. We remained friends throughout the years. I looked up to him, but still, we were in the same boat because we were all in Pittsburgh trying to make it. Just knowing him and the little things I played with him in town here was just beautiful. Ray has always been pleasant, always smiling and conscientious about his music. He was a great musician, and he was just Ray. He was sort of a jolly guy who just loved to play. He was serious about his music.[16]

When asked about the Pittsburgh music scene, both Harper and Brooks mentioned the union and the celebrated jam sessions that took place there. Harper recalls:

> There was a club [The Musicians' Club] that when any of the musicians would come to town, Lionel Hampton, any of them, you name them . . . Count Basie. They always hung out there at night, and we would have sessions there. It was one of those clubs that was hard to describe because everybody played there, including Thelonious Monk.

Brooks elaborated:

> We had one of the nicest musicians' clubs in the country. We would go down there, and everyone could have rehearsals. We used to have jam sessions, and we'd start at four or five o'clock in the evening. We would play all night. Guys would go home, go to sleep, and come back the next day, and guys would still be playing the same jam session. Somebody with a big band would come into town, and naturally, they would want to find out where the musicians were. They would come to the Musicians' Club and see big Tommy Turrentine and other musicians. There were so many guys who could play, and we would just wipe those guys out. People from all over the country would come here and talk about us.
>
> There wasn't a lot of money, but there were a lot of places to play. We practiced all day, and we'd go out on jobs, and it was like going to a feast. It was for the joy of the music, and everybody enjoyed each other, and everybody tried to learn. Everybody would teach each other, not only the Black musicians but also the white musician. The white musicians were friends with us during that time, and we all got along beautifully. We respected each other. We played together. Everything changed later on, but during that time, it was a different thing.

When asked about some of the local musicians and groups Ray Brown might have worked with, they mention an older swing saxophonist named Henry Foster and his group, the Krazy Katz. Harper remembers working with Brown in the group and states that: "Ray and I came up under him, and he did many things like the Elks Club and the Masonic Temple. Things like that, and he knew a bunch of numbers. He had four pieces. He had three rhythm [section instruments], and he played sax." Both Harper and Brooks also remember playing with a group led by a man known as Little Charlie. Brooks recalled:

> Little Charlie was a guy who was like four feet tall. When I was fourteen years old, he was the one that I'd sneak out the window at night and play at a place called the Melody Bar. Ray Brown would sit in, and we'd play down there. Little Charlie was a little saxophone player, and he sort of taught me, and I guess Ray, too, because he was older than us, you know. He was instrumental.

They also remember working with Brown in a "commercial group" led by saxophonist Leroy Brown and his group, the Brown Buddies. They also recall working with Fred Evert's Big Band, which, according to Brooks, was the "only black big band at that time that got any substantial (work)." Other mentioned names included pianist Tiny Trent and drummer Honey Boy Minor. Brooks also mentioned a pianist he knew as Fritz Jones, who later came to fame after adopting his Muslim name Ahmad Jamal.

During his 1996 interview with Ted Panken, Brown recalls his formative years in Pittsburgh.[17]

When did you start gigging on the bass?

When I got to high school, a guy who I used to deliver papers to named Henry Foster was looking for some guys, and I said, "Hey, I play the bass, and my friend plays the piano" – a guy named Walt Harper. He hired both of us, and we started working with them on Friday and Saturday and Sunday, making $3 a night. That was a lot of money then. There were no taxes either.

What type of places would you play, and who was coming to hear you?

Just local people. I don't know . . . A lot of that stuff is dim now in terms of me giving you accuracy about the people showing up. All I can remember is playing and learning the tunes.

Was it piano-bass-and-drums?

Piano, bass and drums, and saxophone.

Do you remember what kind of repertoire you were playing at the time? Did you ever have room for features for yourself?

Not really, no. But we played just the tunes of the day. "Tea For Two," "Satchel Mouth Baby," and "Honeysuckle Rose."

And all this time, you're still going to the theaters to hear the big bands?

Oh yeah. When I got to high school, we started playing hooky to hear . . . We were listening to Lester Young, Bud Powell with Cootie Williams, Oscar Pettiford with Charlie Barnet, way before he ever joined Duke Ellington.

In Pittsburgh, what was the top level of bass playing you could hear when you were coming up?

I guess the top bass players were a guy named Bass McMahon, who wound up playing with Eckstine's band. Then a guy who wound up here in New York, who they called Crusher, named Carl Pruitt, and he was with Roy Eldridge's band. They were the top guys in Pittsburgh.

After making his first public appearance at seventeen and working with local figures, Ray Brown was soon known around town. While still in high school, established bands began to seek his services. Brown was anxious to join a touring unit and found his first opportunity with territory bandleader Jimmy Hinsley. Brown recalls:

> So Hinsley came through [Pittsburgh], and he was jammin', and I came up and sat in, and he said, "Hey kid, I like the way you play, you looking for a job?" I said, "Not until I get out of school." I'd already been through a scene with Cootie Williams' band. They had this big show that came into the Stanley Theater downtown. Cootie Williams' Band with Ella Fitzgerald and the Ink Spots and Ralph Brown's Show. The bass player got his draft notice somewhere on the road, and he refused to acknowledge it, and when the band hit Pittsburgh the first day, they picked him off and took him directly to camp. So they had to get a bass player from Pittsburgh. There was a good bass player, his name was Carl Pruitt, and he did the Williams Theater, but the jacket that the bass player had didn't fit Pruitt, who was too husky for it. The jacket fit me, and they offered me the job. I went home and told my folks that I had this marvelous job, my big chance, and my mother said, "You can't go to work 'till you finish school; your brother is going to college. Don't you want to go to college?" I said, "No." She said, then you must finish high school." My father said, "Yep, you got to." And so, I had a double coronary and three fits, and then I got over it. So, when Hinsley came along and offered me a job, instead of saying, "Yes," I just said, "No, I got to finish school first." So, he said, "When do you finish school?" I guess it was about six months, so he said that when I finished school, I could join his band. I finished school in June, and in July, I joined him in Buffalo, New York.[18]

Following his graduation in 1944, Ray Brown left Pittsburgh to tour with Jimmy Hinsley. Ray Brown's yearbook quote read as follows: "The right man is the one who seizes the moment."

2 Working the Territory
1944–1945

The road was a crucial experience for young jazz musicians like Ray Brown. Here, developing musicians could bond with and learn from more experienced performers. By showcasing their abilities in different territories, they could also catch the eye of other, perhaps more prominent, bandleaders. It was not uncommon for musicians to move quickly from band to band in pursuit of a higher profile or better pay. Being on the road could be an exciting proposition at times, but there were negatives, too, such as long, uncomfortable bus rides, poor living conditions, and lengthy periods of separation from family and friends. African American musicians in the 1940s also faced bigotry and segregation, especially while traveling into the South. Besides which, touring musicians ran the risk of being fired at a moment's notice: bandleaders were sometimes forced to fold mid-tour when their finances could no longer hold up – in many cases, they were at the mercy of crooked promoters and club owners who took advantage of traveling acts. So road musicians could find themselves out of a job with little money and no means of getting home.

It was in Buffalo, NY, with the Jimmy Hinsley Sextet, that Ray Brown, fresh out of high school, began the first of his many road experiences. Little is known about Hinsley other than that he was a territory bandleader who played the saxophone. Pianist Walt Harper remembers the band as a rhythm and blues group, and he also recalls the Turrentine brothers from Pittsburgh being members. According to Ray Brown, Hinsley also performed in Wilmington, Baltimore, and Indianapolis. This was a crucial experience in Ray Brown's development: not only was he getting his first taste of the road but it was during this time that he met pianist Hank Jones. Ray recalls:

> When I joined Jimmy Hinsley's band in '44 when I first left home, we went into Buffalo, New York. We were at a nightclub called the Moonglow. We were there for a couple of months, and I got a room at the YMCA . . . The second day I was at the "Y," I think I slept late, and I came down just after lunch. I came down the steps that passed the cafeteria, and the cafeteria door was closed. There was a piano in the cafeteria; I had seen it, you know. I was comin' down these steps, and I heard this record that my father had bought when I was a kid of Art Tatum playing "Begin the Beguine," and I paused outside the door. I just stood there and listened to it. It got to the end, and it kept going. I opened the door and went in, and

here's a guy sitting there playing the piano. I said, "Hey man, I thought that was a record." He said, "You know this record?" I said, "Yeah, Art Tatum, we have it at home." Then I introduced myself. It was Hank Jones, and he was on a gig playing with another band in Buffalo. So we became good friends. I used to bring my bass home every night, and we used to practice in the cafeteria.[19]

Hank Jones tells a similar story.

> We first met in Buffalo, NY. I was there working at a little bar called the Anchor Bar with a trio. Not my trio but with another group, and Ray was working in another part of town with a band from Pittsburgh. We were both staying at the YMCA, and there was a piano in the dining room. Every day we would be down there and have lunch, and after, we would have a little jam session. At the time, he was seventeen years old. That was back around 1943 or '44, I guess. That's how we first met. We met accidentally. I was down there working on the piano; he came down to hear me play. He went to get his bass . . . He was a Tatum fan as I was at the time, and I still am. We started to compare notes and so forth, and that is how our relationship and friendship began. I've known him all those years . . . Hinsley was the group I think he was with when I met him. I think they were out of Pittsburgh. I'm not sure. They might have been from someplace in Boston. I don't recall ever hearing the group, as a matter of fact. When they worked in Buffalo, we never got a chance to hear them because we worked the same hours they did.
>
> What happened was that after we ended our sets at the same time each night, we would meet and go over to hear Art Tatum if he was in town . . . At the time we met [Ray Brown], he was young, eager, and inquisitive. A very, very dedicated player and musician. I believe that those characteristics carried on throughout his career. Later on, I believe he became more, let's say, assertive. He became a leader in his own right, but when you become a leader, you naturally become a little more assertive.[20]

As with most of Ray Brown's essential connections, it was a chance meeting that led to a long-standing musical partnership. Ray and Hank would work together at different periods throughout their impressive careers. While pianists like Hank Jones were developing in Tatum's mold, the bass world had lost its most influential figure when Jimmy Blanton died in 1942. Blanton's unfortunate passing meant that Brown needed to find a new leading influence, and it was while he was on the road with Hinsley that Ray Brown discovered the great bass innovator Oscar Pettiford. In a 1976 interview for *DownBeat*, Brown recalled, "When I was with Jimmy Hinsley, I heard Oscar Pettiford's solo on 'The Man I Love' on a Baltimore jukebox. I listened to it and said, 'Jesus Christ! If that's the way they are playing bass in New York, I'm not going there.'"[21]

Oscar Pettiford was born on September 30, 1922, in Okmulgee, Oklahoma, on a Native American reservation. As a teen, Pettiford joined his ten siblings in a family band that gained popularity in Minneapolis. Around this time, Oscar met the exceptional bassist Milt Hinton, who had found fame as a long-standing member of Cab Calloway's orchestra, beginning in 1936. Hinton took a keen interest in the young bassist and served as Pettiford's mentor during a pivotal time in which the latter was questioning whether he actually wanted to pursue music. Thanks to the encouragement of Milt Hinton and the recordings of Jimmy Blanton and others, Oscar Pettiford found inspiration to continue.

Following a stint with Charlie Barnet in 1942, in 1943 Pettiford joined Roy Eldridge's band. Around this time, the bassist was a key figure in the development of bebop as a style, co-leading a group with Dizzy Gillespie in 1943 and leading legendary jam sessions around New York City. Pettiford soon gained notice as New York's newest bass star when he developed a more virtuosic approach to bass soloing in which he replicated the vocabulary and technicality of the top saxophone and trumpet soloists of his day. In doing so, Pettiford earned recognition as the finest technician and most influential bassist since Jimmy Blanton.

In 1945, Pettiford joined the Duke Ellington Orchestra, replacing the often-overlooked bassist Junior Raglin, who had joined Ellington after the onset of Blanton's fatal illness in 1941. During this period, Pettiford also performed with Woody Herman, Charlie Shavers, and Louie Bellson and led several of his own bands.

Oscar Pettiford was also one of the few bassists of his generation to compose for jazz, and his originals – like "Tricrotism," "Bohemia after Dark," and "Laverne Walk" – have been studied by generations of jazz bassists and are considered bebop classics. Pettiford eventually settled in Europe in the late '50s; in 1960, aged only thirty-seven, he died of a virus closely related to polio.

Oscar Pettiford is still remembered for his many bass innovations. His technical prowess opened up new melodic possibilities for the bass, and his ability to deliver horn-like improvisations and melodic lines at rapid tempos inspired a generation of bassists, which included Ray Brown, Charles Mingus, and Paul Chambers. Ray Brown had a competitive nature; while he was with Hinsley, he had grown determined to match Pettiford's talents and anticipated a time when the two would come face to face. In preparation, he studied Pettiford's solos as well as those by other top bassists like Slam Stewart and Milt Hinton.

Ray remained with Jimmy Hinsley's group for somewhere between six and eight months, a tenure that was abruptly halted when the band got stranded in Indianapolis. He was faced with two options: go home to Pittsburgh or remain in Indianapolis. For the time being, Brown decided to stick around Indianapolis.

In his *Cadence* interview, Brown explains:

> I had just left home and didn't want to go back, so I decided to stick it out. About three or four of us musicians conned a guy who had a nightclub that was closed into opening it up. We did pretty good business, so we were working three or four nights a week, and then Snookum Russell came to town. Indianapolis was a place where a lot of territory bands came in, and musicians stayed around there because they could always get picked up. So Snookum Russell was out for a couple of months. He had some tours going, so he picked me up and a couple of other guys. We then went to Pittsburgh, and we played in a theater. I got four or five guys from Pittsburgh: drummer Joe Harris, trombone player William Davis, Tommy Turrentine, Stanley's older brother, so I got a bunch of guys jobs.[22]

Snookum Russell, Brown's next significant employer, was a bandleader and a pianist from New Orleans who had a scaled-down big-band unit. Legendary trombonist J.J. Johnson and trumpet star Fats Navarro were both members of the Snookum Russell Orchestra at one time. Russell's orchestra was known for its extensive touring; when Brown was in the group, the unit traveled throughout the South and passed the Mason–Dixon line. Brown was very quickly made aware of the horrible conditions many African Americans suffered in the South. When *DownBeat* asked him about the tour, Brown judged the conditions to be "Bad! There is no other way to describe it – bad."[23]

Throughout his life, Brown was cautious when speaking about racism to the print media. In fact, Brown always chose his words in much the same way as he chose his notes on the fingerboard – carefully. Perhaps he elected to monitor himself when discussing racism because he had many white friends and business contacts. Brown was always business-minded, and he may have felt that a militant stance on the subject would be detrimental to his career.

Snookum Russell was well aware of Brown's growing talents and quickly promoted his new young bass phenomenon. He advertised Ray Brown as the "World's Greatest Bass Player," an epithet sure to gain Brown some attention. One of Russell's main attractions was a feature between Brown and tenor saxophonist Charles Harmon. The two would walk out in front of the bandstand and play a version of "Sometimes I'm Happy," recreating Slam Stewart and Lester Young's solos from their famous 1943 recording, Ray bowing his solo as per the original. The act also included Snookum Russell and Ray Brown playing pieces drawn from the duo recordings of Jimmy Blanton and Duke Ellington. Unfortunately, there are no recordings of Brown's performances at this crucial juncture of his career.

In his 1996 interview with Ted Panken, Ray Brown reflected on his time with Snookum Russell's band:

> I guess you could call it almost a commercial jazz band. He covered the hits of the day. If Lucky Millinder had a hit with Bull Moose Jackson, "Who Threw the Whiskey in the Well," we would be doing that. What happened was, I joined Snookum, and then he found out that I knew all of this stuff

that Jimmy Blanton and Duke Ellington had done, so he started doing it between the two of us – because he, of course, loved Duke Ellington. So he started featuring me doing the Blanton stuff. There was a saxophone player in that band named Charles Carman(?) out of Sandusky, Ohio, and this guy was a Lester Young freak. He knew everything Lester Young ever made – every note! When I met him, and we were talking (after he'd been in the band for a little while), he said, "Do you know anything about Prez?" I said, "Sure." He said, "What do you know about him?" I said, "Well, what do you want to know?" He said, "Do you know any of his solos?" I said, "Call one."[24]

After only a few months with Snookum Russell, Brown was setting his eyes on New York, the epicenter of jazz creation and development since the late 1920s. It may have been tenor saxophonist Eddie "Lockjaw" Davis who inspired Brown to relocate: in the Dizzy Gillespie documentary *To Bop Or Not To Be*, Ray Brown remembers:

> I saw Lockjaw Davis in St. Louis. He was with Andy Kirk's band. He told me, he said, "You play good, kid." He said, "You should go to New York," and I said, "Oh, I don't know if I'm good enough for that," and he said, "No. Go ahead, you go. You'll work it; you'll make it."[25]

3 Dizzy, Bird, and Bop
1945–1946

In 1945, while working in Florida with Snookum Russell, Ray Brown and at least four of his bandmates decided to relocate to New York. His bandmates all backed down at the last minute, but eighteen-year-old Brown took his bass, some sandwiches, and his dreams of becoming the world's greatest bassist on a railroad coach to New York, the jazz center of the world. As with most of Brown's decisions, there was careful thought and pre-planning behind this move. To generate interest, Brown was able to use Snookum Russell's advertising to his advantage. Brown explains:

> I took about sixty or eighty of those flyers [with the "World's Greatest Bass Player" hook] and mailed them with a letter to these agencies in jazz magazines telling them I was looking to come to New York for a job, but I gave my home address in Pittsburgh. Then I called my mother three or four weeks later, and she said I had gotten three job offers from big bands and the most prominent one was from Andy Kirk's Orchestra. [Brown also received offers from Lucky Millinder's and Billy Eckstine's Orchestras.][26]

Ray Brown vividly remembered the trip to New York.

> I arrived in New York after a day-and-a-half train trip. And I had my luggage, which was one suitcase, and my bass . . . I got off the train, I got on a subway, and I went up and got off at 168th and Amsterdam. My mother's sister, my aunt, lived in Amsterdam at 166th. I carried my bass and bag down the two blocks, and then she lived up on the third floor. I went up there. She had told my mother that if I came to New York, I could stay with her until I got myself situated. She had a son the same age as I, and she had a couple of kids. So I put my stuff in a room and then she gave me some dinner. I had dinner with my two cousins and my aunt. While we were eating dinner, I asked my cousin, "Do you know where 52nd Street is?" He said, "Sure." I said, "Can we go down there after we eat?" He says, "Yeah, I'll take you down." So we finished eating and left, got on another subway, and went downtown.
>
> He took me around there, and I looked in the first place; it was the Three Deuces. I don't remember who was playing there at the time . . . I think it was Don Byas and Benny Harris. They had two groups in each club. And then the headliner at the Downbeat, the next club, was Billie Holiday and Art Tatum. Not too shabby. The next club was Coleman Hawkins and

he was playing with a rhythm section of Denzil Best, Al McKibbon, and Thelonious Monk. He [Coleman Hawkins] only showed up on Saturday night and played "Body and Soul" and left again . . . At intermission at the club, there was a singer named Billy Daniels. The guy playing piano for him was a guy that I knew called Hank Jones, who is one of the premier pianists even as I speak. Hank and I lived in the YMCA in Buffalo years before, when I first left home, my first job. So I said to my cousin, "Come on, let's go in there; I'm going to see if I can find Hank because I know him." So I walked in, he was in the back, and we talked for a few minutes, and he said, "Sit down," and we sat at an empty table.

We're talking about what we had been doing since we hadn't seen each other, and he looked up, and he said, "Oh, Dizzy Gillespie is coming through the door." I said, "Wow." I said, "Introduce me to him, I want to meet him." So Dizzy came in, and he said, "Hey, Diz." Diz walked over. He said, "I want you to meet a friend of mine." He said, "The kid's a bass player, just got into town." Dizzy looked at me, and he said, "Yeah, how are you?" He said, "Can you play?" . . . Hank said, "Yeah, he's a great bass player." So Dizzy said to me, "You want a job?" I said, "Yeah." So he gave me a card out of his pocket and said, "Be at my house tomorrow at seven pm." I had already gotten a job. I had three job offers with three bands that I had sent away for . . . [but] I go to Dizzy Gillespie's house the next day, and there are four guys there: Dizzy Gillespie, Charlie Parker, Bud Powell, and Max Roach.

Charlie Parker, I had seen with Jay McShann. Bud Powell, I had seen with Cootie Williams' band. Max Roach, I had seen in the theater with Benny Carter, and Dizzy I had seen with Cab [Calloway]. So I had seen all these people, and I had heard them on record, but this was the first time [I met them]. Then they started to play. It scared me to death. I mean, I never heard anything like this before. But they played really fast, and that's something I could do. So I guess maybe that's why they kept me. But anyway [Dizzy] said, "Okay, you'll do." We are going to work, and he told me when. I went back up to my aunt's the next day, and I called my mother. She said, "Which one of the bands did you take?" I said, "Uh, I didn't take any of those." She said, "Well, what did you do?" I said, "I'm with Dizzy Gillespie." She said, "Who?"[27]

Ray Brown's first meeting with Gillespie took place on October 12, 1945, one day before his nineteenth birthday. When Ray first met Dizzy Gillespie, the trumpeter was preparing a bebop band for an upcoming six-week engagement at Billy Berg's Supper Club in Los Angeles, where he intended to introduce his group to a West Coast audience. Although the circumstances under which Brown was hired for Gillespie's band might seem like pure chance, he proved to be the perfect bassist for Gillespie and Parker's energetic music: not only could he play fast and long, but his technical development meant he was able to improvise in a bebop context. Before meeting Gillespie, Brown had little familiarity with the bebop style and repertoire. But he did possess a willingness to learn, and Gillespie was willing to teach. Dizzy Gillespie soon became Ray Brown's most influential mentor.

Ray Brown got the job because Curly Russell, Gillespie's previous bassist, had decided that he needed a break from the road. So, after only two days in New York, not only had Ray secured a job but he had been accepted into an exclusive school of sound scientists aiming to advance the style they had developed.

Before the California trip, the band's line-up was Ray Brown, pianist Bud Powell, drummer Max Roach, Charlie Parker, and Dizzy Gillespie. But a series of dramatic events resulted in only three of these five making the trip; and only two of those would return from the West Coast. Ray Brown remembered performing with the original all-star line-up before they left. In the following interview transcription, interviewer Phil Schaap appears to be shocked to receive this information:

> **Brown:** We worked in New York at the Spotlite, we played a theater in Boston, and we played the Brown Derby in Washington, DC. These were warm-ups getting ready for California.[28]
>
> **Schaap** (excited)**:** With Bird [Parker] and Bud?
>
> **Brown:** Yeah. And then all the problems began. Prior to us leaving, Bud and Max both ran into some personal problems, so we had to take Al Haig and Stan Levey. We took a train out to Los Angeles. We rehearsed on the train with the new guys.

Although Brown does not elaborate on Powell's and Roach's "personal problems," he did mention that the "problems" involved drugs. This is plausible, since both Max Roach and Bud Powell are known to have struggled with substance abuse. Drummer Stan Levey and pianist Al Haig were both gifted musicians who had worked with Parker and Gillespie at the Three Deuces on 52nd Street beginning in March 1945 and were familiar with the repertoire. Gillespie presented his new music to a California audience while dealing with the pressures of both incorporating new band members and with presenting an integrated band, something that was still relatively controversial in 1945. Before leaving for California, Gillespie also picked up vibraphonist Milt Jackson to enhance the group's sound. Ray and Milt became fast friends, forming a musical connection that would endure for decades.

Dizzy Gillespie's Rebop Six opened at Billy Berg's Club on December 10, 1945, and remained there until February 3, 1946. Tenor saxophonist Lucky Thompson was also added to the band during the six-week engagement. As he continued his interview with Schaap, Brown recalled the Billy Berg experience:

> **Brown:** The music was so far out to the people in California that they called us "The Men from Mars." Billy Berg said, "Unless you guys can

commercialize a little more, I'm going to have to close this engagement out." We were supposed to be there for six weeks, and he was trying to close us out after two weeks. He said, "You know, you guys are going to have to sing or do something." So, Charlie Parker wrote some little arrangements where everybody in the band was singing "When I Grow Too Old to Dream" and a couple of other things. He wrote these arrangements out himself, and then they brought in [saxophonist] Lucky Thompson also . . . We completed the six weeks.

They had three acts on the bill. They had Slim Gaillard, but it wasn't Slim and Slam [Stewart]; it was Slim and Bam [Brown], which was more comedy than music . . . Then they had a piano player also called Harry the Hipster Gibson who would sing songs like "Who Put the Benzedrine in Mrs. Murphy's Ovaltine?" [Laughs] All these people were very popular in California and were well liked.

Schaap: So they had two novelty acts and one band playing new jazz?

Brown: Yeah, bebop. It's like having Chinese food in a kosher restaurant, you know.

Schaap: If Bird wasn't always there, you always had the six pieces? Is that the story, the background behind Lucky Thompson being hired?

Brown: Well, no. Billy Berg thought that the tenor saxophone would make us sound a little more commercial and that Lucky would play a style more to the liking of the people who came into the establishment. The problem, of course, was that Dizzy and Charlie Parker played as one person, so it's very hard to fit someone new in there anyway. The only guy that I ever heard that felt comfortable with the two of them was Don Byas, who used to come to sit in with us every night on 52nd Street.

Schaap: Do you remember anything more about these vocal numbers . . . ?

Brown: We just sang all together, you know. I mean there wasn't a singer in the band, so we had to sing together.

Schaap: Was Billy Berg satisfied [with the singing]?

Brown: Well, all I can tell you is that we stayed the six weeks. So something worked out, you know. We were just trying to make this thing last so we wouldn't have to go back [to New York].

Schaap: Were you miffed, though, a little bit about this foolish [suggestion]? He should have let the Dizzy Gillespie Band be the Dizzy Gillespie Band.

Brown: Well, if he brought us all the way from New York, he should let them do what they do, you know. He must have had some idea what they did before he brought them out there unless someone sold him on this. I don't think Billy Berg was somebody who could assess music anyway. Billy Berg probably listened to what people said when they heard the music, but I don't think he had any ear for what was really going on.

At the time of Gillespie's trip to California, bebop was still a relatively new sound to West Coast ears, albeit – despite what older research and dramatic representations like the movie *Bird* might have us believe – not entirely unknown. The presence of East Coast innovators like Gillespie and Parker, bop's most innovative experimentalists, generated a great deal of interest on the West Coast, especially among musicians and enthusiasts, but it wouldn't have been the first time most had heard it.

Alyn Shipton, in his book *On Jazz*, shares interview excerpts from trumpeter Clora Bryant, who recalls hearing musicians like Howard McGhee, Teddy Edwards, and drummer Roy Porter playing bop at the Downbeat Club on Central Avenue in early 1945. Teddy Edwards also reflects that "there was music all up and down on Central Avenue." He remembers sitting in with local musicians like saxophonists Wardell Gray and Sonny Criss, who were already experimenting with bebop vocabulary in clubs and sessions before Parker and Gillespie's arrival.[29]

In fact, Gillespie's sextet was not even the first group to present modern material at Billy Berg's club. John Chilton, in his book *The Song of the Hawk: The Life and Recordings of Coleman Hawkins*, recounts that Coleman Hawkins' band with Howard McGhee, Oscar Pettiford, Charles Thompson, and Denzil Best played bop material at the club at their opening engagement on February 1, 1945. In the book, McGhee states, "I guess Coleman was the one who opened the West Coast up as far as modern sounds in jazz."[30]

Working with Gillespie and Parker in Los Angeles gave Ray's reputation a considerable boost. On December 29, 1945, Dizzy Gillespie's sextet was recorded at NBC Studios in Hollywood for the radio program *Jubilee*, which was broadcast for the Armed Forces Radio Service. Hosted by the jive-talking Ernie "Bubbles" Whitman, the *Jubilee* program was the first all-African American variety show. The show premiered in the late 1930s on CBS Radio but later moved to NBC, and *Jubilee* had become a favorite of troops overseas during World War II. The *Jubilee* session is the first recorded evidence we have of Ray Brown. It reveals Brown's ability to play fast cohesive walking bass lines behind two of the greatest masters of jazz: Gillespie and Parker.

The sextet performed only three tunes for the broadcast. The first was a tightly arranged original Parker–Gillespie composition called "Shaw 'Nuff," taken at a breakneck tempo to showcase the two maestros at their best. The group followed with Gillespie's "Groovin' High," a modern take on Paul Whiteman's hit "Whispering." Without introduction, Milt Jackson is added for a version of "Dizzy Atmosphere," a Gillespie original based on the chord changes of George Gershwin's classic "I Got Rhythm" ("rhythm changes": a common thirty-two-bar chord progression used for many jazz standards). The band plays the melody of this selection at an impressively fast tempo. Comparing these three tracks with Gillespie and Parker's earlier recordings from the year, it is clear that Ray Brown is already proving his ability to match and maybe even surpass the group's original bassist Curly Russell.

While in Los Angeles, Ray Brown also had the opportunity to enter a studio for the first time when he was invited to record with the Dodo Marmarosa Trio for the Atomic Records label on January 11, 1946. Like Ray Brown, pianist Dodo (Michael) Marmarosa was born in Pittsburgh. Since Marmarosa was only one year older than Brown, it is reasonable to assume that the two might have known each other before this date. By 1945, Marmarosa had toured with some of the most famous white swing bands, including those led by Artie Shaw, Gene Krupa, and Tommy Dorsey. Following these stints, the pianist settled in Los Angeles, where he began to work with musicians like Lester Young, Howard McGhee, and later Charlie Parker. Marmarosa had an excellent harmonic and inventive piano style that foreshadowed what would later be known as "cool jazz." Unfortunately, he suffered from psychological instability, which derailed much of his career.

Not only would the January 11, 1946, session mark Brown's debut in a commercial recording studio but it was also the first record made by Marmarosa as a leader. Joining Marmarosa and Brown on the recording was drummer Jackie Mills, who was a few years older than Marmorasa and Brown and had previously worked with swing bands led by Charlie Barnet and Boyd Raeburn. Marmorasa recorded an original composition for the session, called "Mellow Mood," on which we hear Ray Brown's first solo on record. His sixteen-bar improvisation comprises a series of cohesive eighth-note runs, triplet figures, and double-timed sixteenth-note phrases before Marmarosa returns to the bridge and finishes out the piece. Overall, the "Mellow Mood" recording is impressive and offers a nice contrast from the more fiery bop music Brown played with Gillespie and Parker. Based on this one recording, it seems reasonable to assume that had Marmarosa, Brown, and Mills continued to perform and develop together, they could have had one of the great trios of the mid-1940s. Around 1950, a second track from the session surfaced with Lucky Thompson added to the trio for an uptempo rendition of "How High the Moon." Thompson's playing is strong on the track, and Ray Brown's walking bass line solid.

On January 24, 1946, the Gillespie band was broadcast live from Billy Berg's Supper Club. The broadcast was hosted by famed singer Rudy Vallée and was aired on the West Coast NBC feed at 7:30 pm. This performance may represent the first time bebop was broadcast on a major network to a national audience. It includes one of Gillespie's most recognizable tunes, "Salt Peanuts," in which the band takes the tune rapidly, and Brown can be heard clearly throughout the recording, especially during the eight-bar break leading into the solo section. The group sounds extremely well rehearsed, and Parker, Jackson, Gillespie, and Levey deliver fantastic performances during their short solo statements.

During their stay in Los Angeles, Gillespie, Brown, and Haig were brought to the studio under the guidance of arranger Johnny Richards. Joining the rhythm section was the Los Angeles jazz drummer Roy Porter, who likely replaced Stan Levey on this session due to union regulations. The record date was meant to pair Gillespie and his sidemen with a group that had six string players, a harpist, and a french horn player. The ensemble recorded four tracks written by Jerome Kern, "The Way You Look Tonight," "Why Do I Love You," "Who," and "All the Things You Are." These recordings were intended to be a tribute to Kern, who had died only a few weeks before, on November 11, 1945. The tracks were recorded by the Paramount label but blocked from release by the Kern estate, who felt that Dizzy Gillespie "strayed too far away from the way the composer had written the songs." The Phoenix label eventually released these tracks in the 1970s, although they mainly went unnoticed at that time. Despite some impressive playing by Gillespie, these tracks are busy and over-orchestrated. None of the tracks has a Ray Brown solo; however, he can be heard clearly in the background and is most impressive on the uptempo "Who" and the more medium-swing "Why Do I Love You." The Richards sessions gave Ray Brown his first chance to record with a large ensemble and with musicians that were not connected to jazz.

Ray Brown's studio session debut with Parker and Gillespie took place on February 5, 1946, for the Dial Records label, at Electro Broadcasting Studios in Glendale, California. Recording with the two most celebrated bop creators, should have been a positive experience for the young bassist, but the session was marked by confusion and miscues. For Ray, the day began as an opportunity to capture his playing with Parker, Gillespie, and Lester Young, arguably the most celebrated tenorist of the 1930s and '40s. But things went wrong from the outset when Lester Young and Milt Jackson failed to arrive at the studio. Lucky Thompson was brought in to replace Young, and guitarist Arvin Garrison served as Jackson's replacement. Alongside these last-minute fill-ins, the piano chair was occupied not by touring member Al Haig but by George Handy. To add to the confusion, Charlie Parker brought an entourage of friends, fans, and hangers-on to the session.

Working through these issues, the group managed to record a George Handy original called "Diggin' Diz," but the disarray led to a recording that sounded sloppy, unpolished, and under-rehearsed. Both Handy and Garrison sound awkward and out of place, and Parker and Gillespie are not at their best. Since the group only managed to record one track, a second session was scheduled for February 7. When Parker, who was struggling with addiction and a mental-health episode, failed to show for the rescheduled session, Dizzy Gillespie's Jazzmen recorded without him. Once again, Lucky Thompson served as Parker's replacement. This session did produce some gems, however, including the uptempo "Dynamo A," with its tight arrangement and fantastic solo statements by Thompson and Gillespie. Although not as impressive as Thompson and Gillespie, Jackson's and Haig's solos are noteworthy. Brown's solid walking bass line against Levey's convincing swing holds the band together.

Other notable tracks from this session include Thelonious Monk's original "Round Midnight," where Brown can be heard clearly as he walks with gentle grace on this harmonically rich ballad. The band also performed a medium-tempo version of Parker's fantastic original "Confirmation." Parker's absence is particularly noticeable on this track, with Thompson failing to negotiate Parker's complex chord changes. Despite a solid solo from Gillespie, "Confirmation" does not fare well as the rhythm section lags. The session also yielded a commercial effort from Gillespie on the remake of the 1934 Rodgers and Hammerstein pop classic "When I Grow Too Old to Dream" – the same tune they were made to sing at Billy Berg's. On the track, Gillespie, Brown, and others sing in unison. This track is notable not because it is particularly strong or innovative but because it shows Gillespie's willingness to conform and entertain. The recordings from the February 5 and February 7 sessions were released on Dial Records under the band name "The Tempo Jazz Men featuring Gabriel on Trumpet." Dial Records may have used the pseudonym to avoid a possible contract breach from Dizzy Gillespie and Charlie Parker.

After six weeks, it had become clear that the West Coast wasn't yet ready for Gillespie's and Parker's brand of East Coast jazz experimentation. While there were some highlights from the Los Angeles trip, like the *Jubilee* broadcast, the group failed to make any notable impact in the city. On February 9, 1946, Gillespie, Brown, Jackson, Haig, and Levey boarded an airplane to return to New York. Charlie Parker traded his ticket for cash, probably to buy drugs, and remained in Los Angeles. The circumstances surrounding the Los Angeles trip led to a fracturing of Gillespie and Parker's relationship and, sadly, the two would never again play together in a working band; however, they would occasionally meet up again after the breakup.

Soon after the split, Charlie Parker signed a one-year exclusive recording contract with Dial Records, and while he did manage to record and perform for the next few months, he grew increasingly more addicted and less stable. On July 29, 1946, a disoriented Parker was found wandering the Civic Hotel lobby naked after a recording session. The saxophonist eventually returned to his room and fell asleep with a lit cigarette, causing a fire. Following the incident, he was forcefully taken by the police to a prison psychiatric ward and eventually to Camarillo State Hospital. Parker remained at Camarillo for several months before re-emerging in February 1947. While a short period followed in which he seemed stable and clean, Parker's demons would continue to challenge him for the rest of his life.

For Ray Brown, the Los Angeles trip must have been confusing. On the positive side, he had played with Dizzy Gillespie and Charlie Parker, two of the biggest names in jazz, made several recordings, took part in a national radio broadcast, and developed a close friendship with Milt Jackson, one of the music's newest young stars. On the flip side, having only been in New York for a short period and having rejected offers from established and consistent bands, Ray Brown had found himself on the road trying to present modern music to an audience that seemed generally unimpressed. He also had to witness the disintegration of Gillespie and Parker's relationship. In Parker, Brown saw the evils of a struggling genius unraveling. In Gillespie, he saw a consummate professional and bandleader with a strong work ethic and an ability to make the best of any situation regardless of the challenges. Thankfully, Ray was not enticed to follow Parker down a hard-living path of late-night partying and drug abuse. Instead, he took note of Gillespie's dedication and savvy and took this as a template for his life and career. He did, however, see a change in Gillespie after the break from Parker. While being interviewed for a Gillespie documentary, Ray explained:

> The biggest change I saw in Dizzy was that after Charlie Parker was gone, he never found anybody to play with, and . . . a part of him seemed to have receded. You'd go to see him, he'd be having a lot of fun and singing and playing and doing all kinds of stuff, but when he and Charlie Parker were playing, man, it was as serious as cancer. I mean, they were nailing it every night.[31]

4 The Dizzy Gillespie Big Band 1946

Before he'd met Ray Brown, Dizzy Gillespie had tried his hand at leading a bebop big band, under the name of the Hepstations. But everything seemed to go wrong for this band; in his autobiography, *To Be Or Not To Bop,* Gillespie described the band as "a mess and a failure."[32] Under the impression he had been booked to play concerts, Gillespie found himself performing at dances. As the Hepstations moved south, they were confronted with audiences expecting blues and danceable swing, but the uncompromising Gillespie went ahead with the modern bop music as intended. But the South was not yet ready for Gillespie's bebop innovations, and the Hepstations were met with hostility. At the end of September 1945, the Hepstations disbanded having been in existence only three months.

On his return from Los Angeles in February 1946, Gillespie set about establishing a big band once again. To do so, he first needed to secure a venue willing to support the group, and he reached an agreement with club owner Clark Monroe. Monroe was more interested in presenting Gillespie's sextet, however, so it was decided that he would begin by presenting Gillespie's combo for eight weeks at the Spotlite Club on 52nd Street. If those eight weeks were a success, Monroe would book the big band for an additional eight weeks at the Spotlite. In Alyn Shipton's book *Groovin' High,* Brown recalls:

> Dizzy called Milt Jackson and me . . . and said he had gotten a big band the year before, and it lasted about three months, and it went belly up, and then he'd got the quintet that we were in. But he told us: "I'm gonna get a big band. It's gonna be different, but if you guys wanna stay, you're welcome." So we said: "Yeah!"[33]

The Gillespie sextet recorded during this period – on February 22, 1946 – with a newly revamped line-up that included Don Byas on tenor, Bill De Arango on guitar, Al Haig on piano, J.C. Heard on drums, and Milt Jackson on vibes. This often-overlooked recording for Victor Records produced four quality bebop tracks. There were two takes of Thelonious Monk's "52nd Street Theme," which was played at a fast bop tempo, and the rhythmic hookup between Ray Brown and J.C. Heard propels the ensemble. Ray Brown is given an eight-bar break and he plays arco: the first recording of Brown using the bow. Another notable track is "Night in Tunisia," Gillespie's most famous composition. While Brown does not solo on the track, he does set up the song by playing the well-known Afro-Cuban ostinato bass figure. The session also yielded a version of "Old Man Rebop," a medium-swing piece featuring Jackson, Byas, Haig, De Arango, and Gillespie as soloists. The final released track from the session was Charlie Parker's bop masterpiece, "Anthropology." The track showcases Jackson's development, Gillespie's prowess, and a fantastic solo by De Arango. Overall, the February 22 session deserves to rank as one of the more exemplary bebop recordings of the mid-1940s.

Gillespie's sextet opened at the Spotlite Club in March 1946 and alternated sets with legendary saxophonist Coleman Hawkins. The booking was a huge success, and Monroe agreed to give Gillespie the extra eight weeks and a chance to reintroduce a bebop big band.

On May 15, 1946, Brown returned to the studio with Gillespie. For this session, Gillespie employed drummer Kenny Clarke and alto saxophonist Sonny Stitt to join Al Haig and Milt Jackson. Gillespie had met Clarke a decade earlier when they worked together in the Teddy Hill Band. During that time, Kenny "Klook" Clarke developed a signature playing style by creating his own technique on the ride cymbal and incorporating accents on the snare and bass drum – known as "bombs" – to increase the music's overall energy. From 1944 to 1946, the beginning of bebop's popularity, Kenny Clarke served in the military and was, therefore, unavailable to record the music he helped create. On completing his military service, Clarke returned to the New York jazz scene and re-established his reputation by working in Gillespie's band.

Sonny Stitt's presence at the May 15 session is also notable. Stitt was the only alto saxophonist of the time who could genuinely match the technicality and virtuosity of Charlie Parker. His early style was so close to that of Parker that many viewed him as a clone, even though Stitt continually claimed he played like that before he had heard Parker.[34] Another key contributor to this session – and future Gillespie works – was arranger Walter "Gil" Fuller. Fuller had worked with Gillespie in Billy Eckstine's orchestra and was one of only a few arrangers able to write quality big-band arrangements of bop charts. Notably, Gillespie and Fuller both seemed enthusiastic to encourage the talents of Ray Brown, the group's sensational young bassist.

The May 15, 1946 session yielded four tunes, which were to remain part of Gillespie's repertoire over the next several months. Ray Brown features most notably on "One Bass Hit (Part 1)," the first of a number of recordings to feature him explicitly, and on which he plays the song's melody against some expertly arranged background figures. Following solos by Gillespie, Jackson, and Stitt, the tune concludes with an impressive call-and-response between Brown and the ensemble. Another essential track showing Ray Brown's ambitiousness is his original offering "That's Earl Brother," with its written angular

Ray Brown with the Dizzy Gillespie Big Band.
Heritage Image Partnership Ltd / Alamy Stock Photo

bop melody containing a short unexpected double-time melodic figure. (The phrase "that's Earl brother" was once used to mean "that's all.") Also released from this session were two vocal numbers, "Oop Bop Sh'Bam" and "A Hand Fulla Gimme," featuring blues vocalist Alice Roberts. The May 15, 1946 session would be Gillespie's final small-group recording as a leader for almost four years.

Within the first few months of working with Gillespie, Ray Brown had already achieved a degree of notoriety. At this point,[35] the bassist was curious to know what Gillespie felt about him as a musician, so he approached him and asked. Brown retold the story in a Gillespie documentary:

> I walked up to Dizzy one day and said, "How am I doing?" He said, "Ok, but you don't play the right notes." "Well," I said, "What do you mean?" and he took me to the piano, and he said, "When we play this chord, you

play that note." And I said, "Yeah, that's what I play." He said, "That's the right note, but that ain't the note I want." Then he revoiced it, and he said, "This is what I want." Then he went through some songs, showing me what he wanted to hear, to play the trumpet. You know, not the voice, not the note to the chord but an alternate. So, that's what Dizzy was doing to the music.[36]

Dizzy Gillespie was determined to make his new big band a success and knew he needed outside help. One of his first decisions was to make Gil Fuller not only an arranger but also a musical director. Knowing that Fuller had a firm hand and the respect of the musicians, he felt he was the man to keep his sidemen in line. As for securing enough material for the band, Gillespie looked to his old employer, singer Billy Eckstine. With his bebop orchestra folding, Eckstine graciously provided Gillespie with microphones, music stands, and charts. Before selecting front-line section players, Gillespie looked first to get his rhythm section in place. He knew that his backline had to provide rhythmic energy, and retaining Ray Brown, Kenny Clarke, and Milt Jackson gave him a solid foundation – but he still needed a pianist. Gillespie first hired Thelonious Monk for the piano chair. Before joining Gillespie, Monk worked with Kenny Clarke as part of the house band at Minton's, a popular jazz venue where bop musicians would go to jam. Monk had also already been recorded as a leader by this time – his unique compositions and advanced chord progressions were critical in developing the harmonic language of bebop. Gillespie might well have chosen Monk not just for his talents as a pianist but for his skills as a composer, too.

In early June 1946, Gillespie debuted his big band at the Spotlite Club on 52nd Street, and a recording exists from the evening. The repertoire included big-band arrangements of material previously recorded by Gillespie's combos as well as new works and arranged standards. While not musically perfect, these Spotlite recordings are of great interest because they reveal the group's embryonic stages; however, it is evident that the band needed more rehearsal. Still, even in these early performances, the group established a unique identity by presenting technical bebop arrangements in a big-band context. The performances on tunes such as "Things to Come," "Ray's Idea," and "Oop Bop Sh'Bam" set the tone for Gillespie's bebop styling and brilliance as a soloist. Kenny Clarke and Ray Brown's rhythmic hookup proved powerful; however, Thelonious Monk sounded less at ease within the section. Ray Brown is most impressive on a new arrangement of "One Bass Hit," which became a perfect vehicle for his solo abilities. Other Ray Brown highlights from the evening include his solo on "Woody 'n' You," and the debut of his original composition "Ray's Idea."

Although Gillespie would sometimes feature Milt Jackson, it became evident that the band needed another impressive soloist. Some time during the Spotlite run, Gillespie added tenor saxophonist James Moody to fill that role, following his release from his military service. Gillespie appreciated Moody's hybrid bebop and swing soloing style, and the saxophonist became one of Gillespie's most important contributors for decades to come. Other notable additions to Gillespie's ensemble at the Spotlite included trumpeter Kenny Dorham and Sonny Stitt and a highlight from these early Spotlite sessions is vocalist Sarah Vaughan joining the band for the ballad "Don't Blame Me."

After about a month with Monk in the band, it became apparent that the painist's unique approach and irresponsible nature were not going to serve Gillespie's vision. Ray Brown remembered the Monk era:

> Monk is a subject in itself. I mean, most piano players in most big bands sit down, and they play with the band, you know. Monk would just sit there . . . and all of a sudden, there'd be a pause from all of the trumpets and everything, and Monk would just go "plink!" like that. And everybody would go "Yeah!" He really was wild, really different. But he didn't stay because most of the time, he would come an hour late, and sometimes he wouldn't show up at all. So we really wanted someone who would be there all the time – and playing all of the time, too! Dizzy was always on time himself, and he knew that [tardiness] doesn't tend to get any better – it usually gets worse.[37]

As a replacement, Kenny Clarke recommended John Lewis, a friend of his from the army. Even though Lewis did not have Monk's daring creative spirit, or the technique of an Art Tatum or a Bud Powell, he did have a steady professional approach as an accompanist. Lewis was also gifted as an arranger and composer, making him a valuable addition. On June 10, 1946, Gillespie took his big band to the studio for the first time, where they recorded "Our Delight" and "Good Dues Blues," the latter a feature for vocalist Alice Roberts. On the medium-swing "Our Delight," Ray Brown's bass is heard clearly, and the ensemble exhibits their mastery of dynamics, a major step forward from the less remarkable Spotlite performances.

On July 9, 1946, the band was back in the studio where Brown got to record his standout feature "One Bass Hit (Part 2)," the most impressive release of his early career. Not only is Brown brilliant during his solo, but Gillespie's solo is equally phenomenal. For this session, the group also recorded a fantastic interpretation of "Ray's Idea" and the highly technical "Things to Come." One less memorable track is a novelty song by Gillespie called "He Beeped When He Should Have Bopped," which is as good an example as any of Gillespie using "novelty" to help sell his music.

On September 25, 1946, Ray Brown got his first opportunity to record as a bandleader. The result was four sides released on three 10" 78 rpm records.[38] Ray Brown used a scaled-down version of the Dizzy Gillespie Big Band for this recording, with Hank Jones sitting in for John Lewis on piano. Additional musicians on the recording were Dizzy Gillespie and Dave Burns on trumpet,

John Brown (no relation) on alto sax, James Moody on tenor, Milt Jackson on vibes, and Joe Harris on drums. Both Burns and John Brown worked as Gillespie orchestra members, and drummer Joe Harris was another Pittsburgh native who often replaced Kenny Clarke in Gillespie's band when the latter was unavailable.

The Bebop Boys recording offers four sides and features three songs written and or co-written by Ray Brown. While *The Bebop Boys'* performances are somewhat unpolished, there are certainly some strong moments. The first track is a Brown original, "For Hecklers Only," a medium swing with Brown foregrounded on the intro, the eight-bar bridge of the melody, and during the solo section. While Brown's statements are impressive, the track is not particularly remarkable. "Smoky Hollow Jump" is another thirty-two-bar bebop tune, written by Brown and Fuller. The song is played at a similar tempo to "For Hecklers Only," and Jackson, Gillespie, and Burns are prominently featured. The next cut is Brown's "Boppin' the Blues," a simple riff-based tune played in a Count Basie style and on which Brown takes a nice solo. The most impressive track is an uptempo piece based on rhythm changes, written by Moody and Burns, called "Moody Speaks." While the album is of importance to the career of Ray Brown as a leader, *The Bebop Boys/Ray Brown's All-Stars* had little commercial impact. Overall, the recording is somewhat sloppily handled, which may have stemmed somewhat from the fact that the session began at 9:00 am, which is early for most gigging jazz musicians.

On November 12, 1946, Gillespie's orchestra was back in the studio to record for the Musicraft label. For this session, Dizzy had a slightly revamped line-up which included James Moody, Joe Harris, and guest vocalist Kenny Hagood. One track issued from this date is an original Gillespie slow swing piece called "Emanon," which served as a healthy counterbalance to Hagood's vocals on the poppy ballad "I Waited for You." As with Gillespie's best material from this era, "Emanon" includes tight horn lines, progressive arrangement, and solos by Gillespie, Jackson, and Moody.

By the end of 1946, not only was Gillespie's orchestra frequently heard on the radio but they were filmed for the movie feature *Jivin' in Bebop*. This showed Gillespie leading his orchestra through several repertoire selections and showcased his dancing, singing, and acting in vaudevillian comedy routines. In some ways, Gillespie's desire to entertain was the antithesis of what many felt bebop truly represented. For bop loyalists, this music was jazz as a stand-alone art form which did not need any outside commercial elements or antics to prove its worth; but Gillespie was a natural entertainer for whom showboating to retain an audience's attention seemed to come easily. While his schtick might have been designed to draw in the audience, Gillespie's clowning never seemed forced, and it appeared to reflect both his own authentic personality as well as his connection to bandleaders he had worked with previously, such as Cab Calloway. While, on the one hand, his routines can be viewed as an extension of racist minstrel traditions, there is also an argument that Gillespie's ability to entertain was crucial in helping to present modernistic music to an audience that might otherwise ignore it. This desire to entertain certainly made him the perfect subject for a film like *Jivin' in Bebop*.

Regardless of its intent, *Jivin' in Bebop* is a fascinating glimpse at one of the finest bebop big bands ever created. The film begins with an introduction by master of ceremonies Freddie Carter, followed by a fantastic version of "Salt Peanuts," in which Gillespie sings and solos. On this track, Joe Harris takes center stage with an impressive extended drum solo. What follows is some comedic banter between Freddie Carter and Gillespie, and these skits continue between each number. The band is most prominently featured on "Oop Bop Sh'Bam," "He Beeped When He Should Have Bopped," "Things to Come," and "One Bass Hit." "One Bass Hit" represents the earliest moment we have of Ray Brown on film, and it is critical viewing for any fan of the bassist.

Singer Helen Humes joins the orchestra for two numbers, and Kenny Hagood appears in "I Waited for You." The movie also centers around stunningly impressive dance routines performed to Gillespie's music, namely "Convulsion," "Shaw 'Nuff," "A Night in Tunisia," "Dynamo A," "Ornithology," "Governor's Square," "Ray's Idea," and "Bag's Boogie." While the low-budget *Jivin in Bebop* is by no means a cinematic masterpiece, it prominently features Gillespie's music and one of the most refined versions of his orchestra.

5 "The New Star"
1947

By 1947, Ray Brown had already sealed his reputation as one of the most impressive bassists in jazz and was a rising star. Since the beginning of the summer of 1946, Brown had been on tour with Gillespie's Hepstations Orchestra, and, while the music was exciting and well suited to New York audiences, the rest of the country did not connect with Gillespie's bop experimentations. After stops in Pennsylvania and Ohio, Ella Fitzgerald and her trio joined the Hepsations tour for dates in Indiana. Bringing a singer of such fame on board was a necessity if they were going to sell the tour: a double billing with Fitzgerald's trio certainly attracted interest and shifted tickets. They remained on tour with Gillespie for several weeks before embarking on their own tour throughout most of August and September. Minus Fitzgerald, Gillespie's orchestra continued throughout the Midwest, performing in St. Louis, Peoria, and, in September, at Chicago's famed Savoy Ballroom.

However, Fitzgerald, following a week of performing just with her own group, returned to the Hepstations tour as a featured singer – at New York's famed Apollo Theater beginning September 21, 1946, and traveling on elsewhere including San Antonio, Galveston, Birmingham, and Atlanta. It was during this time that Ray Brown developed a romantic connection with the acclaimed singer, leading eventually to marriage and a musical partnership.

When the tour returned to the Apollo on January 17, 1947, Fitzgerald – who had accepted an offer to join the Cootie Williams band at the Paramount Theater – was replaced for a week by Sarah Vaughan, who, notwithstanding her incredible talents, was not nearly as well known as Ella at this point in her career. Musically, however, Vaughan's style at the time was a better fit with the bebop genre than Fitzgerald's, who was still mainly known for singing cutesie novelty hits. Although short-lived, Fitzgerald's time with Gillespie's orchestra had a profound impact on her style, building a stronger connection with bebop repertoire and phrasing.

It became evident early on that Gillespie's orchestra was going to have financial struggles, which resulted from several factors. To begin, selling a group of all-African-American musicians nationally in the late 1940s was a difficult prospect in any case. In addition, Gillespie's music was modernistic and not always well received by those who came to dance. Other factors included the general costs associated with running a big band, including travel expenses, equipment costs, and salaries for the musicians and arrangers. In the face of all this, Gillespie's agent Billy Shaw was determined, and worked diligently and creatively to keep the band afloat until 1950.

In addition to performing with the large group, Gillespie's rhythm section of Ray Brown, Milt Jackson, John Lewis, and Kenny Clarke became a separate working unit in their own right. Brown recalled how this came about:

> There were very few soloists in the band to do the bulk of the soloing. We didn't have a prominent trumpet soloist besides Dizzy, and in the saxophone section [for much of the time] we really only had James Moody. So most of the "All-Stars" were in the rhythm section, and there were enough of us to write things to feature us. The brass players, especially the trumpets, had high notes and lots of them. Just screaming figures and more and more high notes, and after about half an hour of that, you'd look over at the trumpet section, and everybody's lip's hanging down, looking like some ground meat. It would be time for an intermission, so Dizzy would say, "Ok, band off!" and we, that's the rhythm section with Milt, would play for fifteen minutes and give the guys a rest. So since we got to doing this every night, we started putting some stuff together.[39]

By the spring of 1947, Gillespie's rhythm section were getting their own gigs and became known as the Atomics of Modern Music, later changed to the Milt Jackson Quartet and eventually settling on the name the Modern Jazz Quartet (MJQ) after Ray Brown departed. With bassist Percy Heath permanently replacing Brown some time between August 18 and 24, 1951, MJQ began incorporating classical music principles and presenting their music in concert hall settings. They eventually became the most commercially successful unit in jazz – with the possible exception of the Oscar Peterson Trio, a group that Ray Brown worked with for nearly fifteen years.

Ray Brown did not participate in any studio recordings in the early part of 1947: his first session that year, with Gillespie's orchestra, was not until August 22. That session yielded four sides, including Ray Brown's feature "Two Bass Hit," written by Dizzy Gillespie and John Lewis. Here, Brown is heard in a call-and-response with the band on the intro, main melody, and an unaccompanied cadenza. The engineer ensured that Brown's bass was well recorded, and he can indeed be heard with great clarity. Other tracks included "Ow!" a strong medium bop, "Oop-Pa-Da," which incorporates silly scat vocals, and "Stay on It," a medium-tempo composition written by Gillespie and Tadd Dameron. This session would be Ray Brown's final studio recording with the Gillespie Orchestra.

While many appreciated bop's innovations, some older jazz writers and musicians remained critical, finding the fast angular melodies, harmonic intricacies, and emphasis on improvisation pretentious and unpalatable. The controversy about bop's "validity" was ongoing, and "battles" between critics, fans, and musicians raged on. One of the most interesting of these battles was heard on two WOR radio broadcasts on September 13 and 20, 1947. Two critics, Barry Ulanov, a bop enthusiast, and Rudi Blesh, a jazz critic who preferred Dixieland, convened their dream bands and let the listening audience be the judges. The "Modernists" that Ulanov assembled for this all-star affair included Dizzy Gillespie, Charlie Parker, clarinetist John LaPorta, guitarist Billy Bauer, pianist Lennie Tristano, drummer Max Roach, and Ray Brown. Blesh countered with his "All-Star Stompers," which included older musicians like cornetist Wild Bill Davidson, trombonist Jimmy Archey, clarinetist Edmond Hall, pianist Ralph Sutton, guitarist Danny Barker, drummer Baby Dodds, and Pops Foster on bass. The two groups played the same numbers and the audience voted for the versions they preferred.

These broadcasts are of particular interest not least because they reunited Gillespie and Parker. Additionally, it gave Brown his first chance to record with Max Roach, one of the finest jazz drummers, and Lennie Tristano, a blind pianist and composer and arguably one of his generation's most gifted and forward-thinking musicians. LaPorta and Bauer's talents should also be noted, although neither man had the same impact on jazz as Parker, Gillespie, Roach, and Tristano.

The September 13 broadcast begins with the band being introduced over Parker and Gillespie's "Koko"; each member is given a short solo break. Unfortunately, the song, one of Parker and Gillespie's most celebrated 1945 creations, was not played in its entirety. The band then breaks into "Hot House," a Tadd Dameron song based on the Cole Porter standard "What Is This Thing Called Love." Hearing Parker and Gillespie deliver melodies in unison – as they do on this track and other early recordings – is one of the greatest pleasures a jazz fan can experience. Parker, who had spent much of the previous year recovering from addiction and mental health problems in Los Angeles, sounds incredible, as does Gillespie. The final track from this broadcast has the band playing the 1930s Broadway classic "Fine and Dandy" at a fast tempo. Unfortunately, the hosts Barry Ulanov and Bruce Elliot talk over the second half of Bauer's solo, Tristano's entire solo, and much of the final melody. Ray Brown is not featured on the broadcast as a soloist, but his superb walking lines help drive the group. As with many live broadcasts at the time, there were some technical issues with the sound. Roach's ride cymbal is way too loud and bleeds into the other microphones, and the piano is seriously out of tune. Notwithstanding these issues, the broadcast is of interest and has historical value.

The September 20, 1947 broadcast also begins with introductions over the "Koko" theme. The band then plays the standard "On the Sunny Side of the Street." Ray Brown gets a chance to play a short four-bar solo on this cut, as does Max Roach. For the second track, the band begins with "Dizzy Atmosphere" before breaking into a fast version of "Tiger Rag," one of the most frequently performed tunes of early jazz. Parker and Gillespie are brilliant in their improvisations, and it is clear they are perfect musical companions.

Milt Jackson and Ray Brown in New York, some time between 1946 and 1948.
Photo by William P. Gottlieb. Archive PL / Alamy Stock Photo

Tristano is equally impressive, and Ray Brown and Max Roach have an incredible rhythm hookup on this track. The recording is truly a highlight. The band then slips into another classic number, "How Deep Is the Ocean," and concludes with a short version of "52nd Street Theme." When the fans' votes came in, the "Modernists" had defeated the "All-Star Stompers."

Another all-star ensemble that included Ray Brown came from a Jazz at the Philharmonic concert at Carnegie Hall. Jazz at the Philharmonic, or JATP, was a concert tour that began in 1944 under promoter and producer Norman Granz's guidance. The show paired some of the biggest names in jazz in a concert setting. Granz did this to market jazz to a larger audience, and, in doing so, took the music out of smaller nightclubs and into large settings, selling more tickets in the process. He also recorded most of these shows and released them first on Mercury Records and later on his own Norgran, Clef, and Verve labels. After his debut with JATP, Ray Brown became a permanent group member, and Norman Granz widely supported the bassist as his career moved forward.

This spirited JATP concert at Carnegie Hall opened on September 27, 1947. Ray Brown appeared with tenor saxophonist Flip Phillips, Illinois Jacquet, trumpeter Howard McGhee, trombonist Bill Harris, pianist Hank Jones, and drummer Jo Jones. Each had come to fame as a member of one of the most famous swing bands: Phillips and Harris with Woody Herman's Orchestra; Jacquet and McGhee with the Lionel Hampton Orchestra; Hank Jones with Billy Eckstine's orchestra; and Jo Jones with Count Basie.

Since these JATP concerts were intended to re-create an onstage jam session, the solos are often extended. For example, the group's recording of the Ellington Orchestra classic "Perdido" took up six record sides and ran for over sixteen minutes. Although all the musicians had strong moments during their improvisations, Jacquet and Phillips seemed to get the most applause. Neither Ray Brown nor Jo Jones is featured as a soloist, but they provide the steady rhythm hookup needed to support the soloists. Also captured that evening was the classic ballad "I Surrender, Dear," the performance of which is excellent and offers a contrast to the more uptempo "Perdido." The very fact that Ray Brown was invited to perform at such an event shows how much his reputation had grown in just a year. He played at least two more nights with JATP at Carnegie Hall, the most critical being on September 29 when Ella Fitzgerald sang for the first time with the unit.

Around the time of the Carnegie Hall Concert, Ray Brown entered the studio with the Flip Phillips and Howard McGhee Boptet, which included Hank Jones and J.C. Heard. The session yielded three tracks: "Cake," "Znarg Blues," and the standard ballad "My Old Flame." Brown is not given any extended solos on these recordings but does play short solo breaks on all except "Znarg Blues." On December 3, 1947, Ray Brown was back in the studio with Jones and Heard for an extended session for Howard McGhee. Also present were James Moody and Milt Jackson. The session yielded nine tracks for Dial Records. Highlights from the recording include "Dorothy," a medium bop original by McGhee which provides a four-bar unaccompanied bass break on the intro and outro. Brown is given a solo on the Hank Jones original "Coolie Rini," and his strong walking lines help push the groove. Another song of note is "Stop Time Blues," an uptempo tune with McGhee, Jackson, Moody, and Jones as soloists.

Ray Brown contributes as a writer on two tracks for the McGhee session. The first of these originals is "Surrender," a clever ballad co-written with Hank Jones; the second composition, "You," is a thirty-two-bar vehicle with some interesting chromaticism[40] in the song's A sections. The track also features a short eight-bar solo by Ray, which, albeit brief, shows the influence of Blanton's playing on his phrasing, tone, and note selections. It is a shame that neither "Surrender" nor "You" were widely used in Brown's career. Overall, the Howard McGhee session is a quality effort. Unfortunately, McGhee struggled with drugs throughout his career and was in and out of the scene.

Brown's final recording of 1947 was on December 20 when he joined a large ensemble to accompany Ella Fitzgerald on several pivotal tracks for Decca Records. Here, Fitzgerald recreated her JATP performance of "How High the Moon," and delivers what many believe to be the most fantastic scat solo ever on record, in which she quotes Charlie Parker's melody from "Ornithology." The recording represented a pivotal transition in her career in which she shifted from pop stylist to a more serious jazz artist. Her relationship with Ray Brown and her connection with Dizzy Gillespie's tour certainly had a bearing on this stylistic change. Another significant track that marks this shift is "My Baby Likes to Bebop," also including scat vocals and with somewhat biographical lyrics, with Ella singing, "My baby likes to bebop, and I like to bebop too." The final track from the session, "No Sense," leans more towards the pop swing tradition that Ella would never entirely abandon.

The commercialization of bebop began as early as 1945, and by late 1947 instrumental bebop had lost much of its earlier purity. Bop attire and vernacular were being commercialized by advertising agencies and American corporations. Bop imitators like Harry the Hipster Gibson and Slim Gaillard were becoming popular by adding ridiculous lyrics to bebop music, often referencing drugs and an underworld counterculture. Bop was also being championed by young white intellectuals, known as beatniks, who seemed most impressed by the heavy use of improvisation. They put their bop heroes on a pedestal and saw the music as freeing and unfettered by pre-existing ideas and principles. Few seemed to properly understand the mathematical precision and theoretical knowledge needed to solo over bop's advanced harmonies.

While bebop began as a serious and innovative underground art form, it was now becoming a parody of itself. Dizzy Gillespie understood the dangers of getting lost in excessive commercialism and looked to redefine his sound. Gillespie had a long-time curiosity about Latin rhythms. His friend, trumpeter Mario Bauza from Cuba, had helped introduce Gillespie to Latin music in the late 1930s and early '40s during their time together in Cab Calloway's orchestra. Some of Gillespie's previous compositions, like "A Night in Tunisia," had flirted with Latin rhythms in a bebop context. But he hadn't yet established himself as a dedicated practitioner of Latin music. With the hiring of the Cuban percussionist Chano Pozo in 1947, Gillespie's orchestra began experimenting more with percussion and Afro-Cuban rhythms.

Ray Brown was not completely satisfied with the new direction Gillespie's orchestra was heading and his tenure ended some time during late 1947, a few months before the new Cubop craze hit the radio airwaves. Brown explains the reason for his departure:

> Chano Pozo just started not long before I left. Matter of fact, one of the things I really never got adjusted to was having conga players, although he [Dizzy] had some of the best ones. Chano playing on "Manteca" or another Latin tune I thought was great, but playing on our arrangements I didn't think was great. It didn't sit real good with me on every song. I mean, this guy's doing all this when we're just trying to swing straight out, and it seemed to inhibit us. I guess I just hadn't got used to doing it.[41]

Another reason for Brown's desire to move away from the Gillespie Orchestra was his developing relationship with Ella Fitzgerald. During an earlier tour with the singer, their relationship had caused tensions within the band. Ray Brown explains:

> I met her on tour, riding a bus all over the country for two or three months. But later on, I think, it was bad for me to show up in a $400 suit and a big Cadillac to come to the job, and the guys are making $67 a week.[42]

So, by the end of 1947, Ray Brown was ready to branch out and was no longer in Gillespie's band. By this point, Gillespie's financial difficulties as a result of a big band's high costs had become more problematic: he even occasionally had to borrow money from Ray Brown and other band members to cover his expenses. Brown had a keen eye for business and must have been able to see the writing on the wall. Gillespie did manage to maintain the big band for a bit longer, however, getting a boost from the Cubop hit "Manteca," which was recorded and released after Brown's departure. But it was not enough to sustain the big band which finally folded in 1950, forcing Gillespie to return to small bands and solo projects.

Ray Brown learned a great deal from Dizzy Gillespie, as did many others, and the two remained lifelong friends and frequent musical companions. Throughout his life, Ray always spoke about his mentor with love and respect. In a documentary about Dizzy Gillespie, Ray Brown explains that:

> Dizzy's worth to the musical community is vast. It's far-reaching, and I don't think it needs to be relegated to bebop. We're talking about music; forget those names and those tags. That's like black and white and Chinese to me, you know. We're talking about music, and he was at the top of the heap . . . [Dizzy was] one of the best that ever did it. Man, that's all you can say.[43]

At the end of the year, Ray Brown was awarded a "New Star" award by *Esquire* magazine. He was now the most sought-after young bassist in jazz.

6 Fitzgerald, Granz, and Peterson
1947–1949

Ella Jane Fitzgerald was born in Newport News, Virginia, in 1917 and had moved to Yonkers, New York, by 1925. Her young life became harder following her mother's death in 1932, when she was placed in the Colored Orphan Asylum. Even as a young girl, Ella had a natural ability to entertain and earned money dancing on street corners. In 1934, she entered her first amateur contest at the Apollo Theater in Harlem, where she sang the pop hit "The Object of My Affection," backed by the Benny Carter Orchestra, and won both the competition and Carter's respect. She went on to win several other similar competitions around Harlem. After a winning performance at the Harlem Opera House in February 1935, the teenage vocalist was introduced to drummer and bandleader Chick Webb, whose orchestra was one of jazz's most celebrated groups at the time and appeared regularly at the famous Savoy Ballroom. After some initial doubts, Webb took a serious interest in Fitzgerald: not only did he hire her for his band but he and his wife welcomed her into their family.

By June that year Fitzgerald had begun recording with Webb's orchestra and her first single, "I'll Chase the Blues Away," was released on the 12th. Although her style would change over the course of her career, her earliest recordings reveal a distinctive timbre of sweet innocence heightened by an excellent sense of pitch. She also had a strong ability to phrase rhythmically. May 1938 saw the release of "A-Tisket, A-Tasket," also with Webb's orchestra: despite the song's childlike simplicity, it became a huge hit. When Chick Webb passed away aged only thirty-four on June 16, 1939, after a lifelong battle with spinal tuberculosis, Fitzgerald took over his orchestra, heading it until 1942, when she decided to go out independently as a soloist. As bebop began to develop in the 1940s, so did Ella Fitzgerald's vocal style. Unlike most swing band vocalists of the late 1930s, Fitzgerald adapted to the new harmonic, rhythmic, and melodic language of bebop and began to incorporate elements of the bop vocabulary into her vocal styling. She emulated the phrasing of instrumentalists like Charlie Parker and Dizzy Gillespie and perfected a scat singing style that would soon become her signature sound. Although Fitzgerald was not the first to put vocal syllables to musical pitches (Louis Armstrong had popularized the technique as early as February 1926 with "Heebie Jeebies"), she was one of the first singers to incorporate bebop phrasing into scat melodies.

Ray Brown first met Ella Fitzgerald in New York some time in 1945 while he was performing with Gillespie on 52nd Street, but this first meeting was not auspicious. Certainly, by this time Brown was aware of Ella Fitzgerald's reputation, but he admitted that he was not initially impressed with her as a singer, recalling, "She was a good singer . . . but at the time, I wasn't really into singers."[44] It wasn't until the Gillespie Orchestra's package tour with Fitzgerald in November and December 1946 that he truly became aware of her talents. Brown explains:

> That's when I really got to hear her, during that tour with Dizzy. It's a different ball game when you're working with somebody. She was amazing, just picking up on everything that the band was doing. It was phenomenal the way she was responding to that band because I don't think she'd ever been around that kind of music before.[45] [She was] working with swing players like Cootie Williams and Andy Kirk.[46]

During the tour, Brown and Fitzgerald grew romantically involved. On December 10, 1947, they were married in Ohio and soon after set up a home in New York at apartment number 47, 104 Ditmars Boulevard, East Elmhurst, Queens. another significant life change quickly followed when they adopted a baby boy from Ella Fitzgerald's half-sister, Frances, naming him Ray Brown Jr.[47]

Because of their busy touring schedule, which included a trip to the West Coast in June and July of 1948, the couple invited Fitzgerald's Aunt Virginia – who had briefly cared for Ella as a child – to live with them to look after their son and their home. Ray Jr. took an interest in music, studying piano by the age of ten. When he showed a desire to play the drums at age fourteen, Ray Sr. arranged for lessons with veteran swing drummers like Bill Douglass and Chuck Flores. Despite his jazz roots, Ray Jr. began playing rock and roll, later admitting that his interest in performing rock music was an act of rebellion. "I used to drive my parents crazy with this. I told my father a few years before he died; you know, a lot of times I played that music 'cause I just wanted to see the look on your face."[48]

Ray Brown Jr. moved to Seattle in 1971, where he continued to study drums with the great Bill Coleman Jr. He also began writing songs and played the piano. By the late 1980s, Ray Brown Jr. had toured much of the world, performing for the United States Department of Defense. He and Rebecca Judd had a daughter named Alice, who was conceived and born in Ketchikan, Alaska.

Beginning in 2001, Ray Jr. embraced his jazz roots with the release of *Slow Down for Love* on SRI Records. His 2008 duet album *Friends and Family* includes guest appearances by many of his parents' past associates, like James Moody, Terry Gibbs, and Maria Muldaur, among others. Also on this album is

Ray Brown Jr.'s second daughter, who went by the stage name "Haylee," singing a version of "A-Tisket, A-Tasket," the song made famous by Ella Fitzgerald, as a tribute to her grandmother.

Looking back at his parents and his childhood, Ray Brown Jr. described his father as a "Disciplined and focused man. He had his habits and routines well in hand. [He loved] music, golf, and family. Not necessarily in that order. Priorities prevailed." He saw their relationship as follows: "There were years I had difficulties. The issues were more with me than him. I was angry at him. Then one day crossing the street, I got about halfway and realized that he had no idea I was angry, and I realized I was only doing damage to myself." Regarding his relationship with his mother, Ella Fitzgerald, Ray Brown Jr. says:

> As with all relationships, it evolved over the years. Looking back, it's easier to see the pain of sacrifices everyone made to move through life. My mother was generous, but she always expected more from me. She recognized and saw things in me that I was unaware of at the time. But recognizing certain strengths in myself later in life has helped me immensely.

When it comes to the influences behind his music, Ray Brown Jr. recalls:

> Unconsciously being at all those concerts and recording sessions; I had an appreciation for music. I can remember being able to go up on stage and play different instruments. Roy Eldridge used to let me play his trumpet. For many years I wanted to play the trumpet. Gus Johnson used to let me play his drums. Mostly I was given the freedom to choose what I wanted to do. In the "formative years," my heart was given to rock, pop, and soul music. It took time and courage for me to move into jazz.

He recalls a time when he was doing a masterclass in Russia, in which "There were the usual questions, and one of the students asked, 'If you could do anything over, what would it be?' My immediate answer was, 'Be nicer to my parents.'" Overall, Ray Brown Jr. believes that his father should be remembered musically as "an innovator and groove maker." As a parent, he sums up his father by calling him, "fair, just and inspiring." At the time of this writing, Ray Brown Jr. announced, "I'm recording a new CD (number 6), but this one is special to me because I'm doing original music again. I had stopped writing for many years, so it's a joy to speak in my voice on my songs again."[49]

Soon after his marriage to Ella Fitzgerald, Ray Brown was forced to make some important career decisions. In mid-January 1948 Dizzy Gillespie invited him to rejoin his group for a European tour. Having never been to Europe, the prospect of taking the job must have seemed attractive to Brown, and, at the time, jazz promoter Norman Granz was also actively pursuing him to tour with Jazz at the Philharmonic (JATP). Knowing that Ella had her own plans to go on the road, Ray decided to stay in New York and turned down both Gillespie's and Granz's attractive offers. Instead, he decided to put a trio together to back Fitzgerald while also taking over managing her career.

So in 1948, Ray Brown had formed his first working trio, which included his old friend Hank Jones on piano and the local New York drummer Charlie Smith, although the following year Smith was replaced by the more experienced Buddy Rich. At this point, Rich, who had worked with such stars as Tommy Dorsey and Harry James, was recognized as one of the great swing drummers. Although the trio was created to accompany Fitzgerald, it was so impressive during instrumental slots that they began receiving bookings without Fitzgerald on off-nights.

In a repeat of events of 1942, 1948 was marked by a recording ban. Concerns about recorded music's popularity and a perceived threat that recordings would replace live musicians led the American Federation of Musicians Unions (AMF) to take measures to secure and encourage the use of live musicians for events and broadcasts – which meant its members were prohibited from making records. So only a few surviving concerts and broadcasts exist of Brown playing with Ella and the trio in the early days. Today some of that material can be heard on the album Ella Fitzgerald, *Royal Roost Sessions with Ray Brown Trio and Quintet* (Cool & Blue CD 112). The Royal Roost was a popular jazz club located at 1580 Broadway, centered in New York's theater district. Fitzgerald was hired at the club for a two-week contract beginning on November 24, 1948, where she performed alternating nights with Lester Young.

The first date of these issued sessions was November 27, 1948, featuring Ella with the Hank Jones and Charlie Smith version of the trio. Ella's scat vocalization is highlighted in the nonsensical "Ool-Ya-Koo," and "Mr. Paganini" is also noteworthy for the famous bebop quotes in her scat melodies. In addition to a set with the rhythm section, Ella and the group are later joined by saxophonists Lester Young and Allen Eager, trombonists Kai Winding and Ted Kelly, trumpeter Jesse Drakes, pianist Fred Jefferson, and drummer Roy Haynes for a lengthy version of "How High the Moon."

A second date from the engagement was broadcast on December 4, 1948. Added to the ensemble on the date was Allen Eager, the great white tenor saxophonist who had previously worked with Woody Herman from the age of fifteen. Ray Brown is featured frequently in instrumental slots, the most impressive being on "I Never Knew," where he opens the tune with ascending bass figures before playing the main melody. After the melody, Eager and Jones play solos before Ray Brown offers his own improvisation, which blends stylistic elements from Jimmy Blanton and Oscar Pettiford. On "Bop Goes the Weasel," Brown can also be heard soloing and singing in an ensemble. The broadcast closes with a swinging version of "Flying Home," a Fitzgerald favorite.

1949 was a whirlwind year for Ray Brown. In addition to touring with Fitzgerald and leading his trio, he was also now back performing with JATP

The Ray Brown Trio (possibly 1948). Left to right: Hank Jones, Ray Brown, Charlie Smith
Ray Brown Papers, Archives Center, National Museum of American History, Smithsonian Institution

and had joined as a regular member. Much like his first meeting with Dizzy Gillespie, Brown's long relationship with JATP founder and record producer Norman Granz began with a situation in which the bassist found himself at the right place at the right time. Brown remembers his first JATP tour:

> Al McKibbon was playin' bass with them [JATP], and he must have gotten the time wrong because he went out to get a sandwich, and the show was getting ready to go on. I'm sitting in [the theater] with my raincoat on, and I looked at Norman Granz, and somebody said, "There's a bass

player over there," and Norman Granz said, "Hey you, get on the stage." I said, "I can't; I'm with Dizzy." He said, "Just get out there; I'll call Dizzy." So, I played the first half. Anyway, I left Dizzy's band, and Norman Granz called me to see if I wanted to go out on tour. That lasted for a long time.[50]

By 1949, Ray Brown was deeply involved with Ella Fitzgerald's career, but he felt he could not turn down Granz's attractive offer to tour with JATP. This must have been a difficult decision because Norman Granz did not hire Ella Fitzgerald for the same tour. Although Granz had made it clear that he had no interest in the singer at the time, she nevertheless went to see her husband perform with JATP in February that year. When she was spotted in the audience and applauded by fans, Granz reluctantly allowed the star vocalist to come up to sing one number. During her stellar performance of "How High the Moon," she added new improvised lyrics and unleashed a virtuosic scat solo that brought the house down. Norman Granz could not help but take note, and from that moment Ella Fitzgerald became one of the most valuable members of JATP, and Norman Granz one of her most important supporters. Within a year she was the tour's main attraction, and Ray was again by her side. Much of Ray Brown and Ella Fitzgerald's future individual successes can be linked directly to Norman Granz's business efforts.

According to biographer Tad Hershorn, Norman Granz set out to accomplish three things in jazz music in the 1940s: "make money, present quality music, and challenge racial segregation – all of which he accomplished."[51] Granz was born in 1918 and grew up among the Jewish minority in Long Beach, California. His strong promotional skills date back to his years as a UCLA student when he began organizing concerts and rallies. By 1942, he was presenting Sunday-night jam session concerts at Billy Berg's Club in Los Angeles, laying down the proviso that the musicians be paid fairly, that the club allowed an integrated audience, and that tables were placed on the dance floor. All three radical demands were met.

Norman Granz championed the idea of jazz as concert music, and began presenting concerts in Los Angeles in 1944. It wasn't long before a series of concerts and concert tours appeared under the title "Jazz at the Philharmonic." The JATP concerts featured many of the most famous jazz musicians of the era, and became known for their long jam sessions and instrumental "battles." Granz recorded many of the JATP performances, releasing them on his own Clef label.

In 1954, Granz established the famous Verve label, and his wealth increased thanks to the success of his recordings and JATP tours. Although he made a great deal of money from jazz, Granz was anything but greedy and shared his money with the musicians who has helped make him wealthy. His generosity and radical approach to civil liberties and musicians' rights have been well documented.

While Norman Granz recorded his musicians frequently and paid them handsomely, he was also stubborn and egotistical with a firm hands-on approach to business. He developed and produced concept-style albums, and some have since accused him of the unnecessary commercialization of serious jazz artists like Charlie Parker. Criticism has also been leveled at Granz for the low recording quality of some of his releases. Regardless, the fact remains that Norman Granz's influence on jazz music is vast and far-reaching. Under Granz's management, a musician could expect first-class treatment and continued popularity. Dizzy Gillespie has said the following about him:

> Norman Granz hired the best musicians and made them fight one another on stage, musically. He paid them top money, and they traveled in first class. He was the first one for whom musicians always traveled that way, lived in the best hotels, and so on, and he was the first to insist that we played in Texas for a nonsegregated audience.[52]

Pianist Hank Jones has also offered his thoughts on Granz:

> He was an entrepreneur. He was responsible in a large sense for breaking down the lines of discrimination in the South. We played many engagements in the South where the audiences were either segregated or people of color were not allowed to enter. Norman Granz specified that at engagements where that happened, that the audience was to be integrated; otherwise, there would be no concert. To my knowledge, he was the only one who did that. Some of the big band bandleaders didn't do that. Count Basie, Duke Ellington, and Jimmie Lunceford's bands didn't do that. They maybe didn't have that kind of power or that kind of persuasion. Anyway, Norman Granz gave you a chance to perform.
>
> Jazz at the Philharmonic got its name from the fact that he brought jazz into the concert hall. People could come dressed in their tuxedos if they wanted to. It elevated the status of jazz. That is the main thing. Not that jazz needed that elevation [as an art form], but it needed it because it brought it to the people who previously said, "Oh well, we don't want to listen to that stuff. That's beneath us, but if it says it will be performed in the concert hall where we go to hear Beethoven and Chopin, the great composers, then maybe it is worth listening to." I think it increased the audience for jazz. Many people who previously were not down to listening to jazz began to listen to it. It helped enormously to popularize the music or make it more accessible, and of course, that doesn't hurt. At that time, I think it sorely needed it.[53]

The recording ban was lifted in 1949, and Ella Fitzgerald and Ray Brown returned to the studio for Decca Records in early January, recording three numbers with an orchestra: "Someone Like You," "I Couldn't Stay Away," and "Old Mother Hubbard." The remainder of Fitzgerald's studio recording that

Ray Brown with Ella Fitzgerald.
Album / Alamy Stock Photo

year did not include Brown or their working trio, as she continued to record with various orchestras and ensembles.

As mentioned, Ray Brown was incredibly busy that year, and as 1949 moved along, he somehow divided his efforts between traveling and performing with Ella Fitzgerald and as a backing musician for JATP artists. The first of the JATP-associated recording sessions was for Charlie Parker, who had recently been included on the JATP tour and was now being managed by Norman Granz. The date, with Hank Jones and drummer Shelly Manne also backing Parker, yielded only one track, "The Bird," which showcases both Parker and Brown as featured soloists. The track may have been recorded from the Carnegie Hall stage, possibly before or after a JATP performance.

Another notable session was on February 29, 1949, for pianist Bud Powell, who was undoubtedly the most gifted bebop pianist, but with whom Ray Brown had not previously recorded. Rounding out the trio was Max Roach; according to Brown, this was the rhythm section that Gillespie first intended to bring to Los Angeles in 1945. For the session, Powell brought uptempo vehicles like "Cherokee," "Tempus Fugit," and "All God's Chillun Got Rhythm," along with more moderate-paced tunes like "Celia" and "Strictly Confidential." These recordings are among Powell's best – an accurate representation of his incredible prowess as a pianist. Since Max Roach chose to play brushes on these selections, Brown's bass can be heard more clearly in the mix, although he is not featured as a soloist. Unfortunately, Powell's career was often derailed by frequent hospitalization as a resut of mental health issues and alcohol abuse; many of his struggles may have resulted from a police officer beating in 1945 and electroconvulsive therapy treatments.

Although the date is unclear, Brown's next session may have been with Flip Phillips and His Orchestra, a session that included such fine musicians as Sonny Criss on the alto saxophone and Kai Winding on the trombone. It was clear that Norman Granz had a genuine affection for Flip Phillips, putting effort into promoting him and featuring him as a JATP member and solo artist. While not considered a jazz innovator, Flip Phillips was a fine saxophone technician who played in a convincing Lester Young swing style. Brown is only briefly showcased on the recording during the intro to "Swinging for Julie" and on "Brownie." The most impressive track from the session is a bop vehicle called "Flip's Idea." Although his tuning is considerably sharp, Sonny Criss plays in a convincing Parker-like style on the track. Ray Brown recorded again with Phillips later that year in a small-group format that included pianist Mickey Crane and drummer Jo Jones, putting down four tracks, including the standard "But Beautiful." Once again, Phillips accurately displays his affection for Lester Young's style. The hardest-swinging number is "Vortex," which briefly foregrounds Brown during the intro.

For much of April 1949, Ray Brown was back at the Royal Roost with Ella and the trio. Several performances from April 15, 23, and 30 have been preserved and issued on the *Royal Roost* album. On a version of "Flying Home" from April 23, trumpeter Howard McGhee, tenor saxophonists Flip Phillips and Brew Moore, and percussionist Machito join Ella and the group on stage. Other notable tracks include "Old Mother Hubbard," "Robbins' Nest," and "In a Mellotone."

A majority of Brown's recorded efforts from 1949 are from the JATP stage at Carnegie Hall. The most notable of these was a midnight concert on September 18, 1949 with some of the most influential figures in jazz history, including Charlie Parker, Lester Young, Coleman Hawkins, Ella Fitzgerald, Buddy Rich, Roy Eldridge, and Hank Jones. Many of that evening's tracks were made available, including a jam session and extended versions of "The Opener," "Lester Leaps In," "Embraceable You," and "The Closer."

The JATP performance also yielded a two-song set featuring the Ray Brown Trio. Brown is featured in the first number, "Ol' Man River," where he plays the melody and solos. "Ol' Man River" is a critical listen for any Ray Brown fan, as it represents his most impressive recorded moment of the year. Hank Jones is also inspiring on his solo, and Buddy Rich causes uproar with his drum breaks. Brown concludes the piece by showing off his technique on a final solo cadenza. For their second track, the trio plays a very uptempo version of the Basie classic "Air Mail Special," which gives way to an astonishing extended drum solo by Buddy Rich, the most virtuosic drum soloist of the swing era.

The evening also included a fine set by Coleman Hawkins with Ray Brown's trio. Hawkins first came to fame as a member of Fletcher Henderson's orchestra in the 1920s; after hearing Louis Armstrong, he revamped his early, more slapstick style to match Armstrong's more blues swing elements and phrasing. As a result, he became one of the first to truly present the possibilities of the tenor saxophone as a solo instrument in jazz. As jazz developed, so did Hawkins, and he adopted a more vertical approach to soloing over each chord change. This approach inspired bop musicians and helped distinguish his talents from the next most celebrated tenorist of his day, Lester Young.

Coleman Hawkins begins his set with "Body and Soul." His recording of the ballad a decade earlier is considered one of the most celebrated modern jazz recordings. He then moves through a repertoire that includes "Rifftide," "Sophisticated Lady," "Stuffy," and "Blues." With this presentation, Hawkins showed that his skills had only strengthened after nearly thirty years in the business.

Another evening feature was Ella Fitzgerald's set backed by the Ray Brown trio, highlights of which include swinging versions of "Robbins' Nest," "Old Mother Hubbard," "I'm Just a Lucky So-and-So," and "Basin Street Blues," where she does an impression of Louis Armstrong. Fitzgerald also showcases her ability to sing the blues on "Black Coffee" and "A New Shade of Blues." The audience grew disruptive during her set, rudely screaming out for her to sing her hit "How High the Moon." At the end of her solo set, Granz brings the entire ensemble out to join her and the trio. To the crowd's great pleasure, he announces the next number, "How High the Moon." The historic evening concludes with the entire ensemble performing the encore, "Perdido."

This same Carnegie Hall concert also marked another historical moment, with Canadian piano virtuoso Oscar Peterson making his long-awaited American debut alongside Ray Brown. Peterson dazzled the New York audience with his versions of "I Only Have Eyes for You," "Fine and Dandy," and "Carnegie Blues." This event launched the beginning of a brotherhood between Oscar Peterson and Ray Brown that would change both men forever: the September 18, 1949 performance might well be the most memorable night of Ray Brown's lengthy career.

Charlie Parker's inclusion on some of the JATP dates must have brought a great sense of joy to Ray Brown. Although their paths had crossed several times since their initial meeting in 1945, it was only after Norman Granz took a stronghold over the saxophonist's career that Brown found more opportunities to work with Parker. When recording Parker, Granz often insisted that he use Ray Brown and the rest of the JATP rhythm section; as a result, some of Parker's finest works from this period are anchored by Brown's bass accompaniment, including the classic album *Charlie Parker with Strings*.

Recorded on November 30, 1949, *Charlie Parker with Strings* was pivotal to Parker's career. Although he had long wanted to record with strings, few expected Parker to actually pull such a session off. First of all, it would include the high costs of hiring an orchestra, a studio, and commissioned arrangements, and, since faith in Parker's likelihood to show up sober – or show up at all – was low, there seemed to be no one willing to support such a project. Thankfully Norman Granz did put his faith in Parker, and, because of this, Parker approached the session with great seriousness. He arrived on time and was prepared. Parker's playing is remarkable, and the album became the saxophonist's most significant commercial success and one of the many essential albums in which Ray Brown participated. To many, the version of "Just Friends" represents Charlie Parker's most outstanding recording of a ballad. Ray Brown has always spoken fondly of Parker and the recording of the album. In the following excerpt, Brown commented on the recording and Parker's ability:

> Bird might have been the most complete player I've ever heard. When I was twelve years old, I saw him in Jay McShann's band; and Parker proved himself to be a fantastic blues player. But by the time he was with Dizzy's band in 1945, his focus was bebop; and he played so well that folks forgot what a great blues player he was. Or with Machito's band, he was great in a Latin jazz setting. When *Charlie Parker with Strings* came out, his ballad playing was so beautiful that people focused on that. He was such a complete player.[54]
>
> I remember that it was amazing how he was able to play with this orchestra [on *Charlie Parker with Strings*]. This was a mix of two completely different thought processes and styles: Mitch Miller [classical

oboist and conductor] and Charlie Parker. I mean, nowhere near each other musically. And the fact that it worked, here's music that people in Omaha would buy. I mean there is just something, some magic about it.[55]

When Ray Brown first met Charlie Parker in 1945, it was during one of Parker's lowest periods. Like many, Brown was in awe of Parker's talents but never truly got to know him well during the challenging Los Angeles trip. Charlie Parker was not a mentor to Ray Brown in the same scholarly way that Dizzy Gillespie was, but, occasionally, Parker did offer some advice to Brown and other younger musicians like Milt Jackson. He often warned Brown and Jackson about the evils of drugs, being aware of how it had compromised his well-being yet he couldn't control his addiction. Brown and Jackson seemed to have taken Parker's advice to heart; both managed to avoid any dangerous drug habits.

Much of what Ray Brown learned from Parker he had to pick up by observing, but he did learn one particular important lesson from Parker about overplaying. Brown explains:

> Bird didn't play endless choruses, and I, for one, wanted to hear more. So once I said to him, "When you play, it feels so good. Why don't you play more?" And he said, "Well, Raymond, I'll tell you. If I played any more, I'd be practicing. And I practice at home."[56]

Throughout his career, Brown was always careful not to overplay, especially during solo spots, having seemingly adopted a similar philosophy to Parker on this issue.

Late 1949 also gives us two curious Mercury Records recording sessions, which place Ray Brown with jazz legend John Coltrane. The first was with Dinah Washington and the Teddy Stewart Orchestra on September 27, 1949. By the late '40s, Dinah Washington had become a break-out star who would eventually be listed among the great jazz vocalists, and the session index lists an impressive ensemble which as well as Ray Brown includes John Coltrane and Jimmy Heath on tenor sax, Freddie Green on guitar, among others. The session yielded four tracks: "Fast Movin' Mama," "Juice Head Man of Mine," "Shukin' and Jivin'," and "The Richest Guy in the Graveyard." Neither Brown nor Coltrane solo on any of the numbers.

The second session was for jump blues vocalist and pianist Billy Valentine and took place in Los Angeles on November 7, 1949. Also included in the ensemble were Johnny Collins on guitar and Specs Powell on drums. This Mercury session also yielded four tracks: "How Long, How Long," "Ain't Gonna Cry No More," "I Want You to Love Me," and "Beer Drinkin' Baby." When Ray Brown was asked about having recorded with John Coltrane, he was adamant that he "never did." In 1949, John Coltrane was yet to become a star, and it is possible that Coltrane failed to make an impression on Brown and that he forgot the particulars of these sessions. If Brown is indeed on these records, they represent the only time that he and Coltrane recorded together.

As the decade was ending, there was no question that Ray Brown had become the most sought-after jazz bassist on the scene. In just one year, Ray Brown had worked with the biggest names in jazz history, backed the most famous vocalist, led his own band, and helped introduce Oscar Peterson, jazz's next major star, on his American debut.

7 Time Changes: Fitzgerald to Peterson
1950

From 1950, Ray Brown and Oscar Peterson began a tight-knit association that continued throughout most of Ray's life. The amount of quality music they have provided is monumental. The two men shared similar musical values, which included tradition over wild experimentation and virtuosity over gimmickry. They both aspired to achieve technical mastery and worked extremely hard at achieving their goals.

Oscar Peterson was born in Montreal, Canada, on August 15, 1925. Fueled by his father's passion for musical education, Peterson's piano training began early, and he developed quickly. While his early training was strictly classical, Peterson's fascination with jazz piano began in his early teens when he first heard Art Tatum. Peterson was determined to match Tatum's technique, and so changed his musical direction and developed an impressive jazz style and repertoire. At fourteen, Peterson won a national amateur talent contest hosted by the Canadian Broadcasting Company, netting him $250 and a slot on a weekly radio program called *Fifteen Minute Piano Ramblings* in Montreal. Having quickly developed a strong reputation around Montreal's St. Antoine district, at seventeen the pianist joined the Johnny Holmes Orchestra and remained with the group for five years.

Oscar Peterson first recorded in Canada in 1946 and soon attracted the attention of famous American musicians like Jimmie Lunceford, Count Basie, Duke Ellington, and Coleman Hawkins. Despite some impressive job offers with top bandleaders, Peterson chose to remain in his native Canada and worked with his own trio at Montreal's Alberta Lounge from fall 1947 through September 1949, enjoying great success. It was during this time that Peterson first met jazz promoter Norman Granz. In an interview, Peterson retold the story of their meeting:

> [Granz] came up to Montreal to promote an upcoming tour of his that was coming through with Jazz at the Philharmonic. He was in a cab on his way back to the airport after doing some promotion prior to the tour. I was doing a fifteen-minute program on the air from the Alberta Lounge, and the cabby happened to have the radio on; and Norman inquired and said

to the cabby, "Who is that?" "What record is that?" And the cabby said, "That's not a record. That's Oscar Peterson." And Norman said, "What are you talking about?" [The cabby] thought Norman was a Montrealer. He said, "Don't you know who Oscar Peterson is?" Granz said, "No." The cabby said, "He's playing at the Alberta Lounge." And Norman said, "Turn around. Never mind the airport. Let's go down there." And he came to the Alberta Lounge, and that's when we first met.[57]

Once he'd heard the Oscar Peterson, Norman Granz instantly had a career plan for pianist. During their initial meeting, the two came to an agreement in which Peterson would finally make his American debut on stage with JATP at Carnegie Hall on September 18, 1949. Carnegie Hall seemed to be the perfect setting in which to introduce himself to the American public: since 1940, it had become a tradition for Granz to introduce a surprise guest at the annual concert there. Previous guests included Lionel Hampton and Billie Holiday, both significant stars.

The concert and Peterson's debut were memorable, especially for Ray Brown, who was the only other musician on stage. Brown and Peterson have often spoken about the debut and why they were only a duo. Ray Brown remembers:

> Buddy [Rich] had a drum solo to play. And you know Buddy, when he plays his solos, he plays till he is exhausted. He just plays until he is two inches from dead. His solos usually came before the intermission . . . Buddy played a solo that night at Carnegie Hall and came off completely wiped out. Norman said, "Okay, I'm going to bring Oscar on." Buddy said, "Norman, I don't think I can go back out there." Norman said, "What am I going to do?" Oscar said, "Ray Brown and I'll do it." So that's how it happened. Out of these things, sometimes good always happens. We went out and played and tore it up anyway. We played "Tenderly," and later on, we went into the studio and made a record of it, and it was a hit record. But that is how the duo started because Buddy was too wiped to play.[58]

Peterson has a different memory of the event:

> Norman Granz wanted me to play solo. He said, "Yeah, all right, you're gonna come on the second half and play solo piano." I said, "Norman, I haven't been playing solo piano recently, and that's another venue altogether," and I said, "Let me use a rhythm section." He said, "No, I want people to hear exactly what you're doing without anything getting in your way." We talked about this for a few minutes, and he said, "I'll make you a concession; you can have Ray Brown, but leave the drums out." Well, mainly I remember that we melded very easily together . . . We didn't have any rehearsal or anything. We just discussed what we were going to play and [*laughingly*] what key it was going to be in, and he said, "We'll lay out an intro, and we'll go for it, you know, which I did, and it was very easy. Immediately it was a fix, as we say.[59]

Notwitstanding the conflicting stories, we know for certain that it was just the two of them on stage and that Peterson's debut was a great success. It was immediately apparent to Oscar Peterson, Ray Brown, Norman Granz, and thousands of fans that Peterson and Brown were a perfect musical match.

Although the Carnegie debut was the first time Brown and Peterson had worked together offcially, the two had already met and jammed together in Montreal when Brown had visited as part of JATP. Peterson had noticed Brown's playing on Gillespie's records as early as 1946 and even told childhood friend bassist Hal Gaylor that someday he would lead a trio with Ray Brown on the bass – a conversation that took place years before the two had ever met. Peterson's foreshadowing was soon to become a reality, but for the time being the pair would have to wait before they worked together again. As 1949 was coming to a close, Oscar Peterson returned to Canada following his Carnegie Hall debut. Ray Brown and his wife Ella Fitzgerald continued to tour with JATP, but a seed had been planted on the evening of September 18, 1949.

As 1950 began, Brown and Fitzgerald were still busily touring and recording together, but it was apparent that their relationship was becoming strained. Brown may have felt somewhat limited by working with a singer, and perhaps backing Ella Fitzgerald was unchallenging for him. The couple recorded twice together at the beginning of the year, the first of these sessions taking place on February 2 for Decca Records, with the Sy Oliver Orchestra backing. While Fitzgerald had proven over the pevious year both a desire and ability to explore bebop and more modernistic elements, her label at that time, Decca, seemed to have little interest in presenting Ella in a setting where she could record extensively in that fashion. Instead, they stuck to the winning formula of Broadway hits, pop ballads, and novelty tunes. So in February, Fitzgerald, Brown, and the Oliver Orchestra recorded a walking ballad called "Baby, Won't You Say You Love Me" and the medium-swing "Don'cha Go 'Way Mad," two commercial offerings on which Fitzgerald sang a duo with Sy Oliver.

On the next of these Decca sessions, on March 3, 1950, Fitzgerald was again backed by the Sy Oliver Orchestra, and here Decca chose to present her singing over a jump blues accompaniment style. Jump blues was a growing trend emerging in the late 1940s as a reaction to bop and the more classically influenced hybrid style known as cool jazz. Jump blues bands favored more straightforward arrangements, simple chord changes, a more danceable drum beat, and a return to swing elements. The style also often incorporated group clapping, and call-and-response patterns associated with the Black church. While it is fun to listen to Fitzgerald and Brown on such tracks as "Solid As a Rock" and "Sugar Foot Rag," it did little to showcase the former's full ability as a serious jazz vocalist. The session also yielded a ridiculous novelty calypso song called "Peas and Rice." The best track from the session is easily Fitzgerald's interpretation of Harold Arlen's "I've Got the World on a String."

Ray Brown had many more musical interests and skills than could be explored in Fitzgerald's group. Feeling creatively handcuffed, Brown sought out small-group opportunities to display his skills. While he remained committed to Fitzgerald's musical efforts, he began to accept various other offers that separated him from his wife. Ella felt strongly that Ray's position was by her side and possibly may not have agreed with her husband's choices.

Norman Granz continued to present Brown with opportunities to support jazz's biggest stars. After the Carnegie Hall debut, Granz was eager to record Oscar Peterson, and, on March 1, 1950, the gifted pianist and Ray Brown recorded together for the first time. The eight-song session showcases Peterson mostly on popular standards and the album was Oscar Peterson's first major hit, with a brilliant interpretation of "Tenderly." Other highlights include "Debut" and "All the Things You Are." Brown is only briefly highlighted as a soloist on the melody of "Where or When." On tunes like "Oscar's Blues" and "In the Middle of a Kiss," Brown's playing is notable on some-call-and response figures where he manipulates double-time and triplet rhythmic figures. These early duo recordings are among Peterson's most pleasing of the early 1950s, showing him as not only one of the most technically gifted pianists in jazz history but as someone capable of incredible harmonic and melodic inventions.

On a later session, in May 1950, Peterson is paired with bassist Major Holley, allowing a comparison between the two performances. While Holley was also an excellent bassist, his quarter-note rhythms have a more staccato (shorter) quality, whereas Brown gives each quarter note its full length. Brown also connects his notes more melodically and interestingly than Holley. Peterson sounds more comfortable with Brown's sense of swing and interacts better with Brown than Holley.

In March 1950, Norman Granz made a series of recordings which included Ray Brown and his trio with Hank Jones and Buddy Rich. The first of these was meant to showcase his JATP saxophonists Flip Phillips, Lester Young, and Charlie Parker. An interesting comparison can be made between the saxophonists when we listen to a recording made around the same time (possibly on the same day). The Flip Phillips sessions further reveal a saxophonist who has an incredible command of the instrument but relies heavily on Lester Young's style and the jump blues gimmickry. In this session, Brown is featured somewhat during his bowed solos on "Feelin' the Blues" and "Lover Come Back to Me." "Blue Room" prominently features Ray Brown throughout and is indicative of the bassist's development. This track ranks among Brown's finest recordings of the early 1950s.

In contrast to the Flip Phillips date, Lester Young's session exhibits the innovator's laid-back phrasing, wonderful tone, and the stylings of a true jazz originator. His style is never excessively showy and certainly less technical than Phillips and Parker; however, Young's playing has an unexplained quality that separates him from other more technical players. Ray Brown is not featured on these recordings as a soloist except for some walking bass line breaks.

The three-song session for Charlie Parker is remarkable. It begins with the walking ballad "Star Eyes," and Parker's interpretation is original, virtuosic, and further exemplifies his astonishing ability to interpret ballads. The second number is simply titled "Blues (Fast)," a piece that seems to have no preconceived arrangement or melody but is an excellent example of how four incredibly gifted musicians can deliver in a jam-session format. The final selection is the 1935 Jimmy McHugh and Dorothy Fields classic "I'm in the Mood for Love," played at a medium swing and on which Brown takes a short solo. Hearing Brown's trio with Parker is an absolute joy.

Ray Brown was likely performing with Ella and his trio throughout most of the spring of 1950, but on July 1 he was back recording for Granz once again. The first of these sessions was for Bud Powell and yielded two tracks. On the first, "Hallelujah," we hear Powell, Brown, and Rich playing in a fast bebop style, the other song being the standard "Tea for Two," three recordings of which were made with only one being issued (Norgran MGN-1036). On this version the group delivers a rubato (out-of-time) intro, before going into a fast swing. These tracks show Powell in his prime and deserve to be lauded as two of the pianist's finest recordings. "Hallelujah" and "Tea for Two" further the argument that Powell was the only true bop pianist who could match Parker and Gillespie's technicality and creativity.

The next session was for Flip Phillips. Joining Brown's trio for this session was famed Basie trumpeter Harry "Sweets" Edison, trombonist Bill Harris, and guitarist Billy Bauer. The session yielded three swing-style tracks: "Be Be," "Dream a Little Dream of Me," and "Bright Blues." This session is a fine example of fantastic front-line musicians playing in the swing style in which they are most comfortable.

On this date, the Ray Brown Trio was also recorded as a self-contained unit in a session that yielded two issued tracks. The first is "Blue Lou," on which Ray Brown plays the melody with the bow, humming the melody in unison with his bow, a style of arco interpretation that had become famous through the playing of Slam Stewart. Following solos by Jones and Rich, Brown returns with an impressive arco solo. The song is tightly arranged and foreshadows Brown's approach to small-group arrangements with his later trios of the 1980s and '90s. The other track issued is a Russian folk number called "Song of the Volga Boatmen." Brown presents the simple melody on this track and takes a masterful solo. The song is a genuine feature for Brown and, quite possibly, with the exception of Gillespie's versions of "Two Bass Hit," his most outstanding solo feature to date. Unfortunately, this session garnered little public interest at the time. Also recorded that day was another impressive Brown feature called "Slow Blues," which was not issued. These tracks are now available on the Ray Brown compilation *The Man: The Complete Recordings 1946–1959* (Fresh Sound Records FSRCD 560).

Ray Brown displays his arco technique.
Album / Alamy Stock Photo

On July 5, 1950, Ray Brown was back recording another string session with Charlie Parker. Joining him in the rhythm section was Buddy Rich and a pianist named Bernie Leighton. While these recordings are not as strong as the 1949 session, Parker's playing is still brilliant and intriguing and the session yielded eight new tracks to add to Parker's catalog. Following the recording, Parker embarked on a series of live performances with the string ensemble, although Ray Brown did not participate in any of these, as Parker's regular bassist at the time, Tommy Potter, handled the responsibilities. For the remainder of the year, despite some personal issues, Parker managed to keep it together just enough to present his "Charlie Parker with Strings" material at clubs like Birdland, the Blue Note, the Apollo, and with JATP at Carnegie Hall.

In August 1950, Oscar Peterson and Ray Brown were back in the studio where they recorded eighteen tracks as a duo. This recording began a pattern whereby Norman Granz seemed obsessed with recording Peterson as frequently as possible to create a backlog of material. Naturally, with such oversaturation, the pianist could not be expected to deliver a masterpiece with every performance. While there was no question of his mastery as a piano virtuoso, some began to criticize Peterson for being formulaic and predictable. Additionally, Brown was most often used only in the more traditional accompanying role of a conventional bassist; rarely was he given lengthy solos on these recordings, and he often chose walking bass lines over counterpunctual melodic statements that might have created more interest. While these recordings failed to document the more daring elements of Peterson's live performances, there are some tracks of considerable interest. The most fascinating of the August recordings is an interpretation of the Russian folk song "Dark Eyes." Unlike other tracks, which followed the standard format of Peterson presenting the melody, then soloing before returning to the theme, "Dark Eyes" "is carefully arranged. It begins with Peterson displaying his early classical training before the song moves between swing, fast double-time statements, and stop-time figures. At one point, Peterson raises the dynamic level to such a high volume that the piano distorts. The Peterson–Brown interpretation of "Dark Eyes" is unexpected and passionate.

On August 15, 1950, Ray Brown and his trio, enhanced by guitarist John Collins, backed Ella Fitzgerald and jump blues vocalist and saxophonist Louis Jordan on the forgettable ballad "You'll Never Be Free." Louis Jordan was one of the most prominent musical personalities of his time. With his group, the Tympany Five, he is widely responsible for popularizing the jump blues craze of the late 1940s and early '50s, which was partially responsible for the slow decline of bebop's popularity. According to Fitzgerald's biographer, Stuart Nicholson, Fitzgerald and Jordan had had an affair from May to August 1938.[60] Even after this short romantic relationship had finished, Fitzgerald continued to record with Jordan over the years prior to this 1950 session.

Given their past relationship, it is possible that this session may have been somewhat uncomfortable for Brown, Fitzgerald, and Jordan.

On August 25, 1950, Ray Brown got his first chance to record with jazz's first great virtuoso and most famous personality, Louis Armstrong. While Armstrong was being presented at this point in his career more as a pop sensation than as the great innovator of jazz, any session with Armstrong guarantees instant joy. The date yielded two tracks, "Dream a Little Dream of Me" and "Can Anyone Explain?" with Ella Fitzgerald and Louis Armstrong singing duets: Fitzgerald's light sweet vocal quality juxtaposed with Armstrong's gravely timbre makes for a perfect contrast, and pairing two of jazz's most recognizable vocalists proved a superb match and a big seller for Decca Records. Although he had never really modernized his trumpet style since the late 1920s, Armstrong's solos always maintained tremendous phrasing and personality that never sounded stale. The arranger for this project, Sy Oliver, does a fantastic job of creating the perfect orchestration to match the vocalists' talents. While Brown is not prominently featured, it must have been an incredible thrill for him to record with jazz's most legendary figure.

On September 16, 1950, JATP embarked on its tenth national tour at Carnegie Hall with its newest member, Oscar Peterson. As the tour moved through every major U.S. and Canadian city, Brown was now performing with both Ella Fitzgerald and Oscar Peterson. Traveling together, Brown and Peterson continued to develop their friendship and tight musical hookup; but, as their friendship grew, Ray Brown's relationship with Ella Fitzgerald continued to suffer. Granz wisely took the opportunity to record the concerts. Oscar Peterson was now one of the main draws of the JATP tour, and he and Brown shone in front of the live audience where the pianist was not limited to the time restraints of the recording studio.

On the compilation Oscar Peterson Duo, *Debut/Mercury Duo Recordings 1949–1951* (Hip-O Select B0012950), we can hear three tracks from the evening, "Gai," "Padovani," and "Tea for Two." Unlike many of his studio recordings at this time, Peterson's playing is daring and innovative as he experiments with odd time phrasings, rapid two-hand unison lines, varied dynamics, and bop styling. The duo has the audience's complete attention, with fans reacting to Peterson's more expressive moments. After "Padovani" and "Tea for Two," which were highlights of the evening, the audience's applause was near deafening. Other highlights captured on the record from the evening were Coleman Hawkins' soulful performances of "Yesterdays," "Hawk's Tune," and "Stuffy," all with the Ray Brown Trio.

Another great pairing occurred around this time when Coleman Hawkins and Charlie Parker, two of the most influential saxophonists of their times, entered the studio together with Ray Brown's trio in October 1950. Later, a video was made of the group miming to their tracks, as had been the case with "soundies" from the era. The video is the longest that exists of Charlie

Parker. Ray Brown can be seen briefly during "Celebrity," with only Parker and Hawkins appearing on "Ballade."

Following the 1950 JATP tour, Oscar Peterson was awarded "Best Pianist" honors in the *DownBeat* magazine poll, an accolade he would continue to receive over the next several years. Granz decided it was time for the pianist to tour the United States as a featured act until the next JATP tour. When Granz and Peterson asked Ray Brown to join Peterson on the road, the bassist was reluctant to accept because he knew it would further strain his marriage. He went ahead and accepted all the same: a decision that may have led directly to his breakup with Fitzgerald.[61]

8 The Oscar Peterson Duo and Early Trio
1950–1952

Touring now as a regular duo, Oscar Peterson and Ray Brown appeared at a club in Washington D.C. called Louis and Alex and then traveled the continent. In his autobiography, *A Jazz Odyssey*, Peterson speaks fondly about those days which he referred to as "The most memorable days of my early musical career." Their relationship developed from friendship to brotherhood as the two performed, traveled, and roomed together. On these duo tours, Peterson and Brown had one common goal: to "Play the world into bad health while having as much fun as possible in the free hours."[62] The two would rehearse whenever possible, determined to prove that they were the best talents on their respective instruments and that, even as a duo, they could deliver music that was both technical and hard-swinging. They also soon realized that they shared a similar sense of humor and enjoyed practical jokes: they would try to outsmart each other whenever possible. As an ongoing joke, they would attempt to unnerve each other before a performance by saying that either Art Tatum or Oscar Pettiford was sitting in the audience – a joke that eventually turned into a reality when Tatum turned up one night to hear Peterson play. Although nervous, Peterson did succeed in performing in front of his idol, and the two piano virtuosos developed mutual respect and friendship, as did Brown and Pettiford.

Musically, the duo was progressing rapidly, but not everything was smooth sailing. On occasion, both men faced racism, mainly as they traveled through the South and parts of Canada. Most Black musicians could not escape harsh treatment, no matter how hard they tried: at times, it was difficult for Brown and Peterson to find a decent place to stay or get a hot meal. In his autobiography, Peterson recalls a number of instances of racism:

> Joe [Woldarsky, manager at the Alberta Lounge] caught my sleeve and said, "Oscar, meet a gentleman who is a great admirer of your music." The man started to rave about my playing before I could say anything and continued for what seemed minutes on end. When he finally stopped, I put out my hand and said something like the usual "Pleased to meet you." At that moment, his facial expression changed abruptly; he recoiled in

anger, his hand jerked away behind his back, and he said, "I could never shake hands with a nigger! I love your playing, but down home in Georgia, we don't allow niggers to even come into a place like this, let alone shake hands with them." . . . My real "education" in bigotry and racial hatred took place when I first toured the south with JATP in 1950 . . . To be insulted, called names, or denied access is one thing, however unacceptable; to live in constant fear of physical harm or even death is quite another.[63]

The duo continued to tour together through 1951 as Granz began planning for a European tour. On January 19, 1951, the pair hit the New York studios to stockpile new material. Most of the ten tracks recorded that day would be released on the 1956 album *Nostalgic Memories* (Clef C-695), with "How High the Moon" serving as the single. Other highlights from the session include "Lover," "Laura," and "Lullaby of the Leaves." While the tracks are pleasant enough, they all conform to the popular three-minute radio format and don't truly showcase Brown's abilities, completely ignoring him as a soloist.

In the March 3, 1951, issue of *Melody Maker*, it was revealed that Norman Granz had abandoned his European JATP tour. Several factors had led to this, foremost of which was Ella Fitzgerald and Ray Brown's reconsideration due to differences they had with Granz about salary. Buddy Rich and Harry Edison also backed out, the former reportedly not wanting to dissolve the big band he was leading at the time. As a result of Fitzgerald's withdrawal, some European promoters wished to cut back on guaranteed payments fearing that attendance might suffer without the concert's biggest draw. In addition to his musician troubles, Granz met with strong resistance from the British Musicians' Union (MU), which had strict guidelines about American musicians performing in the United Kingdom: no American artists could play within their jurisdiction unless there was a reciprocal agreement in which an equivalent cohort of British musicians gained work in the United States. Although he tried to strike a deal with the MU, which included a proposed concert in aid of its Musicians' Benevolent Fund or any charity of their choice, his requests were denied. So, instead of Europe, JATP's eleventh tour was another foray around the United States.

By the summer of 1951, Ray Brown and Ella Fitzgerald were estranged, and Oscar Peterson was having trouble obtaining the necessary work permits from the Canadian government to tour. Things eventually worked out, with Brown and Fitzgerald reconciling their differences for the time being and Peterson securing an arrangement that allowed him to travel with JATP. So, on September 14, 1951, JATP kicked off a ten-week, forty-eight-concert tour with Ella Fitzgerald and Oscar Peterson billed as the attractions.

Granz used the opportunity to add to his catalog of recordings based on the JATP tours. The first of these to include Ray Brown was a big-band session led by Cuban-born composer and arranger Chico O'Farrill on August 7, 1951. Through his work with Machito, Stan Kenton, Benny Goodman, and Dizzy Gillespie, O'Farrill helped incorporate Afro-Cuban elements into jazz. The four selections recorded that day would be included in the 1956 release *Chico O'Farrill: Jazz North of the Border and South of the Border* (Clef MG C-699). These excellent recordings display O'Farrill's superb ability as an arranger. The session also included such jazz stars as Roy Eldridge and Flip Phillips, serving as the primary soloists. Working with Brown in the rhythm section were Jo Jones on drums, Billy Bauer on guitar, and Ralph Burns on piano.

On the same day as the O'Farrill session, Brown recorded eight further tracks with Ralph Burns not only as pianist but leader, arranger, and composer too. This unique session included a string section and ensemble with French horn and the magnificent talents of alto saxophonist Lee Konitz. Both Burns and Konitz were connected with the newly celebrated "cool jazz" movement, which added more subdued textures, arrangement characteristics, and classical elements to jazz. The cool style was adopted and popularized by Miles Davis on his classic 1949 and 1950 recordings that led to the album *The Birth of Cool*. Hearing Ray Brown perform in the "cool" context is fascinating and further displays his versatility. The tracks recorded were released on the 1952 album *Free Forms by Ralph Burns* (Mercury MG C-115). Ralph Burns and this album are certainly worthy of more attention.

On August 8, 1951, Brown recorded at RCA Victor's 24th Street Studios in New York City, with Charlie Parker and an ensemble that included Red Rodney on trumpet, John Lewis on piano, and Kenny Clarke on drums. Parker's sax is considerably sharp on the record, and while Rodney is a fine player, his talents are not those of Dizzy Gillespie. For the session, Brown can be heard soloing on "Si Si" and "Swedish Schnapps." A highlight of the session is Charlie Parker's version of "Lover Man," a much more exemplary recording of the ballad than his version from July 26, 1946, from the night of his Los Angeles breakdown. Much of the material from this session was released on *The Magnificent Charlie Parker* (Clef MG C-646).

Ray Brown was part of another landmark session on August 24, 1951, when he recorded with Milt Jackson, John Lewis, and Kenny Clarke. Many consider this the first recording of the Modern Jazz Quartet (MJQ), one of the most celebrated and successful instrumental jazz groups, who had begun to develop their signature sound as members of Dizzy Gillespie's orchestra. The date yielded four excellent tracks under the band and album name *The Milt Jackson Quartet* (Dee Gee 1002): "Milt Meets Sid," "D&E," "Yesterdays," and "Between the Devil and the Deep Blue Sea." The group has a nice hookup and an overall sound that mixes cool jazz, blues, and swing. It would have been interesting if Ray Brown had continued to develop with MJQ – which he could have done had he not been focusing his attention at this time on helping the careers of Ella Fitzgerald and Oscar Peterson. Not long after bassist Percy Heath took over from Brown in the group, the Milt Jackson Quartet changed its name but kept the same initials – and in 1952 the Modern Jazz Quartet was born. Ray Brown had helped the group develop its early sound and is usually credited as a founding member.

On November 23, 1951, Decca brought Louis Armstrong and Ella Fitzgerald back to a Los Angeles studio to record with Dave Barbour's orchestra. The session yielded four forgettable commercial numbers in "Necessary Evil," "Oops" (Decca 27901), "Would You Like to Take a Walk?" and "Who Walks In When I Walk Out?" (Decca 28552). In this large ensemble, Brown serves only as an accompanist. It had become apparent by the time of this recording that Fitzgerald and Brown were following two very different musical paths.

Having worked for the best part of two years as a duo, at Norman Granz's behest Peterson and Brown recorded with a third member. While in Los Angeles, on November 25, 1951, guitarist Barney Kessel joined them to record five tracks in a session that would become the first of many Oscar Peterson Trio recordings. Kessel was an established Los Angeles musician who had already worked with stars like Lester Young, Charlie Parker, and Artie Shaw. Adding a third harmonic voice was a breath of fresh air and offered new arrangement possibilities. Since both Peterson and Brown were great admirers of the work of Nat King Cole and Art Tatum's trio, which also used piano–bass–guitar instrumentation, adding a guitarist made perfect sense.

Oscar Peterson likely felt that using another linear melodic instrument would add interesting harmonic textures; Ray Brown had already proven to Peterson that he could assume the rhythmic responsibilities without a drummer. Besides its melodic and harmonic possibilities, the guitar could also be used as an effective rhythmic instrument and in fact was initially employed for just such a purpose on its earliest appearance in Dixieland and swing bands. Brown is briefly featured on the ballad "It's Easy to Remember"; one of the more surprising tracks, "Until the Real Thing Comes Along," features Peterson as a vocalist on which he reveals an ability to sing in the style of Nat King Cole.[64]

Still committed to Fitzgerald's career, Ray Brown began 1952 with a January 4 studio date for Fitzgerald and the Decca label, which resulted in two tracks, "Air Mail Special" (Decca 28126) and "Rough Ridin'" (Decca 27948). There is a unique sound to these recordings thanks to the inclusion of organist Bill Doggett and the Ray Charles Singers. Fitzgerald's scat vocalizations are on full display on both tracks.

In 1952, Granz persuaded Peterson to permanently add a third member to his group. Although the duo format had worked well for a while, club owners were complaining about the high price they were paying for just two musicians. The problem, of course, was finding the right musician. At first, Peterson chose to go with a familiar face and hired drummer Charlie Smith, who had previously worked with Brown and Fitzgerald in their trio, as well as one of Peterson's own earlier trios. Smith was a fine and experienced drummer, but didn't remain with the group for long; according to Peterson, Smith was reluctant to travel.[65]

Following Smith's departure, Peterson decided that a guitarist might better suit his group and hired Irving Ashby, who had worked with the Nat Cole Trio. In the March 21, 1952 issue of *DownBeat,* an announcement was made that Ashby was now a regular member of the Oscar Peterson Trio. By then, the trio had already gone into the studio to record the album *Oscar Peterson Plays Pretty* (Columbia Clef Series 33C-1037) in Los Angeles on January 26, 1952. The date yielded eight sides which included popular standards like "You Go to My Head," "They Can't Take That Away from Me," and "These Foolish Things (Remind Me of You)." Ashby adds an excellent light swing to these numbers but is underutilized and rarely featured. This session would be Ashby's only recording as a trio member.

Peterson writes:

> Irving Ashby entered our group as a very well-known player in his own right. Having spent many years with Nat King Cole's group, he came in with confidence, which was fully deserved; however, he was also somewhat apprehensive... During his tenure with the group, I noticed a very interesting thing: there was an unspoken rivalry between Irving and Ray. It was not exactly a war, but it most certainly was a matter of neither one giving way to the other. Ray was always willing to play any lines required of him, no matter how difficult, whereas Irving seemed to feel that we did not need as many linear statements being made by both bass and guitar. Irving's presence meant that the trio swung in a notably mellow fashion. He never pretended to be a great uptempo player, but he sure could mellow into a righteous groove if the tempo was put anywhere within his liking. He brought a rich and swinging melodic feel to the group.[66]

It soon became apparent that Oscar Peterson's trio required a guitarist who could swing at any tempo and one who could provide melodic statements and counterpoint with confidence. The most obvious choice was Barney Kessel, but at this point in his career he was comfortably established in Los Angeles as a freelance musician and disliked traveling. So he and Peterson struck a deal whereby Kessel would join the group only for a year, an arrangement that would give Peterson enough time to get established and search for an eventual replacement.

On February 26, 1952, Peterson, Brown, and Kessel entered a Los Angeles studio where they recorded ten tracks, eight of which are augmented by drummer Alvin Stoller. Hearing Oscar Peterson with a drummer and guitarist is another welcome change which helped add some variety to his rapidly growing catalog. These recordings are also notable because six of these selections' running time is well over ten minutes. Here, Peterson and the ensemble get a chance to explore, and hearing these musicians in a more informal jam-session context is an absolute pleasure. Peterson's and Kessel's abilities as soloists are fully showcased. The addition of a drummer freed Brown from the heavy responsibility of being the principal rhythmic element within the ensemble. While not featured frequently as a soloist, Brown plays some impressive breaks on "Tea for Two" and "Body and Soul." Once again, Oscar Peterson does his Nat King Cole vocal impression on two tracks, "Too Marvelous for Words" and "But Not for Me."[67]

The next noteworthy studio date for Ray Brown was a big-band recording on March 25, 1952 for Charlie Parker, backed by the Joe Lippman Orchestra. The session took place in a studio located at First Ave. and East 44th Street in New York City, and the ensemble included Flip Phillips, Oscar Peterson, and guitarist Freddie Green. Hearing Parker in a big-band context is of particular interest, primarily since he is widely associated with the birth of bebop and the eventual breakdown of the swing big band's popularity. This recording most certainly upset many bop enthusiasts. On the recording, Parker is fantastic in his interpretations of "Night and Day," "Almost Like Being in Love," "I Can't Get Started," and "What Is This Thing Called Love." These tracks were originally released as *Charlie Parker Big Band* (Mercury MGC-609).

The next day, Ray Brown was in Los Angeles, where he would record with legendary vocalist Billie Holiday for the first time. Through the 1930s and 1940s, Holiday was one of jazz's biggest names and best-selling vocalists. Unlike Fitzgerald, though, she had a limited vocal range: her genius was not one of technicality but a matchless ability to interpret standard material with her signature bluesy and laid-back phrasing. At this point, Holiday was making a comeback after years of drug and alcohol abuse had led to a nearly year-long imprisonment beginning in 1947. The incarceration and the loss of her cabaret card made it impossible for her to perform anywhere alcohol was sold. Joining Ray Brown on the session were trumpeter Charlie Shavers, Flip Phillips, Oscar Peterson, Barney Kessel, and Alvin Stoller. In April, a second session with almost the same ensemble[68] produced fifteen more fantastic tracks. These sessions are among Holiday's finest of her later career, and Ray Brown's bass has an excellent presence throughout. Highlights from the session include "East of the Sun (West of the Moon)," "You Go to My Head," and "I Only Have Eyes for You." Much of the material recorded that day was released on the album *Solitude: Songs by Billie Holiday* (Clef MGC-690).

At some time around now, presumably the same week as the first Holiday session, Brown, Peterson, and Kessel recorded four tracks with the Nick Esposito Sextet (Clef EP-190). Esposito began his career as a violinist with the Chicago Symphony and was the first jazz guitarist ever featured with the New York Philharmonic. In addition to his career as a performer, he was a guitar luthier who made several improvements to the instrument and invented the adjustable bridge and double-cutaway guitar shape. Also included in this recording is Flip Phillips, trombonist Bennie Green, and drummer J.C. Heard. Brown's next effort was a session for Flip Phillips, likely made the same day as the Esposito recordings. Included in the group were Shavers, Stoller, Peterson, and Kessel.

In March of 1952, Norman Granz made the long-awaited announcement that he was finally able to organize a European JATP tour, and one of his featured acts would be the newly formatted Oscar Peterson Trio. The fourteen-date tour kicked off in Stockholm on March 30, with the troupe moving through Gothenburg, Malmö, Copenhagen, Paris, Brussels, Geneva, Zurich, Frankfurt, Amsterdam, The Hague, and Lausanne. The tour concluded with two shows in Frankfurt on April 19 for an audience of primarily American service members. This experience marked the first of many international tours that Ray Brown would participate in throughout his career.[69]

In either late May or early June 1952, Peterson's new trio was recorded in Los Angeles. The session features Peterson as a singer on "It Makes a Difference to Me" and "Autumn in New York," but the group is most impressive on the instrumental selections like "Pettiford's Tune (Little Boy)" (which has Brown as a soloist), "You Go to My Head," "Thou Swell," "Willow Weep for Me," and "Minor Blues." They benefit from the kinds of tight arrangements that were sometimes lacking in many of the trio's more rushed, short-form commercial efforts.[70]

In either late June or early July 1952, Granz and his musicians joined the Peterson trio for a JATP studio recording, a session that included Charlie Shavers, Benny Carter, Johnny Hodges, Charlie Parker, Flip Phillips, Ben Webster, Oscar Peterson, Barney Kessel, Ray Brown, and J.C. Heard. Marking a departure from previous JATP live recordings, Granz brought his all-star cast into a Los Angeles studio. With little use of arrangement or preconceived organization, the musicians approached the session as if it was a pickup-style jam session. It's notable among JATP recordings for the absence of the intrusive crowd noises, each musician being heard clearly and allowed to perform without the pressure of having to impress a large audience. One of the exceptional moments on these *Norman Granz Jam Session*[71] albums is a medley in which each musician is featured on a ballad of their choosing. Ray Brown went for "The Man I Love," a tune often associated with Ella Fitzgerald, on which he proved that he still could maintain interest as a soloist. Another notable moment was "Funky Blues," which pitted alto legends Charlie Parker, Johnny Hodges, and Benny Carter against one another.

Ray Brown's next studio appearance was on July 22, 1952 with a small-group format for tenor saxophone specialist Illinois Jacquet. At nineteen, Jacquet came to fame as a member of the Lionel Hampton Orchestra, with which he recorded one of the most famous tenor solos of all time on the hard-swinging "Flying Home." The solo was celebrated for his use of an overblowing technique known as "honking," a method that would often be emulated in jump blues. By 1944, Jacquet led his own band, where he continued to showcase the full thick tone of his saxophone in a jump blues style that would later influence early rhythm and blues and rock and roll. The session is of interest also because of Count Basie's presence on the jazz organ.

Count Basie was one of the true legends of swing, most notable for his work as a leader and pianist. His music greatly influenced Brown as a child, so this encounter must have been a memorable one for the bassist. Also included in the ensemble were Hank Jones on piano, Freddie Green on guitar, and Jimmy Crawford on drums. The session produced four solid tracks, "Lean Baby," "Somewhere Along the Way," "The Cool Rage," and "Port of Rico," which appeared on *Collates No. 2* (Mercury MGC-129), a 1953 Illinois Jacquet LP that brought together prior single releases.

Brown may well have enjoyed an even bigger thrill when he and Oscar Peterson recorded one track with the Basie Big Band on that same date for an uptempo number called "Be My Guest." That same date also yielded two more small-group tracks, the first being "Blues for the Count and Oscar," with Basie on organ and Peterson on piano. Also in the ensemble were Eddie "Lockjaw" Davis and Paul Quinichette, two of the era's finest tenor saxophonists. Brown takes a solo on this cut. On the second track, "Extended Blues," Basie plays the piano while Peterson takes over on the organ. Although Brown is not a primary soloist on the July 22 recordings with Basie, these tracks should not be overlooked as they establish a connection between Brown and the jazz legend Basie. The tracks were initially issued on the Oscar Peterson with Count Basie 45 rpm *The Count and Oscar* (Columbia SEB-10060).

On July 27, 1952 Brown was back recording with the great Billie Holiday in New York City with an ensemble that included Peterson, Freddie Green, Gus Johnson on drums, Joe Newman on trumpet, and Paul Quinichette. The group recorded six standards for the session. While Holiday's voice shows signs of wear attributable to hard living, her vocal timbre has a pleasing smokey quality, particularly on ballads and blues like "My Man" and "Stormy Weather." Ray Brown is briefly featured playing a bowed intro on "Lover Come Back to Me." Most of the material from the day was released on the Billie Holiday album *Recital* (Clef MGC-686). On August 4, 1952 Ray Brown was recorded on the album *Lester Young with the Oscar Peterson Trio* (Norgran).[72] Drummer J.C. Heard was also added to the ensemble to enhance the rhythmic energy. The recording resulted in one of Lester Young's finest efforts from the latter part of his career. Brown's only solo from the album is on the track "Indiana."

When JATP returned for their annual Carnegie Hall performance on September 13, 1952, the line-up included Roy Eldridge, Charlie Shavers, Benny Carter, Flip Phillips, Lester Young, Oscar Peterson, Barney Kessel, Ray Brown, and Buddy Rich on drums. The unit was recorded live, with several tracks appearing on the album *Norman Granz' Jazz at the Philharmonic Vol. 15* (Mercury MG VOL. 15).

On September 18, 1952 alto sax master Benny Carter recorded seven fantastic tracks with an ensemble that included Oscar Peterson's trio and Buddy Rich. Three of the tracks, "Isn't It Romantic," "Some Other Spring," and "These Things You Left Me," also included a string section. Benny Carter was a true marvel in jazz. He was not only celebrated as an alto player but was an outstanding trumpet player, arranger, composer, and bandleader with a recording career lasting an astonishing seventy years. Carter sounds tremendous on these recordings.

In December of 1952, the Oscar Peterson Trio recorded an astounding forty-two tracks as Norman Granz continued to stockpile material for the archives. Unfortunately, the effects of recording fatigue make many of these tracks sound flat, despite the obvious talents of Peterson, Brown, and Kessel. Most of the material was recorded for the *Oscar Peterson Plays* series and can be heard on 1953 releases like *Oscar Peterson Plays . . . the Jerome Kern Song Book* (Verve V6-2056), . . . *the Cole Porter Song Book* (Verve VS-6083), . . . *the George Gershwin Song Book* (Verve MG V-2054), . . . *the Irving Berlin Song Book* (Mercury MG C-604) and . . . *the Duke Ellington Song Book* (Mercury MG-C-606). These tracks fall into the three-minute radio single format, with Brown rarely foregrounded and Peterson and Kessel not overly experimental. There are some highlights, however, including "I Got Rhythm," "Willow Weep for Me," "Oh Lady Be Good," "Blue Skies," and "Rockin' in Rhythm."

December 4 also yielded another session for Benny Carter,[73] followed by a December 13 Roy Eldridge date with the Oscar Peterson Trio.[74] J.C. Heard is again on both recordings. Peterson plays organ on the Eldridge date, which adds further interest to these recordings. As well as some oustanding trumpet playing, Eldridge can also be heard scatting on "Rocking Chair."

One of the more unusual Oscar Peterson Trio sessions was in December 1952, at Radio Recorders Studio in Hollywood, when they recorded in an ensemble backing actor, dancer, songwriter, and singer Fred Astaire on thirty-eight tracks. The bulk of these recordings served as a retrospective of hit songs from Fred Astaire's extraordinary film and stage career. Astaire sings in a pleasant crooning style throughout, although struggling at times with certain intervals and failing to match the abilities of singers like Bing Crosby or Frank Sinatra. Astaire seems most comfortable with medium-swing numbers like "Puttin' on the Ritz," "Steppin' Out with My Baby," and "Top Hat, White Tie and Tails." Ray Brown only really comes to the fore on the Astaire recordings on a bowed intro and melody on "Oh, Lady Be Good." The most exciting moments are when Astaire tap-dances along with the band on "(Ad Lib) Fast Dance," "(Ad Lib) Medium Dance," and "(Ad Lib) Slow Dance." Additionally, the ensemble delivers a few swinging longer-form instrumental numbers like "Jam Session" and "The Astaire Blues." These recordings are now available on the compilation *The Astaire Story* (Mercury MGC-1001/4).

After the Astaire session, the Peterson trio recorded nine more tracks for the *Oscar Peterson Plays* series, all for the Irving Berlin LP (Mercury MG C-604). Once again, the group keeps to the three-minute format and takes few risks with the material.

As 1952 came to a close, Ray Brown emerged as one of the most sought-after and well-known bassists in the business, a consummate professional who could enhance any performance or session. It was also becoming apparent that Ray Brown and Ella Fitzgerald's relationship was coming to an end: Ray was now primarily choosing work with no Ella by his side.

9 Navigating the Changes: Transitions
1953

After 1952's hectic recording schedule, Ray Brown's and Oscar Peterson's studio activities slackened off come 1953. In fact, Brown's first studio session of the year wasn't until April 20, in New York, when the Oscar Peterson Trio with drummer Jo Jones backed Roy Eldridge on four sides which would feature on the album *Dale's Wail* (Clef MGC-705) credited to Roy Eldridge and His Orchestra Featuring Oscar Peterson/Jo Jones. Peterson is on organ for this recording, a welcome change after his extensive piano recordings to end the previous year. Eldridge is in fine form, using a Harmon mute on "Love for Sale" and "Dale's Wail." Consistent with many of his recordings, Eldridge shows off his remarkable capacity for playing in the upper register on tunes like "Dale's Wail" and "Oscar's Arrangement."

The next day, the Oscar Peterson Trio returned to the studio for a session featuring Ben Webster. Peterson was back on the piano for this recording, and the group was enhanced with J.C. Heard on the drums. The session resulted in some of Webster's most exemplary small-group playing on record. It would be combined with later recordings for the 1957 *King of the Tenors* compilation (Verve MGV-8020). Webster's gravelly, breathy tone is well represented on each track. One of the highlights is the saxophonist's re-creation of his classic solo on "Cotton Tail," which he first recorded as a member of the Ellington Orchestra in 1940. He is equally brilliant on the folk ballad "Danny Boy."

On May 21, 1953 the Oscar Peterson Trio was back in the studio recording standard material with Peterson as vocalist. While his vocal talents do not come close to his virtuosity as a pianist, he again proves reasonably competent. It is interesting to hear how the group takes a more understated "cool" approach when backing Peterson as a vocalist. These tracks are on the 1954 release *Oscar Peterson Sings* (Clef MGC-145). This recording is also notable for being the last official session in which Barney Kessel served as a member of the trio.

When Barney Kessel's one-year agreement with Peterson ended, both Peterson and Brown knew that finding a guitarist capable of filling Kessel's shoes would not be easy. One name that came to mind was Herb Ellis, who at that time was playing in a trio known as the Soft Winds, a group based in Buffalo and sharing the same instrumentation as Peterson's trio. When Peterson approached him, however, he was reluctant, first of all because he was unsure that he could match the technical skills of Peterson and Brown but also because he was uneasy about Peterson and Brown's reputation for playing practical jokes. He made it clear to Peterson that "he enjoyed a good laugh, but there were certain boundaries beyond which he was not prepared to go."[75] But Ellis overcame his concerns and accepted Peterson's offer. After his first rehearsal with the trio and some light hazing in which both Peterson and Brown ambushed the guitarist in his hotel room, it was apparent that Ellis could match Peterson and Brown both musically and personally. The first "classic" Oscar Peterson Trio was born.

With Herb Ellis on board, the trio looked to expand its skills and repertoire. Peterson remained the group's primary soloist, while Brown and Ellis developed rhythmic concepts that provided a strong swing element and an ability to manipulate dynamics and tempos. Ellis also showed his skills by playing advanced melodic and harmonic counterpoints against Peterson's fiery piano runs. Brown and Ellis's rhythmic hookup developed as a result of long periods of intense rehearsal. In doing so, the two grew inseparable and developed a lifelong friendship, becoming like brothers. Within months, the Oscar Peterson Trio was not only matching the musical abilities of the guitar trios that preceded it but taking the format in new directions by focusing on the intricacies of small-group arrangements. The trio expanded its repertoire and often changed songs' keys just to challenge themselves. All three members were fully committed to the development of the group.

As Ellis and Brown's friendship began to grow, Oscar Peterson took the opportunity to challenge his bandmates. His musical demands often seemed technically impossible, and even unreasonable at times, but meeting them was a matter of pride. The two usually found a way to fulfill Peterson's most strenuous demands and went to great lengths to prove to Peterson that they could handle any challenge.

As the Oscar Peterson Trio took a new shape, so did Ray Brown's personal life. It had been evident for several years that Brown and Fitzgerald's marriage was in decline, and by 1953 the couple gave up trying. On August 28, Ella Fitzgerald and Ray Brown divorced in Juarez, Mexico, where the process was much quicker than in the United States. Although they could not survive romantically, they remained close friends and musical companions until Fitzgerald died in 1996.

Both Fitzgerald and Brown have openly discussed their divorce in interviews. In a documentary video Fitzgerald revealed:

> It was beautiful while it lasted. We were both going different ways. We never saw each other because he was here and I was there . . . You know, the first three years were wonderful because he was a wonderful person.[76]

Ray Brown also spoke about the breakup and admitted that "It was awkward for a few minutes. But that's all. We never had any big differences after that; of course, we had our son, Ray Brown Jr."[77]

Oscar Peterson gave his thoughts on why Fitzgerald and Brown's marriage did not last:

> Well, I think the road took its toll, the traveling. She was also doing her gigs on the road. My trio, with Ray, was on the road doing our gigs, and we were in opposite parts of the country at different times. So, they didn't get to see each other very often. It's tough to keep any marriage together doing that . . . Ray was in Ella's group, and Ray was doing what he did best [accompanying], and he was playing bass for her group. He was also a very talented soloist, and I think that being with my group gave him a chance to explore other avenues solo-wise.[78]

Ray Brown has always been complimentary about Ella Fitzgerald's talents when speaking with the press, summing up his thoughts with: "The bottom line is that she was always a pleasure to work with, musically." He goes on:

> Once Ella got her music fine-tuned, back in the '40s with that combination of bebop, ballads, and swing, she just became a complete singer. She had great pitch, a great ear, and an ability to grab hold of whatever was going on, a completely natural musician.[79]

As September 1953 began, Ray and Oscar were back working with JATP. Granz's stars now included Roy Eldridge, Dizzy Gillespie, Johnny Hodges, Illinois Jacquet, Flip Phillips, Ben Webster, Lionel Hampton, Oscar Peterson, and Buddy Rich. JATP was recorded on September 2, 1953 and, with each member given a solo spot, the tracks are lengthy, ranging from thirteen minutes to over twenty minutes on "Ballad Melody." While the performers are all brilliant, the length of the recordings and the lack of variation and experimentation can make for a challenging listen. The variety when it comes is from the solos of Lionel Hampton and Dizzy Gillespie.[80]

Granz also recorded Lionel Hampton with only Brown, Peterson, and Rich on the same day. The session yielded six tracks and, in contrast to the all-star session, the Lionel Hampton quartet session is interactive and hard-swinging. Peterson and Hampton push each other to new heights: they can be heard moaning, groaning, and vocalizing throughout each track. Once again, the rhythmic hookup between Ray Brown and Buddy Rich is perfect. Ray is given a chance to solo on the tracks "Always" and "S'Wonderful." This recording might well be Hampton's most extraordinary small-group effort after his days with Benny Goodman. Buddy Rich is particularly impressive during his solo on "Air Mail Special." These recordings are now available on *The Complete Lionel Hampton Quartets and Quintets with Oscar Peterson on Verve* (Verve 314 559 797-2 QS01).

On September 4, 1953, Ray Brown reunited with Hank Jones in a trio that included the guitarist Johnny Smith to record four tracks, in which three were Hank Jones originals: "Thad's Pad," "Things Are So Pretty in the Spring," and "Odd Number." Hearing Brown perform in a different ensemble but with the same instrumentation as the Oscar Peterson Trio allows an interesting comparison. On "Thad's Pad," Brown is more prominently featured than on many of Peterson's more commercial efforts, playing countermelodies and solo statements. On this recording, Jones, Smith, and Brown take a more "cool" approach, and the ensemble focuses on feel, orchestration, and texture rather than on a display of virtuosic solos by the leader. Hank Jones delivers some fantastic reharmonization and chord sequences throughout the four tracks. Ray Brown is most impressive during his solo on "Odd Number." Overall, the session proved to be one of Brown's finest recordings of the year. These tracks can be heard on the 1956 Hank Jones album *Urbanity* (Clef MG C-707).

On September 10, 1953 Ray Brown recorded for the first time with Gene Krupa. Krupa had emerged as a major star in the 1930s while playing drums with the Benny Goodman Orchestra and Trio. He left Goodman in 1938 to create his famous big band, which he was forced to break up after a public marijuana possession arrest in 1943. Following a short jail sentence, Krupa returned to sideman work and small-group efforts, retaining his status as one of the the swing era's most explosive drummers. Included on the Krupa recording is pianist Teddy Wilson, one of the most impressive and influential swing-era pianists. Wilson also came to fame as a member of Goodman's trio, beginning in 1935. The Goodman–Krupa–Wilson trio represented a landmark in jazz: the first time a prominent white bandleader welcomed an African American musician – i.e. Wilson – into his band.

The Krupa session is also of interest because it was the first of many times that Ray Brown would record with Herb Ellis. This all-star ensemble also included Ben Webster on tenor, Charlie Shavers on trumpet, and Bill Harris on trombone. The recording yielded eight tracks for the album *The Exciting Gene Krupa* (Clef MG-C687). Krupa is most impressive as a soloist on "Jungle Drums" and "Showcase." As expected, Ben Webster and Charlie Shavers excel as featured soloists.

Brown was back in the studio for a September 17, 1953 session for Johnny Hodges. Along with Brown, the rhythm section included Leroy Lovett on piano and J.C. Heard on drums, with a front line of Emmett Berry on trumpet, Lawrence Brown on trombone, and Arthur Clarke on tenor saxophone. This was the period (1951–1955) in which Hodges had departed from Duke Ellington to pursue solo efforts. As with many of these solo projects, the music is in the Ellington style. This three-song session included "Easy Going Bounce," "Indiana," and "Johnny's Blues."[81] The selections offer some comfortable swing but are not particularly innovative or forward-looking. Hodges eventually returned to Ellington's band and remained with the group until his death in 1970.

On September 19, 1953 Ray Brown returned to Carnegie Hall as part of the JATP project. The new all-star line-up now included Roy Eldridge, Charlie Shavers, Bill Harris, Benny Carter, Willie Smith, Flip Phillips, Ben Webster, Lester Young, Oscar Peterson, Herb Ellis, and a combination of J.C. Heard, Buddy Rich, and Gene Krupa on drums. Recordings from the show have been captured on the now somewhat rare albums *Jazz at the Philharmonic Vol. 9* (1956; Verve MG-VOL. 9) and *Vol. 16* (1954 Clef MG-VOL. 16).

On the same evening, Brown reunited with ex-wife Ella Fitzgerald for a performance of "Bill" and "Why Don't You Do Right." Interestingly, Oscar Peterson is not not on piano, being replaced by Raymond Tunia, who often served as Fitzgerald's accompanist at the time. Buddy Rich occupies the drum chair on these tracks. It is apparent from the audience's response that Ella Fitzgerald's appearance was a highlight. Tracks from that evening and other Fitzgerald shows are available on the 2016 compilation album *Jazz at the Philharmonic: The Ella Fitzgerald Set* (Verve B0024612-02).

In the fall of 1953, JATP embarked on its thirteenth tour, which included stops in the U.S.A., Canada, Hawaii, Australia, and Japan. The troupes' November 18 show at Tokyo's Nichigeki Theater was particularly well received and archived on the 1972 album release *J.A.T.P in Tokyo (Live at the Nichigeki Theatre 1953)* (Pablo Live 2620 104). These recordings included several selections from the Oscar Peterson Trio sets. It was also evident by the audience's response that the Tokyo crowd was enthusiastic about American jazz. Peterson and the trio are masterful in their interpretation of "Tenderly" and on standards like "That Old Black Magic," "Alone Together," and "Swingin' Till the Girls Come Home." One of the finest moments from the Tokyo concerts is the trio's interpretation of "Sushi Blues," where Brown provides a perfect walking bass line. Peterson also delivers some of his most impressive and inventive improvisations to date on that track. Brown's intro and outro to "Alone Together" display a new direction for the trio that showcases more subtle arrangement characteristics, including detailed attention to time feel, song form, and rhythmic variations. Brown and Herb Ellis both solo on "Swingin' Till the Girls Come Home." This set exhibits the great music and the possibilities of Peterson's trio of the time.

Also archived from the Japanese tour and appearing on that album was Ella Fitzgerald's set, with Brown, Ellis, Tunia, and Heard serving as her accompanists. One cannot help but wonder if Fitzgerald's decision not to work with Peterson confirms speculations that she partially blamed Peterson and Brown's close friendship and constant touring for their breakup. Brown can't have been unaffected to hear Fitzgerald singing lyrics like "he never treats me sweet and gentle the way he should" and "he don't love me like I love him" during "I Got it Bad and That Ain't Good." As with most of Fitzgerald's JATP performances, it is clear from the applause that she was the show's star. Her set included her signature hits like "Oh, Lady Be Good" and "How High the Moon," and impressed with her scat solo on "Smooth Sailin'" and her Armstrong impression during "Frim Fram Sauce."

One of Brown's more exciting sessions of the year was a recording with female Japanese pianist Toshiko Akiyoshi on her 1954 debut album *Toshiko's Piano* (Norgran MGN-22). Akiyoshi was "discovered" in Japan by Oscar Peterson during the tour, who brought her to the attention of Norman Granz, so a quickly organized two-day session on November 13 and 14, 1953 saw her recording with Brown, Ellis, and Heard. Although somewhat heavy-handed at times, Akiyoshi's piano playing reveals a strong bebop knowledge combined with some elements of Japanese folk music. Highlights from this session include "Shadrack" and the Akiyoshi original "Salidado." Brown's only solo spot is on "Toshiko's Blues." Akiyoshi, who subsequently moved to the United States, has had a fantastic career in jazz and has been nominated for fourteen Grammy Awards.

This first Japanese tour had a profound effect on Ray Brown, as he recalls:

> Going to Japan was the biggest thing that had ever hit there, jazz-wise. We had a two- or three-hour ticker-tape parade through the streets from the airport in open cars. We went to Europe as well, but going to Europe doesn't set you up for going to the Orient because everything was different. And the Japan of 1953 wasn't the same thing as Japan in the 1990s. But we didn't have any adjustment problems. When people are eager to see you – it's always comfortable to go somewhere where people want to see you.[82]

Throughout much of his later career, Japan would serve as a second home for Ray Brown, and he was often asked to back Japanese artists on record and on stage.

Following the trip to Japan, the Oscar Peterson Trio returned to Los Angeles. On December 6 and 7, Oscar Peterson and Ray Brown entered the studio with Barney Kessel to record over thirty-five tracks that would be issued on numerous *Oscar Peterson Plays* compilation albums. Granz's choice of Kessel over Ellis for these sessions may have resulted from the former's knowledge of the extensive material as well as Granz's level of comfort with the more experienced guitarist. The bulk of these recordings are now featured in the collection *The Complete Clef/Mercury Recordings of the Oscar Peterson Trio* (Mosaic MD7-241).

But in a larger-group ensemble, Granz seemed to be okay with including Ellis. On December 9, 1953, the working trio entered a Los Angeles studio for a session that featured Dizzy Gillespie and tenor saxophonist Stan Getz, along with drummer Max Roach. Getz first came to prominence as a member of Woody Herman's famed "Four Brothers" saxophone section and later achieved superstardom in the mid-1960s when he helped popularize bossa nova. A true highlight from this session comes from a two-part funky Afro-Cuban number called "Siboney." Brown begins "Siboney (Part 1)" with a funky bass line which eventually shifts to a fast walk. Gillespie is brilliant as the featured soloist. The piece ends with Brown reverting to the original Afro-Cuban groove. "Siboney (Part 2)" features Stan Getz and offers a Latin-flavored opening before shifting to a more uptempo swing. The piece ends with Brown's original bass line from "Part 1." Another highlight from the session is the seriously uptempo "Impromptu." These fine recordings were released in 1955 as *Diz and Getz* (Norgran MBN-1050).

Soon after the Gillespie–Getz sessions, the Oscar Peterson Trio and drummer Alvin Stoller recorded several tracks with Roy Eldridge. Highlights from the session are a soulful swing called "Feeling a Draft" and the Ellington classic "Echoes of Harlem," in which Eldridge seems to channel the spirit of Ellington trumpet star Cootie Williams. These tracks would initially be issued as 45 rpm singles and later on the 1978 Roy Eldridge compilation *Dale's Wail*.

Herb Ellis had recorded with the Oscar Peterson Trio live during a JATP concert and as a backing session musician in support of other musicians with Peterson and Brown. However, he had yet to record with just the trio for a studio session. That didn't take place until December 10, 1953, when the group recorded "I Want to Be Happy" and "Great Day" for the compilation *Oscar Peterson Plays Vincent Youmans* (Clef MGC-625) and "Manhattan" for the album *Oscar Peterson Plays Richard Rodgers* (Clef MGC-624). The group also recorded "Tenderly," which remained unissued. Also unissued was material recorded by the trio with Ellis on a session that took place on December 16. The only other Oscar Peterson Trio studio track with Ellis to be released was from a December 31 session that produced a version of "I Won't Dance," which appeared on the album *Oscar Peterson Plays Jerome Kern* (Clef MGC-623). In general, these early tracks with the new trio are somewhat flat and reserved compared to its live and later material.

While Herb Ellis was still securing his reputation and getting his feet wet with the Oscar Peterson Trio, Ray Brown was further cementing his acceptance and recognition as one of the most celebrated bassists in jazz. When *DownBeat* magazine released its annual readers' poll winners at the end of 1953, Ray was ranked number one for the first time in the bass category, beating bassist Eddie Safranski by fifty-four votes. Safranski, who was mostly known for his work with Stan Kenton and Benny Goodman, had topped the poll from 1946 to 1953. In the piano category, Oscar Peterson dominated with 1,136 votes, Dave Brubeck coming second with 613. Herb Ellis appeared on the poll for the first time with a ninth-place finish. As for the Oscar Peterson Trio, the band made fourth place (400 votes) in the "Instrumental Combos" category and was several hundred votes behind groups led by Dave Brubeck (973), George Shearing (956), and Gerry Mulligan (797). The fourth-place finish was a huge jump from the group's twelfth place in 1952 (with 77 votes).

10 The Studio Recordings of the First Classic Oscar Peterson Trio 1954–1958

By 1954, after several months of working and touring as a member of the Oscar Peterson Trio the previous year, Herb Ellis was growing more comfortable in his role. It had become clear that his dedication and skills made him an excellent replacement for Barney Kessel and he had established himself as the correct choice as they moved forward. Through an extensive and grueling rehearsal, touring, and recording schedule, Peterson, Brown, and Ellis were functioning as a unified musical entity, focused on expanding their repertoire, arrangements, and overall sense of swing. While Peterson led many impressive trios, it is this first "classic" trio with Ellis that is most often remembered with admiration. It wasn't just about Peterson's virtuosic talents as a soloist but the carefully crafted arrangements as well, the trio's vast repertoire, and the confident and personalized propulsion of swing created by Brown and Ellis without the help of a drummer.

Always a great opportunist, Norman Granz knew he had something special with this new line-up. By 1954, Peterson was a major star and one of Granz's most marketable clients. Through his work with the trio and his now many studio credits, Ray Brown had gained a reputation as a musician capable of providing solid bass accompaniments to anyone who required his services. He was also a reliable soloist who could impress when given the opportunity. In Ellis, Granz and the trio had a rising star on the electric guitar whose interests seemed aligned with Peterson's visions for his group and whose selflessness allowed him to work in a supportive role while applying his skills as a soloist. In return, Peterson and the trio had a deep trust in Granz's advice and direction.

As he had done the previous year, Granz promoted the Peterson trio in three ways. First, he showcased the group as a distinct entity, setting up extensive tours and recording sessions, thus creating a back catalog of material that would serve Granz for years to come. Second, he continued to use the group as a house rhythm section for his celebrated national and international JATP tours. Third, he continued to call on the trio as a backing rhythm section to support new studio recordings by vocalists and instrumentalists.

When it came to recording the Oscar Peterson Trio in its own right, Granz did so at a feverish pace, and it seemed as though he wanted a trio version of every one of his favorite standards. Since many of these cuts were released on 78 rpm records, they were often limited to a radio-friendly format of around three minutes, leaving little room for experimentation or solos from Brown or Ellis. As a result, many of these studio efforts sound rushed or flat. Some other cuts, however, placed importance on arrangement, emphasizing dynamics and rhythmic feel. A majority of the studio work from the trio was suitable for the conceptual *Oscar Peterson Plays* series of albums.

After the December trio sessions of 1953, the Oscar Peterson Trio did not record together as a separate unit until April 27, 1954, in New York. Many of the eleven tracks from that date are popular ballads, with seven pieces issued on the album *Pastel Moods by Oscar Peterson* (Verve MGV-2004). The album combines songs from this session with a Los Angeles session from January 26, 1952, with Irving Ashby on guitar. The original album liner notes pay Peterson a backhanded compliment: "One can't help but possibly notice the size of Oscar Peterson. He is a huge mammoth of a man, yet this great height and overall size is belied by the gentle, almost caressing touch he gives the piano." The trio takes few risks on the session, but all the tracks are played with an air of elegance and sophistication, consistent with the tastes of many casual jazz fans. Tracks from the session have also been issued on the albums *Recital by Oscar Peterson* (Clef MGC-694) and *Romance: The Vocal Styling of Oscar Peterson* (Verve MGV-2012).

Coming off a successful fall 1954 JATP tour, the Oscar Peterson Trio became the Oscar Peterson Quartet on October 27, when guest drummer Louie Bellson was added to record seven tracks in Los Angeles. Tracks from this session found their way onto compilation albums like *Recital by Oscar Peterson*, *An Oscar for Peterson* (American Recording Society G-415), and *Piano Interpretations* by Oscar Peterson, Art Tatum, Teddy Wilson, and Bud Powell (Norgran MGN-1036).

Although the trio functioned perfectly well without drums, Granz often saw fit to augment the group's recordings with drummers from his JATP troupe. The hookup between Brown and Bellson, two of the finest accompanists, is particularly successful on "Singin' in the Rain." Bellson plays the uptempo swing using brushes, allowing Brown's bass to cut through more prominently. Their driving swing feel is a perfect underlying groove for Peterson and Ellis, who play fine solos. Bellson is showcased on the track, trading four-bar solo breaks with Peterson.

On November 15, 1954, the Oscar Peterson Trio recorded an astounding twenty-two tracks in just one day. All tunes from this session were issued on two albums: *Oscar Peterson Plays Harry Warren* (Clef MGC-648) and *Oscar Peterson Plays Harold Arlen* (Clef MGC-649). Harry Warren was a noted American composer and one of the first songwriters to write primarily for film. In his six-decade career, Warren wrote over 800 songs for over 300 films. The Warren material most used by jazz musicians includes standards such as "Lullaby of Broadway," "The More I See You," and "There Will Never Be Another You." Brown's only feature on the album is a sixteen-bar solo on "I Only Have Eyes for You," in which he uses eighth-note scale fragments centered on the mid-range of the instrument. Also of note is Brown's short descending solo cadenza to end the piece. During this period, Brown's solo style was continuing to be shaped by the innovations of Oscar Pettiford, who was still considered by many to be the finest bass soloist of the time.

In the studio, the Peterson trio was most interesting when revealing their intricate arrangements, as on their version of "Chattanooga Choo Choo." The piece's strength comes from strong predetermined characteristics such as stop-time figures and time feel changes. Unfortunately, given the amount of material the group was being asked to record in a day, many of the tracks on these *Oscar Peterson Plays* recordings lack such detail, nor do they evince the kind of experimentation that the group was capable of given more time.

Like Warren, Harold Arlen made a solid contribution to the American Songbook, and much of his work is heavily favored by jazz musicians. Tunes like "Come Rain Or Come Shine," "Let's Fall in Love," and "Stormy Weather" have been widely recorded by numerous jazz legends. By the time of his death in 1986, Arlen had written well over 500 songs, mainly for stage and film. Like the Warren session, Brown is given only one short solo on one track: "As Long As I Live." While most of the material on *Oscar Peterson Plays Harold Arlen* is somewhat formulaic, the group does impress during "It's Only a Paper Moon," playing some well-placed rhythmic hits on the head, followed by inspired solos by Peterson and Ellis. Herb Ellis provides some further rhythmic interest by using the guitar in a percussive way, playing muted notes on his strings. This was to become a signature of his playing style.

The following day the Peterson trio was back in the studio to record an additional thirteen tracks, of which nine appeared on the album *Oscar Peterson Plays Jimmy McHugh* (Clef MGC-650). Jimmy McHugh was also a celebrated songsmith, who operated during the 1920s and 1930s, frequently with lyricist Dorothy Fields. The album's most impressive track is "Digga Digga Doo," which stands out for its hard swinging and overall spirit. In contrast to the previous day's tracks, Ray Brown is featured more prominently on the *McHugh* album, and can be heard taking a short solo on "I Can't Believe That You're in Love with Me," "I'm in the Mood for Love," and "You're a Sweetheart," and a more extensive solo on "I Can't Give You Anything but Love." While not overly showy, this latter solo has some well-placed melodic phrasing and thematic characteristics, even throwing in a quote from "The Surrey with the Fringe on Top."

Although the Oscar Peterson studio recordings sold well, particularly among the casual jazz fan demographic, the trio's live releases held most interest for enthusiasts and critics. As revealed in the next chapter, the Oscar Peterson Trio was recorded on a number of live JATP concert albums and collections, and, although these recordings are notable in tracking the group's development, they are often limited to a small selection of tracks. A more extensive representation of the group at this time can be found on some full-length live releases, the first of which from a November 8, 1955 performance at the Los Angeles club Zardi's Jazzland (a venue on Hollywood Boulevard operating from 1950–1957). The double album *The Oscar Peterson Trio at Zardi's* (Pablo Records 2PACD-2620-118-2) is often cited as one of Peterson's finest live releases. It fully represents how perfectly the trio functioned without the influence or interference of record executives, producers, and studio engineers.

Overall, thirty live tracks comprising nearly two-and-a-half hours of music have been preserved from the evening. Analysis of this material provides evidence of Brown's continued incremental development as a melodic entity and soloist. For his solo on "There's a Small Hotel," he pays particular attention to rhythmic pacing: while the majority of the solo is played using typical eighth-note rhythms, Brown incorporates some well-placed double-time bebop licks and triplet figures. He also delivers some strong improvisation on the final bridge and a solo cadenza. One of the stand-out moments of the evening is the arrangement of the Peterson original "Noreen's Nocturne," the shifting themes and countermelodies of which, at times, place Ray Brown at the forefront. The tune is furthermore a testament to Peterson's ability as a composer, which was only partially realized by 1955, when the material was still largely rooted in interpretations of standards.

Another highlight from the evening is "Easy Does It," which appeared on the album *Oscar Peterson Plays Count Basie* (Clef MGC-708), an arrangement that the trio would perform regularly over the next few years. A study of Brown's bass lines on the various versions of this tune reveals that he preconceived the descending walking line that accompanies the song's main melody. The track features an eight-bar Ray Brown solo, which, although brief, shows a combination of double-timed bebop lines played with great precision. There is evidence of Brown expanding his range as he moves higher up into the thumb position to play a high C (octave 3) with complete accuracy to conclude the piece. Brown is also heavily featured on "Swinging on a Star," where he further displays his skills as a soloist.

Most of the tracks on *At Zardi's* contain at least fragmentary Ray Brown featured moments. However, it seems that Peterson's arrangements were designed to offer Brown solos over only specific sections of the form rather than having the bassist improvise at length over a full chorus. The notable exception is Brown's entire chorus solo on "Honeysuckle Rose," which, along with several other tunes from the evening, Peterson points out as a fan request. Overall, *At Zardi's* is a privileged glimpse into how Oscar Peterson's trio approached the many smaller club dates they performed at the time. Had it not been held back from release until 1994, it may have been more highly celebrated as a classic.

The Oscar Peterson Trio did not record again in the studio as an independent unit until December 27, 1955, more than a year after the lengthy sessions of November 15 and 16, 1954. To enhance the group, Buddy Rich was brought in to record the album *Oscar Peterson Plays Count Basie*. Of all the *Oscar Peterson Plays* material from this period, the *Basie* album is possibly the most inspirational. The interest derives from several factors. First and foremost, many of the tracks on this long-play record far exceed the three-minute limitation that had become commonplace in other similar Peterson extended-play records. With the extra time, the group interact further, and the soloists have more time to explore. Additionally, Basie's bluesy and straightforward approach to composition is ideally suited for interpretation and for the trio's hard-swinging style. Furthermore, each track is carefully arranged with a focus on rhythm, orchestration, dynamics, and purpose.

Buddy Rich, who had previously recorded with Count Basie's Octet,[83] was perfectly equipped for this role. His hookup with Brown and Ellis is pure perfection, leaving the listener to wonder what more the group could have achieved if Rich were to have been made a more permanent member. The *Count Basie* album clearly indicates that, when afforded the required time, Peterson's group could craft impressive small-group jazz arrangements as well as anyone in the business. The inclusion of solo spots and featured bass figures on tracks like "Easy Does It," "Blues for Basie," and "Topsy" demonstrate Peterson's willingness to give his bassist more featured moments.

Noted jazz critic Scott Yanow sums up the *Basie* album:

> On the face of it, pianist Oscar Peterson (whose virtuosity always allowed him to play an infinite amount of notes) and Count Basie (who made inventive use of silence and space by emphasizing single rhythmic sounds) would seem to have had little in common. However, they both swung, and there was a definite overlapping in their repertoire. Peterson's Basie tribute is a near-masterpiece. With guitarist Herb Ellis, bassist Ray Brown, and guest drummer Buddy Rich all playing quite sympathetically, Peterson's arrangements make the nine Basie-associated songs (along with Peterson's original "Blues for Basie") all sound quite fresh and lightly swinging.[84]

Although the "classic" trio remained intact for nearly two more years, *Oscar Peterson Plays Count Basie* would be the trio's final full-length studio recording.

Norman Granz was happy to continue using the Peterson trio as a backing unit, but by 1956 he must have felt he had stockpiled enough of their studio recordings and instead decided to focus on capturing the band live. On August 8, 1956 the trio recorded a live album that epitomizes all their brilliance: the group's signature album *At the Stratford Shakespearean Festival* (Clef MGC-751),[85] from a concert performed in Peterson's hometown of Ontario, Canada. That evening, the Peterson trio played opposite the latest star addition to Granz's roster, the Modern Jazz Quartet. Throughout the performance, the audience is attentive, quietly taking in each note and subtle nuance of the arrangements; however, the conclusion of each song is met with explosive applause. The crowd was particularly spirited because Oscar Peterson was one of their greatest hometown heroes, and his return was a celebrated event.

Such circumstances allowed the Peterson trio to play and explore without restriction. With the audience's full engagement, the trio took full advantage of dynamics and group interplay on a familiar repertoire of tightly arranged standards and Peterson originals. Many feel that the Oscar Peterson Trio's spirit and sense of swing have never been better documented than on the *Stratford Shakespearean Festival* album. Ray Brown is prominently featured in nearly every song, a welcome change from previous live recordings on which he is generally only offered shorter solo breaks.

One such highlight is "How High the Moon," a song often associated with Ella Fitzgerald. Here, the bassist is featured on a melodic two-chorus improvisation – with a solo that is often cited as one of his best. The improvisation has been studied by nearly every developing jazz bassist as if it were a classical etude. "How High the Moon" begins with Peterson and Brown trading two-bar solo statements, in which Brown displays some impressive eighth-note runs, triplet figures, and blues licks. Following the introduction, Ellis joins as Peterson states the melody, with Brown providing broken walk lines and countermelodies over a moderate tempo. Ellis then plays a one-chorus solo before he begins his improvisation.

Brown enters his solo by quoting the classic "They All Laughed," followed by some well-organized phrases, including a slightly behind-the-beat eighth-note run on its sixth measure. To end the first sixteenth bar (half-chorus), Brown jumps into the upper register sliding into a high B, demonstrating his range on the instrument. On measure 17, the second half of the first chorus, Brown begins by quoting Charlie Parker's bop classic "Moose the Mooche," before breaking into a fiery half-chorus of cleanly played double-time bop figures and a series of well-placed accented pull-offs.

For the first half of the second chorus, he begins again with a simple melodic statement and a short series of resting points before impressing further with double-time figures, rhythmic motifs, and some scale-like upper structure figures. Brown concludes his solo with bop licks and a four-bar statement which is again purposely played behind the beat to add tension to the solo's finale.

This conclusion is met with great applause and by the beginning of Peterson's improvisation, supported by a steady walking bass line and quarter-note chord "chops" by Ellis. The entire bass line and solo to "How High the Moon" is included in Mathew Rybicki's transcription book, *Ray Brown: Legendary Jazz Bassist.* In his "Song Notes" section, Rybicki writes:

> This bass solo is considered by many to be one of the best, if not the best, bass solo ever recorded . . . he plays what is, to me, one of the most technically challenging and musically satisfying bass solos on record.[86]

"Gypsy in My Soul" is another track of particular interest. The track is a fine example of the small-group arrangement characteristics of the group and how, at times, the band could function as co-equals. Here, Ray Brown displays a series of right-hand "flutter" techniques, introductory melodic statements, inner-working countermelodies, and his signature hard-driving walking bass lines. Ellis is also particularly impressive during his solo.

Another feature of the evening is an ambitious classically influenced programmed jazz suite called "Daisy's Dream." Oscar Peterson introduces the work by saying that the composition was inspired by John Lewis of the Modern Jazz Quartet; he tells the audience that the music

> tells the story of a young girl who is given a music box. The girl falls asleep to the tune played by the music box and dreams that the figurine at the top of the box comes to life, commences to dance with her, and takes her through several musical idioms, such as a waltz and jazz idiom. Finally, she is awakened by the original theme of the box.

The piece is beautifully written and performed; however, Ray Brown's arco playing is, at times, flat and lacks the more traditional classical vibrato common among concert bassists. While it took a while to develop, Ray continued to work on his arco playing throughout his career. Although he became steadily more proficient, he never truly reached the level of consistency as an arco player that would be required of a featured symphonic bassist.

Nonetheless, the *Stratford Shakespearean Festival* album is a must-listen for any jazz fan: it ranks among the great live jazz trio albums. It is also a critical album for tracking the development of Ray Brown's playing and popularity.

Over the next few months, although the Peterson trio did not record another featured album, several of their performances were recorded and eventually released on Norman Granz compilations, and the group was seen on a Los Angeles broadcast on KABC-TV. The *Stars of Jazz* program of March 4, 1957 featured performances of "A Gal in Calico," "Time after Time," and "Seven Come Eleven."[87]

In 1958, the Oscar Peterson Trio recorded another live album, one of their finest, at the Concertgebouw in Amsterdam, Holland, on April 12. On the original liner notes of *The Oscar Peterson Trio at the Concertgebouw* (Verve MGV-8268), Norman Granz reveals:

> It never occurred to me to record the concert in Europe as I had done for so many years with Jazz at the Philharmonic in America. Fortunately, a rabid jazz fan in Amsterdam recorded the concert that I presented at Concertgebouw and afterward presented me with the tapes. On these

tapes is some of the most exciting jazz and certainly the most exciting trio music that I've heard in years.

On this performance, Ellis shows remarkable confidence and development as a soloist, thereby pushing Peterson and Brown to new heights during their improvisations. Ray Brown is most heavily featured on "Bluesology" and "Daahoud." Although his bass sounds distant on this amateur recording, you can still hear how his solo ideas on "Bluesology" are well connected and phrased. The audience picks up on the finer moments from Brown's improvisation, providing applause and encouragement as he creates.

Possibly the group's most impressive moments on the album are on their interpretation of Clifford Brown's "Daahoud," which demonstrates the significance to the trio's overall presentation and sound of specific arrangement details. Brown's solo on the track displays his further command of pacing and blues phrasing. Another highlight is the group's uptempo interpretation of Bud Powell's "Budo." This track, and the album as a whole, best represent Herb Ellis's development during his time with the Peterson trio. His playing on "Budo" shows an advanced ability to provide rapid, well-connected bop phrasing mixed with downhome Texas-style blues.

After an extensive European tour with JATP through the spring, Oscar Peterson returned to Toronto to present his polished trio at the intimate Town Hall Tavern Club on July 5, 1958. The result was the live album *On the Town with the Oscar Peterson Trio* (Verve MGV-8287). The clinking of glasses and audience conversation is a distraction throughout the recording, although some argue that these ambient noises add to the organic experience of a record such as this.

As with all Oscar Peterson Trio live performances from this era, *On the Town* is a worthwhile listen; however, these performances lack the energy and interaction of the *Zardi's*, *Stratford*, and *Concertgebouw* concerts. This lack of enthusiasm may indicate that the band felt underappreciated by the audience's lackluster response, especially after the fanfare they had been used to receiving, particularly in Europe.

Apart from "The Champ," other highlights from the album were denied listeners until the expanded CD version (Verve 5170247), namely "Joy Spring," and "Gal in Calico." Although it is not his best work, Brown's strongest solo on the record is on "Our Love is Here to Stay" also held back until the later release). His fine improvisation is rewarded by just some delayed, scattered applause. *On the Town* was to be the final full-length album by the original classic Oscar Peterson Trio.

One of the trio's final appearances was a return performance on the *Stars of Jazz* program on KABC-TV on August 18, 1958.[88] While this chapter has laid out the key recording of the Oscar Peterson Trio, most of which were issued during the time they were a working unit, many videos and recordings released by collectors continue to appear on social media outlets.

Towards the end of 1958, Herb Ellis decided to leave the trio having served as its guitarist for about five years. He had grown tired of the constant traveling and had decided to move to Los Angeles, to concentrate on studio activities – a path that Ray Brown would later pursue. Oscar Peterson explains:

> Well, he [Ellis] decided to settle in LA, and I think he grew tired of traveling because we were traveling as a trio. Then the fall would come, and we'd go on tour with Norman Granz's Jazz at the Philharmonic, and we were on the road most of the year.[89]

While it must have been tough for Peterson and Brown to learn of Ellis's decision, the split was amicable. Although no longer a group member, Ellis would reunite with Peterson and Brown throughout his career, including a brief reunion, starting around 1990. Many see the line-up with Ellis as Oscar Peterson's most creative effort. In an interview for *DownBeat*, Ray Brown said:

> I enjoyed playing in all the groups, but I think probably the best one we had . . . was the group with Herb Ellis. If I could have had $5 an hour for the time we put in rehearsing, I could have retired. You've got to realize we had a repertoire of maybe 200 arrangements. And they were tough, complex things. We would rehearse as much as six hours a day in addition to playing at night.[90]

11 The JATP Tours and Records 1954–1958

While the Oscar Peterson Trio released many fine studio and live albums, as we saw in the previous chapter its value also came as a backing rhythm section for Norman Granz's JATP tours and studio efforts. Ray Brown's connection with JATP is an essential part of his overall story. After the trio's tour of fall 1947, he joined the JATP troupe and from 1949 became a regular and valued member, eventually becoming its longest-tenured bassist.

When Norman Granz began presenting his JATP concerts in 1944, Johnny Miller and Red Callender first appeared as bassists. Miller served as the bassist in the famed Nat King Cole Trio from 1943 to 1948, the group on which Oscar Peterson patterned his earliest trios, during which time the Cole trio made many of their most famous recordings. With Cole, Johnny Miller demonstrated an ability to keep solid time without a drummer but was rarely ever heard doing much more than serving a timekeeping role.

Red Callender was technically more gifted and versatile than Johnny Miller. In the early 1940s, he too recorded with Nat King Cole, and also with Erroll Garner, Charlie Parker, and Dexter Gordon. Although Callender could have continued moving forward exclusively as a jazz musician, in the early 1950s he decided instead to focus his activities as a Los Angeles session musician. In doing so, he became one of the first African American bassists and one of the first "jazz" musicians to succeed as a commercial studio musician. Following this groundbreaking path, and with later encouragement from Callender himself, Ray Brown would eventually follow a similar route as a studio musician. Before Brown became a regular JATP member in 1949, he was preceded by John Simmons, Tiny "Bam" Brown, Oscar Pettiford, Charles Mingus, Billy Harnott, Curly Russell, Chubby Jackson, Slam Stewart, Rodney Richardson, Al McKibbon, Charlie Drayton, and Benny Fonville, who all played bass with JATP. While all these were undoubtedly skilled musicians, it was in Brown that Granz finally discovered the perfect bassist for his concerts.

When he first appeared with JATP in 1947, Ray Brown was one of the newest stars in jazz, which may have been a deliberate departure for Granz, who mainly gave a platform to veteran musicians. Brown's stamina and solid timekeeping provided a perfect accompaniment, which many of Granz's stars appreciated. In 1954, Brown was still only in his twenties, yet already he had acquired a certain gravitas from his past experience and mounting recording credits. Alongside Brown's technical skills, Granz almost certainly appreciated Ray Brown's enthusiasm and professionalism. The connection between the two men was important and long-lasting. In Granz, Ray Brown found a music-business mentor: to some degree, Brown's business acumen was as impressive as his bass playing. From Granz's point of view, Ray Brown was his first-call option for many years: Granz knew that Brown could handle any session and would enhance any musical situation.

By 1954, JATP – which was dedicated to showcasing the stars of jazz, a virtual one-stop shop concert for fans looking to hear their most beloved musical heroes – was a well-oiled machine. With his JATP tours, Norman Granz was realizing a dream: to spread jazz music worldwide by presenting an integrated cast of musicians to an integrated audience in a concert environment, breaking down traditional norms and racist practices. The JATP tours, and Granz's involvement with his work, afforded Ray Brown a certain level of career comfort. From late 1953 to 1958, the Peterson trio remained one of the featured acts, as well as being used to back the many stars of the JATP shows both on stage and in the studio.

On February 6, 1954, JATP kicked off an exhaustive four-week run across Europe with a concert in Brussels. The troupe had only two days off. This was at the time when Norman Granz was Ella Fitzgerald's manager. For the European JATP, Granz featured past JATP performers like Ella Fitzgerald, Benny Carter, Roy Eldridge, Charlie Shavers, and Bill Harris, as well as the Peterson trio. New additions included Stan Getz, Louie Bellson, and John Lewis. To Granz's frustration, JATP was not permitted to perform in England, as the British Musicians' Union would not forego their strict reciprocal exchange policy, even though JATP had performed a benefit show in England a year before to raise money for the victims of a terrible flood which had killed over 300 British citizens.[91]

The national U.S. tour of September and October 1954 included two new additions: the celebrated early superstar of the vibraphone, Lionel Hampton, and clarinet master Buddy DeFranco. Adding extra interest to the New York appearances was the inclusion of Lester Young, plus a set of Charlie Parker playing with strings at both Carnegie Hall and Newark's Mosque Theater. The return of Dizzy Gillespie to the JATP stage was a further bonus. The challenge for Granz was that he was competing with other jazz package tours like the Birdland Stars of 1955, the Sarah Vaughan and Stan Getz Festival of Modern American Jazz, Norman Granz's own Ellington, Brubeck and Mulligan package, and Machito's Mambo Tour, which Granz's brother, Irving, was promoting. Despite the competition, the JATP tour, which involved thirty-seven dates, grossed $380,000, an improvement on his national numbers a year before.

Between the international and national JATP tours, the Peterson trio performed on July 8, 1954 at the First Newport Jazz Festival, on a bill that included Billie Holiday, Dizzy Gillespie, Ella Fitzgerald, Erroll Garner, Gene Krupa, Lennie Tristano, Stan Kenton, and Teddy Wilson. To his credit, Granz did not block members of the JATP troupe from performing at the Newport Festival, even though the festival did not precisely align with his personal interests.

On September 17, 1954 the entire opening night concert at Bushnell Memorial Auditorium in Hartford, Connecticut, was archived and released in 1955 as *Norman Granz's Jazz at the Philharmonic Vol. 17* (Clef MG VOL. 17). Granz would routinely introduce the performers at the beginning of each show; the announcement of the name Ray Brown brought a solid round of applause, as did the mention of Dizzy Gillespie. As Alyn Shipton says in *Groovin' High*:

> the collaboration between Norman Granz and Dizzy happened at a mutually beneficial time for them both, and the relationship between Dizzy and this mercurial entrepreneur one year his junior was of crucial importance in reviving his fortunes. Granz needed stellar musicians of Dizzy's calibre whom he could accommodate in his Jazz at the Philharmonic tours, record for his label, and promote aggressively alongside other key musicians . . . Dizzy himself needed a dramatic career turnaround to rescue him from the doldrums where he had been since the big band broke up in 1950.[92]

Ray Brown must have been thrilled to reconnect with his most significant musical mentor on this and subsequent tours.

Recorded at Bushnell are selections from the Peterson trio's set, including a Herb Ellis showcase on the Django Reinhardt classic "Nuages." It is a pleasure to hear Ellis featured in such a way, especially since he was often limited on the trio's studio recordings. Other selections from their set are impressive uptempo versions of "Love for Sale" and "Avalon." A true highlight is the tightly arranged uptempo "Come to the Mardi Gras," which offers several time feel changes that shift from a Latin-tinged groove to a driving swing. The response from the crowd following the number is overwhelming, and these live recordings are essential in tracking the development of the Peterson trio with Ellis. The 1954 Bushnell concert included Roy Eldridge, Bill Harris, Flip Phillips, Ben Webster, and Louie Bellson. As with most JATP performances, the show began with a jam-session-style presentation featuring high-flying swing numbers and a ballad medley. A particularly impressive moment was Louie Bellson's featured drum solo.

Following the all-star jam, guests Buddy DeFranco and Lionel Hampton were featured, along with the Peterson trio plus Buddy Rich. The ensemble received an enthusiastic, well-deserved fanfare on "Flying Home," which was the final number of their set. DeFranco also appeared with the same group that evening without Hampton. Through his fantastic interpretation of tunes like "I'll Remember April," "Now's the Time," "Avalon," and others, DeFranco shows why he is generally considered one of the most impressive clarinetists of the bop and post-bop eras.

One of the features of the 1954 JATP Bushnell concert was a set by Ella Fitzgerald. As before, Fitzgerald chose to use her own piano accompanist, Raymond Tunia, along with Ray Brown and Buddy Rich. Recordings from her set included a tune called "The Man That Got Away," an interesting choice given Fitzgerald and Brown's relationship. Other songs included "Hernando's Hideaway," "Later," and "A Foggy Day."

Not every stop during the tour went as planned, especially when the group traveled to the South: the 1954 national tour coincided with a period of widespread racial tension with the Civil Rights Movement exerting itself. Much of the country became further divided when, on May 17, 1954, the Supreme Court desegregated schools as part of the *Brown vs. Board of Education* ruling. The decision led to a backlash among many disagreeable bigoted residents of southern states, bringing racially fueled rallies and violence.

During a JATP concert in Charleston, North Carolina, on September 27, 1954, Granz noticed that the concert's African American participants were sectioned off into the theater's balcony. A persistent social activist, Granz demanded that the theater be integrated. If his demands were not met, he would cancel the performance; so, reluctantly, the theater manager allowed many of those in the balcony to move to the middle of the theater.

During the show, a crowd of bigoted angry locals began to gather outside the stage door. When Granz got word of the growing mob, he told his off-stage musicians to exit. As numerous musicians left the theater, Ella Fitzgerald appeared on stage with only her rhythm section, which included Ray Brown. With a spotlight illuminating only Fitzgerald, Ray Brown and Raymond Tunia snuck off the dark stage leaving Ella to sing with just Louie Bellson behind her. As they were playing their final number, a crew member began to break down Bellson's drum set leaving only the snare. When it was over, Fitzgerald and Bellson exited the theater in limos while the unsuspecting audience waited for another number, which never came.

A studio recording of the complete JATP ensemble of the time, minus Ella Fitzgerald, was recorded on October 30, 1954, in which the group plays in the typical jam-style format. The first of these releases included only "Stompin' at the Savoy (Parts 1 and 2)," which took up two entire sides of the album *Norman Granz' Jam Session #6* (Clef MGC-4006). The second release, *Norman Granz' Jam Session #9* (Verve MGV-8196) includes only two tracks, "Lullaby in Rhythm" and "Funky Blues," which each took up an album side. In such jam-style sessions, a certain degree of interest derives from analyzing the stylistic differences among soloists improvising on the same song. The opportunity to hear Eldridge and Gillespie play together in this format is particularly notable. For Ray Brown and the rhythm section, these lengthy sessions show incredible stamina. Providing a steady time feel over multiple choruses without losing the changes requires excellent focus and experience.

On February 7, 1955, JATP opened its fourth European tour with two evening concerts in Stockholm. Along with the Oscar Peterson Trio, the tour included Ella Fitzgerald, Roy Eldridge, Dizzy Gillespie, Louie Bellson, Bill Harris, Flip Phillips, and Buddy DeFranco. The only new addition was pianist Don Abney, who was now serving as Fitzgerald's accompanist. These shows were followed by performances in Copenhagen, West Berlin, Frankfurt, Munich, Stuttgart, Zurich, Basel, Geneva, Lyon, and Paris. The tour involved forty-two consecutive dates. Tracks from the Stockholm performances are now available on *The Exciting Battle: J.A.T.P. Stockholm '55* (Pablo 2310-713).

The European tour was successful, but also not without its issues and controversy. One particularly troubling situation nearly ended Ellis's tenure with the tour, and that of the Oscar Peterson Trio, when Ellis was too drunk to catch the flight from New York on the morning he was to leave for Europe, and ended up in the hospital. Ellis disappeared into a second alcoholic fog for about a month in New York the following year. However, following a meeting with Peterson, Ellis firmed up his commitment to Alcoholics Anonymous and swore off drinking. "Oscar and Norman were great," Ellis said. "If they had not wanted me to come back, I don't know what would have happened to me." Granz even extended kindness to Ellis by giving him a gift of an expensive watch when Ellis made his return and committed to sobriety.[93]

When asked if he ever considered replacing Ellis, Oscar Peterson responded:

> I did at one time when he was away for quite a while. He missed a European tour, and when I returned, the AA [Alcoholics Anonymous] was going up one side of me and down another because they felt that I had been encouraging him by being too lenient. I considered replacing him, but we loved Herbie and were concerned about what would happen to him. When I came back from Europe, we had quite a long talk, and I laid it out on the table cold turkey for him. [I told him] that he had to find himself, or he would sacrifice any further performances with the group, which he did. After some time apart from the trio, in which guitarist Kenny Burrell served as his replacement, Herb Ellis eventually kicked his habit and continued with the group.[94]

Another challenge for JATP in 1955 came when members of the group struggled to find suitable lodging in West Berlin; only after Granz made claims of racism on a radio station were premium rooms found for the performers. The West Berlin performance was well received, and selections from the show can be heard on the import *USA All-Stars in Berlin, February 1955* (Jazz Band EBCD 2113-2). The recording includes two tracks from the Peterson trio's set. The first is the group's fine arrangement of "Easy Does It," which reveals a more chamber-like approach. Ray Brown's playing includes a fine arpeggiated bass solo written into the arrangement. The group pays particular attention to dynamics within the piece, and the audience, which is vocal throughout, rewards the trio with a deafening round of applause. The other track is a breakneck version of "Seven Come Eleven." The track is also tightly arranged and demonstrates Ellis's strengths as a soloist. These two tracks offer one of the finest representations of the trio to this point. For many in the JATP audiences, the Oscar Peterson Trio's more focused approach may have been a welcome change from the lengthy jam sessions that began each evening.

Other challenges during the tour included the issuing of work permits and European Musicians' Union restrictions on American musicians. As for the shows themselves, one particularly troubling moment occurred when the group performed their final shows at Le Théâtre des Champs-Elysées in Paris. Clarinetist Buddy DeFranco was booed off stage by a rowdy Parisian audience, who seemed to have a distaste for the clarinet in jazz and possibly a sense of reverse racism for DeFranco as a white musician playing "Black music."

The issue with DeFranco might have also been musical, stemming from his apparent missing of the ending to "Just One of Those Things." The audience also seemed to take offense with his decision to play "April in Paris," a song that the Parisian audience held dear. Granz somehow managed to subdue the crowd by stopping the performance, walking onto the stage with a stopwatch and a chair, and sitting down. He told the audience that "they were either going to listen to two hours of music or two hours of yelling and booing." After some time, the audience calmed down and chose to listen to more music. Later, DeFranco told Granz biographer Tadd Hershorn that in Paris there was a group of jazz players that booed because they had a problem with any clarinetist assembling a group. "So it was kind of a conspiracy. I went back to Paris several times after that and never had trouble."[95]

As in the national 1954 tour, some racial issues arose when touring the American South in 1955. On October 7, Granz spotted a segregated audience in Houston's Music Hall. After receiving much resistance to hs attempts to integrate the audience, Granz personally removed the "Whites" and "Negro" signs from the theater. Granz's behavior – and JATP's presence – brought police officers round, who burst into Ella Fitzgerald's dressing room and caught Illinois Jacquet and Dizzy Gillespie shooting dice. When Granz tried to block the officers from searching the bathroom out of concern that they would plant drugs on the musicians, an officer put a gun to the promoter's chest and threatened to shoot him. At the end of the performance, Granz, Fitzgerald, Gillespie, Jacquet, and Fitzgerald's cousin Georgiana Henry were all booked by officers before returning for a second performance. When seeing a large group of reporters and photographers gathered at the police station, it was clear to Granz that the arrest was a preconceived setup. Although the bail was set at only $10 each, Granz spent over $2,000 in legal fees to remove the charges.[96]

There were also issues at a show in San Antonio, where a fight broke out between two young men in the audience. Additionally, the audience had to be reprimanded by Granz to stop shouting during Fitzgerald's set and to stop smoking in the theater. Overall, though, the tour made an encouraging return, grossing $588,000 for the promoter. An October 1955 performance at the Chicago Opera House recorded on October 2, 1955 saw a JATP performance of a set that had become somewhat formulaic, the band presenting lengthy versions of jam-style blues, swing tunes, a ballad medley, and a drum solo.

Of these tracks, the ones of the most interest in evaluating Ray Brown are from the Oscar Peterson Trio's five-song set, which included versions of "Anything Goes," "Baby, Baby All the Time," "Budo," "Easy Does It," and "Sunday." Unlike the more jam-oriented material of the evening, the Peterson trio demonstrates continued interest in crafting arrangements while still impressing with superior technique as soloists. These five tracks were issued on *Jazz at the Philharmonic 1955: Volume 2* (Columbia 33CX 10079).

The 1956 JATP international spring tour was a six-week run with a slightly scaled-down unit of only the Oscar Peterson Trio, Ella Fitzgerald, Roy Eldridge, Dizzy Gillespie, Flip Phillips, Illinois Jacquet, and Don Abney, who was still serving as an accompanist for Fitzgerald. The tour included stops in Oslo, Gothenburg, Copenhagen, Malmö, Kiel, Amsterdam, Hamburg, Zurich, Manheim, Karlsruhe, Vienna, Berlin, Hannover, Essen, Cologne, Düsseldorf, and Frankfurt. Around the time of the tour, Granz was being investigated by the FBI as part of the McCarthy trials for his earlier connection to the Communist Party. Along with Granz, the FBI sought to interview thirty-five musicians, of which only six complied. The rest chose to assert their First and Fifth Amendment rights and refused to testify. To avoid a subpoena, Granz decided to go abroad and took up residence for a time in Mexico and then Paris. Granz eventually met with agents, and the matter was all but dropped, and Granz avoided any government "blacklist" which had prevented others in the entertainment field from working. Granz did admit that he had attended a few meetings at private homes and accepted an invitation some ten years earlier to join the musicians' branch of the Communist Party. He did so because their propaganda seemed to align with his interest in fighting racial discrimination at the time. He refused to offer any names to the agents, and the incident did not seem to have any significant permanent lasting effects.

Between the international and national tours of 1956, on August 15 Ray Brown and JATP appeared at the Hollywood Bowl, a scenic outside venue overlooking the beautiful Hollywood hills, first opened in 1922. The JATP event marked the highest attendance at the venue to date. The evening included performances by stars including Louis Armstrong, Ella Fitzgerald, Art Tatum, Roy Eldridge, and Oscar Peterson. As he often did, Norman Granz began the concert by laying out the evening's events. He then introduced the members of the opening jam in the following order: Buddy Rich, Ray Brown, Herb Ellis, Oscar Peterson, Flip Phillips, Illinois Jacquet, Harry Edison, and Roy Eldridge. The musicians then broke into a lengthy version of "Honeysuckle Rose," "Ballad Medley," and "Jumping at the Woodside."

After the jam, Art Tatum is introduced, and proceeds to play a fantastic set of solo piano pieces. Ella Fitzgerald is then presented, with a group that including West Coast bassist Joe Mondragon. With Granz's increased activities in Los Angeles, Mondragon was now serving as Norman Granz's most recorded house bassist, thus somewhat limiting Ray Brown's studio credits. While Mondragon is a fine accompanying bassist, he could never match Ray Brown's popularity.

After Fitzgerald's celebrated set, the Peterson trio took the stage and performed a repertoire that included "9:20 Special" and the tightly arranged "How About You." The next performer was Louis Armstrong, who presented a Dixieland-style set with Ella Fitzgerald joining him for several songs. For the final number of the evening, the Peterson trio returned to the stage to join Armstrong and Fitzgerald on "When the Saints Go Marching In." The star-studded event was a fantastic success. Music from the evening is now available on the album *Jazz at the Hollywood Bowl* (Verve MGV-8231-2).

After the resounding success of the 1955 Newport Jazz Festival, Granz's competitive instincts may have inspired him to enhance his JATP roster with a more modernistic group. To this end, he signed up the Modern Jazz Quartet to the tour. Even by virtue of their name alone, the MJQ brought to the tour a forward-looking and modernizing direction. Guitarist Clinton "Skeeter" Best also performed with the MJQ as a guest artist. The remaining touring unit included Ella Fitzgerald, the Oscar Peterson Trio, Dizzy Gillespie, Sonny Stitt, Stan Getz, Illinois Jacquet, Flip Phillips, Jo Jones, and Gene Krupa. Kicking off at Carnegie Hall on September 15, 1956, the tour moved through most major U.S. cities, with the group performing thirty-five concerts in thirty-one days. The inclusion of Stan Getz and the MJQ afforded JATP a modern counterbalance to the veteran members of the tour like Flip Phillips and Gene Krupa.

As 1957 came round, JATP continued to be well received by international audiences who apparently still valued swing-based music and the veteran musicians who played it. The 1957 tour began with some difficulty because Ella Fitzgerald was ill, and the concerts from April to June had to be postponed. When the tour finally kicked off, the troupe included a familiar cast of Ella Fitzgerald, the Oscar Peterson Trio, Roy Eldridge, Jo Jones, and Don Abney. The only new addition to the tour was violinist Stuff Smith, a somewhat forgotten figure in jazz, whom Granz was now supporting. Absent from the tour was Flip Phillips, who had not missed a JATP tour since 1944. Dates for these performances included stops in Italy, Germany, Switzerland, Spain, France, Holland, and Scandinavia.

Three tracks by Stuff Smith with the Oscar Peterson Trio and Jo Jones were recorded on May 2 at the Salle Pleyel in Paris and eventually released on the Stéphane Grappelli and Stuff Smith album *Violins No End* (Pablo 2310-907). The unusual experience of hearing the trio back a violinist is of interest, mainly because with three string instruments – violin, guitar, and bass – the players must take care to remain in the correct registers of their instruments to avoid harmonic clashes.

Parisian-born Stéphane Grappelli was the most celebrated jazz violinist; along with Django Reinhardt in the 1930s he helped introduce a style that is often referred to as "gypsy jazz." The style used only string instruments, usually eschewing reeds or brass. In more traditional American-based jazz subgenres, the violin has often been considered a novelty instrument, despite its roots in the jazz idiom dating back to early New Orleans. Stuff Smith was one of the earliest practitioners of jazz violin, and he gained some notoriety when he played with popular Midwest bandleader Alphonse Trent in the 1920s. Before the tour, Stuff Smith had already worked with bop innovators such as Coleman Hawkins, Charlie Parker, and Dizzy Gillespie; however, his style was still heavily based in swing. It is also interesting to note that many sources credit Smith with being the first violinist to use electric amplification.

Norman Granz seemed to have a real fascination with Stuff Smith at the time, and recorded the violinist regularly. While accompanying Smith, Brown plays a pizzicato solo on "Desert Sands," which delivers well-connected phrase sequences and a nice contrast to Smith's arco melodies. Through his career, Brown would continue to work with violinists, including Stéphane Grappelli and classical virtuoso Itzhak Perlman.

On July 7, 1957, the Peterson trio returned to the celebrated Newport Jazz Festival; several selections from the performance are included on the album *The Oscar Peterson Trio with Roy Eldridge, Sonny Stitt and Jo Jones, At Newport* (Verve MGV-8239). The most notable selection was a fantastic new arrangement of Clifford Brown's "Joyous Spring." The tune was a tribute to the virtuosic trumpeter who died tragically in a car accident at only twenty-five on June 26, 1956. The group's four-song set concludes with a spirited version of "52nd Street Theme," a staple in their set since their outstanding performance at the Stratford Shakespearean Festival in 1956.

Domestically, 1957 represented a period of transition for JATP and Norman Granz. That year, Granz along with a record-breaking fifty thousand fans attended the Newport Festival, and it had now become evident that Granz had become noticeably agitated by the festival's success. Since 1954, several of Granz's managed artists had appeared at Newport, and Granz recorded some of the performances for eventual release. However, a strange dynamic was at play between Newport Festival organizer George Wein and Norman Granz. As Newport began to surpass his JATP tours in terms of popularity and critical attention, Granz became increasingly critical of the festival in the press and through "private" conversation. His big gripe was about the

Jazz at the Philharmonic, 1952. Left to right (back): Gene Krupa, Ella Fitzgerald, Ray Brown, J.C. Heard, Barney Kessel, Oscar Peterson, and Lester Young; (front): Flip Phillips, Charlie Shavers, and Willie Smith

Allstar Picture Library Ltd / Alamy Stock Photo

way the musicians were treated: they weren't granted the same amenities that Granz provided on JATP tours. Nevertheless, despite his efforts to include more modern musicians in his domestic JATP tours, Granz was losing his grip on maintaining general interest in his JATP tours, and their popularity was waning.

For the 1957 tour, Granz pulled out all the stops by including as many musicians of interest as possible. The national JATP tour kicked off on September 14 with a line-up that included Ella Fitzgerald, the Oscar Peterson Trio, the Modern Jazz Quartet, Roy Eldridge, Lester Young, Stan Getz, Coleman Hawkins, J.J. Johnson. Illinois Jacquet, Flip Phillips, and Jo Jones. Despite all efforts, many theaters remained half full; at places like Boston Symphony Hall, where hitherto JATP would sell out two nights, they could not even sell one night of tickets. After the final performance at Shrine Auditorium in Los Angeles on October 25, 1957, Granz decided that JATP would no longer tour in the States and that his focus would remain on promoting the careers of Ella Fitzgerald and the Oscar Peterson Trio. Part of the lack of interest may have come from the fact that the U.S. was on the brink of the 1958 Eisenhower Recession, which saw a downturn in employment, income, and production. With this economic uncertainty, many were careful with their entertainment spending.

Although the 1957 national tour was not particularly successful, the music was still high-quality. Granz recorded and released a good amount of material from the performances at the Chicago Opera House on October 19 and Shrine Auditorium on October 25. One such release, *Ella Fitzgerald at the Opera House* (Verve MGV-8264), includes selections from Ella Fitzgerald with the Peterson trio and Jo Jones at the Chicago Opera House with added tracks from the Shrine with Connie Kay replacing Jones on drums.

Also from the Chicago Opera and Shrine are recorded sets by trombone master J.J Johnson alongside Stan Getz with the Oscar Peterson Trio. The Chicago set includes drummer Connie Kay, and Louie Bellson occupies the drum throne for the Shrine performance. The pairing of Johnson and Getz, two new additions to Granz's JATP roster, is a welcome addition to the JATP catalog of recordings. Both sets reveal two fantastic and focused soloists whose styles complement each other. These performances were issued on *Stan Getz and J.J. Johnson at the Opera House* (Verve MGV-8265).

Also released from the Chicago show was the recording *The JATP All-Stars at the Opera House* (Verve MGV-8267). Interestingly, Ray Brown was replaced by bassist Percy Heath on the Chicago jam but reinstated at the Shrine performance, yet Peterson performed on both.

The Oscar Peterson Trio's and the Modern Jazz Quartet's sets were also recorded from the Chicago Opera House performance and released on the album *The Modern Jazz Quartet and the Oscar Peterson Trio at the Opera House* (Verve MGV-8269). By 1957, the Peterson trio and the MJQ were two of the most successful touring jazz units and favorites among even the most casual jazz fan, whose primary preference in music might be more classically oriented. When Granz first added the MJQ to his fall 1956 JATP tour, alongside the Peterson trio, it drew comparisons between two of the most successful and beloved groups in jazz.

The initial release of *The Modern Jazz Quartet and the Oscar Peterson Trio at the Opera House* offered three cuts from the MJQ on side A and five from the Peterson trio on side B. In comparing the two groups AllMusic reviewer Scott Yanow states: "While the MJQ sounds much more introverted than the more exuberant Oscar Peterson Trio, the two popular groups have more similarities than differences."[97]

The popularity and presence of the MJQ on tour might have encouraged the Oscar Peterson Trio to step up their game, and the trio is in fine form throughout their short set, which includes "Should I," "Big Fat Mama," "Indiana," "Joy Spring," and "Elevation."

On "Big Fat Mama," Brown plays one of his finest solos to date. What makes it particularly interesting is how he intermingles bluesy statements and bebop licks through focused phrasing in which he provides specific resting points. As a soloist, Brown is most successful when he tries not to overtly display his technicality. As his career progressed, Brown developed a deeper understanding that it was through focused phrasing and more selective displays of virtuosity that his solos made their strongest connections with audiences. This approach served him particularly well when his technical skills began to be matched and further surpassed by other younger bassists whose talents seemed unachievable by those of Brown's generation. Whatever the era, Ray Brown could always evince a level of technical ability that remained impressive. However, for many, Brown's tastefulness not his technicality was the true source of inspiration.

The Oscar Peterson Trio at the Chicago Opera House represents one of the finest live releases by the "classic" trio on the JATP stage.

The 1958 European tour, which kicked off in April and lasted through early May, included Ella Fitzgerald, the Oscar Peterson Trio, Coleman Hawkins, Roy Eldridge, Sonny Stitt, Stan Getz, Dizzy Gillespie, and Gus Johnson on drums. Also on the tour were pianist Lou Levy (who had taken over as Ella Fitzgerald's accompanist), well-known session bassist Max Bennett, and drummer Gus Johnson. Included too were Welsh stride pianist Dill Jones and his trio with English bassist Malcolm Cecil and drummer Danny Craig. Sitting in with their group was clarinetist Dave Shepherd. Although Granz had struggled in the past getting JATP to England, he was able to include dates in London, Bristol, Newcastle, and Sheffield in 1958. The inclusion of Dill Jones's trio was part of a concession between Granz and the British Musician's Union to allow for performances in England. This tour would mark Ellis's final JATP performance with the Oscar Peterson Trio.

In place of a JATP national tour, Granz wisely presented a more scaled-down one-month tour billed as "An Evening with Ella Fitzgerald and the Oscar Peterson Trio." The decision to continue to feature the trio in this fashion must have been a welcome relief for the group, especially since the decision to drop the national tour would provide a degree of uncertainty for the many musicians Granz employed.

12 The Classic Oscar Peterson Trio with Singers 1954–1958

The Oscar Peterson Trio was often used by Norman Granz to back singers both on the JATP stage and on record. A level of restraint is required to do this well. Peterson could mesmerize an audience with his technical ability and virtuosity but he had the discipline to simplify his playing and provide clear harmonies behind vocalists. Ray Brown was responsible both for generating a forward-moving pulse and, from a harmonic point of view, laying down a root-based foundation. Over the years, he proved himself one of the finest and most consistent accompanists for singers, keeping impeccable time and delivering well-crafted bass lines, a solid intonation, and a round-focused tone. Herb Ellis, an accomplished soloist, would often have to move even further into the background when working with singers. His responsibilities included providing harmonic sequences and fragmented background figures, all the while taking great care not to clash with Peterson's chording or the bass register. The trio handled this work with regality and grace, allowing vocalists to showcase their talents and make some of their finest recordings.

Granz was very discerning in selecting his vocalists for JATP performances. From 1944, these included Carolyn Richards, Slim Gaillard and Bam Brown, Billie Holiday, Helen Humes, Sarah Vaughan, and Kenny "Pancho" Hagood. Ella Fitzgerald officially joined JATP in 1949, serving as the tour's featured vocalist, which is why the Oscar Peterson Trio was so closely connected with Fitzgerald during this period. As we've seen, Ray Brown's relationship with Ella Fitzgerald was complex, but, as touring JATP members, Ray and Ella couldn't avoid having a working relationship even when their personal one was suffering.

As the first JATP tour of 1954 began, Fitzgerald and Brown had been divorced for less than six months. Brown was now dating Cecilia Connor from Detroit: later that year (August 13, 1954), the two would marry. Their marriage lasted nearly 48 years until Ray Brown's passing. Cecilia describes how she met her husband:

> I'm from Detroit and lived across the street from Milt Jackson. He had four brothers, five boys, and no girls, so I considered myself adopted [by

the Jacksons]. When my husband and Milt were with Dizzy Gillespie, they became close. Whenever Dizzy came to Detroit, Milt would have him over to the house with the band, and he [Milt] introduced me to my husband. That was before he married Ella.[98]

While there were undoubtedly moments of awkwardness between Fitzgerald and Brown in 1954, the two were able to put their differences aside and continue to make quality music. With each passing tour and year, the former couple rebuilt a friendship. Of course, they also were co-parenting Ray Brown Jr. When it came to music, Granz knew that Fitzgerald and Brown were perfectly matched, and he continued to showcase Fitzgerald with Ray Brown backing.

By 1954, Ella Fitzgerald had sold over 20 million records, which ranked her among the most popular singers of her time. When Granz took over the management of Fitzgerald, he got her out of her recording contract with Decca and in 1956 she began recording for his Verve label. Like the Oscar Peterson Trio, Ella Fitzgerald recorded numerous albums for a *Songbook* series, singing the most popular tunes of the most famous composers. The majority of Fitzgerald's recording sessions in 1954–56 are found on her popular albums *Ella Fitzgerald Sings the Cole Porter Song Book* (Verve MGV-4001-2) and *Ella Fitzgerald Sings the Rodgers and Hart Song Book* (Verve MGV-4002-2). Both were recorded in Los Angeles with larger studio orchestras, most frequently with Joe Mondragon on bass. Although not serving as her bassist in the studio during these years, Brown continued to back Fitzgerald at JATP performances.

In 1956 Granz recorded an entire album of duets between Ella Fitzgerald and Louis Armstrong (who was never a touring member of JATP but did participate in the August 15, 1956 performance of JATP at the Hollywood Bowl). A day after this celebrated performance, the Oscar Peterson Trio and Buddy Rich entered the new Capitol Studios in Los Angeles to back Ella and Louis for one of their careers' most commercially successful projects. The session yielded eleven standards that included light swings and ballads. The successful pairing of two of the most innovative and beloved vocalists, supported by the brilliant rhythm section, produced the celebrated album *Ella and Louis* (Verve MGV-4003). In addition to his characteristic vocals, Armstrong is also impressive on his trumpet solos, primarily played in the older Dixieland style of interpretation and phrasing. Highlights include popular hits like "They Can't Take That Away from Me," "A Foggy Day," and "Cheek to Cheek."

Norman Granz knew he had a good thing with Fitzgerald and Armstrong and continued to record the singers with the backing of the Peterson trio. So, on July 23, 1957, the trio was back in Los Angeles to record another album with the two stars, but with Louie Bellson in place of Rich. As before, we have American Songbook classics accompanied by a top-notch rhythm section. This material would later appear on the double album *Ella and Louis Again*

(Verve MGV 4006-2).[99] The same rhythm section was also used to record three tracks with Ella Fitzgerald alone: "It Happens Every Spring," "Comes Love," and "Ill Wind."

A July 31, 1957 session at Radio Recorders Studio (again with the same rhythm section) yielded four more tracks, including "Makin' Whoopee," "I Get a Kick Out of You," "Let's Do It (Let's Fall in Love)," and "Willow Weep for Me." On the same day, Ray Brown also recorded with Count Basie alums Lester Young and Harry Edison. One can only imagine what a young Ray Brown would have thought if he had been told that he would be recording with his childhood stars, Armstrong, Young, and Edison, all in one day!

There was a final Armstrong–Fitzgerald session with the Peterson trio and Louie Bellson on August 13, 1957. Today, all the Fitzgerald and Armstrong duets are available on *The Complete Ella Fitzgerald and Louis Armstrong on Verve* (Verve 537-284-2).

On October 17, 1957, the trio, along with Ben Webster and drummer Alvin Stoller, recorded five Ellington tunes with Ella Fitzgerald for her upcoming release *Ella Fitzgerald Sings the Duke Ellington Song Book* (Vol. 2) (Verve MGV-4009-2). A further evaluation of the Peterson trio's backing of Ella Fitzgerald can be made from several live JATP recordings of the period. While Ray Brown is not heavily featured on these Fitzgerald–Armstrong recordings, they show how perfectly Brown, Peterson, and Ellis could accompany without being flashy. Brown's musical connection with Fitzgerald would continue for some years.

Despite their very different vocal styles, the singer Ella Fitzgerald was most frequently compared to was Billie Holiday. Although the latter had not appeared with JATP since 1945 she recorded for Granz in 1952, with Ray Brown backing. According to *Verve: The Sound of America*,[100] "In 1954, Billie toured Europe and seemed happier than she had been in years, perhaps because she had a new lover named Billy McKay, who at least kept drugs out of her life." Sadly for Holiday, the happiness did not continue, she and McKay began to fight frequently and Holiday returned to the addictions that would end her life.

The trio of Peterson, Brown, and Ellis recorded a date with Holiday in New York on April 14, 1954, with Charlie Shavers on trumpet and Ed Shaughnessy on drums. The session yielded Holiday's classic version of "How Deep Is the Ocean," plus "I Cried for You" and an uptempo revisit of "What a Little Moonlight Can Do." These tracks were eventually released on *Recital by Billie Holiday* (Clef MG C-686) in 1956. After a long struggle with addiction, Billie Holiday passed away on July 17, 1959, aged only forty-four.

The Peterson trio and Ray Brown had a long-running association with drummer Buddy Rich, who also recorded several times as a vocalist. Ray's first studio session of 1955 was on January 26 in New York, for a vocal recording featuring Rich, which reveal the drummer's pleasant crooning style. Accompanying are the Peterson trio with the Howard Gibeling Orchestra and trumpeter Lee Castle. Like Oscar Peterson, who also sang on occasion, Buddy Rich would never truly break through as a vocal star. Material from these sessions was initially issued on the Norgran label as *Sing and Swing with Buddy Rich* (Norgran MGN-1031) and "Everything Happens to Me" b/w "Sure Thing" (Norgan 144).

On December 29, 1955, the Oscar Peterson Trio with Alvin Stoller recorded again with film legend Fred Astaire on two tracks: "I Won't Dance" and "They Can't Take That Away from Me," which reaffirm that Astaire was best suited for stage and screen, as his ability as a jazz vocalist can best be described as mediocre. Granz can't have been thrilled with the performances as they remained unissued until the 2017 CD release of Fred Astaire and Oscar Peterson, *The Astaire Story* (Verve B0026605-02). This would be the trio's final attempt to record with the icon.

After the Astaire session, Peterson, Ellis, Brown, and Stoller remained in the studio to work with vocalist Toni Harper. Harper was a former child star, and it is quite possible that Norman Granz saw a parallel between her and Ella Fitzgerald. Unlike Fitzgerald, Harper did not succeed as a lasting commercial recording artist despite having a fine voice and beautiful looks. After several attempts at solo fame in her early and mid-twenties, Harper retired from the business at only twenty-nine. But these 1955 recordings of popular standards reveal a gifted singer who deserved wider recognition. The session led to her debut album *Toni* (Verve MGV-2001).

One of the more fascinating singers the Peterson trio backed was Anita O'Day. During the 1940s she emerged as one of the more popular female vocalists while working with the West Coast bandleaders Gene Krupa, Woody Herman, and Stan Kenton. O'Day first signed with Norman Granz in 1952 and began recording for his Norgran label. Plagued by heroin addiction, O'Day had many ups and downs in her career but managed to prevail, enjoying a career as a recording artist for over sixty years.

The Peterson trio first recorded with O'Day on January 31, 1957, in Chicago at Universal Recording Studio, sessions that resulted in her album *Anita Sings the Most* by Anita O'Day and Her Rhythm Section (Verve MGV-8259). Enhancing the group was O'Day's touring drummer John Poole. The album reveals the uniqueness that resulted from the singer's smokey voice and lack of classical vibrato (the legacy of a botched childhood tonsillectomy). Her individualistic sound perfectly serves the American Songbook repertoire and *Sings the Most* is regarded as one of her finest albums.

In their final year as a working trio, Peterson, Brown, and Ellis, along with drummer Alvin Stoller, recorded with Dorothy Dandridge. The session took place at Radio Recorders Studio in Hollywood on January 19 and 20, 1958. Dandridge was already a major star when the group recorded these tracks.[101] Having developed her reputation as a singer, actor, and dancer at venues like the Cotton Club and the Apollo, Dandridge's fame grew after a performance in the title role of the 1954 film *Carmen Jones*. It earned her an Academy

Award nomination, making her the first African American film star nominated for Best Actress. In 1959, she was nominated for a Golden Globe for *Porgy and Bess.*

Smooth Operator reveals Dandridge's ability to deliver jazz ballads convincingly, and the album ought to rank among one of the stronger records of American Songbook ballads. Ray Brown is prominently featured on "That Old Feeling" – at times accompanying the singer alone as well as offering focused and impressive solo fills and runs. Another notable Brown moment is on "The Nearness of You," with some heavily active bass lines against Dandridge's melody. Creating some interest is the decision to have Peterson play the celesta on "I've Grown Accustomed to Your Face." Overall, Dandridge and the ensemble are well represented on *Smooth Operator.* Sadly, Dorothy Dandridge died in 1965 of a possibly accidental overdose when the groundbreaking entertainer was only forty-two years old.

13 The Session Recordings of the Classic Oscar Peterson Trio
1954–1958

Following the emergence of bebop, much of the interest in small-group jazz was based on the individuality of soloists. With a greater focus on improvisation, solos now tended to be lengthier on record and in concerts. During this era, when it came to recording or performing, featured musicians were often pitted with pickup bands and rhythm sections made up of sidemen who were not part of any working unit. This heavy reliance on individual journeymen musicians was a notable change from the big-band era, in which orchestras were built on the consistency of their members.

A significant element of a big band's sound came from its rhythm section, which functioned as a unit to create a distinctive feel and concept. Since orchestra members toured and recorded together frequently, soloists would be comfortable with the rhythm section before entering a recording studio. Many small-group recordings during the big-band era were created by showcasing one or more featured band soloists with their regular rhythm section. This consistency and overall band concept began to be lost lost as the big bands folded in the late 1940s.

Similar to the touring big-band rhythm sections of the past, the Oscar Peterson Trio developed a signature time feel and concept adaptable to the many star instrumentalists they would back in the studio. This level of steadiness and specificity was achieved through countless hours of touring, recording, analyzing, and practicing. By using the Peterson trio as a studio backing band, a leader was all but guaranteed a characteristic group sound based on the rhythmic traditions of swing and bop. The trio also came with the strengths of its three individualistic soloists, with Peterson being the most virtuosic. While many jazz record producers had their favorite individual rhythm section players, few of these units matched what the Oscar Peterson Trio had to offer.

When recording instrumentalists as leaders, Granz had a vision and concept that worked pretty well. A pattern developed, in which Granz would sign a soloist who had already achieved a degree of fame, add the Oscar Peterson Trio, hire a skilled drummer to hold it all together, and record. In doing this, Granz knew he could create a solid recording and moreover do so quickly thereby cutting studio costs. Using this formula, Granz would attract attention (and sales) both from the fan base of the soloist or bandleader and that of the Oscar Peterson Trio.

As time passed, and with a wealth of older jazz recordings still available, new consumers might often feel overwhelmed by the amount of material by artists such as Louis Armstrong, Ella Fitzgerald, Lester Young, Ben Webster, or Stan Getz. Trying to pick the "right" record could be perplexing, so record buyers would often look at who else was on the album. When an artist had the Oscar Peterson Trio behind them, the record basically came with an assurance that it would be a solid purchase and often among the artist's best recordings.

With regard to Ray Brown specifically, a certain steadiness and sound was expected and delivered. The jazz literature –as well as anecdotally from other musicians – often cites Brown as jazz's finest accompanist and hardest-swinging bassist. While these labels testify to his reputation, they demand further evaluation. As discussed in the previous chapter, the success of Brown as a singer's accompanist had much to do with his impeccable time, well-crafted bass lines, solid intonation, and round-focused tone. These same factors applied when Ray Brown backed instrumental soloists, but in these cases, he was afforded additional freedoms. Working with instrumentalists generally allows a higher level of interplay than with singers, whose needs – and those of their lyrics – can stifle such creativity.

There is a push–pull factor in being an accompanying bassist, and a responsibility that comes with the instrument's foundational role as the ensemble's lowest voice and one of its principal rhythmic entities. On the surface – and in rudimentary discussions on the role of the bassist – the concepts are simple: play steady time, and offer note choices that best outline the chord changes. Many bassists have had fine careers by largely adhering to these basic principles. But, at its core, jazz is based on improvisation, which reaches beyond just the principal soloist. A creative bassist will find possibilities in the accompaniment far beyond just providing a walking bass line. For example, at times, they can break the steadiness of walking time by adding eighth notes, sixteenth notes, triplet figures, syncopations, rests, pedal tones, countermelodies, and alternate time feels. By breaking from the standard walking rhythm or two-feel pattern over a basic swing feel, the bassist provides new rhythmic information and moments of interest and interaction. The issue then becomes one of frequency. What is the perfect balance between adding alternate rhythmic concepts without overstepping the primary role in servicing the soloist?

Another factor lies in choosing the appropriate notes. Bass lines have a shape and a direction generally intended to outline the basic harmony laid out by the composer. The soloist then creates melodic interest from notes that best fit into each chord or key. Chords are often built from the bottom up, with the lowest note holding more weight than the intervals placed above it. A bassist can imply inversions or alternate chords by choosing notes that are not the chord's root. In doing this, a new harmony can be genreated, offering the soloist a new structure to explore. Once again, the question is one of frequency and preparation. To successfully "prepare" alternate note choices without losing the overall direction of a line, the bassist must carefully locate the notes that both precede and follow a unique or alternate choice. Another question arises: when is it appropriate to break from your primary role as a rhythm section player to provide counter-statements with which the soloist can interact?

There is no one rule in jazz regarding interaction as a bassist. It is a matter of context, so more questions need to be asked: Who am I backing? What do they require me to create? How much interaction are the remaining members of the group implying?

Brown was a master of addressing these questions. During the period we've been discussing, he mainly backed musicians who had already developed a unique vocabulary, specific style, and a strong reputation. Through study, experience, and instinct, he was masterful in figuring out the best way to work and interact with each soloist within his role in the trio. He generally found the perfect balance between servicing such a soloist while offering subtle musical suggestions and without becoming overwhelming. In this way, Ray Brown was unique: no other bassist could adapt with the same ease.

Although Ray Brown's lines were based on functionality and interaction with the group, they also worked independently, even taken out of the context in which they were created. A useful way to evaluate a Ray Brown bass line is to isolate it from the surrounding voices and listen to it as if it were a monophonic melody, analyzing its melodic shape, harmonic direction, and rhythmic movement. But such an analysis can only go so far in explaining the greatness of Brown's playing, as intangible elements and a personal touch define all great jazz musicians.

Many significant innovations in jazz improvisation were made by saxophonists. And these players became some of the biggest stars. The Oscar Peterson Trio backed many of the most noteworthy in the studio and on JATP tours between 1954 and 1958. One cannot discuss tenor saxophonists in jazz without mentioning the "Big Three": Lester Young, Coleman Hawkins, and Ben Webster, among the most celebrated stars of the swing era and beyond, each with his specific sound and approach. Of the three, Young is possibly the most intriguing.

Lester Young came to national fame as the principal tenor saxophonist soloist with Count Basie's band in the mid and late 1930s and is often cited as the most influential jazz soloist after Louis Armstrong and before Charlie Parker. In Basie's orchestra and in small groups, Young regularly worked with one of jazz's most celebrated swing rhythm sections: bassist Walter Page, drummer Jo Jones, guitarist Freddie Green and Basie on piano. Together this unit developed a rhythmic energy centered around new concepts in swing. Its success arose from Page's shift from a more traditional Dixieland two feel into patterns that incorporated more consistent four-beat walking bass lines.[102] In addition, Jo Jones revolutionized swing drumming by keeping 4/4 time on his cymbal rather than on the bass drum. He then used the bass and snare drums more for accents and effects. Freddie Green's role within the group was to play quarter-note rhythms with an accent on beats two and four, using smooth voice leading to outline each harmonic shift. With Green providing a more powerful rhythmic pulse, Basie often limited his playing to sparse colorations and short melodic statements. Basie's rhythm section heavily inspired Ray Brown, and the overall model for his time feel can be traced to Walter Page. Even as a drummerless trio, Peterson's group strove for the same drive as Basie's rhythm section, and their accompaniment style fit perfectly into Lester Young's lyrical approach.

Granz took an interest in producing Young in the mid-1940s when the saxophonist's career was disrupted by his military service. Young was court-martialed for possession of narcotics and sentenced to a year of hard labor in 1945. The experience was traumatic for him, and there wre concerns over how he would recover musically and psychologically from the situation. Norman Granz, who tried to no avail to make a case to the draft board that Young was unfit for military service, helped him get his career back on track almost immediately after his release. With Young having initially returned to the Aladdin label, Granz organized additional recordings for him in 1947 and added him to his JATP tour. Ray Brown began recording with Lester Young in 1950, and the Oscar Peterson Quartet supported him on record for the first time in 1952. On November 1, 1955, the Oscar Peterson Trio with Buddy Rich recorded with Lester Young and Harry Edison at Radio Recorders Studio in Los Angeles.[103] The session yielded eight tracks initially released on the album *Pres and Sweets* (Norgran MGN-1043). The recording was a reunion of sorts as both Young and Edison had worked together as star soloists in the Count Basie Orchestra.

While the group sounds solid and professional, neither Young nor Edison take many risks during their improvisations. Young's decision to play it safe may have stemmed from the fact that he was suffering a mental-health decline that hospitalized him later in the month. By this point in his career, his playing could be sporadic and formulaic. Although arguments have been made about the deterioration of Young's playing, regardless Young retained a specific approach and musical personality that always added interest to a session. The general consensus that Young's playing was diminished may be more accurately modified by saying that his playing had become uneven, as there are some fantastic recordings of Young from this latter period of his career.

In contrast, trumpeter Harry "Sweets" Edison was playing consistently at a high level at this point in his career and had many years and albums ahead of him, several of which included Ray Brown. After dozens of recent 1955 sessions without a bass solo, Brown was finally featured on "She's Funny That Way." His solo begins with a descending scale-like pattern followed by clear behind-the-beat eighth-note statements played in a phrasing pattern which seems inspired by Young's approach and presence. Young, Edison, and the Peterson trio recorded again on July 31, 1957, again at Radio Recorders Studio, with Louie Bellson replacing Rich. Some of this material was included in the release Harry Edison and Lester Young, *Going for Myself* (Verve MGV-8298). Of particular interest is Lester Young's clarinet work on "St. Tropez" and his interpretation of "Our Love Is Here to Stay." Today, Brown's studio recordings with Lester Young can be evaluated on *The Complete Lester Young Studio Sessions on Verve* (Verve 314 547 087-2). Sadly, Lester Young died aged only forty-nine in 1959.

One of the saxophonists Ray Brown worked with most during this period was Ben Webster, and in fact many of the latter's finest small-group recordings were made with Ray behind him. Before recording with the Peterson Trio, Webster had enjoyed the support of many fine rhythm sections, most notably as a member of Duke Ellington's Orchestra from 1940 to 1943, with a section that included bassist Jimmy Blanton, drummer Sonny Greer, guitarist Fred Guy, and Ellington or Billy Strayhorn on piano. There was seemingly nothing that rhythm section was incapable of at the time. The unit could deliver some of the hardest-driving, danceable swing and also play with a great deal of subtlety and coloration to enhance Ellington's more harmonically rich and highly arranged, classically based works. On several recordings, the Peterson trio showed comparable versatility during this period.

Webster had appeared on some Norman Granz jams as early as 1942 but did not join as a JATP touring member until 1953, and that same year he first recorded with the Oscar Peterson Trio. On October 15, 1957, Webster recorded with the trio and drummer Stan Levey for what became one of his most celebrated albums, *Soulville* (as the Ben Webster Quintet; Verve MGV-8274). Here, Webster showcases his bluesy and soulful approach as he works through a set of standards and ballads. Some of the most notable elements of Webster's playing are his ballad interpretation, breathy tone, laid-back phrasing, and rich timbre, which are all on display here, and the Peterson quartet perfectly supports Webster on these recordings.

Brown's bass is well recorded on *Soulville,* and he is heard as a soloist on the title track, where his improvising is a perfect example of his work over a slow blues, delivering characteristic licks focused around the blues scale. Brown is also featured on "Makin' Whoopee," first offering some bass figures in the introduction and then displaying more bop-oriented double-time figures during his short eight-bar solo. One of the fascinating aspects of later reissues of the album is hearing Ben Webster play piano on "Who," "Boogie

Woogie," and "Roses of Picardy." While he is no match for Peterson, Webster plays in a convincing boogie-woogie style.

Of the "Big Three" tenor masters, Coleman Hawkins' playing was the most modernistic. His move to a more vertical approach to improvising in the late 1930s inspired the development of bebop. Hawkins first came to fame as a member of Fletcher Henderson's Orchestra. Henderson is often credited as the bandleader who most impacted the early sound and practices of swing big bands. As a leader, pianist, arranger, and composer, his orchestra fused African American jazz music and spirit into more traditional white popular songs. This was first achieved by using accomplished arrangers like Don Redman and Benny Carter and (at different times) adding several key soloists including Hawkins, Louis Armstrong, Roy Eldridge, and Chu Berry. For some time, Henderson's rhythm section included bassist John Kirby and drummer Walter Johnson, a section whose characteristic was an ability to shift easily between commercially based "sweet" arrangements and swinging "hot" charts. The Peterson trio had this same flexibility.

Hawkins first appeared with JATP in 1945 and was part of many subsequent tours and recordings. By 1954, Brown had already recorded with the tenorist, but it was not until October 16, 1957 that Hawkins was teamed up in the studio with the Peterson trio, along with drummer Alvin Stoller. This material resulted in the classic *The Genius of Coleman Hawkins* (Verve MGV-8261), with highlights including "My Melancholy Baby" and "In a Mellotone," which perfectly display Hawkins' shifting swing-to-bop approach. Of added interest are the Latin-inspired "Begin the Beguine" and "I Never Had a Chance."[104] Unlike the Webster session, Hawkins' set leaves less of a role for Peterson as a soloist, and Ellis and Brown are not featured beyond their expertly handled accompaniment.

Ben Webster joined the group in the studio later that day, resulting in yet another classic, *Coleman Hawkins Encounters Ben Webster* (Verve MGV-8327). This pairing provides an excellent opportunity to compare the styles of the two masters. While all-star sessions sometimes fail to connect, possibly because of the pressure of trying to compete, these recordings reveal two fully realized tenor soloists who each seem comfortable in their style and approach. Whether it's the boogie "Blues for Yolande," the ballads "It Never Entered My Mind" and "Prisoner of Love," or the more Latin-based "Rosita," both Hawkins and Webster create a vibe and musical connection that is worthy of high praise. *Coleman Hawkins Encounters Ben Webster* is a perfect example of how Oscar Peterson's quartet enhances both tenorists' creative prowess and energy without being over-assertive.

Another tenor saxophonist of note who worked with the trio is Stan Getz, who possessed remarkable prowess coupled with a beautiful tone and a laid-back style reminiscent of Lester Young. Getz first came to prominence in the mid and late 1940s playing with bandleaders such as Stan Kenton, Jimmy Dorsey, and Benny Goodman.

In 1947 Getz began working with Woody Herman's band, where he became the most celebrated member of Herman's famed saxophone unit known as "The Four Brothers." At various times Herman's rhythms section included Oscar Pettiford on bass, Lou Levy on piano, Shelly Manne on drums, and Terry Gibbs on vibraphone. Herman required rhythm sections to be able to shift seamlessly between swing, bop, and West Coast cool. While never truly part of this latter scene, the Peterson trio had enough sensibility to incorporate a more "cool" approach when required.

Following his stint with Herman, Getz worked more as a leader and small-group performer and signed with Norman Granz in 1952. Although he had many personal and career ups and downs, Getz continued to record throughout the 1950s for Granz and, on a number of these occasions, with Ray Brown. Before accompanying Getz as a leader, the Oscar Peterson Trio recorded with him as co-leader on the album *Diz and Getz* in 1955, and on an August 1, 1957 Los Angeles recording known as *Jazz Giants 1958* credited to Stan Getz, Gerry Mulligan, Harry Edison, and Louie Bellson with the Oscar Peterson Trio (Verve MGV-8248). The juxtaposition of these musicians works quite well, and of the many Norman Granz all-star jams *Jazz Giants 1958* ranks among the best, mainly because of the distinct differences between the approach and timbre of Gerry Mulligan on baritone sax, Stan Getz on tenor and Harry Edison on trumpet. A true Ray Brown highlight is on the opening track, "Chocolate Sundae," the introduction of which exhibits his range, creativity, and technicality on a solo featuring signature characteristics, such as slides and note bends. He is also featured on a ballad medley where he plays a solo interpretation of "Makin' Whoopee," where for the first several measures he adheres to the written melody before moving into a more soloistic approach in which he only occasionally refers to the written line.

On October 10, 1957, Getz was to be found on his own with the Oscar Peterson Trio at Capitol Studios in Los Angeles. The result was *Stan Getz and the Oscar Peterson Trio* (Verve MGV-8251), a signature recording in Getz's career. Of all the . . . *and the Oscar Peterson Trio* albums, this is among the finest, and also noteworthy in that no drummer was added, thus offering a true representation of the Peterson trio as a stand-alone rhythmic unit. From the outset, the album is hard-swinging: the opening track, "I Want to Be Happy," has excellent exploratory solos by both Getz and Peterson. On the now-expected "Ballad Melody," which became a showpiece of Norman Granz-produced projects, Ray Brown interprets "I Can't Get Started" with only the backing of Herb Ellis. Once again, he shines on these ballad presentations, perfectly balancing the song's written melody with a display of improvisation and technicality. Ray is also given a solo spot on the album's final cut, "Bronx Blues," another example of how the bassist approaches an improvisation over a slow blues.

As with many of his solos during this period, Brown reaches into the bass's higher (thumb) position but does not remain there for any real length of time. Interestingly, many of Brown's heroes, such as Jimmy Blanton and Oscar Pettiford, rarely explored this higher range, and emerging bassist Paul Chambers also tended to avoid the thumb position. Charles Mingus would explore this higher register at times during this period, too, but often treated this register more as an effect than a viable means of melodic improvisation. Around this time, a young white bassist from New Jersey named Scott LaFaro would be the first to explore the possibilities of the thumb position, thus setting a new standard for jazz bass improvisation. Sadly, LaFaro died in a car crash in 1961 aged only twenty-five. Brown's comfort with thumb-position soloing would develop slowly, and it would be some years before he more frequently played longer solo phrases in higher positions.

In addition to Young, Webster, Hawkins, and Getz, Peterson also worked with other familiar saxophonists on albums like Benny Carter, Dizzy Gillespie, and Bill Harris, *New Jazz Sounds* (1955; Norgran MGN-1044),[105] *The Flip Phillips Quintet* (1955; Clef MGC-637), *Rock with Flip* (1956; Clef MGC-740), and Sonny Stitt, *Only the Blues* (1958; Verve MGV-8250). Of these sessions, Brown is only foregrounded on the medium-tempo "A Foggy Day," from a 1954 Benny Carter recording, on which he plays a full chorus of solo with only the backing of Bobby White on brushes and light comping from Peterson and Ellis.[106] Despite a fragmented harmonic backdrop, this solo shows a vertical approach in which he references the harmonic possibilities of the chord changes while still maintaining a linear direction.

Since jazz's beginnings, the cornet and trumpet have served as featured instruments for improvisation, and during this period the Peterson trio backed some of the finest players. No discussion of jazz trumpeters can omit Louis Armstrong, jazz's first great innovator and celebrity. Despite changing trends in jazz and his reluctance to engage with more modern styles, Armstrong remained one of the most celebrated jazz stars until his death in 1971. By the mid-1950s, Armstrong was singing a lot more, but he still retained the ability and personality as a trumpet player to continually impress. In addition to the famed duo sessions of Fitzgerald and Armstrong, the Oscar Peterson Trio with Louie Bellson was recorded independently with Louis Armstrong in Los Angeles on July 31, 1957, and again in Chicago on October 14, 1957. Tracks from the session were released in 1959 under the album title *Louis Armstrong Meets Oscar Peterson* (Verve MGV-8322); they show that, although Armstrong was no longer pushing the boundaries, his interpretations of pop standards could still bring joy. They do little to reveal Ray Brown's development but are nonetheless a reflection of his professionalism and steadiness.

One of the trumpeters Ray Brown and the Oscar Peterson Trio recorded with most frequently was Roy Eldridge. Once considered an untouchable technician until Gillespie emerged in the early 1940s, Eldridge's skills, competitive spirit, and charisma never seemed to diminish. Eldridge was an early addition to the JATP tours and began working consistently with the troupe in 1944. Having performed numerous shows with Eldridge on the JATP stage, Ray Brown first recorded with the trumpeter in 1951. In 1952, Eldridge recorded with the Oscar Peterson Trio with Barney Kessel and then again with Herb Ellis in December 1953. On September 14, 1954 Eldridge joined Buddy Rich and the Peterson trio to create *Little Jazz* (Clef MGC-683).[107] Eldridge's playing on the album is top-notch: he continues to impress with his command and control of the trumpet as a solo vehicle, particularly when he ventures into the instrument's higher register. Ray Brown and the Oscar Peterson Quartet mostly play a supportive role.

Brown's most significant mentor, Dizzy Gillespie, first appeared with JATP in January 1946. After struggling to keep a bebop big band afloat, Gillespie mainly returned to small-group work in the early 1950s and then began recording for Granz, where he was often paired with Roy Eldridge or Harry Edison. His first studio session for Granz with the Oscar Peterson Trio came on October 29, 1954, in New York City with Roy Eldridge and Louie Bellson for a series of tracks for the albums *Roy and Diz* (Clef MGC-641) and *Roy and Diz #2* (Clef MGC-671). The recording had a longer jam session-style format, and, while it is interesting to hear two of jazz's greatest trumpeters battling, the session lacked preparation and direction. Ray Brown is briefly featured on the intro of "Trumpet Blues," where he plays an out-of-time solo in the opening before he moves into a fast walk. "Limehouse Blues" is most impressive because of its incredibly rapid tempo, again showing Brown's ability to walk fast and well-connected bass lines for lengthy periods. Ray Brown would repeatedly record with Gillespie throughout the trumpeter's long career.

Harry "Sweets" Edison was a masterful trumpeter who found fame as a featured soloist in Count Basie's Orchestra from 1938 to 1950. When the Basie band temporarily disbanded in 1950, Edison performed with JATP. He subsequently settled on the West Coast, becoming a sought-after studio musician and joining a short but growing list of African American jazz musicians moving more toward commercial studio work. The Harry Edison Sextet, including the Oscar Peterson Trio, Ben Webster, and Alvin Stoller, was recorded in Los Angeles on March 5, 1957. For this five-song session, Barney Kessel was used instead of Ellis on all but one number, "Blues for Bill Basie." On March 30, 1957 the group, now with Ellis, recorded three more numbers supporting the Harry Edison album *Gee, Baby Ain't I Good to You* (Verve MGV-8211). Ray Brown would further record with Edison throughout their careers on both Los Angeles studio dates and jazz records.

One of Norman Granz's greatest gifts was his ability to get stars to go head-to-head both on stage and on record. When Granz set up a session on November 2, 1955 with Edison, Eldridge, and Gillespie he was able to present three of the most impactful jazz trumpeters on one album, *Tour de Force: The Trumpets of Roy Eldridge, Dizzy Gillespie, and Harry Edison* (Verve MGV-8212). Supporting them was the Oscar Peterson Trio with Buddy Rich. Issued from the session were the lengthy tracks "Tour de Force" and "Steeplechase." A "Ballad Medley" was also recorded but not issued.

While singers, saxophonists, trumpeters, and pianists are most frequently recorded as bandleaders on jazz recordings, other instrumentalists were also given opportunities to record as leaders for Norman Granz, with the backing of the Peterson trio. Lionel Hampton was one of the artists the trio most frequently shared the studio with during this period. Hampton had come to fame as the vibraphonist in Benny Goodman's Quartet and Orchestra from 1937 to 1941. A prolific freelance player, by 1940 Hampton had also begun leading his own big band, where he showcased his talents on the vibes and as a singer and drummer. With the band, Hampton's music helped popularize jump blues, a more hard-driving hybrid style that relied heavily on swing and blues elements. Hampton's band continued to score numerous jukebox hits for the next several years.

After recording a session for Clef in 1953 with Brown and Peterson, Hampton joined JATP in 1954 and began recording more frequently with the trio. Overall, the combination of Hampton, Peterson, and Brown, would record over six spirited hours of music in just one year, as heard on the compilation *The Complete Lionel Hampton Quartets and Quintets with Oscar Peterson on Verve* (Verve 314 559 797-2). The first of these sessions took place on April 12, 1954, and included Buddy Rich. Unlike the more radio-friendly ventures, the length of these recordings allowed Brown more solo space to improvise. Hampton's encouraging moans and grunts suggested that the group appreciated the extended jam-style format. Ray Brown is most heavily featured on "Love for Sale" and "Willow Weep for Me." In general, his solo style on these tracks was still patterned after the Oscar Pettiford model of bop-style licks in a scale-like fashion. Brown would continue to incorporate Pettiford's style throughout his career but would often do so in a fragmented way through shorter phrases that were interspersed with more personalized licks, melodic statements, and techniques such as slides, double stops, hammer-ons, and pull-offs.

The next day, clarinet master Buddy DeFranco was added to the group for a similar jam-style series of recordings, resulting in the 1954 release of *The Lionel Hampton Quintet* (Clef MGC-628). Granz again allowed for even more space and exploration on the record, yielding a version of "Flying Home" that lasted over seventeen minutes! For this session, Brown can be heard soloing on "These Foolish Things," where at times he blends a more lyrical approach with heavier note runs, a formula that served him well. The bassist is also featured at the end of "Je Ne Sais Pas," where he plays a fiery solo displaying a combination of bop and blues phrasing. On September 13, 1954, Peterson, Brown, and Rich recorded nine more tracks with Hampton in New York. These recordings lack the energy and interest of the sessions from earlier in the year. The song of most interest to a Ray Brown enthusiast is "When the Saints Go Marching In," which includes a rare lead vocal by the bassist. While in no way a master vocalist, Brown's voice has a certain quality that works for the song. There is no indication that Ray Brown had any ambitions to work as a singer.

Two days later, Herb Ellis was finally invited to join Hampton in the studio. The session supplied several more memorable moments, with Hampton and the Peterson trio maintained a magnificent connection. Ray Brown's most notable feature from this date is his solo on the standard "But Beautiful," where his phrasing is precise and well connected. Another track of note is "Hamp's Boogie Woogie," which sees the vibraphonist and the Peterson trio playing in a jump blues context, representing a momentary departure from the trio's more bop- and swing-related material. Despite an obvious strong connection between the musicians, Hampton did not record with the trio after 1954.

After recording with the trio and Lionel Hampton, Buddy DeFranco led his own session with the backing of the Oscar Peterson Trio and Louie Bellson on October 29, 1954. The result was the 1957 album *Buddy DeFranco and the Oscar Peterson Quartet* (Verve MG-8210). Hearing the trio supporting a clarinetist is a welcome sonic change. An album highlight includes the walking ballad "Easy to Love," which features a Ray Brown solo. His improvisation is not flawless, as his intonation gets a little "pitchy" in some areas, but overall his ideas and phrases are clear and expressive.

On December 6–7, 1954, in Los Angeles, Ray Brown was part of a large ensemble featuring Buddy DeFranco and Oscar Peterson. The session was arranged and conducted by Russell Garcia,[108] and the result was an often-overlooked album *Buddy DeFranco and Oscar Peterson Play George Gershwin* (Norgran MGN-1016). Hearing the trio participate in this format, alongside a string section, was a fresh departure from their regular and often rushed Granz sessions. While string sessions can often sound forced and fail to hit the mark, Peterson and DeFranco do a fantastic job servicing Gershwin's material. While Brown is not prominently featured on the album, the record is undoubtedly recommended, being another instance in which Brown is at ease among the classically schooled, which can sometimes be intimidating for a jazz musician.

There is often a special bond between a drummer and a bassist. Brown was often the bassist that most drummers wanted to work with, so when a drummer was allowed to lead a session Ray was the obvious person to call. Buddy Rich was the drummer most associated with Ray Brown early in his career. Rich served as a member of the Ray Brown Trio in 1949, was included on multiple JATP tours, and was used to accompany the Oscar Peterson Trio on dozens of recordings. After an earlier 1955 recording session with Buddy Rich featured as a singer, Brown and Peterson returned to the studio in New York on May 16, 1955 for a new project with Rich as leader, where he returned once again to the drum throne. Replacing Ellis on the guitar was Freddie Green. Ray Brown is featured on a great interpretation of "This Is Always," where he further displays his ability to hold the listener's interest as an interpreter of popular melodies. An evaluation of these tracks and other Buddy Rich-led sessions from the era can be heard on the box set *Argo, Emarcy and Verve Small Group Buddy Rich Sessions* (Mosaic Records MD7-232).

Drummer Gene Krupa began working with JATP in 1945, where at times he served as the drummer alongside Buddy Rich. On tours, the two participated in staged drum battles which became a popular feature of the show. Before joining JATP, Krupa achieved international fame as a member of the Benny Goodman Orchestra from 1934 to 1938, which he left to form his own big band, which was derailed when he was arrested for marijuana possession in 1943. On November 1, 1955, Granz set up a Los Angeles studio session geared towards drum enthusiasts when he recorded the Gene Krupa and Buddy Rich Nonet. This session is noteworthy, since a jazz group with two drummers is a rarity, especially two as talented as Rich and Krupa. The backing musicians were Eldridge, Gillespie, Jacquet, Phillips, and the Oscar Peterson Trio, and the tracks from the session can be heard on the album *Krupa and Rich* (Clef MGC-684). As with many of Granz's jam-style recordings, the songs are lengthy and rely heavily on improvisation. The session represents another unique sideman project for Ray Brown.

Although Norman Granz seemed most impressed by jazz soloists, he was able to recognize the genius of the forward-looking composer, arranger, and pianist Ralph Burns. On February 4, 1955, the Oscar Peterson Trio participated in a large ensemble session for Burns in New York. The result was a brilliant showcase called *Ralph Burns among the JATPs* (Norgran MGN-1028). Other notable ensemble members on the recording are Roy Eldridge, Bill Harris, Flip Phillips, Al Cohn, and Louie Bellson. Ray Brown is featured heavily as a soloist on "Pimlico," opening with some signature blues-based licks along with an extensive solo in which he primarily plays eighth-note patterns, triplet figures, and double-time licks.

Violinists are under-represented in jazz and were absent from Norman Granz's catalog and JATP tours until 1957, when he began showcasing violinist Stuff Smith. On March 7 and 12, 1957, Smith recorded with a group that included Oscar Peterson, Ray Brown, Barney Kessel, and Alvin Stoller at Glen Glenn Studios in Hollywood, California. The material would be included on two Verve releases, *Stuff Smith* (Verve MGV-8206), which came out at the time, and the much later *Stuff Smith–Dizzy Gillespie–Oscar Peterson* (Verve 314 521 676-2). These recordings are a fine display of Smith's ability and further reveal how the Peterson trio can adapt their playing as accompanists so as not to overpower the situation. Kessel is particularly impressive and soulful throughout the session, and hearing him reunite with Brown and Peterson attracts further interest in the recordings.

For Ray Brown fans, the Stuff Smith recordings are of value because he solos on nearly every track. Some of Brown's finest moments come on "Desert Sand," on which his solo offers clear phrases with short periods of rest to let each melodic statement sink in, a growing trend in his solos from around this time. Another fine representative track is the ballad "Body and Soul," on which his improvisation begins by quoting the popular standard "Too Marvelous for Words," before going into a solo that exhibits the totality of his ability, including fast bop-like runs, bluesy inflections, and clear melodic passages. A close listen reveals Brown taking deliberate breaths at times throughout, a technique that bassists sometimes use to emulate the breathing and phrasing of a horn player. His solo on "Body and Soul" is also masterful and surpasses the technicality of Jimmy Blanton's famed duo interpretation of the tune recorded with Duke Ellington in 1940. The Stuff Smith recordings overall reveal Ray Brown's development as a soloist at a time when he was truly coming to grips with how to perfectly blend technicality and taste with each improvisation.

The most famed violinist in jazz was Stéphane Grappelli. From 1934 to 1939, along with the genius guitarist Django Reinhardt, he rose to international fame in the Quintette du Hot Club de France. While on tour with JATP in France, Norman Granz took the opportunity to record Grappelli and Stuff Smith with the Oscar Peterson Trio and drummer Jo Jones at Studios Barclay, Paris, France, on May 4, 1957. The result is the aforementioned *Violins No End*, which was held from release until 1984. While the recording had little commercial impact, it provides an exciting example of two of the most significant jazz violinists supported by a superb rhythm section. On the record, Ray Brown plays well-crafted solos on "Don't Get Around Much Anymore" and "Chapeau Blues." Both solos show Ray Brown's further maturing as a soloist.

At this point, Brown seems to have gathered a series of signature licks and techniques; however, he never relies entirely on his bag of tricks, and intersperses pre-worked material along with more exploratory runs and melodic sequences. Overall, the album is pleasurable and hard-swinging, especially the uptempo "The Lady Is a Tramp." The *Violins No End* recording also includes some live material from the Salle Pleyel in Paris, as discussed earlier.

After working as a member of the Oscar Peterson Trio for two years, Herb Ellis was given his first chance to record as a leader in Los Angeles on December 28, 1955. The result was *Ellis in Wonderland* (Norgran MGN-1081). From the session, Ellis is most impressive in his ballad interpretation of the standard "It Could Happen to You." Brown's only featured moment in the first session is on "Pogo," where he doubles the song's melody and plays some tasteful solo breaks. A second session for the album took place on January 3, 1956. Unlike the tracks recorded in December, these are more carefully arranged, mixing cool jazz styling and swing. Ray Brown is featured briefly on the Ellis originals "Detour Ahead" and "Ellis in Wonderland." On his eight-measure solo for "Detour Ahead," he mainly patterns his ideas into one-bar phrases; for the more uptempo "Ellis in Wonderland," he engages in some nice countermelody interplay with Jimmy Giuffre. This level of detail is impressive, refreshing, and widely different from much of the Oscar Peterson Trio's work of previous years. In sum, *Ellis in Wonderland* should be seen as one of the best jazz releases of 1956.

In addition to his work with the trio, Oscar Peterson had a few opportunities to record as a leader in more extensive group settings during the "classic trio" period, and Ray Brown and Herb Ellis would often be included in these large ensembles. One such recording was in Los Angeles on December 30, 1955, where Peterson recorded with the Russell Garcia Orchestra. As with many jazz and orchestral pairings, these recordings are sanitized and overly commercial. The material from this session was released on the Oscar Peterson album *In a Romantic Mood* (Verve MGV-2002). Another orchestral presentation with Peterson and the trio was recorded in Los Angeles on March 28, 1957. This dated-sounding project coupled Oscar Peterson as a pianist and vocalist with the Buddy Bregman Orchestra, with the tracks later surfacing on the Oscar Peterson album *Soft Sands* (Verve MGV-2079), a forgettable recording saturated with commercial-sounding strings and stale arrangements.

While in Paris with JATP, the trio, along with Roy Eldridge, Dizzy Gillespie, Stan Getz, Coleman Hawkins, and drummer Gus Johnson, took part in a recording session on May 1, 1958 for the French-Italian film *Les Tricheurs* directed by Marcel Carné. The music incorporates traditional jazz as part of its soundtrack. The film, which dealt with adolescent free love, was highly controversial and banned in some regions of France. Despite criticism, *Les Tricheurs* won the Grand Prix du Cinema Français and was a resounding success. Nearly five million people watched the film, and therefore listened to Brown's bass playing.[109] The experience, and the response, may well have been what opened his eyes to the possibility of more commercial studio work, a path he would be fully exploring by 1965.

14 Sideman Sessions without Peterson 1955–1958

Ray Brown's association with Oscar Peterson and JATP being so strong, it is easy to forget that Brown was a sought-after session bassist even before his pairing with Peterson in 1952. Although the bulk of his activities from 1954 to 1958 were tied to Peterson and JATP, he was still used independently as a bassist on several projects that did not involve the pianist. With or without Peterson, Brown's approach to session work remained relatively consistent throughout his career: providing a solid swing-based rhythmic function along with a strong propulsion of the beat; in doing so, he would choose notes that spoke to harmonic accuracy alongside a melodic sense of shape and direction. Additionally, his tone was always solid and present, which reflected the strength of his technique. The roundness of his tone was partly due to the large size of his hands and his ability to strike each note with the meatiest part of the side of his index finger. If called on by a leader to solo, Ray Brown would always impress but rarely overshadow the skills of the bandleader, which added additional value to his presence on records. These abilities, coupled with his preparedness, ambitiousness, and overall professionalism, made him the perfect choice for almost any mainstream jazz recording.

Brown's first recording session of 1954 took place on February 2 in New York City with the Gene Krupa Sextet. The ensemble included all-star jazzmen such as Charlie Shavers, Bill Harris, Eddie "Lockjaw" Davis, and Teddy Wilson. The choice of Wilson over Peterson was likely because, as members of the Benny Goodman small groups and orchestra, Wilson and Krupa had developed a tight rhythmic hookup. The session can be described as a typical throwback swing recording presented by outstanding seasoned musicians. Brown's most memorable moments come during a tightly arranged Shavers original, "Windy," on which he improvises on the final eight-bar bridge in the bebop style, contrasting with some of the more swing-based solos on the record. On the lengthy "Ballad Melody," Brown is featured on "Tenderly," keeping close to the song's original medley for the first two A sections and bridge although nonetheless adding some rhythmic interpretation and melodic figures during resting points in the original written line. For the final A section, he deviates from the melody and improvises around the harmonic structures. Tracks from this session were issued on the Gene Krupa Sextet's *Album #3* (Clef MGC-631).

Ray Brown's next session without Peterson was on March 30, 1954 at Fine Sound Studio in New York, with Ben Webster as leader along with Teddy Wilson and drummer Jo Jones. The quartet recorded four fine ballads, "Love's Away," "You're Mine, You!" "My Funny Valentine," and "Sophisticated Lady." Ray Brown can be heard playing arco for much of the session, a technique he often struggled with early on. However, after working with various classical masters along the way, he eventually showed more consistency and competence. Ben Webster again shows how to play ballads with expressive beauty and grace. These tracks were released on the 1955 album Ben Webster with Strings, *Music for Loving* (Norgran MGN-1018) and later on a similarly titled expanded collection (Verve 314 527 774-2).

After working with past associates throughout most of 1954, Ray Brown finally added some new musicians to his résumé when he recorded with guitar virtuoso Tal Farlow in a session that included drummer Chico Hamilton and pianist Gerry Wiggins, both significant contributors to the West Coast jazz scene. The result was a brilliant album, *The Artistry of Tal Farlow* (Norgran MGN-1014). Before 1954, Farlow worked in the famous Red Norvo Trio (alongside bassist Charles Mingus) and later was a member of Artie Shaw's small group, the Gramercy Five. His guitar playing has agility and harmonic inventiveness and this album reveals some wonderful interplay, various tempo changes, and tight small-group arrangements. Brown's most impressive solo is on "Tal's Blues," where he takes more melodic and harmonic risks than he did in Peterson's trio. The album's highlight is "Cherokee," played at breakneck speed, and which displays Brown's ability to provide a steady walk at a nearly impossible tempo.

On February 11, 1956, Brown participated in another fine session for Tal Farlow with Oscar Pettiford and his old friend Hank Jones. Also included was drummer Henry Bellson (Louie's brother). On these recordings, Pettiford plays pizzicato cello throughout. The cello was not commonly used in jazz, and Pettiford tuned his cello like a bass. Ray Brown took a serious interest in Pettiford's cello work and subsequently began to experiment with the instrument. Norman Granz must not have been particularly fond of these recordings, as they remained unissued until the 1984 Tal Farlow album, *Poppin' and Burnin'* (Verve 815 236-1). While these tracks had little commercial impact, they were undoubtedly pivotal to Ray Brown's development and are an absolute must-listen for any bassist because they pair Pettiford and Brown. Additionally, the juxtaposition of guitar, cello, and bass creates a unique musical palette rarely heard in jazz. Pettiford shows that he is equally impressive on the cello, with the instrument's smaller size and higher pitch only serving to augment his agility and bop interpretation. Ray Brown is given solo opportunities on "I Wished on the Moon," "Swingin' Till the Girls Come Home," and "Bernie's Tune." Much of his solo inspiration and phrasing can be linked to

Pettiford, and hearing the two improvise on the same album and the same track, as they do on "Bernie's Tune," provides an opportunity to examine their similarities. Farlow is particularly impressive on "The Way You Look Tonight," which is performed with only Jones and Brown. It is refreshing to hear Ray Brown participate in a somewhat more experimental recording session.

The next day, Brown showed up for a session with Louie Bellson and His Orchestra, which featured vocalist Pearl Bailey on two tracks. By the time of this recording, Bailey was a Broadway star and married to Bellson. The tracks "Tired" and "Go Back Where You Stayed Last Night" demonstrate why Pearl Bailey should be remembered as one of America's finest female entertainers and vocalists. The two tracks were initially issued on either side of a 45 rpm single (His Master's Voice 45 POP.244).

Beginning in September 1956, Ray Brown participated in four further studio sessions without Peterson, the first on September 11 for a trio recording featuring vocalist and pianist Blossom Dearie, resulting in her eponymous American debut album (Verve MGV-2037). Joining Ray Brown on the album was drummer Jo Jones. The session continued the next day, with Herb Ellis added to the ensemble. While these recordings would mark Dearie's debut as a leader, the singer with the soft girlish voice had already succeeded in Paris singing with vocal groups like the Blue Flames and the Blue Stars. She also scored a hit in 1952 with King Pleasure on the tune "Moody's Mood for Love." One of Dearie's striking attributes as a vocalist was her ability to sing in both English and French, evidenced in "I Won't Dance," "Comment Allez-Vous," and "Tout Doucement." As a pianist, Dearie's interpretations and improvisations are simplistic, especially compared to Oscar Peterson's virtuosity, and overall the album is lacking in contrast and experimentation.

Ray Brown would record with Dearie twice more during this period, the first time on September 12–13, 1957 when along with Herb Ellis and Jo Jones he recorded several tunes with the singer in New York. Tracks from the date resulted in the Verve release *Give Him the Ooh-La-La* (Verve MGV-2081). The bassist's most memorable moment is on the standard "Just One of Those Things," where he plays alone behind Dearie for the entire first verse.

Exactly one year later in 1958, and again on September 12–13, Brown backed Dearie in New York City for her upcoming album *Once Upon a Summertime* (Verve MGV-2111). Also on the album were Mundell Lowe on guitar and Ed Thigpen, a reasonably new drummer on the scene. Brown is more active on this recording than on his previous projects with Dearie, and he can be heard soloing on "Teach Me Tonight." For the improvisation, Brown creates his solo against only the fine brushwork of Thigpen. After opening with an interpretation of the melody, the bassist builds the rhythmic intensity to offer impressive note-heavy statements. This album is significant in Brown's career because it is the first session in which he was paired with Ed Thigpen. Their hookup is instantly noteworthy, especially on tunes like "If I Were a Bell," "We're Together," "Down with Love," and "Love Is Here to Stay."

Thigpen would soon become one of Ray Brown's most important musical companions as the drummer in the Oscar Peterson Trio.

On September 13, 1956, Ray Brown was reunited with pianist Bud Powell for a trio session at Fine Sounds Studio in New York which included drummer Osie Johnson. The album was initially released in 1958 as the Bud Powell Trio, *Blues in the Closet* (Verve MGV-8218). This session took place less than three months after Powell's brother, pianist Richie Powell, and the young trumpet virtuoso Clifford Brown had died in a car accident. By the time of this recording, Bud Powell was taking regular treatments of thorazine to deal with his schizophrenia after spending time in psychiatric facilities. Despite the tragedies in his life, Bud Powell's virtuosic abilities still could impress, as they do on these recordings. Highlights include incredibly uptempo numbers like "Be-Bop," "Fifty-Second Street Theme," and "I Know That You Know." Brown is most prominently featured on Oscar Pettiford's original "Swingin' Till the Girls Come Home," playing the song's melody and trading four-bar statements with Osie Johnson.

The next day, Ray Brown recorded with the Sonny Stitt Quartet, with Stitt on both tenor and alto sax, pianist Jimmy Jones and drummer Jo Jones. "I Know That You Know" and "Twelfth Street Rag" offer examples of how Stitt continued to play with incredible dexterity similar to Charlie Parker. Brown is most prominently featured on the soulful "Down Home Blues." His solo begins with a fast right-index-finger flutter technique, followed by blues licks, bop quotes, and a triplet pull-off figure which he now included in many of his solos around this period. The album would be released in 1957 as *New York Jazz* (Verve MGV-8219). Both the Stitt and Powell recordings confirm that when masters play bebop, it can still sound fresh and exciting.

On October 16, 1956, Ray Brown was in Los Angeles to record an Illinois Jacquet session featuring Roy Eldridge, Jimmy Jones, Herb Ellis, and Jo Jones at Radio Recorders Studio. It is somewhat curious that Oscar Peterson was not present for this or Brown's several previous sessions. Unlike the two more bop-oriented sessions with Powell and Stitt, the Jacquet session was more of a traditional swing affair. Jacquet exhibits his signature tone on the tenor and precise phrasing throughout the recording of his *Swing's the Thing* (Clef MGC-750).

Over the previous few years, Norman Granz had supervised most of Brown's recordings, but in 1957 the bassist also began recording for Lester Koenig's Contemporary label. Established in Los Angeles in 1951, Contemporary Records was critical in popularizing West Coast jazz musicians like Chet Baker, Art Pepper, and Shelly Manne. Unlike Norman Granz, Koenig had a less hands-on approach to repertoire and focused more on presenting jazz in the highest available recording quality.

The first Contemporary albums with Ray Brown on them began with Sonny Rollins' *Way Out West* (Contemporary Records C3530). By 1957, Rollins had become one of jazz's most outstanding and innovative tenor soloists, bridging the gap between Coleman Hawkins and John Coltrane. After emerging on the New York jazz scene in 1949, Rollins was imprisoned for most of 1950 on an armed robbery charge and in 1952 for heroin possession. Despite hiatuses in his early career, Rollins attracted attention while working with Miles Davis, Charlie Parker, Thelonious Monk, and the Modern Jazz Quartet. In 1956, Rollins became fully established as a leader by releasing his breakthrough album *Saxophone Colossus* (Prestige PRLP-7079).

On *Way Out West*, Sonny Rollins broke new ground in jazz by including a mix of cowboy folk classics and jazz standards with a chordless ensemble of just saxophone, bass, and drums. The absence of a principal harmonic instrument gives *Way Out West* a more open and experimental quality than anything recorded by the Oscar Peterson Trio. The unique instrumentation forced Brown to provide the harmonic material needed for Rollins to create his masterful solos. Playing drums on the album is Shelly Manne. By this point, Manne had led some great jazz combos and developed a strong reputation in Los Angeles; beginning around this period, he was to become one of Ray Brown's most significant musical partners. As a drummer, he is never overly flashy but relies on his subtlety and creativity to provide perfect rhythmic backdrops. Manne's lighter style of playing, often using brushes, allowed Brown to fully showcase his fantastic tone and timbre.

The *Way Out West* session began at 3:00 am on March 7, 1957, in order to accommodate everyone's busy schedule. Today, *Way Out West* is considered a classic and ranks among both Sonny Rollins' and Ray Brown's most outstanding achievements. Rollins' solos throughout are inventive, forward-looking, and fresh. Brown is featured as a soloist on every track, and he seems to feed off Rollins' creativity. One perfect example of Brown's approach on the album comes from the song "I'm an Old Cowhand," where Rollins and Brown engage in a back-and-forth musical conversation during the song's melody, trading solo statements and fragmented melodic ideas. Throughout Rollins' improvisation, Ray Brown provides a solid walk with note choices that accurately represent the implied harmonic structures of the tune; however, he does not always start on the root of the chords he is implying. Brown's marvelous ability to approach non-root or chord tone notes is handled mainly by providing well-connected half-step or whole-step motion.

From a rhythm point of view, Ray rarely plays more than three measures with only quarter-note rhythms; he adds eighth notes and syncopation to his lines for variety. He is particularly gifted at incorporating an expanded range when walking bass lines and will sometimes slip into the upper-structure third octave on the bass with ease and clarity. Playing high up in the "thumb" position is a challenge for many bassists because the notes are spaced more closely than in the lower register. On his solo on "I'm an Old Cowhand," Brown delivers precise phrasing and a display of range, grace notes, pull-offs, and slides. He does this without harmonic backing; playing in this chordless format affords him a great deal of freedom and also added responsibility.

Although the contrast between cowboy songs, standards, and Rollins' originals makes for a nice variety, the album may have worked even better conceptually if Rollins had only stuck with the novelty of presenting all cowboy songs. Regardless of this slight critique, the overall spirit of *Way Out West* is infectious. The work ranks as one of Ray Brown's most memorable albums as a sideman.

On October 11–12, 1957, Herb Ellis recorded the material for his *Nothing but Blues* album (Verve MGV-8252) with Stan Getz, Roy Eldridge, Ray Brown, and Stan Levey. The album displays Ellis's Texas blues roots, with the guitarist producing blues figures throughout the recording through his use of note bends, double-stop figures, and blues scales mixed with melodic bebop lines. Brown is given writing credits on three tunes, "Pap's Blues," "Blues for Janet," and "Blues for Junior." The first two are slow downhome blues with a call-and-response between Ellis and the two horns. By contrast, "Blues for Junior" is more arranged, and performed in the hard bop style of Art Blakey's Jazz Messengers. While these tunes are somewhat simplistic, they show Ray Brown's renewed interest in composition. Although he did write more intricate songs, a large portion of his recorded and published works are based on standard twelve-bar blues chord changes.

Also on October 12, Brown was in the studio with pianist Lou Levy and drummer Stan Levey for a session resulting in material for the album *Getz Meets Mulligan in Hi-Fi* (Verve MGV-8249). The pairing of the laid-back styles of Gerry Mulligan and Stan Getz is of immediate interest. Their connection is evident from the opening track, "Let's Fall in Love," both men displaying a focused, improvised direction enhanced by a gorgeous tone and timbre. Mulligan and Getz are particularly impressive when they play conversational countermelodies. Adding to the interest is Getz and Mulligan's switching of primary instruments. Getz is featured on baritone sax and Mulligan on tenor for the album's first three tracks, "Let's Fall in Love," "Anything Goes," and "Too Close for Comfort."

Brown solos on the closing track of the 1991 CD edition (Verve 8493922), "I Didn't Know What Time It Was," his playing centered mainly in the instrument's mid to upper-mid register, where he plays eighth-note structures. His accompaniment throughout the album is solid, and he has an excellent connection with Lou Levy, whose piano style is more spacious than Peterson's. Both Mulligan and Getz are brilliant throughout, and overall *Getz Meets Mulligan* is a fine artistic achievement and another notable Ray Brown sideman session.

On December 12, 1957 Ray Brown recorded for the first time with violinist and double bassist John Frigo, resulting in Frigo's debut as a leader, *I Love John Frigo . . . He Swings* (Mercury MG-20285). Born in Chicago, John Frigo first gained notoriety working with Chico Marx's Orchestra, where he performed a comedy routine on the violin. While serving in the coast guard during World War II, he played in a band with Al Haig and Kai Winding.

After his service, he played with Jimmy Dorsey before joining Soft Winds with Herb Ellis and pianist Lou Carter. When Ellis left Soft Winds to join the Oscar Peterson Trio, Frigo returned to Chicago, where he worked primarily as a studio bassist, arranger, and fiddler with the Sage Riders, the house band for the radio program *National Barn Dance*.

Accompanying Frigo on his leadership debut were Ray Brown, Herb Ellis, Cy Touff on bass trumpet, Dick Marx on piano, and celeste, and Norm Jeffries on drums. Although mostly disregarded, *I Love John Frigo* deserves more attention, mainly because of Frigo's incredible talents, the unique nature of the instrumentation, and the album's carefully crafted arrangements. One of the more exciting tracks for comparison is Frigo's "Big Me – Little Me," where Frigo overdubs himself as he trades solo statements on both violin and bass. Although known more for his work as a violinist, Frigo proves quite remarkable as a bassist. He would not record again as a leader until 1988 but appeared several times with Ray Brown in the 1980s in a side project known as Triple Treat with pianist Monty Alexander and Herb Ellis.

15 Bass Hits! *This Is Ray Brown* and the Poll Winners 1956–1958

For years Ray Brown had been providing superb accompaniment for others, but except for a few sides recorded in 1946 as *The Bebop Boys/Ray Brown's All-Stars* (see Chapter 4), he had still not yet released a full album as a leader. However, on November 21 and 23, 1956, he finally got an opportunity to record his first major label release as a leader: *Bass Hit!* (Verve MGV-8022). For this, he returned to his roots as a big-band bassist. Conceptually, the recording was intended to foreground the bass as a lead instrument within a large-group context, in the same way that Brown had been featured with the Dizzy Gillespie Orchestra on "One Bass Hit" and "Two Bass Hit" over a decade before. In the original liner notes, Brown reveals:

> First of all, I wanted to make an album that would be worth hearing musically. That's the most important thing, overall. After that, I wanted to show that the bass can produce interesting music on its own, and for that, I take some solos, but I didn't want the bass hogging the scene, either.

For this record, Norman Granz hired arranger Marty Paich, a noted Los Angeles composer and pianist who had already worked with Mel Tormé and Peggy Lee. The chosen band for the project included Pete Candoli, Harry Edison, and Ray Linn (trumpets); Herbie Harper (trombone); Jimmy Giuffre (clarinet, tenor, and baritone sax); Jack Dulong and Herb Geller (alto sax); Bill Holman (tenor sax); Jimmy Rowles (piano); Herb Ellis (guitar); and Alvin Stoller (drums), all of whom appeared on the first November 21 session. Two days later, Conrad Gozzo replaced Candoli on trumpet and Mel Lewis replaced Stoller on drums.

Bass Hit! opens with a short unaccompanied bass theme followed by Paich's slick arrangements of the Paich and Brown original "Blues for Sylvia," named after Paich's sister-in-law. The second track is the Cole Porter original "All of You," with Brown playing the song's melody and providing countermelodies and further improvisation. Next is the ballad "Everything I Have Is

Yours," which showcases Brown on the melody, along with unaccompanied solo statements, double-stop figures, and call-and-response solo patterns. Side A of the original record concludes with a swinging arrangement of "Will You Still Be Mine," where Brown again provides the melody and a masterful solo.

Side B of *Bass Hit!* opens with a medium-swing Brown original called "Little Toe," a nickname he used for his wife, Cecilia. Instead of complete improvised statements, Brown trades four-bar passages with Harry Edison. The standard "Alone Together" follows, which begins with Brown playing unaccompanied chords on the bass. Chordal playing is a technique that bass players hesitate to attempt, being challenging to execute while staying in tune. Brown then plays the melody against light orchestration. The next cut, "Solo for Unaccompanied Bass," is a veritable display of mastery and inventiveness. The piece is organized by several themes, including a return to the album's opening theme. "Solo for Unaccompanied Bass" must rank among one of Brown's most remarkable creations and one of his most exploratory efforts. After the impressive solo display, the music transitions into the beautiful ballad "My Foolish Heart." The final track on the album is the bop-inspired Paich and Brown original "Blues for Lorraine," named for Paich's daughter. The piece concludes with the unaccompanied intro solo themes. Additional material from the original sessions, including several uptempo versions of "After You've Gone," has been released on reissues of the album.

Bass Hit! was critical in re-establishing Ray Brown as a leader and showcasing the bass as a solo instrument. It also proved that, despite the emergence of bassists like Charles Mingus, Paul Chambers, and Scott LaFaro, Brown still ranked as one of the most outstanding and impactful bass technicians. Thankfully, *Bass Hit!* was not the last time Brown recorded as a leader, and more such recordings were to come on which he could fully display his technicality, imagination, and versatility.

In fact, as soon as February 27 and 28 of the same year (1958), Brown was recording his second album as a leader for Norman Granz: *This Is Ray Brown* (Verve MGV-8290). Unlike *Bass Hit!*, these recordings feature a small group: Jerome Richardson on flute, Oscar Peterson on organ and piano, guitarist Herb Ellis, and drummer Osie Johnson. The choice of flute and organ is unique and may have been made in order to differentiate his album from Oscar Peterson Trio efforts. The album's first track, "Bric A Brac," one of three Ray Brown originals, is an uptempo swing number with a lengthy solo by the bassist, replete with signature licks, blues statements, and bop runs.

The second track, another Brown original, called "Upstairs Blues," begins with a soulful unaccompanied intro by Brown before settling into a slow blues. After a strong solo by Richardson, Ray shows his incredible skills in soloing over the blues, a perfect vehicle for the bassist who delivers a solo that must rank as one of his most finely paced and constructed. The song concludes with a short outro by Brown. The album's third track is Brown's version of the fast-tempo classic "Indiana (Back Home Again in Indiana)." Once again, his interpretation of the melody and bop-style solo is impressive. Oscar Peterson is back on the piano for this track, where he sounds most at home. After Ellis's solo, Brown is again featured on the final melody. Side A concludes with the Hoagy Carmichael ballad "The Nearness of You," where Peterson returns to the organ. Richardson plays the original melody, and Brown solos somewhat frantically against the written line. In his improvisation, Brown continues to show off his technique by presenting double-time phrasing and bop licks.

Side B of *This Is Ray Brown* begins with a lengthy version of the Strayhorn/Ellington classic "Take the A Train." With Richardson stating the melody and Peterson on the piano, the piece is presented as a traditional swing number. Consistent with the era in which the song was written, Brown's solo statements are more rooted in the swing tradition, possibly as a tribute to Jimmy Blanton. The next track, another credited to Brown, called "Cool Walk," sees one of Brown's steady walking lines, centered around his solid time feel, his clear tone, and the balance between vertical note choices to fit each chord and linear movement. Brown takes a lengthy improvisation against the rhythm section following Richardson's solo. The final track is the 1941 hit "Jim." This nine-minute version begins with Peterson on the organ before Brown interprets the melody and plays a lengthy solo.

This Is Ray Brown is a significant record for the bassist being the first of his many full-length small-group releases as a leader. Additionally, Brown's recent sideman efforts around this time had rarely featured him as a soloist, so here we get to appreciate his continued development as a bassist and his desire to present original material. *Bass Hits!* and *This Is Ray Brown* established Ray Brown's reputation for carrying a leadership role while also allowing him to step outside of his entrenched association with Oscar Peterson.

While Ray did have some input as a member of the Oscar Peterson Trio, it was clear that Peterson had the final say as to the direction of the band. So, possibly in order to further his ambitions as a leader or at least an equal member, Ray took part in several co-leader/group efforts throughout his career. One of the best examples of this was with a group known as the Poll Winners, a collaborative trio with Barney Kessel and Shelly Manne, who made their first recordings, *The Poll Winners* (Contemporary Records C3535), on March 18–19, 1957 in Los Angeles for the Contemporary label. This album would be the first of five released by the group.

The concept came together when Brown, Kessel, and Manne were named winners of the three major jazz polls, *DownBeat*, *Metronome*, and *Playboy*, in 1956 and 1957. Despite its ridiculous cover art, which shows the three men dressed in suits holding giant candy cane-type poles, the music is perfectly conceived, arranged, and performed. *DownBeat* reviewer Don Gold gave the album 4½ stars out of 5 and summed it up with the following comments in a 1958 review:

> There is very little that must be said about the value of the Poll Winners. It is virtuosity without the air of sacrifice or an air of relaxed enjoyment. There are splendid solos by each member, making this a ball for listeners and an unintended instructional record for guitarists and drummers. These are the sounds of musicians who enjoy playing together. This is The Rhythm Section, and it's the Melodic Section too. Definitely recommended.[110]

Each track on *The Poll Winners* album is arranged, distinguishing it from Granz's more jam session-style recordings. The record is a career highlight for Brown and a sign of how he would later pattern his trios as a leader. The album begins with the Clifford Brown original "Jordu," with its syncopated hits on the melody, followed by an impressive solo by Barney Kessel, whose playing is showing greater confidence than it did in his Peterson trio days. Manne's brushwork is also notable, and his hookup with Brown is pure perfection, exemplified by a section in which they trade four-bar statements, after which the band quickly shifts into a quasi-Latin groove, a masterclass in small-group orchestration and arrangement. Side A of the original LP is completed by the standards "Satin Doll," "It Could Happen to You," and a hard-swinging version of "Mean to Me." Each includes a Ray Brown solo.

A highlight from Side B is "Green Dolphin Street," which begins with a unique feel created by an ostinato bass line, some muted statements by Kessel and light cymbal work by Manne. The tune is notable for its back-and-forth between Latin and swing time feels, which the group executes masterfully. The rhythmic backdrop created by Manne and Kessel gives Brown a contrasting feel to play against during his solo.

The next track, "You Go to My Head," is a perfect example of how detailed and worked-out the Poll Winners arrangements were. Kessel engages in conversational interplay throughout, which allows each musician to take the lead as a soloist. By dropping in and out strategically, Shelly Manne only enhances the arrangements. Few drummers had such an awareness of how to use time and space to best serve a song. The piece concludes with a solo cadenza by Brown.

In short, the *Poll Winners* is a fantastic achievement based on crafted arrangements, a group concept, and the power and energy of swing-era principles. On this and future Poll Winners recordings, Ray Brown gets opportunities to showcase his bass playing as a co-equal member, often breaking free from the role of a straightforward accompanist.

On August 19 and 21, 1958, Brown was back in a Los Angeles studio with Barney Kessel and Shelly Manne to record the album *The Poll Winners Ride Again* (Contemporary Records C3556). Along with their first recording, this work must be considered one of the great Ray Brown recordings of the era. The continued critical success of these Poll Winners projects was the direct result of an intangible connection characterized by subtlety and detail. Regrettably, the group was never a working band outside of the studio.

The album begins with a swinging original by Kessel called "Bee Deedle Dee Do," on which Brown shows his ability to pace a solo in his use of organized phrasing and dynamics. The second track, "Volare," has shifting melodic themes, fermatas, bowed bass lines, and subtle brushwork. The beautiful ballad "Spring Is Here" follows, which contains a Ray Brown solo and concludes with some of his arco work. Side A of the original album ends with "The Surrey with the Fringe on Top." It begins with a fiery solo intro by Brown, and a bass interpretation of the song's main verses played against some exploratory reharmonization provided by Kessel.

Side B begins with the Brown original "Custard Puff," a favorite among his fans. The slow swing, carefully crafted arrangement details and challenging bass solo make this track an album highlight. Next is the novelty number "When the Red Robin Comes Bob Bob Bobbin' Along," followed by Kessel's original "Foreign Intrigue," and a reworking of the bluesy ballad "Angel Eyes." The album concludes with a somewhat comical uptempo version of "The Merry Go Round Broke Down," a fitting number to match the album cover art, which shows the trio on a merry-go-round. This sophomore effort demonstrated that the unity and connectivity displayed in the group's first effort could be repeated and expanded.

On November 2, 1959 they recorded the album *Poll Winners Three!* (Contemporary Records S7576). In addition to fantastic versions of the standards "Soft Winds," "Easy Living," and "Mack the Knife," each member of the group provided an original track. "Crisis," by Barney Kessel, begins with Brown setting a funky groove which shifts into a Latin feel before settling into a fast walking swing. The trio's ability to seamlessly change time feels and interact together is perfectly exemplified on the track.

Shelly Manne's offering, "The Little Rhumba," is equally impressive. After a well-arranged intro that showcases Brown, the music falls into a light rhumba before shifting seamlessly into a swing feel. After an impressive drum solo, Ray Brown offers his improvisation. The piece concludes with a return to the rhumba. Brown brings us his original blues, "Minor Mystery," which begins with the bassist presenting the melody using a technique called col legno or striking the string with the back of the bow. This was not a practice commonly used by Brown (or many other jazz bass players), but it is particularly useful as an effect. He takes an extensive bluesy solo on the track, mainly by means of shorter phrases and clear melodic ideas. He returns to the col legno melody to end the piece. Brown's solo is a fine offering that shows clear direction and focus.

Between August 30 and September 1, 1960 came the recording of the Poll Winners' fourth album, *Exploring the Scene!* (Contemporary Records M3581). The departure here is that each track is a tune written and released by contemporaries and new jazz innovators. Many of the composers included were seen by fans and critics as alternative, or a reaction, to the older styles of swing and bebop that characterized the music of the Oscar Peterson Trio.

The album begins with a medium-swing vehicle by pianist Ray Bryant called "Little Suzie." Bryant had been active on the jazz scene since 1946; after working with leaders like Charlie Parker, Dizzy Gillespie, and Sonny Stitt, he became associated with the hard bop genre through his work with Art Blakey, Sonny Rollins, and others. Bryant would later record with Ray Brown.

Track 2, Dave Brubeck's "The Duke," is one of the album highlights. Brubeck came to prominence in the mid-1950s offering his brand of cool jazz to college campuses and festivals. His 1959 signature album, *Time Out* (Columbia CL-1397), made the pianist/composer a superstar, peaking at number two on the Billboard pop charts and the first jazz album to sell a million copies. Much of the interest in the album came from Brubeck's use of unconventional time signatures. "The Duke," however, first appeared on Brubeck's 1956 release *Brubeck Plays Brubeck* (Columbia CL-878) and gained further notice when it was included on Miles Davis's 1957 masterpiece *Miles Ahead* (Columbia CL-1041). The Poll Winners presented the tune in the subdued "cool" style for which Brubeck was known, with Brown's solo showing his growing maturity as he furthers his use of precise phrases and clarity and control, avoiding style without substance.

Track 3 is a new arrangement of the modal masterpiece "So What," from Miles Davis's 1959 *Kind of Blue* (Columbia CS8163), one of the most beloved and best-selling jazz records of all time. By eliminating advanced chord changes and providing only fragmented harmonic material, Miles Davis and his colleagues, including John Coltrane, Julian "Cannonball" Adderley, and Bill Evans, created a more "open" sound, breaking from the bop tradition. As in Davis's original recording, the bass is featured in the song's main melody. But, unlike in the Miles version, there is a bass solo. It is interesting to hear how he approaches a song with just a two-chord harmonic structure.

The next track is the Erroll Garner classic ballad "Misty," written in 1954. Garner, like Brown, was from Pittsburgh. Although the piano virtuoso had been on the scene for many years, his live album *Concert by the Sea* (Columbia CL-883), first released in 1955, had sold over one million copies by 1958, helping to make Garner one of the most popular jazz figures of the mid to late 1950s. Brown is featured on the song's bridge and chooses to reinterpret the original melody with impressive double-time figures. He also uses the bow to conclude the piece.

What follows is "Doodlin'" by Horace Silver, a twelve-bar blues initially released in 1954, and a critical work in influencing the hard bop movement, in which Silver was a leading figure. Through his work with the Jazz Messengers, which he co-led for a time with Art Blakey, the group released the celebrated album *Horace Silver and the Jazz Messengers* (Blue Note BLP-1518), including both the jukebox hit "The Preacher" and "Doodlin'." Through his work with the Messengers and his own celebrated groups, Silver strove to return jazz music to its African American roots, a counter-reaction to the more subdued "cool jazz" music popularized on the West Coast. Horace Silver remained a popular figure in jazz for over sixty years.

Side B of the original album begins with John Lewis's cool jazz classic "The Golden Striker." As previously discussed, John Lewis was a former bandmate of Brown's in Gillespie's band and later served as the leader and principal composer of the Modern Jazz Quartet. The introduction to "The Golden Striker" features a beautifully bowed statement by Ray Brown. Albeit a short sample, it is evidence that Brown has progressed as an arco player. His playing is much more in tune than prior bowed examples, and his tone is rich.

The next track is Neil Hefti's acclaimed composition "Lil' Darlin'." The song was composed and performed by Count Basie's Orchestra in 1957 and is one of the critical compositions that presented a significant shift from Basie's more hard-hitting blues interpretations that made him famous in the 1930s. With its relaxed feel and open melody, "Lil' Darlin'" is one of the most recognizable jazz pieces from the 1950s. Brown is again featured as a soloist.

The next cut is "The Blessing" by Ornette Coleman. With his free jazz interpretations, Coleman completely changed the possibilities for jazz in 1959 with his album *The Shape of Jazz to Come* (Atlantic SD-1317) and, later, *Free Jazz* (Atlantic SD-1364). "The Blessing" comes from Coleman's 1958 debut, *Something Else!!!!* (Contemporary C3551). It is one of Coleman's more "traditional" works, and the Poll Winners' interpretation sounds somewhat formal and standard. Brown takes a lengthy solo on the piece. He would later be vocal in his distaste for "free jazz."

The album concludes with "This Here" by pianist Bobby Timmons. As with Horace Silver, Timmons was a key contributor to the hard bop movement popular in the mid-1950s and early 1960s. "This Here" was the title track of Timmons's first release as a leader, *This Here Is Bobby Timmons* (Riverside RLP-1164). Brown is again prominently featured, trading solo statements with the consistently inventive drumming of Shelly Manne. *Exploring the Scene!* works well as a concept album and displays Ray Brown's willingness to adapt to the many jazz subgenres happening at the time.

After a fifteen-year absence, the Poll Winners recorded their final album, *Straight Ahead* (Contemporary Records S7635), on July 12, 1975. Interviewed for the album's liner notes, Brown reveals:

> The main difference about my playing is that I have grown emotionally. I think I am entering a new phase where I can construct solos better than I ever did. You know, for years, I was with Oscar Peterson, and of course, I played solos then, but I think my main thing was a concept of time because we didn't have drums for so long, and I was the drummer and the bass player so to speak. In listening to this record, I found, just personally, that I have grown some emotionally in that, I give myself a chance to think more when I'm soloing. As Lester Young always used to say, "Tell me a story." He didn't care if you want to play only five notes in eight bars if they meant something.

I haven't had a chance to practice for any length of time in the last couple of years due to the fact that I'm doing a lot of different things like managing Quincy Jones and co-producing his records, but I find myself now wanting to play more. I had almost stopped playing for a while, but now I'm back into it. Probably I'm more relaxed now than when I used to come out here and make my records, in those days, I was always on the road. Since 1966 I've lived in Los Angeles, and I'm going home to bed every night in my own home, and that relaxes you, you know.

Barney and Shelly have always been easy to play with. I worked with Barney in Oscar's trio, and I work with Shelly regularly now in the L.A. Four with Laurindo Almeida and Bud Shank.

I think at the age of the guys in the group, we've all reached a certain point where the only thing we need is the inspiration to play. When the three of us get together, that inspiration is there, and I think we do play close to our potential.

Ray Brown is featured heavily throughout *Straight Ahead*, which includes the standards "Caravan," "Someday My Prince Will Come," and "Laura," as well as the Kessel originals "Blue Boy" and "One Foot off the Curb." The one original offering from Ray Brown is "Two Cents," which is performed as a medium-swing piece, with Barney Kessel playing the main melody. Kessel follows with a solo before Brown takes over as the soloist. The bassist then plays the melody to conclude the piece. Although it is a fine album, *Straight Ahead* does not capture the same spirit that the group had on their first four releases.

16 The Second Classic Oscar Peterson Trio (Part 1) 1959–1961

Naturally, with the departure of Herb Ellis late in 1958 the future of the Oscar Peterson Trio was uncertain. Throughout the years, Oscar Peterson's music had relied on solo virtuosity, rhythmic swing, and engaging small-group arrangements placed over a repertoire that mainly included jazz standards. With the loss of Ellis – and the changing environment of jazz – the trio was now forced to adapt. In his biography, Oscar Peterson explains:

> Herb Ellis's departure from the trio for the West Coast created a terrible void. The group with Herb and Ray had become such a well-oiled intuitive outfit, and Herb's guitar such a matchless and central component in all our arrangements that I found it hard to imagine starting over with a completely new group, let alone a group containing not guitar but drums. I spoke disappointedly to various close friends, wondering aloud what my next move would be. The person to come up with the most lucid evaluation of the situation – wouldn't you know it? – Norman Granz... After asking about my future plans, he at once demolished my worries about finding another guitarist by issuing a completely new challenge. He informed me that many people – players and listeners alike – were curious to see if I could retain my command of the piano and the group if Ray's immense sound were to be complemented by a drummer. This challenge was couched with great tact, for he never suggested a lack of faith in me. On the contrary, he believed I would greatly benefit from the change.[111]

The shift from guitar to drums in the trio heralded a new era for the Oscar Peterson Trio. As we have seen, many of its past recordings had been enhanced by the addition of drummers, including Buddy Rich, Stan Levey, Louie Bellson, J.C Heard, Alvin Stoller, and Connie Kay. But Peterson now needed to find a permanent drummer who was not only willing to take on a grueling touring schedule but able to fit into an established group. To temporarily fill the drum chair, Peterson hired Gene Gammage on November 21 and 22, 1958 to record the concept album *Oscar Peterson Plays My Fair Lady* (Verve MGV-2119), thus beginning a new series of *Peterson Plays* albums for Verve. Before this, Gammage had recorded with Peterson in 1957 for the album *Soft Sands*. Unlike many of the later Peterson presentations with Ellis, *My Fair Lady* lacks the characteristic arrangements and cohesiveness for which the group had become known. On the album, the trio is best represented on the hard-swinging "Get Me to the Church on Time," on which Ray Brown plays the main melody, and on the album's signature number, "I Could Have Danced All Night."

Shortly after the stint with Gammage, Oscar Peterson hired drummer Ed Thigpen, on Ray Brown's suggestion. Ed Thigpen discusses his first meeting with Ray Brown:

> I got to New York in the early '50s . . . I had heard about Ray Brown, but I still hadn't seen him. until I went into the army, and that's when I met him. I was in Korea and went on an R+R from Korea to Japan to Tokyo. When I got there, I discovered that Jazz at the Philharmonic was there. Ben Webster and Benny Carter were on the program, and of course I knew about Ella. I knew about the artists that were there, but not really that well. I knew them because I played with Ben Webster before and Benny Carter.
>
> I went to the concert, and I got backstage, and that's when I met Ray Brown. He was a nice guy and took me out after the concert. I was still drinking milkshakes at the time, and then we went to a jam session. That's when I first heard the trio [with Ellis], and I told him that night, I said, "You know it would be nice if you guys had a drummer also in your group, and I would like to be the one." I was brash. He said, "Well, you never know, kid [*laughs*]." I believe that was in January 1954. So, when I left the army in February of '54, I went back with Dinah [Washington] and went to New York. Some time went by, and I wound up settling in New York, and then I ran into him again. It was on a record date with Blossom Dearie. I was working with Billy Taylor, and that's when I heard the Stratford record, which was burning. I said, "Wow, man, that is really something." Then somehow, we wound up on a record date together.[112]

He goes on to describe how he became a member of the Oscar Peterson Trio:

> Ray recommended me for it. He was going through this transition after Herbie had left. A lot of it had to do with Ray. I remember Ray and Oscar coming into the Hickory House from time to time, where I was playing, to have a steak and so forth. Ellington and many people used to go there to eat, but I didn't know he was also checking me out [*laughs*]. It was a highlight, let's face it.

Soon after joining the Oscar Peterson Trio, Ed Thigpen came to recognize the pressure of being a new voice in one of the most successful jazz units ever. By this time, Peterson and Brown had firmly secured their reputation-wheras Thigpen was a rising star, under the microscope both of the public and his new bandmates. Peterson and Brown were perfectionists with one goal: to continue to have the world's hardest-swinging trio. They would stop at nothing to achieve perfection and would not accept a half-hearted effort from anybody, especially a young lion like Thigpen.

Thigpen talked about the pressures he felt when he joined the trio and how he found his role with the group:

> The pressure is the fact that all of a sudden you're with two geniuses at the top of their game, and you have to come in and plant another instrument into [the dynamic] of the group . . . [Herb Ellis and the guitar] were very successful in that group . . . Musically that group had such an identity, and I had to find a way to make the drum set fit within that context, and Oscar is a taskmaster. He knew what he wanted, and he was a leader. He is a great arranger, but it was left up to me to find the parts, the sound, and the type of feel.
>
> One of the best cases I can give you was about our time feel. The first week I [joined] we worked a gig in Boston at Storyville. The first week was great, man. It was just cooking. I forget where the second week was, but I said, "Boy, this is going to be beautiful." I was mesmerized by how they played, but it felt so good. So, Ray said, "We're going to have to work on our time." I said, "No problem, we'll have it in two weeks, man. Don't worry. I got it. Everything's cool." Shoot, five years later, we were still practicing daily [*laughs*]. However, we built something unique. So, if there was pressure, it was from that aspect. It's like when you play at that level, you know this thing is possible. So, the pressure might be in being able to be consistent. It takes time to be able to do that.
>
> We didn't use a lot of notated music. It was memorizing the intricate parts because we had some complex arrangements. Particularly on *West Side Story*, those things were very involved. A lot of the things were relatively open, but some were very involved, and you know [Oscar], he was very exact because you know he has perfect recall. Perfect pitch, perfect everything. So, he knew what he wanted, and if you deviated too much from certain basic things, which I tended to do . . . I would be exploring around and carrying on [*laughs*]. That didn't sit too well sometimes. When I said being a taskmaster, I didn't mean it negatively because he was brought up that way and was hard on himself. You know, it wasn't like I was the only one getting it. He and Ray had been a team. They had been together for fifteen years before I even got there.[113] So I was finding my role. It all paid off and pays off even to this day, so I'm grateful for it. My role was primarily to punctuate and keep time because Peterson was the primary soloist. I was there to mark things. I had to be not subservient, but sometimes I had to hold back in certain areas. You know where maybe I would have liked to have done something else, but it wouldn't have fit. Oscar's a stylist. So, everything doesn't fit with everybody.

Much like Oscar Peterson and Ray Brown, Ed Thigpen's style incorporated sensitivity, rhythmic interplay, and technical virtuosity. The inclusion of drums allowed Ray Brown more freedom, and the bassist was now given more solo opportunities. Additionally, the absence of another melodic string instrument allowed Brown to further create bass lines without worrying about a harmonic or range clash between the bass and the guitar. The same elements that allowed him more freedom also limited his role in the group because he was no longer looked upon as the group's most vital rhythmic force.

With Thigpen in the trio, Norman Granz now had a cohesive working unit available to back soloists on recordings without the added responsibility of finding a drummer who could comply with the trio's tight schedule. Of course, Granz took full advantage of his new house rhythm section and set about producing new recordings with the trio backing. Granz's fascination with the "Great American Songbook" inspired the producer to record the newly formatted Oscar Peterson Trio playing their versions of songs from popular Broadway shows and the works of other popular American songwriters.

Granz would also showcase the newly formed Peterson trio on international JATP tours and domestic concerts. Surprisingly, Ray Brown was absent for the beginning of the spring 1959 JATP tour for the first time since becoming a permanent member. Replacing Brown was bassist Jimmy Gannons. The troupe included familiar faces like Ella Fitzgerald, Oscar Peterson, Herb Ellis, Sonny Stitt, Roy Eldridge, Gene Krupa, and Stan Getz, along with newcomers like Ed Thigpen, Eddie Wasserman (sax and clarinet), Ronnie Ball (piano), Joe Gordon (trumpet), Richie Gordon (tenor sax), Russ Freeman (piano), and Monty Budwig (bass).

By May 18, 1959, Ray Brown rejoined Peterson and Thigpen in Paris to record two albums on the same day. The first session resulted in the album *Sonny Stitt Sits in with the Oscar Peterson Trio* (Verve MGV-8344.) Whether playing alto or tenor saxophone, Stitt is brilliant throughout, proving that he was still among the most impressive saxophone technicians and undoubtedly one of the most authentic bop interpreters. Unlike Charlie Parker, with whom Stitt is nearly always compared, Stitt now had two different approaches depending on whether playing tenor or alto: more bop-style phrasing on the alto, and a more swing/bluesy approach on the tenor. On the highly energetic "I Can't Give You Anything but Love," Brown plays a repeated bluesy bass note figure in the introduction which morphs into a more note-heavy bop line. Following solos by Stitt and Peterson, Ray is featured as a soloist and plays with great confidence and connectivity. Hs improvisation ends with what was now becoming his signature triplet-figure pull-off lick.

Brown is also featured as a soloist on Peterson's often-used arrangement of "Easy Does It," with a statement that is bluesy and perfectly suited to the overall spirit of the tune. One of the finest moments on the record comes during "Moten Swing," when both Peterson and Thigpen drop out mid-song to allow some nice interplay between Stitt and Brown. Despite having worked together for just a few short months, the strong hookup between Peterson, Brown, and Thigpen is instantly recognizable and evident in this recording, Thigpen's first with the group.

On the same day, the Oscar Peterson Trio proceeded to record seventeen more numbers, many of which would appear on the album *A Jazz Portrait*

The Oscar Peterson Trio performing as part of the Jazz at the Philharmonic series, Concertgebouw, Amsterdam, April 11, 1959. Peterson in action at the piano, with Ray Brown to the right and drummer Ed Thigpen behind Brown.

BNA Photographic / Alamy Stock Photo

of Frank Sinatra by the Oscar Peterson Trio (Verve MGV-8334). It is easy to disregard *A Jazz Portrait* and other similar albums as commercial trivia. However, Peterson and the trio are so remarkable in their abilities that, even though many of their more commercial works lack exploration and innovation, they still offer a robust archive of cohesiveness and dexterity. An evaluation of "You Make Me Feel So Young" and "The Tender Trap" reveals the development of Thigpen's role within the group and his sense of swing. Brown is particularly impressive on "The Tender Trap," interacting with Peterson through a series of solo fills.

From July 14 to August 9, 1959 Norman Granz took full advantage of the newly revamped Oscar Peterson Trio by making a series of cookie-cutter *Oscar Peterson Plays . . . Song Book* recordings resulting in numerous 1959 releases like *Oscar Peterson Plays the Duke Ellington Song Book* (Verve MGV-2055), . . . *the George Gershwin Song Book* (Verve MGV-2054), . . . *the Richard Rodgers Songbook* (Verve MGV-2057), . . . *the Jerome Kern Song Book* (Verve MGV-2056), . . . *the Cole Porter Song Book* (Verve MGV-2052), . . . *the Harry Warren and Vincent Youmans Song Books* (Verve MGV-2059), . . . *the Irving*

Berlin Song Book (Verve MGV-2053), . . . *the Harold Arlen Song Book* (Verve MGV-2060), and . . . *the Jimmy McHugh Song Book* (Verve MGV-2061).

Later releases included *The Jazz Soul of Oscar Peterson* (1960; Verve MGV-8351), *Thoroughly Modern 'Twenties* (1967; Verve V/V6-8700), and *Oscars: Oscar Peterson Plays the Academy Awards* (1969; Verve V6-8775). These albums are not to be confused with similar earlier *Oscar Peterson Plays* albums recorded by Peterson's earlier trios. In total, the group recorded an astonishing 114 tracks from July 14 to August 9, 1959. This volume of material saturated the jazz market.

Most of the recordings produced during this time followed a concise format: Peterson presented the melody before soloing and returning to the theme. It resulted in shorter tracks, mostly under the three-minute mark, leaving little space for Ray Brown to solo.

Some credit must be given to the Peterson trio for their ability to play such varied material. However, many found such extensive recording of jazz standards counterproductive to the advancement of jazz as a creative force. These concept albums allowed limited space for solo experimentation, and seemed aimed more at the casual jazz listener than the serious jazz fan. Although the songbook albums sold well, many judged these commercial efforts as second-rate.

Some took offense to the group's popularity, and the Oscar Peterson Trio soon became a target for criticism from musicians and writers. Miles Davis has been quoted as saying that Peterson sounds as if he had to "learn" the blues, implying that Peterson could never sound like a natural jazz musician. In a *DownBeat* blindfold test, Charles Mingus listened to a recording by Buddy DeFranco and Oscar Peterson and was quoted as saying, "No Stars! Because this is supposed to be a jazz review, and I don't think that's jazz!"[114] Critic Max Harrison wrote the following in his *Jazz Journal Magazine*:

> His [Peterson's] improvisations often seem to be haphazard structures of more or less complexity imposed upon the material without much thought and not arising from any overall conceptions. Most of us have been bored by the monotony of Peterson's mechanical posturings.[115]

A later review by Whitney Balliett, a jazz critic at the *New Yorker*, was especially harsh. In 1966 he wrote, "Peterson's playing continues to be a pudding made from the leavings of Art Tatum, Nat Cole, and Teddy Wilson."[116]

While many writers were quick to dismiss Peterson's work as being uninventive and overly technical, Ray Brown was rarely criticized in the same fashion. Since he was so closely linked to Peterson, it might be assumed that Ray Brown was guilty by association, yet he was rarely singled out as a target for criticism. In fact, in the following review, taken from Martin Williams' book *Where's the Melody?*, the critic attacks Peterson while praising Brown:

> Quite often, his [Peterson's] dexterity seems to be a detriment. He cannot resist, it seems, obvious triplets, scale, and arpeggio runs as they occur to him, and time and again, he will interrupt the perfectly respectable musical structure he has been building to run off such pianistic platitudes. One might almost say that Peterson's melodic vocabulary is a stockpile of clichés that he seems to know every stockpile riff and lick in the history of jazz. Further, his improvisations frequently just string them together . . . There could probably be no more sufficient contrast to such cliché mongering than the presence of bassist Ray Brown in Peterson's group. Brown's virtues are many – his sound, his excellent and sympathetic swing, his joyous and natural commitment to the act of playing.

In interviews with Ed Thigpen and Oscar Peterson, both men discussed this period of intense recording and harsh criticism. Thigpen remembers:

> We used to roll those things off like nothing We did twelve albums in two-and-a-half or three weeks. That was the "Songbook" series. Let's face it: Oscar's a great improviser, and the melodies and the tunes weren't that long. It wasn't that intricate or involved. A few things were [complicated] like when we did "Goodbye J.D.," but for most tunes, you come up with the arrangement quickly. It's like good athletes. They are in shape, know the games, and know the game's rules, so they react. So, you know your skills are together, so it's not [hard] . . . that's the way recording was. It was a whole different ball game in those days than it is now, with the high technology. A lot of that had complicated the issue of playing some live music . . . We worked every day for nine-and-a half months out of the year. So, when you play that much, it is no big deal to run into the studio to do something, because you know where you're going.[117]

Oscar Peterson recalls:

> On occasion [the criticism] was unfair, but you learn to ignore that because the bottom line is your public. If they like what you are doing and they keep showing up, that's the bottom line. You're in the entertainment business, and I don't mean funny hats . . . Most of the critics don't play anyway. You're baring your soul when you hit the bandstand. Everybody's human and everybody would like to get all good reviews, and some things you feel are unfair, but there were a lot of discussions from time to time. If there was anything resentful in a critique, it was when it wasn't constructive. If it's constructive criticism, you weigh it, but if it's from out in the left field because some guy is biased, then it hurts sometimes. It's annoying because these people have a license to defame your integrity, but [yet] you have no source of a rebuttal. Even if you want to bother with it, you can't get tied down with that because, as I said before, as the lines are around the corner, that's the bottom line. Critics get a freebie. Critics don't play [*laughing*]. I don't write, and they don't play, so I ignore them, and they ignore me. That's the way I look at it . . . You know, when you're up there trying to do what you believe in, you don't listen to those various

comments, whatever they may be. They may irk you for ten minutes, but it will not make you change your intent. Not me, certainly, or Ray.[118]

While the songbook recordings from 1959 are intended as commercial efforts, it would be unfair to dismiss this critical period of the group's and Ray Brown's development. In listening to these various albums, some gems can be found. Despite the brevity of these radio-friendly cuts, Ray Brown's presence is strongly felt, and his bass is generally recorded with rich clarity, especially on *Oscar Peterson Plays the Cole Porter Song Book*.

One masterwork from these Chicago sessions is *The Jazz Soul of Oscar Peterson*, on which the trio reached some of its most incredible moments of experimentation and interpretation. *Jazz Soul* offers a group concept in which the trio sounds carefully prepared as they glide smoothly through clever arrangements. One song of note is a carefully reworked version of the Gillespie tune "Con Alma," which finds Brown playing countermelodies, unison lines, and bass solos. Thigpen is also impressive in his ability to add rhythmic coloration through his cymbal work, and he seems to give purpose to each component of the drum set. "Close Your Eyes" is also wonderfully constructed in its use of metric modulation, key changes, and added interludes. Unlike the other songbook recordings, the group is given ample space to explore. Peterson's experiments on the Spanish-influenced "The Maidens of Cadiz" last nearly eight minutes. The album closes with Gillespie's bebop classic "Woody 'n' You," taken at a brisk tempo.

Despite the trio's careful attentiveness on *The Jazz Soul of Oscar Peterson*, London *Observer* writer Benny Green (not to be confused with the musicians of the same name) took jabs at Peterson in his liner notes for the album. Even his compliments can be regarded as backhanded. Green writes:

> [Peterson's] all-conquering technical facility can itself be a double-edged sword, for if it can indeed sometimes take your breath away, it can at other times conjure up a vision of a very fast runner sprinting full pelt up a cul-de-sac. There have been occasions in the past when Peterson has seemed to me to be steamrolling all his raw material into one great Petersonian pulp. But the shortcomings are worth gambling on because when Peterson really hits his stride, there is nobody in the whole range of jazz quite so brilliant.

The Peterson trio returned to a Los Angeles studio on October 12, 1959 to work on another masterpiece when they recorded music from George Gershwin's innovative American folk opera *Porgy and Bess*.[119] The trio's interpretation of this classic material is remarkable for its overall sense of swing and space. Much like the previous songbook albums, the arrangements on *Oscar Peterson Plays Porgy and Bess* (Verve MGV-8340) were conceived during the recording session. However, in contrast to those earlier cookie-cutter recordings, *Porgy and Bess* offers a much more interesting range of jazz interpretations – less conventional than expected and expertly performed and arranged.

Ray Brown is featured prominently on the opening number "I Got Plenty o' Nuttin'," beginning the track with a repeated bass figure before presenting the main melody against only the brushwork of Thigpen and then giving way to Peterson on the bridge. The bassist returns to play the melodic line on the last A section. Brown then settles into a fantastic walking line which provides the perfect rhythmic feel and melodic shape for Peterson to take the lead. Brown returns to the melody to conclude the song.

On "There's a Boat Dat's Leavin' Soon for New York," Ray Brown is given ample solo space. He offers signature licks, upper-structure statements, and clear and often concise phrases in his improvisations. His solo on this track – as with Peterson's approach on the album as a whole – seems to intentionally not overwhelm but instead best service the spirit of each number and the album's overall concept and feel. The intangible spirit and connectivity heard here among the trio are extraordinary, making it one of the Oscar Peterson Trio's finest and most creative efforts from this era.

On November 5, 1959 they were back in the studio for an ambitious big-band effort led by Russell Garcia. Hearing them in such a context is undoubtedly of interest. A highlight from the album is the uptempo Ray Bryant original "Cubano Chant," a recent addition to the Peterson songbook. The pairing of the trio against the full orchestra works particularly well on this track, especially during a call-and-response section between Peterson and the orchestra. Also of note is the lightly textured ballad "Stockholm Sweetnin'," which demonstrates Garcia's ability as an arranger of ballads. These recordings were released as *Swinging Brass with the Oscar Peterson Trio* (Verve MGV-8364).

The next day the trio recorded their final album of the year, *Ben Webster Meets Oscar Peterson* (Verve MGV-8349). As with previous releases with the saxophonist, Webster retains a strong musical connection with the Peterson trio. Many rank this album as one of the tenorist's most impressive works. Unlike some of his contemporaries, Webster never looked to alter his style to suit the rapidly changing trends in jazz, and this album is a testament to a sound and an approach that are timeless. Ray Brown is given solo space on "The Touch of Your Lips," "Bye Bye Blackbird," and "This Can't Be Love." His improvisations embody a similar grace to those of Webster.

As 1959 was coming to an end, the jazz scene was changing dramatically. Without question, jazz had now been surpassed by rock and roll as the day's most celebrated music. Jazz, the genre that had once been America's most popular form and a vehicle for dancing, had now become viewed as "art" music. Moving away from the commercial elements of swing, jazz musicians were now looking for new ways to present their music. Throughout 1959, classic albums were either recorded or released that tested the boundaries of the genre, such as Miles Davis's *Kind of Blue*, John Coltrane's *Giant Steps* (Atlantic SD-1311), Dave Brubeck's *Time Out*, the Bill Evans Trio's *Portrait* in Jazz (Riverside RLP 12-315), Charles Mingus's *Mingus Ah Um* (Columbia CS-8171), Art Blakey and the Jazz Messengers' eponymous album (Blue Note BLP-4003), and, most notably, Ornette Coleman's free jazz exploration *The Shape of Jazz to Come*. While the Oscar Peterson Trio still delivered fantastic music and adopted some characteristics of these contemporaries, they mainly presented straight-ahead jazz based on swing and bop traditions. With new talent emerging, the group were now looking like part of jazz's old school.

As the new decade began, manager and promoter Norman Granz, now living in Switzerland, was only putting on JATP concerts overseas. With a new focus, Granz scaled back his Oscar Peterson Trio recording in 1960, and instead chose to release the trio's stockpile of material from 1959. The absence of studio time was a shocking change of direction for the trio. Granz set up only one studio date for the group in 1960 in which they recorded compositions from the musical *Fiorello!* Debuting on Broadway in 1959, *Fiorello!* tells the story of former New York City Mayor Fiorello H. LaGuardia. Since none of the songs from the musical became part of the popular standard repertoire, the Oscar Peterson Trio album *Fiorello!* (Verve VSTC-238) has been broadly ignored by jazz enthusiasts, but, as with *Porgy and Bess*, the trio takes more care on the album than was the case with most of the *Peterson Plays* records. Highlights include "Home Again," "'Til Tomorrow," and "Politics and Poker." *Fiorello!* is in fact an excellent record deserving of more attention.

Beginning on March 21, 1960, at the Paris Olympic Theater, Granz opened his *Miles Davis and the JATP All-Stars Tour* with a line-up that included the Davis Quintet with John Coltrane on sax, Wynton Kelly on piano, Jimmy Cobb on drums, and the extraordinary Paul Chambers on bass. The twenty-two-city tour also included the Oscar Peterson Trio and the Stan Getz Quartet. There are a few Oscar Peterson Trio recordings from the tour, including an April 8 performance in Zurich which was released as Volume 30 of the Swiss Radio Days Jazz Series (TCB Records TCB 02302), and an April 30 concert issued as *Paris Jazz Concert Part 1* (LaserLight Digital 17417). Both performances are remarkable glimpses into how the trio sounded live, documenting Thigpen's development, and the further use of Ray Brown as a secondary soloist. Some time during the year, the Peterson trio also recorded in Canada at CBC Studios, resulting in another impressive album: *Oscar Peterson Trio Live at CBC Studios, 1960* (Just a Memory JAS 9507-2).

With less time being spent in the studio, Ray Brown, Oscar Peterson, and Ed Thigpen took their professional careers in a new direction by instructing students at the Advanced School of Contemporary Music in Toronto. Peterson had founded the Advanced School in his home, before moving it into a Toronto facility. The school's faculty included the Oscar Peterson Trio, Butch Watanabe, and composer Phil Nimmons. Although there is a surplus of jazz programs in colleges and universities today, it was unusual to find such a program in 1960.

The school lasted only a short time, for several reasons. For one, the program was plagued by financial problems from the outset. Secondly, the faculty found balancing their busy touring schedules and teaching responsibilities challenging. Oscar Peterson and Ed Thigpen discussed the school and why it eventually became impossible to run. Peterson remembers:

> Actually, the school started in my house in Toronto at the time. We had a guy named Phil Nimmons who had a group of his own here called "Nimmons and Nine." Phil, Ray, and I got together and decided it would be good to give young players a chance to operate with people operating in the [jazz] medium. So, we formed the Advanced School of Contemporary Music. It started as holding the first sessions in my home, in the basement, and then finally, we took quarters downtown and ran the school from there.
>
> It became almost impossible because we couldn't spend that much time. One day, Norman commented, "You guys are gonna have to decide whether you want to be performers or teachers." He said, "It's gonna take too much of your time." We had to hold auditions and listen to all the tapes that were sent in. We had to set up the curriculum. We had to be there when the students arrived, and then we had to adjudicate what they had done when it was all over. This takes a lot of time, which we didn't have. We had to give up an awful lot of road time, so we decided that we couldn't sacrifice that time.[120]

Ed Thigpen remembers:

> I was invited to join the faculty, and that's why I moved to Canada, and Ray moved up there too. He and Oscar had this idea. You know, John Lewis had this school where he was the musical director, and evidently, they got the idea to start a school in Canada because they could stay home more, and Ray would move up there. I think the first reason was to have a home base where they could be more [grounded]. They had done some teaching, and I had done some stuff with Billy Taylor. As far as I could see, that was the beginning of it. But we started getting so busy on the road that we couldn't keep it up for more than two years . . . We had people enrolled from all over the world, and it started with the rhythm section, and then there were arranging classes with Phil Nimmons. So that's the nucleus of the orchestra right there, and it was fun to do it . . . You know, the group continued to get more and more popular, and we had more and more commitments. You can't run a school all of the time and be on the road and not be there.[121]

After its initial opening in 1960, the Advanced School of Contemporary Music decreased its yearly activities and eventually closed some time in 1964. Former students like pianist Mike Longo and bassist Jay Leonhart remained active in jazz. Brown's position at the school also helped spark further teaching opportunities, and he stayed involved in jazz education throughout his career. His interest in teaching led to the 1963 publication of his *Ray Brown's Bass Method*, which is still among the most used bass method books today. Later in his career, he released an instruction video titled *The Art of Playing the Bass* and participated in several masterclasses and lectures.

In December of 1960, the future of many of Granz's recording artists was in jeopardy when he sold his Verve label and the rights to his Mercury, Clef, Norgran, and Down Home masters for $2.8 million to MGM. With the sale, Granz agreed to stay as a consultant for a year, but, shortly after the purchase, MGM bought in a new artist and repertoire chief named Creed Taylor. Taylor, who had previously served as the head of Bethlehem Records and ABC-Paramount, had an excellent reputation for turning profits. For years, Norman Granz charitably served as a virtual economic lifeline for dozens of important jazz figures who were no longer commercially successful. Taylor was less tolerant, and he decided to thoroughly restructure the label. He fired nearly every Verve artist from the past except top sellers like Ella Fitzgerald, Oscar Peterson, Johnny Hodges, and Stan Getz. Creed Taylor's primary interest was producing more commercially viable music. While no longer in control of recording, Granz retained several of his artists, including Oscar Peterson and Ella Fitzgerald, as their manager.

While many past Verve artists were left with a feeling of disappointment and uncertainty, the Oscar Peterson Trio did not need to worry. With a smaller roster of artists, Creed Taylor could focus more attention on the group. In addition, the trio could now produce albums that were less rushed and with more emphasis on sound quality and marketability. This new approach led to some of the Oscar Peterson Trio's most commercially successful works and brought the group to its highest level of fame.

In 1961, Verve Records decided to capture the Oscar Peterson Trio live instead of offering studio productions. They did so at the London House in Chicago, where the trio performed between July 27 and August 6. After sifting through the volume of recorded material, four LPs were eventually released, including *The Trio: Live from Chicago* (Verve V/V6-8420), *The Sound of the Trio* (Verve V/V6-8480), *Put on a Happy Face* (Verve V/V6-8660), and *Something Warm* (Verve V/V6-8681). Eventually, the complete recordings were released in a box set titled *The London House Sessions* (Verve 314 531 766-2).

In listening to these recordings, it becomes apparent that not all audiences gave the trio the proper respect they deserved. Additionally, the piano was terribly out of tune. At points, Oscar Peterson is polite but vocal about his irritation with the noisy audience. However, in some cases, the sounds of silverware clinking, light chatter, and the occasional telephone rings give these recordings a personal feel. Fortunately, there were also nights at the London House engagements where the audience was cooperative and responsive, and at which point the trio sounded particularly inspired.

The London House recordings offer many highlights, and Ray Brown is particularly impressive in his ability to provide countermelodies and solo statements. In addition, his rhythmic hookup with Ed Thigpen is a forward-moving foundation that continues to define fundamental swing. Ray Brown is particularly impressive soloing on "Sometimes I'm Happy," "Daahoud," "Cubano Chant," and "Tricrotism." Most striking is the band's ability to produce coherent statements on very uptempo numbers like "Woody 'n' You" and "Swamp Fire."

Ray Brown's composition "Gravy Waltz" also makes its first recorded appearance. Although several of his compositions made their way onto his solo efforts, it was rare for a Ray Brown original to appear on an Oscar Peterson date. "Gravy Waltz" is a clever tune played in 3/4 time with a bluesy feel that incorporates triplet figures, and the distinct-sounding sharp four-chord gives the music a unique harmonic texture. "Gravy Waltz" is Ray Brown's most famous composition, being used as the theme song for *The Steve Allen Show*, a popular television show in the 1960s. Allen is also given compositional credit for writing "Gravy Waltz," as he later wrote lyrics for the piece. In 1963, Brown and Allen received a Grammy award for their composition in the "Best Original Jazz Composition" category.

Creed Taylor, like Granz, found value in using the Oscar Peterson Trio to back other artists, and the group made a series of fine recordings with Milt Jackson on September 15 and 18 in New York City, resulting in the Oscar Peterson Trio with Milt Jackson, *Very Tall* (Verve V/V6-8429). Surprisingly, given their fame and the fact that they were both Verve/MGM artists, this was the first time Jackson had recorded with Peterson. However, Ray Brown and Milt Jackson were close friends and had recorded together before, beginning with their days working with Dizzy Gillespie.

The most unusual track on *Very Tall* is the group's take on the traditional folk song "John Brown's Body," a famous Civil War Union song referencing extreme abolitionist leader John Brown, who attempted to lead a slave uprising after conducting a raid on Harper's Ferry Armory in October 1859. The song's melody is set to Julie Howe's "Battle Hymn of the Republic." Combining traditional folk melodies with jazz can often lead to a successful blend of American traditions. Brown is best represented on Milt Jackson's original "Reunion Blues," playing the song's melody before shifting into a funky bass line and settling into a confident walking line. The session would be Brown's last of the year.[122]

17 The Second Classic Oscar Peterson Trio (Part 2) 1962–1965

The Oscar Peterson Trio's first recording of 1962 was on January 24–25 in New York City when the group undertook the difficult task of reworking Leonard Bernstein's popular 1957 musical *West Side Story*. At this time, the members still had their teaching responsibilities at the Contemporary School, and finding the time to get together to rehearse had become difficult. All the same, the group took special care in rearranging and rehearsing the music for this effort. In a departure from the other songbook albums, on *West Side Story* (Verve V/V6-8454) the trio pays extraordinary detail to the arrangements while leaving enough space for improvisation. Brown's lengthy solo on "Jet Song" incorporates some laid-back eighth note statements and several of the characteristic individual figures that often find their way into his improvisations — personal "clichés" that lend Brown's solos their individuality. *West Side Story* is one of the finest of the Oscar Peterson Trio's concept albums.

Following the recording of *West Side Story*, the Oscar Peterson Trio continued a pattern of touring and teaching. The group would not enter the studio again until June 13, 1962, when they began a three-day recording series for Oscar Peterson's big-band album, *Bursting Out with the All-Star Big Band!* (Verve V/V6-8476) The sessions were arranged and conducted by Ernie Wilkins and included an all-star cast of twenty-six musicians, including legends like Nat Adderley, Roy Eldridge, Clark Terry, Cannonball Adderley, and James Moody. This album is fascinating because Peterson was rarely featured in a big-band context. Ray Brown is most prominently featured on the Oscar Pettiford classic "Tricrotism," where he impresses with solo bop statements in the introduction, trading eight-bar phrases with Peterson. This tightly arranged version of the tune is taken at a much faster tempo than the famed version by Oscar Pettiford and Lucky Thompson released in 1956, and the over-eleven-minute-long version recorded by the Peterson trio at the London House in 1961. Unlike the previous version, the *Bursting Out* "Tricrotism" does not include an extended bass solo.

One notable characteristic of the big-band version is the shifting opening theme played in four keys during the song's outro. "Tricrotism" would remain part of Ray Brown's repertoire, and analysis of his takes on the tune make for an interesting comparison. Another fantastic showpiece on the album is the Cuban-influenced "Manteca," made famous by Dizzy Gillespie's Big Band, and which Ray had recorded with Gillespie in December 1947, shortly before he left the orchestra.

On September 25–27, 1962 the Oscar Peterson Trio recorded the album *Affinity* (Verve V/V6-8516) in Chicago. It testifies to the group's development, specifically in adding small-group arrangement details to their re-creations of standards and new materials. The fact that the album was recorded over three consecutive days shows that Creed Taylor and producer Jim Davis, who had worked as a producer on their last few releases, were committed to capturing the group at their best. Although rarely discussed as a classic, *Affinity!* is the Peterson trio at its finest. One only has to listen to "This Could Be the Start of Something," "Six and Four," and "Tangerine" to appreciate the trio's direction and cohesiveness.

Much of the strength of the recording can be attributed to Ed Thigpen, who is playing with new confidence and less restraint, adding more fills, time feels, and accents. *Affinity!* also marks the first studio recording of Brown's "Gravy Waltz" (as discussed in Chapter 16). One of the more interesting cuts on the album is the Bill Evans composition "Waltz for Debbie," and not just because it is a fantastic performance: Bill Evans' lighter touch was often seen as a reactionary contrast to Oscar Peterson's note-heavy hard-driving approach. And Scott LaFaro was the bassist in the Bill Evans Trio from 1960 to 1961, during which time he expanded the instrument's role by playing in a more conversational style, breaking away from the hard-driving, consistent walking bass line accompaniment style that often characterized the playing of Ray Brown. Additionally, LaFaro expanded the higher range of the bass and impressed listeners with his exceptional technique and exploratory phrasing. With his upper-structure playing, rapid solo phrases and contrapuntal lines, he was the first significant figure to offer a clear fundamental shift in the possibilities of jazz bass virtuosity. LaFaro's interpretations of "Waltz for Debbie" can be heard on the Bill Evans compilation *The Complete Village Vanguard Sessions, 1961* (Riverside 3RCD-4443-2).

On December 15 and 16, 1962 the Peterson trio took part in their final studio session of the year in Los Angeles. Although his activities with Verve had become limited by now, Norman Granz nonetheless worked as producer on what would become *Night Train* (Verve V/V6-8538), which has remained the Oscar Peterson Trio's most beloved album. If a music fan had only one Oscar Peterson Trio record in their collection, it was most likely *Night Train*. Simply put, it is a classic and often listed among the best of all jazz recordings. The album's beauty lies in the group's overall sound and approach to swing and blues numbers. Essentially, the album exemplifies traditional small-group jazz played with perfection.

On many of his albums Peterson is sometimes unable to contain his technical ability, but on *Night Train* he shows restraint, playing more precise phrases that are as suited to the tastes of the casual listener as to those of the serious jazz enthusiast. That is not to say that Peterson's performance is not impressive; his ability to limit the use of highly technical solo passages only serves to testify to his growth as a musician. Similarly, Ray Brown seems to have taken a great deal of care in formulating his bass lines and solos. Holding it all together is Ed Thigpen, whose time feel and well-placed accents exemplify swing drumming.

Ray Brown has solos on "Night Train," "Bags' Groove," and "Honey Dripper," each of which is a perfect reflection of his current approach to jazz improvisation, balancing a repertoire of equal parts swing, blues, bop, and signature licks. One of the more notable cuts is the gospel-based Peterson original, "Hymn to Freedom," which reveals a new, more ambitious direction as a composer. Overall, *Night Train* is successful because it showcases the group's tremendous precision and unity; while their style draws from an earlier generation, they never sound formulaic or sterile.

By 1963, Oscar Peterson and Ray Brown were not being called upon to record as much as they had been, very likely because plenty of stockpiled material was still waiting for release. Although not so well represented in the studio, the group still toured regularly. The first recording assignment of 1963 paired the group with singer and actor Bill Henderson. Henderson's soulful voice first came to notice in his native Chicago when he was performing with pianist Ramsey Lewis. In the late 1950s, he moved to New York, scoring a hit with a vocal version of Horace Silver's "Señor Blues." Recorded in February 1963, the album *Bill Henderson with the Oscar Peterson Trio* (MGM E/SE-4128) is an enjoyable listen and something of a departure at this point as they hadn't recorded with a singer for some time.

Bill Henderson's vocal style sits somewhere between rhythm and blues and swing. On this record, he is most impressive on uptempo numbers like "You Are My Sunshine," "The Lamp Is Low," and "A Lot of Livin' to Do." This session is notable because it marks the first *vocal* recording of Ray Brown's "Gravy Waltz," which, as we saw in the previous chapter, had lyrics added by Steve Allen. It is the only Ray Brown song to have made any commercial outside impact, and it has been recorded by dozens of artists, including Sarah Vaughan, Quincy Jones, Shirley Scott, Chet Atkins, and the Andrews Sisters. Besides retaining a career as a recording artist, Henderson began acting in the 1970s. A reliable character actor, Bill Henderson's credits include minor roles in films like *City Slickers*, *Clue*, *Fletch*, *White Men Can't Jump*, and *Lethal Weapon 4*.

In March of 1963, the trio was back in Europe, where they were again recorded at the L'Olympia theater in Paris on the 22nd with Roy Eldridge, eventuallly seeing the light of day on *Paris Jazz Concert Part 2* (LaserLight Digital 17418.) The group's next studio recording would be in New York on August 3, 1963. For this date, the trio recorded a spirited Peterson composition called "Hallelujah Time" to serve as a second track for his 45 rpm single

Ray Brown with Oscar Peterson, 1965.
Heritage Image Partnership Ltd / Alamy Stock Photo

"Hallelujah Time" b/w "Hymn to Freedom" (Verve VK-10302). Peterson would frequently perform both pieces in concert around this time.

On November 8 and 10, 1963 the trio was at Radio Recorders Studio in Los Angeles again to participate in a large-group recording with the Nelson Riddle Orchestra. The result was the Verve release of *Oscar Peterson & Nelson Riddle* (Verve V/V6-8562), representing another commercial-sounding effort in which a classical orchestra merged with a jazz rhythm section. A good portion of the material is somewhat sanitized and would likely be described by some as "elevator music." The merging of styles worked best on the ballads "Come Sunday" and "Goodbye." Of the more swinging numbers, "A Sleeping Bee" is the most enjoyable because Riddle's arrangement incorporates more traditional big-band characteristics.

American popular music would change forever when the Beatles arrived in America on February 7, 1964. Beatlemania led to a further "British Invasion" of bands into America, including the Rolling Stones, the Animals, the Kinks, the Yardbirds, and the Dave Clark Five. It was notable that they often played watered-down versions of American blues and rhythm and blues. Soon, however, they found their own creative voices, often with a whimsical brand of English nostalgia blended with psychedelic rock forms. These groups effectively reintroduced American music to a larger, more integrated U.S. audience unaware of its origins. Simultaneously, popular soul and rhythm and blues artists were were finding a new level of fame within the Black community, notably those on the Motown label under the direction of hitmaker Berry Gordy, such as Smokey Robinson and the Miracles, the Temptations, Marvin Gaye, Diana Ross and the Supremes, among many others.

This put jazz musicians under further pressure to retain younger audiences both in the U.S. and abroad. In response, many began to tour more frequently in Europe, where swing-based jazz continued to be more widely appreciated. Other jazz figures brought the spirit of rock and roll music into jazz, more heavily incorporating rhythm and blues rhythms and repertoire. Within a few years, forward-looking musicians, with Miles Davis in the vanguard, would be integrating electric instruments into jazz, leaving traditional acoustic jazz bands like the Oscar Peterson Trio looking increasingly old-fashioned and unpopular.

Despite the landscape change, the Oscar Peterson Trio continued to do what they did best: hard-swinging standards mixed with original material. On February 27–28, 1964 the trio recorded another fine traditional-sounding album, *The Oscar Peterson Trio Plays* (Verve V/V6-8591). The group sounds polished, especially on the standard "Fly Me to the Moon," where Peterson incorporates a complete reharmonization and tight reworking of the structure without losing the melodic line. Ray Brown is heavily featured on "Let's Fall in Love," where he is afforded an extended solo and can be heard vocalizing during the improvisation.

Brown's bass is more present in the mix on the *Trio Plays* recording than on many other contemporary releases. Throughout the album, the trio retains its small-group arrangement characteristics, such as rhythmic hits and attention to dynamics, to retain a group sound. The *Trio Plays* album is solid overall and shows the trio at its zenith. However, the group's approach in the studio was now becoming almost too polished and predictable, especially for those fans who favored more exploratory musicians like John Coltrane, Charles Mingus, Wayne Shorter, Jackie McLean, and Horace Silver, all of whom would produce more forward-looking albums that year.

For much of the spring and early summer of 1964, the Oscar Peterson Trio traveled throughout Europe and the Far East. Several subsequent releases document the group live from this period, including: *Paris Jazz Concert Part 2* from the Théâtre des Champs-Elysées, April 25–26, *The Oscar Peterson Trio in Tokyo, 1964* (Pablo VDJ-25008-9), from Ōtemachi Sankei Hall, Tokyo, Japan, June 2, 1964; *Hallelujah Time!* (Moon Records MCD050-2), from London (no specific date); and *Live and at Its Best* (Point 2620532) from Ljubljana, Yugoslavia, July 29.

The group also recorded in Germany at the private home of Hans Georg Brunner-Schwer, resulting in the later release of *Easy Walker!* (Prestige PRST 7690). Brunner-Schwer was an audio engineer and a huge fan of pianists, notably Oscar Peterson. He would fund private concerts in his house and record them at his professional-quality domestic studio using only the finest equipment and technology. He would later form MPS Records in 1968 and release several Peterson recordings.

After extensive touring, the trio returned to New York and joined Clark Terry in the studio on August 1, 1964. The result is the ten-song Mercury Records release *Oscar Peterson Trio + One* (Mercury MG-20975). Previously, Clark Terry had worked with Duke Ellington, Count Basie, and others, then, beginning in 1962, he started a ten-year engagement as a member of the Tonight Show Band but continued his work as a sideman and session player. Throughout his impressive fifty-year career, Terry made over 900 jazz recordings. While he is not always included among the most influential trumpeters in jazz, Terry is a great talent and stylist who can enhance any musical situation.

Clark Terry holds the listener's attention throughout *Oscar Peterson Trio + One* by switching between trumpet, flugelhorn, and singing. Peterson demonstrates his new expanded interest in writing by adding three original pieces, "Blues for Smedley," "Squeaky's Blues," and "Roundalay." Two of the more interesting tracks on the album are "Mumbles" and "Incoherent Blues," on which Clark Terry showcases his unique and, at times, ridiculous-sounding scat-style singing, where he mumbles the melodies instead of providing a more traditional syllabic approach. Ray Brown is most impressive as a soloist on "Blues for Smedley," with his blues lines and well-placed phrases. He also provides some funky bass lines on "Squeaky's Blues."

On September 9, 1964, Oscar Peterson recorded *Canadiana Suite* (Limelight LM-82010), his first album of all original material with the trio. Separated into eight movements, *Canadiana Suite* was inspired by the Canadian landscapes that Peterson loved. The album was released in 1965 on Limelight Records, a Mercury subsidiary headed by Quincy Jones. Widely ignored today, *Canadiana Suite* is one of the Peterson trio's most exemplary efforts and shows the pianist's growth as a composer. Ray Brown is particularly inspirational as a soloist on "Place St. Henri," "Wheatland," and "Laurentide Waltz."

One of the Oscar Peterson Trio's most enjoyed albums is *We Get Requests* (Verve V/V6-8606). The album resulted from several sessions at RCA Studios in New York between October 19 and November 20, 1964, and is significant as the trio's final release on Verve, which had supported the group for fourteen years. The finely crafted arrangements and interpretations of jazz standards reveal a group so comfortable with each other that there was an almost telepathic connection. The one original is Peterson's "Goodbye J.D." Brown is most impressive during solos on the ballad "My Only Love," with a series of double-time phrases. "You Look Good to Me" is also notable and begins and ends with Brown's arco figures, followed by some pizzicato lines phrased in the bop style against the main melody.

1965 began as usual for Ray Brown and the Peterson trio. The group all seemed to be very much on the same page as they continued to tour throughout the beginning of the year. For much of the first part of 1965 they were in Europe, and several performances from that time have been captured on video and on record, including *Nightingale* (Jazz Birdies of Paradise J-Bop 047), which includes two Peterson originals, "Place St. Henri" and "Nightingale," along with two standards, "My Only Love" and "Yours Is My Heart Alone," from a London performance of January 23.

On May 10, the trio were again taking advantage of Hans Georg Brunner-Schwer's private studio, where they recorded at least four tracks, including "Gravy Waltz," "Three O'Clock in the Morning Blues," "Squeaky's Blues," and "Tenderly." These would eventually be released on *Exclusively for My Friends: The Lost Tapes* (MPS Records 314 529 096-2).

On May 12, 1965 the trio performed in Germany, resulting in the subsequent release of *May 1965: Münchner Jazzstage* (Lantower Records), which captures an enthusiastic audience and the trio at their best. Highlights are "Wheatland" and "Place St. Henri" from Peterson's *Canadiana Suite*. On the latter both Brown and Thigpen play well-connected solos, and Brown is also prominently featured on "You Look Good to Me" in a similar fashion to the *We Get Requests* album. His solo on the track reveals a heightened sense of sophistication and melodicism.

On May 29, 1965 the trio was recorded at the Tivoli Gardens Concert Hall in Copenhagen, Denmark, resulting in the live album *Eloquence* (Limelight LM-82023), their final live release with Ed Thigpen. The brilliant recording displays the unity, focus, and mastery of tempo, dynamics, and arrangements that the Peterson trio had achieved over the past five-plus years. Ray Brown is prominently featured throughout the concert and is most brilliant as a soloist on "Autumn Leaves," "Misty," "Younger Than Springtime," and "Moanin'." One highlight of the evening is the group's presentation of John Lewis's "Django," which incorporates well-placed dynamic and rhythmic elements. *Eloquence* presents a trio that has achieved its highest level of mastery.

It was during 1965 that Ed Thigpen expressed his desire to leave. The drummer explains:

> It was mutual. Oscar wanted a change. Most groups, like Miles Davis, used to change all the time . . . I was going through a change myself because, as great as that experience was, there were some other things I was hearing that were not applicable to the situation. Everybody was growing, and everybody had new ideas. Maybe there just comes a time to move on, and it becomes mutual. You can go into all kinds of scenarios, but basically, I feel that it was a time that had run its course . . . By [listening to] my performances, obviously, I was ready for a change because I started doing things that weren't applicable to the situation. I had just heard Tony Williams, and I heard some other folks that were doing things that made me say, "Wait a minute [*laughs*]; music is going another way." . . . If you have my *Out of the Storm* record [Verve V6-8663], you can hear where my head was. That was the first thing I did. It was my first solo project. So, you can see where my head was.[123]

After departing, Ed Thigpen joined Ella Fitzgerald for about a year, whereafter he went to Los Angeles as a studio musician, recording with commercial stars like Pat Boone, Peggy Lee, Johnny Mathis, and Andy Williams. In 1968, he rejoined Fitzgerald for four years before settling in Copenhagen where he continued teaching and performing.

With Ed Thigpen no longer in the group, Oscar Peterson and Ray Brown briefly reunited with Herb Ellis in Los Angeles on October 28, 1965 for the Nat King Cole tribute album *With Respect to Nat* (Limelight LS-86029). Here Peterson sings Nat Cole's hits just as he had done as a developing musician in Canada. While the album is a fitting tribute to Nat King Cole, the trio plays close to the original Cole trio's style, and the album is not among Peterson's most impressive works. As for Ellis, no permanent reformation of the classic line-up was up for discussion.

Soon after the departure of Thigpen, Ray Brown expressed his desire to move on. Ray Brown has given many reasons for leaving the group that had provided him wealth, experience, and fame. In one of a number of his recollections on the subject he says:

> Some of those tours were really punishing – we'd come to Europe and do sixty-two one-nighters in sixty-five days, and then I'd start to think, "Hey! I don't need this much money!" . . . I think Oscar and I built something between us that will always stand up musically. It was just that one day I looked up and realized that I'd turned forty, and although the money was great, the tour schedules were heavy. So, I decided to quit.[124]

In the November 4, 1965 edition of *DownBeat* magazine, an article announced Ray Brown's decision:

> Ray Brown, who has won more awards for excellence than any other bassist, will be available for a New Year's Eve gig. He will leave the Oscar Peterson Trio in December after nearly 15 years with the pianist. The parting is amicable. Brown's leaving had been rumored for several months and gained added impetus when drummer Ed Thigpen left the Peterson group in June. Thigpen, who was replaced by Louis Hayes, had been with the trio, one of the most tightly-knit in jazz, for five years. Brown reportedly will settle in Los Angeles.

Before leaving the group, Ray Brown recorded for a final time with the trio, which now had Louis Hayes on drums. Before joining Peterson in 1965, Hayes had already developed a reputation as one of jazz's finest drummers and regularly worked with Horace Silver and Cannonball Adderley. They recorded at Chicago Sound Studios on December 3, 1965 and the results can be heard on Peterson's album *Blues Etude* (Limelight LM-82039). Here, Hayes sounds confident but does forcibly push the tempo at times. While they played well enough together, it can't be ignored that Ray Brown spent thousands of hours developing his rhythmic hookup with Ed Thigpen. Perhaps given more time, Brown and Hayes would have formulated a groove that could have served the direction of Oscar Peterson.

Naturally, the departure of Ray Brown was difficult for Peterson to endure. However, he did find first-rate replacements in Sam Jones and Niels-Henning Ørsted-Pedersen, to mention two in particular. Throughout their long history, Ray Brown and Oscar Peterson formed a personal and musical brotherhood that continued throughout their lives. Though Ray Brown left Peterson's trio late in 1965, he would continue to record and appear with Peterson on many occasions. Even after Peterson suffered a severe stroke that partially paralyzed him in 1993, the musical hookup between Ray Brown and Oscar Peterson never seemed to fade.

Oscar Peterson has said of Ray Brown: "He's like a brother to me . . . If I had to sum up Ray in a sentence, I'd say this: 'He's the epitome of forethought. Sympathetic forethought.'"[125]

18 Solo and Sideman Sessions 1959–1965

While playing with the second "classic" Oscar Peterson Trio, Ray Brown continued to work as a sideman and leader. Before drummer Ed Thigpen had recorded with the Peterson trio, he visited the studio with Ray Brown and guitarist Kenny Burrell for a Blossom Dearie session. The result was the album *Blossom Dearie Sings Comden and Green* (Verve VS-6050), on which Ray is heard most prominently on "Just in Time" and "The Party's Over," although overall the record is not remarkable. Brown and Thigpen recorded again with Dearie on May 21–22, 1959; this time, her former husband the Belgian reed specialist Bobby Jaspar was added to the ensemble. The result was an album, *My Gentleman Friend* (Verve MG VS-6112), on which Dearie is at her most interesting when she sings in French, as she does with "Chez Moi," "Boum," and L'Étang."

On April 9, 1959, the same day as one of those Blossom Dearie sessions, Brown was asked to participate in pianist Junior Mance's first album as a leader, *Junior: Junior Mance and His Swinging Piano* (Verve MGV-8319). Mance had previously worked with Gene Ammons, Lester Young, Cannonball Adderley, Dinah Washington, and, most recently, Dizzy Gillespie. Knowing that Mance wanted to embark on a solo career, and with Lalo Schifrin waiting to take his place in the Gillespie quintet, Dizzy helped secure this trio session for him with Norman Granz.[126] With a style combining swing and blues, Mance went on to have a successful recording and touring career. Lex Humphries, an emerging New York City drummer who would eventually record with jazz revolutionaries like John Coltrane and Sun Ra, rounded out the ensemble.

There is an appreciable hookup between Mance, Brown, and Humphries throughout the record, and hearing Ray Brown in a trio setting without Oscar Peterson is always of interest. Brown's bass is well recorded throughout *Junior*, and his walking lines mesh well with Mance's phrasing, touch, and sense of swing. Surprisingly, Brown is not widely used as a soloist on the record, but he does add fills and countermelodies to advance the musical conversation. His one extensive solo takes place on the slow and soulful "Blues for Beverlee," on which he allows a good amount of space to begin with and does an exceptional job of repeating and building off short themes. He avoids the trap of overplaying and so his improvisation works well within the tune's overall feel and framework.

If recording two albums in a day was not enough, Ray Brown was asked to complete a third on that same day when he was included on an all-star jam-style album called *Ben Webster and His Associates* (Verve MG VS-6056), with Roy Eldridge (trumpet), Coleman Hawkins, Budd Johnson, and Ben Webster (tenor saxophones), Jimmy Jones (piano), Les Spann (guitar), and Jo Jones (drums). With some tracks lasting nearly twenty minutes, Ray Brown had his work cut out, especially since the bass is a physically demanding instrument that has been known to cause many hand injuries. It is simply astounding that Brown had the stamina to record so many tracks in one day and still manage to sound fresh.

Following the lengthy Oscar Peterson songbook sessions of 1959, Brown participated in a trio recording with reeds specialist Jimmy Giuffre and master guitarist Jim Hall on August 6–7. Of all Ray Brown's "cool jazz" projects the album *The Easy Way* by the Jimmy Giuffre 3 (Verve MG V-8337) is the small-group recording most characteristic of this more relaxed jazz style. With its shifting harmonies, compositional details, lighter texture, and use of space, *The Easy Way* exemplifies the conversational nature and lyricism of the "cool" approach; it is a testament to Brown's versatility that he plays so effectively in that genre. He is featured regularly throughout the album and is simply masterful. *The Easy Way* ought to be considered one of Brown's most inspired projects and one of the great jazz albums of the late 1950s.

A project such as this helped distance Brown from the harsh criticism that often followed Oscar Peterson. On the site *All About Jazz*, Joshua Weiner wrote:

> The almost psychic interplay here between Giuffre and Hall is typical of the 3, but Brown is a real surprise. He sounds glad to be liberated from the relative stricture of Oscar Peterson's Trio, fitting seamlessly into Giuffre's conception while still providing a strong, swinging pulse. The subtlety between this recording is quite a contrast from many of Peterson's projects. It is unfortunate that, Brown was not more active in more "cool" chamber jazz projects after this album.[127]

One of the most memorable Ray Brown recordings of 1960 was *Cannonball Adderley and the Poll-Winners* (Riverside Records RS 9355), an all-star session that included Cannonball Adderley on alto sax, Victor Feldman on vibes and piano, Wes Montgomery on guitar, and Louis Hayes on drums. The sessions were split between a May 21 recording at Fugazi Hall in San Francisco and a second session on June 5 at United Recording in Los Angeles.

By 1960, Adderley, Feldman, Montgomery, and Hayes were considered to be among their respective instruments' most impressive voices. Mostly a jam-style session album, the unique qualities of the musicians on *Cannonball*

Adderley and the Poll-Winners is awe-inspiring. Ray Brown's playing is prominent, and his bass is well recorded throughout. On the opening track, "The Chant," Brown is heard playing the song's main melody, and the bassist is also featured as a soloist on several tracks, including "Lolita" and "Yours Is My Heart Alone." His most impressive solo comes on the bebop blues "Au Privave." The solo offers some bop phrasing but is not overly showy, and Brown's playing is enhanced by the light comping of Montgomery's guitar and Hayes's simple hi-hat click on beats two and four. Ray Brown, like most bassists, benefits from a lighter background texture to allow the nuances of the bass's tone to cut through on recordings.

On June 1, 1960, an unissued Verve session including Ray Brown was listed in session catalogs: a Los Angeles recording for Johnny Hodges and His Orchestra which included former and current Duke Ellington Orchestra members Lawrence Brown, Booty Wood, and Ben Webster. Ed Thigpen and pianist Jimmy Rowles joined Ray Brown in the rhythm sections. While it's unknown why the session was unissued, it was nonetheless a significant one, being the first time he worked with Jimmy Rowles. Rowles and Brown would later be frequent collaborators.

One of Brown's lesser-known recordings also took place on June 1 and 2 for pianist Joyce Collins, in a trio with drummer Frank Butler. The session resulted in her debut album *Girl Here Plays Mean Piano* (Jazzland JLP 24). Collins's career mostly centered around Los Angeles and Las Vegas and her most notable appearances were in television studio bands for *The Mary Tyler Moore Show* and *The Bob Newhart Show* in the 1950s. Interestingly, the album lists Ray Brown under the pseudonym Ray Green, which might have something to do with the album being on Jazzland Records, a subsidiary of Riverside Records, and Norman Granz's approval might have been required. Even though the album had little impact, the project is impressive, with Brown featured on several tracks like "Walkin'," where he begins his solo with a gentle walk before offering some bluesy lines and bop sequences. For his solo on "Day In, Day Out," he takes a different approach and improvises with fire and enthusiasm, incorporating longer phrases and increased rhythmic pacing during breaks.

It was during this period, on November 2, 1959, that Ray Brown embarked on one of his most ambitious efforts: an album that featured him entirely on the cello. Several years earlier, Oscar Pettiford had introduced him to the cello as a vehicle for jazz improvisation. Although Pettiford's cello recordings impressed him, Brown cites Keter Betts as the man who made him change his mind about the instrument. In the liner notes to his *Jazz Cello* (Verve V6-8390) album, Brown describes how he got into playing the instrument some time in 1959:

> Keter stopped by to see me, and he was running late, and he left the cello there, saying he'd pick it up the next day, but before he left he said, "Why

don't you try it out? You might like it." Well, I did. We had sessions, and I found it [the cello] was a nice, easy, and clear means of expression that I kept at it all week and played it between shows. Yet when we left for Washington, I didn't think about it again, that is, not until we returned there in 1960 when I went to a party where I borrowed the cello and jammed all night.

The other bassist of note who experimented with jazz cello was Harry Babasin, who made the first jazz cello recordings in 1947 with Dodo Marmarosa's trio. Another jazz cellist to have some impact was Fred Katz, who played in drummer Chico Hamilton's quintet in the mid-1950s. Unlike Brown and Pettiford, who played pizzicato, Katz was a classically trained cellist who played the instrument using the traditional arco technique.[128]

While Brown enjoyed playing Keter Betts's cello, he needed a hybrid version of the instrument to better suit his needs. He contacted the Kay Bass Company and asked them to build him a cello that would feel and tune like a bass, only an octave higher. As a result, Brown became the inventor and endorser of the Kay Jazz Cello, which, although never gaining widespread popularity, led to the development of other hybrid bass instruments, such as the tenor bass guitar. Brown felt the instrument he designed allowed him greater scope and facility. He also found lines that were difficult to execute on the bass to be much easier on the cello. In addition, the instrument lent itself to more clarity on recordings than the bass.

For the *Jazz Cello* album, Brown chose mostly standard material, because "Since we were introducing what you might call a new sound, I at least wanted tunes the public would know."[129] And on standards like "Ain't Misbehavin'" and "Tangerine" he handles the melody masterfully. On the album Brown is accompanied by a ten-piece band, including Don Fagerquist (trumpet), Harry Betts (trombone), Jack Cave (French horn), Bob Cooper, Meredith Flory, Bill Hood, and Paul Horn (saxophones), Jimmy Rowles (piano), Joe Mondragon (bass), and Richard Shanahan (drums). Russ Garcia handled the arrangements and ensured that Brown was allowed ample space to create and develop.

The *Jazz Cello* album begins with Brown presenting the melody on "Tangerine," From the first note, the instrument's tone and timbre are of great interest, with the higher octave affording Brown's statement more clarity. Overall, the music is rather over-arranged and has a slick Hollywood-type feel, which was characteristic of Garcia's writing style at the time. Ray Brown plays melodies and solos on nearly every tune on the record, the cello extending his vocabulary and technique. Although Brown is impressive throughout, the album lacks a strong secondary soloist, and the arrangements could have been better suited to the project. Nonetheless, *Jazz Cello* is an essential album for Ray Brown as it demonstrates his desire to create and display his originality while still recognizing the jazz tradition. Other notable bassists who picked up the cello include Sam Jones, Percy Heath, Dave Holland, and Mike

Richmond. Ron Carter also played cello, but in his case cello had been his first instrument before switching to bass.

On January 22, 1960 Ray Brown began recording his most exemplary big-band project resulting in the album *Ray Brown with the All-Star Big Band. Guest Soloist: Cannonball Adderley* (Verve V6-8444), and for which he enlisted some of the finest names in jazz: Nat Adderley, Joe Newman, Ernie Royal, and Clark Terry (trumpet); Jimmy Cleveland, Paul Faulise, Melba Liston, and Britt Woodman (trombone); Cannonball Adderley and Earl Warren (alto sax); Budd Johnson and Seldon Powell (tenor sax); Yusef Lateef (tenor sax and flute); Jerome Richardson (baritone sax and flute); Hank Jones (piano); Sam Jones (bass); and Osie Johnson (drums). The recordings were conducted and arranged by Ernie Wilkins and Al Cohn.

This first session had Ray Brown playing cello on "My One and Only Love," "Two for the Blues," and "Baubles, Bangles, and Beads." Ray Brown is nothing short of amazing in his melodic interpretations and improvisations, and having Cannonball and Nat Adderley as secondary soloists adds to the recordings' brilliance. The next day the band returned to record six more tracks to finish the record. Tommy Flanagan replaced Hank Jones on piano for this session, and bassist Sam Jones was no longer present as Ray Brown was on bass.

On the opening track, "Work Song," Ray Brown trades melodic statements with Cannonball Adderley and the orchestra to begin the piece. Wilkins' orchestration is on full display throughout the track, and both Adderley brothers are impressive on their solos. After the alto and trumpet solos, Brown is featured with only the light accompaniment of Osie Johnson's cymbal before several other members of the band filter into the background. The piece concludes with a high-energy interlude and outro chorus. This track is a career highlight for Ray Brown. Track 2 is an uptempo swing piece titled "It All Happened in Monterey," a notable moment on which is when Brown and Cannonball Adderley play a written unison solo. What follows is an impressive version of the ballad "My One and Only Love" as cello vehicle. Next, Brown is featured on Oscar Pettiford's technical masterpiece "Tricrotism," a showcase piece for the bass which Brown would perform frequently.

Side B begins with the Ray Brown original "Thumb String," named for his use of an advanced right-hand technique that involves strumming chords with his thumb. The second track is another Brown original called "Cannon Bilt," a medium swing which begins with Brown trading melodic statements with the orchestra in a similar way to on "Work Song." Next up is the cello feature "Two for the Blues," which, unsurprisingly, is a blues, performed and arranged in the Basie style but with the jazz cello taking center stage. Nat Adderley's solo is particularly inspiring. A tight arrangement on the medium uptempo standard "Day In Day Out" sees both Cannonball Adderley and Ray Brown foregrounded for short solo statements. The final track is a cello interpretation of "Baubles, Bangles, and Beads," on which Brown is again engaged in a call-and-response with the orchestra. The song is a showpiece for Ernie

Wilkins' skills as an arranger and is characterized by a strong swing feel with solid solo statements by Ray Brown and Cannonball Adderley. In sum, *Ray Brown with the All-Star Big Band* is a masterwork and must be considered one of the all-time finest bass (and cello) player-led albums as well as one of the outstanding big-band albums of the 1960s. For several years to come, Ray continued to be heard on jazz cello although he never found an opportunity to use it with the Oscar Peterson Trio.

A mystery "unissued" Ray Brown session with "others" is listed on the Verve catalog for February 11, 1963. It references two tracks, "Etude" and "I Know You So Well." It would be interesting to hear these cuts; however, with so much recorded Ray Brown material available, there seems to be little interest in unearthing unissued material.

On October 28 and 29, 1963 Ray Brown reunited with ex-wife Ella Fitzgerald for an New York City blues session with Roy Eldridge on trumpet, Herb Ellis on guitar, Wild Bill Davis on organ – adding a gospel quality to the recordings – and drummer Gus Johnson. From 1945 to 1949, Wild Bill Davis worked in Chicago as a member of Louis Jordan's Tympany Five, a popular jump blues group often credited for bridging jazz music and early rock and roll before residing on the East Coast in the 1950s, frequently performing in New York and Atlantic City.

If there was one familiar criticism of Ella Fitzgerald early on, it was that she lacked the traditional blues spirit that characterized vocalists like Bessie Smith and Billie Holiday. With the release of these tracks, which appeared on the album *These Are the Blues* (Verve V6-4062), Ella proved that she *could* sing the blues with authenticity and with the spirit of the style. Brown is featured as a soloist on "You Don't Know My Mind," capturing the blues spirit in his one-chorus improvisation. Coming out of the solo, Fitzgerald sings the line, "He said he didn't want me, I wasn't good enough." Once again, one can't help wondering if blues lyrics like these held any poignancy for Brown and Fitzgerald, given their past relationship.

On December 18, 1963, Ray Brown connected with pianist André Previn, Herb Ellis, and Shelly Manne in a Hollywood studio to record the album *4 to Go!* (Columbia CS 8818). Previn was a famed German American pianist, composer, and conductor who must be regarded as one of the most gifted musicians of the twentieth century. He first found fame as an arranger and composer for Metro-Goldwyn-Mayer's film works. He also conducted the London Symphony Orchestra, the Pittsburgh Symphony Orchestra, the Los Angeles Philharmonic, the Royal Philharmonic, and the Oslo Philharmonic.

Few classical musicians could convincingly cross over from classical performance to jazz, mainly because classically trained musicians are intensively trained to reproduce written music with precision, leaving little room for improvisation. But Previn was among the few equally comfortable with classical and jazz idioms. Throughout *4 to Go!* Previn reveals that not only can he sound authentic as a jazz pianist but could also be highly creative and forward-looking. The juxtaposition of Previn with Ray Brown, Herb Ellis, and Shelly Manne makes for an impressive line-up.

The group performs several standards on the record, with each member providing an original composition. Herb Ellis offers a funky blues, "Life Is a Ball," with a unison head between himself and Brown before eventually settling into a hard swing. Shelly Manne contributes "Intersection," with shifting time feels and a modal interlude. Previn's "Don't Sing Along" is equally brilliant in demonstrating the group's ability to move comfortably between rhythmic feels and accents. Previn's playing throughout the tune is imaginative and modernistic. Ray Brown offered his composition "I Know You Oh So Well," on which he presents the melody before giving way to Previn on the bridge. For the standards, the group reinterprets "No Moon at All," "Bye Bye Blackbird," "It's Easy to Remember," "You're Impossible," and "Oh, What a Beautiful Mornin.'" *4 to Go!* ranks as one of Ray Brown's finest recordings of the era.

Ray Brown began his 1964 studio activities as a co-leader of a quintet with Milt Jackson, resulting in the ambitious album Ray Brown/Milt Jackson, *Much in Common* (Verve V6-8580), recorded at A&R Studios in New York over two dates. The first session on January 13 included Wild Bill Davis on organ, Kenny Burrell on guitar, Albert "Tootie" Heath on drums, and famed gospel vocalist Marion Williams and saw the unit performing gospel and spirituals. On January 14, Hank Jones replaced Bill Davis and Williams did not participate.

Much in Common begins with Ray Brown delivering the melody on his original title track; there are well-played solos by Kenny Burrell and Bill Davis before Brown takes center stage as a soloist. For the second cut, Brown introduces "When the Saints Go Marching In" with a short bass intro before Marion Williams' spirited vocals and Jackson's solo. The third track, "I'm Going to Live the Life I Sing About," is a vocal showcase which truly captures the gospel spirit. Track 4 is the Ray Brown slow blues "Gravy Blues," with Brown and Jackson trading solos. Side A concludes with an uptempo version of the famous spiritual "Swing Low, Sweet Chariot," sung by Williams.

Side B begins with Ray Brown stating the melody on the classic "What Kind of Fool Am I?" Milt Jackson and Hank Jones take solos before Brown interprets the final theme. Marion Williams returns for the next track, a moving interpretation of "Sometimes I Feel Like a Motherless Child," followed by "Just for the Thrill," a Milt Jackson feature. The ballad "Nancy (with a Smiling Face) comes next and features Milt Jackson and Ray Brown as soloists. The album concludes with Williams presenting a short uptempo version of "Give Me That Old Time Religion." The album is a little disjointed conceptually with its blend of standards and gospel vocals. Separating the more standard tracks from the gospel numbers might have given the album more cohesion.

From August 31 through September 5, 1964 Ray Brown recorded with Sammy Davis Jr. and the Count Basie Orchestra in New York. He was paired with a rhythm section of Count Basie (piano), Freddie Green (guitar), Sonny

Payne (drums), and Emil Richards (percussion). Handling the arrangements were Quincy Jones and George Rhodes. The sessions led to the album Sammy Davis and Count Basie, *Our Shining Hour* (Verve V6-8605). With his ability to sing, dance, and act, Sammy Davis Jr., "Mr. Showbusiness," was one of America's most beloved entertainers throughout the mid-twentieth century. At this time, arranger Quincy Jones was beginning to establish himself as one of the most influential figures in the music industry. Jones and Ray Brown eventually formed a business relationship critical to both men's success. While he is not prominently featured on the record, Ray Brown's bass is recorded clearly on *Our Shining Hour*. His hookup with the rhythm section is solid and characteristic of the swinging "Basie sound." The most interesting track is "Bill Basie Won't You Please Come Home," where Sammy Davis can be heard tap-dancing with the band.

Ray Brown began 1965 in New York City, where he embarked on another studio collaboration with Milt Jackson, on January 4–5. For this recording, Brown and Jackson were featured in a big band that included Ernie Royal, Clark Terry, and Snooky Young (trumpet); Jimmy Cleveland and Urbie Green (trombone); Jimmy Heath, Jerome Richardson, and Phil Woods (reeds); Hank Jones (piano); and Grady Tate (drums). The album was arranged by Oliver Nelson and Jimmy Heath, two of the most gifted jazz arrangers on the scene. These recordings would result in the Verve release *Ray Brown/Milt Jackson* (Verve V6-8615).

Ray Brown provides two original compositions for the album, including the medium-tempo original "Lined with a Groove," which serves as a showcase for Ray Brown and Clark Terry. The second of his compositions is "Just Can't Fool Myself," a bluesy swing with a fine arrangement. Two of the more memorable cuts on the album are the hard-swinging "Now Hear My Meaning" by Jimmy Woods and the more subdued "In a Crowd" by John Lewis. Although the album does little to push the boundaries of jazz, as bassist/bandleader Charles Mingus was doing at the time, it is always a treat to hear an album that features a bassist of incredible skill. Indeed, by 1965 it was clear that Ray Brown had many talents and ambitions that extended beyond his role as the bassist of the Oscar Peterson Trio.

19 Commercial Studio Efforts 1966–1969

Ray Brown's career contacts came out of a combination of good timing and a strong reputation. While Brown was forced to make on-the-fly decisions in his early days, he thought and planned long and hard before leaving the Oscar Peterson Trio and moving to Los Angeles in 1966. One of the many professional connections he had made during his years and travels with JATP and the Peterson trio was the popular film and studio composer Henry Mancini. Whenever Ray Brown was in LA with the Peterson trio, Mancini would call on him to do various commercial recordings and studio dates. He was assured by Mancini, and others, that he could find steady work in Los Angeles if he relocated.

After eighteen years on the road with JATP and Peterson, he was ready for something more relaxed. Wisely, he ensured he was prepared, both financially and mentally, before relocating to the West Coast. In *DownBeat*, Brown admitted to Leonard Feather, "I had prepared myself that in the event that I didn't work for six months, we [he and Cecilia] could still eat." In the event, he was over-prepared because he found work immediately in LA. He explains:

> Prior to me moving to California, there were very few Blacks playing in the studios. Benny Carter and Buddy Collette had led the way, and everyone had gotten used to Black guys in those orchestras. I had arrived there at a good time because all the studios had just gotten rid of their permanent orchestras. For years every studio had its own orchestra with the musicians and staff arrangers on one-year contracts, and they played whatever music was required for each picture that was made. When I came to California, it marked the beginning of a new era when lots of jazz guys started doing movie music and interesting stuff.[130]

Throughout the mid to late 1960s, Brown appeared nightly with studio orchestras on television shows hosted by popular entertainers including the Smothers Brothers, Pat Boone, Merv Griffith, Steve Allen, Joey Bishop, Frank Sinatra, and Red Skelton. He would also play on non-jazz-related pop recordings. His consistent studio activities linked him with the "Wrecking Crew," although he is rarely listed as a member. The "Wrecking Crew" is a name given to a group of Los Angeles-based session musicians heavily active in the 1960s and '70s. Most of the players were solid readers and had jazz or classical backgrounds. Other upright bassists in the crew were Red Callender, Jimmy Bond, Chuck Berghofer, and Lyle Ritz.

Brown supplemented his many playing engagements with other music business activities, such as managing Quincy Jones and the Modern Jazz Quartet. He started a publishing company, *Ray Brown Music*, and released instructional materials, including his book *Ray Brown's Bass Method*, and sheet music. Later, he released a three-part series of instructional videotapes called *The Art of the Bass*, which featured Brown with prominent bassists like Milt Hinton, Jeff Clayton, and François Rabbath. He was also becoming more active as a teacher, privately and at the University of California. Within a short period, he proved himself a significant force in a city full of superstars. While many jazz artists of his generation had difficulty finding work, Brown flourished.

By 1966, Ray Brown was working more than ever, and his bass was being heard on everything from commercial jingles to film scores, television shows, and albums by a wide range of artists. He was not always credited on session dates so many of his commercial efforts during this time remain a mystery. Still, if you went to the movies, watched television, or listened to the radio, it would have been nearly impossible not to hear Ray Brown. David Meeker's book *Jazz in the Movies*[131] and various web sources offer several titles in which the bassist participated; in some cases, he is even given credit as a composer. Some of the more famous television and film projects Brown played on included the television theme songs to *Mission Impossible, Mannix,* and the movie *Husbands*. He later wrote music for *The Bill Cosby Show, Sanford and Sons,* and *Ironside*. At some point during this time, he even purchased an electric bass to increase his studio adaptability.

Much of Brown's session work came from Henry Mancini and Quincy Jones. Mancini is generally recognized as one of the most successful film composers, having won over twenty Grammy awards, including a Lifetime Achievement Award. He has also been celebrated with four Academy Awards and a Golden Globe. Mancini was also an extremely popular recording artist from 1960 to 1980, dominating the "easy listening" genre.

On February 21–22, 1966 Ray Brown was in the studio with Mancini to work on the album *Mancini '67: The Big Band Sound of Henry Mancini* (RCA Victor LSP 3694). Here, besides his original "Turtles," Mancini arranged material by other composers, with his arrangements paying tribute to the commercial 1940s swing bands of Glenn Miller, Tommy Dorsey, Jimmy Dorsey, and Artie Shaw. Joining Ray in the rhythm section were pianist Jimmy Rowles, drummer Jack Sperling, with Larry Bunker on vibes, Bob Bain on guitar, and Milt Holland on percussion. Highlights include "Satin Doll," "Autumn Nocturne," "The House of the Rising Sun," and "Cherokee."

Between February 12 and 14 of 1968 Brown recorded again for Mancini for the soundtrack to the comedy film *The Party* (RCA Victor LSP-3997). This soundtrack comprises various genres ranging from sultry ballads, jazz swing, vocal numbers, and funky grooves. The more groove-based material – "The Party," "Chicken Little Was Right," and "Birdie Num-Num" – undoubtedly inspired by James Brown's music, provides the most interest. Ray's only solo is at the end of the modern swing "Wiggy," where he plays a walking bass line solo. Also included in the recording band were frequent collaborators like Jimmy Rowles, Plas Johnson, Shelly Manne, and Larry Bunker. Due to the general loose nature of its acting, *The Party* has become a cult classic; however, by using "brownface" to portray an Indian character, actor Peter Sellers – and director Blake Edwards – attracted criticism.[132]

Another of the more recognizable movie projects was Mancini's soundtrack for *Peter Gunn*. It began as a popular television series, running from 1958 to 1961, notable for being the first televised detective program the main character of which was created specifically for television rather than being adapted from other media. In 1967, the film version was recorded and released, with music that is among Henry Mancini's most famous works. The soundtrack led to the release of the album *Gunn . . . Number One!* (RCA Victor LSP 3840). Mancini essentially updated music from the original series for the soundtrack, and these adaptations included a degree of jazz improvisation. Along with Ray Brown, his ensemble for this project included saxophonists Ted Nash, Bud Shank, and Plas Johnson, trumpeter Pete Candoli, trombonist Dick Nash, pianist Jimmy Rowles, drummer Shelly Manne, guitarist Bob Bain, and vibraphonist Larry Bunker. Ray Brown is only briefly foregrounded on "A Quiet Happening" during a final solo cadenza and on the intro of "I Like the Look."

Another Mancini recording from this period (1969) was *Six Hours Past Sunset* (RCA Victor LSP-4239), a smooth and heavily orchestrated effort that showcases Mancini as a pianist. One of the more notable aspects of his piano style is the laid-back phrasing that blends classical and jazz elements. Ray Brown is mainly situated in the background of this album.

The other major avenue for film work was Quincy Jones, and the most successful recording on which Ray Brown took part in 1967 was Jones's soundtrack to the murder mystery *In the Heat of the Night* (United Artists Records UAS 5160), a movie starring Sidney Poitier and Rod Steiger which collected five Academy Awards, including Best Picture and Best Actor (Steiger). The music was composed, arranged, and conducted by Quincy Jones and won a Grammy award for Best Soundtrack. Along with Ray Brown, a host of outstanding musicians from different genres participated in the recording, including Don Elliott (trumpet, mellophone, vocals, and bongos); Bud Shank (reeds); Roland Kirk (flute); Bobby Scott (piano); Billy Preston (organ); Glen Campbell (guitar and banjo); Carol Kaye (electric bass); and Earl Palmer (drums).

The most famed song was the title track, "In the Heat of the Night," sung by Ray Charles, which reached number thirty-three on the *Billboard* Hot 100 chart and number twenty-one on the Hot Rhythm and Blues Singles chart. Ray Charles, considered an American treasure as a vocalist and pianist, incorporated gospel, jazz, blues, and rhythm and blues. Also deserving of special praise is Roland Kirk, whose flute playing is featured throughout the soundtrack. Like Ray Charles, Kirk was a blind musician with lofty goals and ambitions. Mainly a jazz performer, the outspoken Kirk played multiple reed and wind instruments and, remarkably, could play up to three at once. His recordings and performances throughout the 1960s and '70s place him among the most inspirational jazz musicians of the second half of the twentieth century.

Another Quincy Jones production that including Ray Brown was the album Quincy Jones and Bill Cosby, *The Original Jam Sessions 1969* (Concord Records CCD-2257-2), recorded between July and September 1969. On this album was the backing music for *The Bill Cosby Show* which aired for two seasons as part of NBC's Sunday night schedule from 1969 until 1971. *The Original Jam Session 1969* represents some of the funkiest upright bass playing heard on record, prime examples being "Hikky-Burr," "Groovy Gravy," and "Jive Den." Equally impressive are the contemporary swing tracks "Oh Happy Day" and "Toe Jam," on both of which Brown solos and on which we hear a bass sound that has changed dramatically. The normal woody tone is replaced by something more amplified, a sound that became associated with many jazz upright players of the late 1960s and early '70s. This recording is also notable because it may have been the first time Jamaican-born pianist Monty Alexander and Ray Brown recorded together. The two would collaborate frequently over the next twenty years.

Although the session list is somewhat vague, Ray Brown played on at least one track for Jones's 1969 soundtrack of the crime film *Lost Man* (UNI Records 73060). On the album's liner notes the bassist is only listed as playing on the final track, "End Title," but he likely played on other tracks as well.

In addition to the film projects, Ray Brown played bass for Quincy Jones's studio album *Walking in Space* (A&M Records SP-9-3023). Recorded between June 18 and 19, 1969, the album includes another mix of fine guest musicians, including such stars as Freddie Hubbard, Roland Kirk, Hubert Laws, Jerome Richardson, J.J. Johnson, Kai Winding, Bernard Purdie, Toots Thielemans, Bob James, and Eric Gale.

On the album's opening track, "Dead End," Brown plays a short unaccompanied solo. The second track, "Walking in Space," like "Dead End," comes from the famous 1968 anti-war musical *Hair*, and Brown begins the twelve-minutes-plus piece. He delivers a busy and groove-based bass line before switching to a walking bass line during solos by Roland Kirk, Freddie Hubbard, Bob James, Eric Gale, and others. The track also features vocalist Valerie Simpson from the famed 1960s group Ashford and Simpson. "Dead End" and "Walking into Space" take up the entire first side of the record.

Side B begins with the classic "Killer Joe." Brown plays the famed ostinato bass line on the double bass, and Chuck Rainey doubles on the electric bass. At times, Brown provides solo fills, momentarily breaking from the written line. Rainey and Brown both play on the next track, "Love and Peace," a bluesy jam showcasing the skilled Eric Gale on guitar. The spacious Johnny Mandel composition "I Never Told You" features Toots Thielemans playing the melody on harmonica. The album concludes with the funky "Oh Happy Day," with what sounds like Chuck Rainey playing an impressive bass line. *Walking in Space* may be best classified as a fusion album, mixing as it does jazz and rock influences and musicians.

Other film projects from this period included a remarkable pairing with North Indian sitar virtuoso Ravi Shankar for the 1968 movie *Charly* (World Pacific Records WPS 21454), a science fiction film starring Cliff Robertson, who plays a character whose intelligence is enhanced through an experimental surgical procedure. Robertson was awarded Best Actor for the film at the Academy Awards. *Charly* represents yet another impactful Hollywood project in which Ray Brown was involved in some small part.

Along with film and television projects, Ray Brown was called upon as a hired hand to perform with some famed singers. Among his session recordings in 1968 are two hit albums by renowned blind Puerto Rican acoustic guitarist and singer José Feliciano: *Feliciano!* (RCA Victor LSP 3957) and *Souled* (RCA Victor LSP 4045). That year, on October 7, Feliciano became a counterculture icon when he performed "The Star-Spangled Banner" during game five of the Major League World Series. His Latin reinterpretation of the anthem was controversial and was understood as a protest against the Vietnam War. Feliciano has since expressed pride in opening the door for other artists who would later attempt their own interpretations of the nation's anthem. Eventually released as a single, his recording of "The Star-Spangled Banner" is now on permanent exhibit in the Baseball Hall of Fame.

The first of the two, *Feliciano!*, was his most successful U.S. album, peaking at number two on the *Billboard* charts. All the tracks are acoustic interpretations of songs by other artists, with his version of the Doors' "Light My Fire" the breakout hit. *Feliciano!* was nominated for Best Album of the Year at the 1969 Grammy Awards, and José Feliciano won the Best New Artist award and Best Pop Male Song of the Year for the track. Alongside Ray Brown on the recording are flutist Jim Horn and percussionist Milt Holland. On the follow-up album *Souled*, Feliciano reinterprets hit songs by Bob Dylan, John Sebastian, Harry Nilsson, and the Bee Gees. The biggest hit from the album was a cover of Tommy Tucker's "Hi-Heel Sneakers." *Feliciano!* and *Souled* might rank as the most listened-to albums Ray Brown participated in. Although primarily situated in the background, Ray Brown's bass is most present in Feliciano's version of the Beatles' "In My Life" from the *Feliciano!* album.

Aiming to match his 1968 successes, in 1969 José Feliciano released the album *10 to 23* (RCA Victor LSP 4185), for which he once again employed Ray Brown to play bass. While it is difficult to be sure, it sounds as if Brown plays some electric bass on the album. The album didn't enjoy the same success as its pedecessors but there are some powerful tracks, including covers of "Little Red Rooster," "Lady Madonna," and "Hey Jude," on which Feliciano displays his remarkable ability as a guitarist. Unfortunately, being over-saturated with strings, some of the material has not dated well.

James Brown was the musician who most influenced Black America in the late 1960s; and Ray Brown could not have been immune to his effect. Through his exceptionally tight uptempo rhythmic music, the "Godfather of Soul" lays claim to have invented funk in the late 1960s, and consistently topped the R&B charts. His 1968 hit "Say it Loud – I'm Black and I'm Proud" served as an anthem for Black youth nationwide. On November 10–11, 1969 James Brown and an eighteen-piece jazz orchestra, which included Ray Brown, recorded his twenty-eighth studio album, James Brown with the Louie Bellson Orchestra, Oliver Nelson Conducting, *Soul on Top* (King Records KS1100), on which we hear James Brown singing standards and big-band arrangements of his past hits. On this record, released in April 1970, Oliver Nelson's arrangements are perfect, and James Brown's voice is remarkable. It contains some of Ray Brown's best electric bass, highlights being "Your Cheating Heart," "It's a Man's, Man's, Man's World," "The Man in the Glass," "September Song," "I Need Your Key (To Turn Me On), "Papa's Got a Brand New Bag," and "There Was a Time."[133]

There are undoubtedly dozens more recordings by known artists to which Ray Brown contributed but sidemen/studio musicians are not always credited. A deep dive into session indexes would be required to discover the entire personnel working on a given album. For example, in his book *Nilsson: The Life of a Singer-Songwriter*, author Alyn Shipton reveals that Ray Brown is playing on "Sleep Late My Lady Friend" on the album *Pandemonium Shadow Show* (RCA Victor LPM-3874), and yet he is not named as a contributor on the original LP sleeve.

During this period, Ray Brown was also part of several studio projects that fall into the "easy listening" bracket, a label given to music made to be accessible and not challenging. One such album is the Alan Copeland Singers, *Cool Country* (1966; ABC Records ABCS-583), a commercial effort pairing studio jazz instrumentalists such as Herb Ellis, Barney Kessel, Harry "Sweets" Edison, and Victor Feldman with the commercial singing group of noted Los Angeles composer and conductor Alan Copeland and his vocal ensemble. The album mainly includes American folk, country, and cowboy songs.

In 1967, Brown was also included on the album the Bob Florence Big Band, *Pet Project* (World Pacific Records WP-1860), which contains twelve commercial jazz arrangements of songs made famous by Petula Clark. Clark was a British vocalist and television personality who had a string of popular hits in the 1960s. Florence was an incredibly gifted arranger, and the songs lend themselves well to a big-band context. Brown can be heard most clearly on "Goin' Out of My Head," Call Me," and "You're the One."

Another commercial release from 1967 was a little-known album called Jimmy Haskell's French Horns, *When Love is Young* (Dot Records DLP-3806). Like Henry Mancini and Bob Florence, Haskell's music was also often filed under "easy listening." He was mainly known as a film composer and worked with various genre-crossing artists such as Ricky Nelson, Elvis Presley, Blondie, and Sheryl Crow. Ray Brown played on portions of the album.

In 1968, Brown was included on the album *Contemporary Sound of Nelson Riddle* (United Artists Records UAS-6670). A well-known arranger, composer, and conductor, Riddle worked primarily with vocalists, including Frank Sinatra, Ella Fitzgerald, Nat King Cole, Dean Martin, and Judy Garland. Like Henry Mancini, Nelson Riddle was celebrated for his work in film and television, wimnning three Grammy awards and an Academy Award. Ray Brown is credited as sharing bass duties with Lyle Ritz and Max Bennett, and it is unclear on which tracks he plays.

20 Jazz Efforts
1966–1969

Although much of Ray Brown's activity was taken up with commercial projects, he was quickly assimilated into the unique California jazz scene. While New York remained the cultural center for jazz in the late 1960s, California had its own particular jazz history. Jazz artists and fans sometimes see the California scene as a relaxing alternative to New York's high energy and quick pace. Numerous jazz artists from the Pacific Coast performed in a style in which melodicism, sound textures, and composition were central. Drummers especially played with a more relaxed touch and focused more on coloration than hard-swinging rhythmic intensity. Jazz audiences that were uncomfortable with bebop's fiery rhythms appreciated this "cool" approach, as purveyed by artists such as Gerry Mulligan, Chet Baker, Stan Getz, Dave Brubeck, Jimmy Giuffre, and Cal Tjader. However, by the mid-1960s, jazz of all stripes was fading in popularity, and jazz artists were increasingly seduced by the financial rewards of studio work.

Ray Brown would never abandon jazz, but by no longer being attached to a working group like the Oscar Peterson Trio, he could branch out into a variety of jazz projects. As the popularity of traditional jazz artists was waning in the mid-1960s, new approaches to jazz music began to surface. Experimentalists such as John Coltrane, Cecil Taylor, and Ornette Coleman attracted attention by breaking down the fundamental rhythmic and harmonic sequences associated with swing and experimenting with modality, free improvisation, and avant-garde ideas. Others experimented with taped sound effects. It was clear that Ray Brown had difficulty coming to grips with these innovations.

For the March 10, 1966 issue of *DownBeat*, Ray Brown was invited onto the popular "Blindfold Test" column and asked to comment on some new, more modern recordings. As the name implies, he was given no information on the recordings before the test. In the piece he expresses his dissatisfaction with recent trends in jazz. These are his comments on Charles Lloyd's "Apex":[134]

> I have a mixed reaction about the chart. I like the way it started off – the original line is fine, but they seemed to get a little away from the structure there for a while. This doesn't bother me, but it is something I've wondered about . . . I haven't played in any of the so-called outside groups, and I wonder if the idea is to play a composed line, a melody line,

and then go outside. I'm just wondering why not start outside and stay outside? Because then you don't have to worry . . . And when they start getting away from it, I have a tendency to think, "oh-oh, they're blowing it." Which is maybe what they want to do . . . They left the structure there for a while, especially when the bass was doing the thing there with the drums. It could have been an interlude; I couldn't tell from the chord structure at all. The saxophone player . . . I don't know . . . had a strange sound. It's the sound of today – is what I mean . . . Personally, I'd like to have seen a few more choruses go by, like the first few they had after the melody line. I'd say about three stars.

And these his comments on Bob James's "Explosions":[135]

Well, let me say first, that's one record you'll never hear in my house! No chance of hearing that at my pad! And if you hear it, I won't be there . . . I figure you're after me when you play that record. You're taking a shot at me for some reason . . . I don't have anything to say about that. I can't say anything, especially about that. I can't say anything categorically about it, because it doesn't fit into anything for me, and I want to be truthful – I just can't hear it. It's beyond me. It's not beyond me technically or harmonically, but it is still beyond me, simply because it represents some type of music which I don't understand. When it first started out, it sounded like background for a Dracula movie or something. No stars.

While acknowledging that music will often frustrate our attempts to classify it into one or other genre, this chapter intends to concentrate on Ray Brown's jazz output. For our purpose, a jazz recording will be defined as one that was conceived with the understanding that a broad, mainstream audience would likely not respond to it, but was instead targeted at the niche audience that comprised jazz listeners. Ray Brown's jazz recordings can be further subdivided into instrumental, live, and vocal.

An early studio engagement in 1966 was a large-group session on March 2 with Benny Carter for his upcoming album *Additions to Further Definitions* (Impulse! AS-9116), a follow-up to his celebrated 1962 release *Further Definitions* (Impulse! AS-12-S). *Additions to Further Definitions*, primarily a traditional swing big-band record, is a vehicle for Carter's alto saxophone playing and demonstrates his skills as a writer and arranger. Brown, who takes a short bop-style solo on "Fantastic, That's You" teamed up here with several past associates: Bud Shank (alto sax); Buddy Collette, Teddy Edwards, and Bill Perkins (tenor sax); Bill Hood (baritone sax); Don Abney (piano); Barney Kessel and Mundell Lowe (guitar); and Alvin Stoller (drums).

Ray Brown remained rooted in more mainstream jazz tastes and values, and rarely strayed from them. His closest attempt at a more open experimental style can be heard on Jack Wilson's album *Something Personal* (Blue Note BST-84251), with Roy Ayers on vibes, Varney Barlow on drums, and Buster Williams on bass and recorded on August 9 and 10, 1966. Here we are treated to more exploratory playing from Ray, on both cello and bass. The album's opening track, a Wilson original, "Most Unsoulful Women," is a modal tune with an unusual ten-bar form and the eighth bar written in a 6/4 time signature. Brown's cello solo against Buster Williams' bass line has a searching quality, and even the most discerning listeners would struggle to guess that they were listening to Ray Brown. The second track, "The Sphinx," credited to free jazz pioneer Ornette Coleman, has an unusual construction: the melodic theme is a seven-bar phrase in which the fifth bar shifts to a 7/4 time signature. Brown again soloes on cello on this fast-tempo tune, and once again the modernism is uncharacteristic of his normal style.

One of the most impressive of Ray Brown's 1966 studio efforts was a September 27 and 28 session with Oliver Nelson for his Impulse! album *Sound Pieces* (Impulse! AS-9129). Although he's not heard on the entire album, Brown plays on an incredibly advanced through-arranged and heavily orchestrated Nelson original called "Sound Pieces for Jazz Orchestra," as well as "Flute Salad" and "The Lady from Girl Talk." Throughout the 1960s, Oliver Nelson not only drew attention for his arranging and saxophone playing but was one of the finest writers of original and forward-looking jazz. In the rhythm section with Brown are Shelly Manne and pianist Mike Melvoin.

Of the many musicians with whom Ray Brown collaborated during this period, saxophonist and flutist Bud Shank must be among the most significant. In December 1966, they recorded together on *Bud Shank and the Sax Section* (Pacific Jazz ST-20110), a solid example of the gifted jazz arrangements of Bob Florence, the group's performances of which make for a fine example of the "California cool" approach laid down in a Los Angeles studios. Highlights include "Summertime," "Take Five," and "I Love Her." The ensemble also included Bill Perkins (alto sax); Bob Cooper and Bob Hardaway (tenor sax); John Lowe and Jack Nimitz (baritone sax); Dennis Budimir (guitar); and Larry Bunker (drums).

The following year Brown recorded again with Shank for *Bud Shank Plays Music from Today's Movies* (World Pacific WP-1864). Shank continues to shine on the alto saxophone with an ensemble of Herb Ellis and Dennis Budimir (guitar); Jimmy Zito (flugelhorn); Mike Melvoin (organ and harpsichord); Frank Capp (drums); and Victor Feldman (vibraphone and percussion). This session was arranged and conducted by Bob Florence and included a studio orchestra. Of all the movie material recorded here, the Michel Legrand composition "Watch What Happens," from the French film *The Umbrellas of Cherbourg*, is the most recognizable today.

One of Shank's most outstanding and now rather overlooked albums is *Windmills of Your Mind: Bud Shank Plays the Music and Arrangements of Michel Legrand* (World Pacific Jazz ST-20157), a 1969 release offering a perfect blend of cool, modern, Latin, modal, and traditional jazz, perfectly arranged and performed. Joining Shank, Legrand, and Brown are Gary Barone, Bud Brisbois, and Conte Candoli (trumpet); Bill Byers (trombone);

Ernie Watts (tenor sax); Artie Kane (organ); Howard Roberts (guitar); and Shelly Manne (drums). Each track is of interest, with highlights including "De Delphine à Lancein," "Watch What Happens," and "Thème d'Elise." Brown and Shank would continue to perform and record together as members of the L.A. Four from 1972 to 1982.

One of Ray Brown's most notable sessions of this period was on February 12 and 13, 1969 for pianist Phineas Newborn Jr.'s album *Please Send Me Someone to Love* (Contemporary Records S7622). Newborn was one of the most skilled pianists of the mid-1950s and 1960s. In Len Lyons's book *The Great Jazz Pianists*, Oscar Peterson said, "If I had to choose the best all-around pianist of anyone who's followed me chronologically, unequivocally . . . I would say Phineas Newborn, Jr."[136] Like Peterson, Newborn Jr. was often criticized for being too technical, and the criticism damaged his fragile psyche and led to several stays at Camarillo State Psychiatric Hospital. He also had physical issues, which included an injured hand, and his output was limited throughout his active years from the mid-1960s till his death at fifty-seven in 1989.

Joining Brown on *Please Send Me Someone to Love* is drummer Elvin Jones, the brother of Thad Jones and Hank Jones. From 1960 to 1966, Elvin Jones came to prominence as a member of John Coltrane's quartet and gained a reputation as one of jazz's most accomplished and energetic drummers. Hearing Brown play in this trio format is a joy. Highlights from the album are the gospel-flavored title track and "Brentwood Blues." The hookup between Brown and the highly gifted Jones is particularly interesting, especially since Jones's long-form experimental playing and recordings are very much in contrast to Ray Brown's more mainstream output.

The same recording date also yielded another fine album – *Harlem Blues* (Contemporary Records GP-3015) – but, for unknown reasons, Contemporary Records held it back from release until 1975. The album begins with the soulful "Harlem Blues" – which is a renaming of "Gravy Waltz" – and also includes the Ray Brown and Gil Fuller classic "Ray's Idea." Brown is most impressive in his nearly three-and-a-half-minute unaccompanied opening statement on "Tenderly," where he proffers a heavily embellished variation on the melody showing his dexterity, fluidity, and imagination. The album's fast-paced closing track, "Cookin' at the Continental," fully demonstrates Newborn's ability to play rapid unison lines with both hands, a prominent feature of his playing. *Please Send Someone to Love* and *Harlem Blues* are both great trio documents and deserving of praise.

On May 13 and 14, 1968 Brown was involved in some of the recording of jazz organ master Jimmy Smith's *Livin' It Up!* (Verve V6-8750). Also listed on the session is electric bassist and renowned session musician Carol Kaye. Jimmy Smith was one of the most popular and consistently recorded jazz artists of the 1960s, regarded as the most influential jazz organist and an essential name in the "soul-jazz" movement. Oliver Nelson arranged the album, and the group also had Howard Roberts on guitar and Larry Bunker on drums. Brown is heard clearly in "Refractions," "The Gentle Rain," "Go Away Little Girl," "Livin' It Up," and "This Nearly Was Mine." The music on *Livin' It Up!* varies between hard-driving soul, blues, and jazz and commercial pop. Regardless of the genre he's working with, Jimmy Smith is remarkable. Ray Brown handles his role perfectly, and frees Smith, who was used to playing in smaller-group formats where he provided the bass notes on the organ, to focus more on the shape and directions of his melodic lines.

One of the strongest complete album projects Ray Brown was involved with during 1968 was an album for Willie Ruff called *The Smooth Side of Ruff* (Columbia CS-9603). Willie Ruff was a fine French horn player who also played double bass. Before the release, Ruff had worked with Miles Davis, Gil Evans, Benny Golson, Quincy Jones, Leonard Cohen, among others, and had also recorded as a co-leader with pianist Dwike Mitchell in the duo Mitchell and Ruff. The legendary John Hammond produced *The Smooth Side of Ruff* as a vehicle for Ruff's versatility as a French horn player, vocalist, and guitarist. Alongside Ray were Ed Thigpen, guitarist Howard Roberts, and Emil Richards on vibes. The album encompasses several styles, including Latin, soul, and jazz.

The Smooth Side of Ruff is an excellent representation of the late 1960s sound, and Brown is well represented on songs like "Sheffield Blues," where he offers an unaccompanied intro to begin the record. On "Mirage Blanc," an ominous-sounding ballad, Brown bows long notes throughout. On "Slim," he plays a groove-based, Latin-flavored, ostinato-style bass line against heavy percussion and Ruff's speech-like vocal styling. The closing track, "Bella Pulcinella," has shifting time feels and a bass solo. It is regrettable that Willie Ruff didn't make more albums in the same vein. From 1971 to 2017, he was a Music Professor at Yale, where he taught ensembles and helped establish the Duke Ellington Fellowship Program. *The Smooth Side of Ruff* is one of the more exemplary late-1960s albums to include Ray Brown.

While he was involved in several exciting projects in 1969, the most notable for Ray Brown enthusiasts has to be the album Milt Jackson with the Ray Brown Big Band, *Memphis Jackson* (Impulse! AS-9193). Brown led his group for three sessions over two days, October 9 and 10, 1969. The tracks for the October 9 session list the following musicians: Milt Jackson (vibes); Ray Brown (conductor, bass); Bud Brisbois and Ollie Mitchell (trumpet); Harry Edison (trumpet, flugelhorn); Jimmy Cleveland (trombone); Kenny Shroyer (bass trombone); Jim Horn (alto sax, flute); Teddy Edwards (tenor sax); John Lowe (baritone sax); Mike Melvoin (electric piano); Fred Robinson (guitar); Wilton Felder (Fender bass); and Carl "Cubby" O'Brien (drums).

Three tracks were recorded on this first session, including Ray Brown's original "Picking Up the Vibrations." The song shifts from a slow soulful groove to a gospel-style funk. It sounds as if Wilton Felder is handling the bass duties on this piece. Another issued track from this early session is "Braddock Breakdown," another Brown original in which he plays funky upright bass before giving way to Felder on the electric bass. This piece has some tight horn lines and a seriously funky groove. The final track from the early session is a Jimmy Heath original, "A Sound for Sore Ears," which begins with a James Brown-influenced groove that perfectly blends soul, funk, and traditional jazz. Four more tracks were recorded on the same day with some line-up changes: John Audino and Buddy Childers (trumpet); Harry Edison (trumpet, flugelhorn); Randy Aldcroft (trombone); John T. Johnson (tuba); Ernie Watts (alto sax); Harold Land (tenor sax); Jim Horn (baritone sax); Mike Melvoin (piano, electric piano); Fred Robinson (guitar); Wilton Felder (Fender bass); and Earl Palmer (drums).

This second session began with "Oh Happy Day," which was arranged by Teddy Edwards. Brown opens the track with slow unaccompanied blues/funk bass lines on the upright. He can then be heard bowing as Felder lays down the groove. The next track is "One Mint Julep (One Way)," for which Brown and Dave Blumberg are credited as co-arrangers and on which Ray Brown handles the melody. Also included is a sequel, "One Mint Julep (The Other Way)," on which Brown plays the same melody but at a brighter tempo before shifting to a more traditional walking bass line during the solos. The same ensemble also recorded the album's opening track, "Uh-Huh," a Ray Brown original funk tune which sets the feel for the entire album, announcing that Ray Brown has decided to incorporate funk and soul into his repertoire. Bob Florence does a great job as an arranger on this piece.

The recordings for *Memphis Jackson* were completed on October 10 with a smaller group of Milt Jackson (vibes); Ray Brown (conductor, bass); Al Aarons (trumpet); Teddy Edwards (tenor sax); Joe Sample (electric piano); Howard Roberts and Fred Robinson (guitar); Wilton Felder (Fender bass); Paul Humphries (drums); and Victor Feldman (percussion). They recorded "Queen Mother Stomp" by Victor Feldman, as well as "Enchanted Lady" and "Memphis Junction" by Milt Jackson. Brown is listed as arranger on all three cuts, and each track offers more uptempo groove-based jazz and funk.

This album is Brown's most memorable large-group session as a leader from this period. It is an outstanding example of instrumental funk and shows Brown's willingness to change direction and get more with the times, especially when it came to funk, soul, and blues, although he still had little interest in free jazz or overdriven guitar rock. It would have been interesting to hear more albums from Ray Brown like *Memphis Jackson*.

There were also several live jazz releases, the most inspired from a January 1968 trio performance with Michel Legrand and Shelly Manne at Manne's Hollywood club, Shelly's Manne-Hole, on North Cahuenga Boulevard. The evening was captured for the album *Michel Legrand at Shelly's Manne-Hole* (Verve V6-8760).

Born in Paris, Michel Legrand was a man of considerable talent. He was a child piano prodigy who studied music at eleven with famed instructor Nadia Boulanger at the renowned Conservatoire de Paris. In the 1960s Legrand began to compose for film and television, eventually building a catalog of over 200 film and television scores. His work earned him three Oscars and five Grammy awards.

Although trained in the classical tradition, Legrand was a phenomenal and inventive jazz pianist who frequently performed and recorded in the genre. Hearing Legrand, Brown, and Manne together in this live context is an absolute treat; and, to judge by the laughter of the three men between tunes, you get the sense that the evening was filled with joy. It must have been a welcome change of pace for the men to work outside the recording studio's confines. Ray Brown is consistently foregrounded throughout the show.

It begins with "The Grand Brown Man," a song listed as being co-written by the trio although it feels more like a free-form jam. Much of the tune is played in the conversational style made famous by the Bill Evans Trio. Ray Brown plays a remarkable solo on this uptempo swing piece, vocalizing his line and matching the pitches. The second tune is the ballad "A Time for Love," where the bassist can be heard playing arco statements in the intro and outro. Still somewhat inconsistent in his higher-register intonation, Brown's final bowed statement is a bit "pitchy." Next up is "Ray's Riff;" true to its name, it begins with a riff played by Brown. Ray Brown is featured as a soloist on the track – with clear blues phrasing followed by a technical display of double-time bebop licks – and again vocalizes at times. The group follows with an interpretation of one of Legrand's most famed compositions, "Watch What Happens." Again, Brown bows long notes on the rubato intro before settling into a contrapuntal bass line which is both functional and conversational.

One of the most impressive presentations of the evening is "My Funny Valentine," which begins with a bass introduction displaying Brown's range, inventiveness, and overall spirit as a bassist. He then settles into a bass line that incorporates flawlessly performed double stops. Legrand joins as a vocalist, singing in a scat style with still only Brown's bass lines to accompany him. Singing turns out to be another of Legrand's talents, albeit lesser known. After some time, Legrand moves to the piano to solo before returning to his singing, ultimately concluding the piece in this way and trading solo statements with Brown. It's a magical moment, and their efforts are rewarded by solid applause. On both the following, "Another Blues" and "Willow Weep for Me," Brown again begins with unaccompanied solo statements. He is featured for a second time on "Willow Weep for Me" when the band drops out midway to afford him room to solo before he resets the groove to allow Legrand to return. The evening concludes with another jam-style original called "Los Gatos," which showcases Brown playing some lines in a minor key before shifting to a flamenco strumming style. *Michel Legrand at Shelly's Manne-Hole* contains some of Ray Brown's most experimental and technically impressive playing.

Another live 1968 recording saw light of day on *Jazz for a Sunday Afternoon, Volume 3: The West Coast Scene* (Solid State Records SS-18037). Here,

Brown is involved in a JATP-style all-star jam on the Thelonious Monk classic "Straight No Chaser." The track lasts over twenty minutes and sees Harry "Sweets" Edison and Bobby Bryant on trumpet, Carl Fontana and Frank Rosolino on trombone, Pete Christlieb and Harold Land on tenor saxophone, Victor Feldman on vibraphone, Tommy Flanagan on piano, and Ed Thigpen on drums. Although lengthy, the solos are inspired throughout, and Ray Brown and Ed Thigpen play with more fire than they generally did with Oscar Peterson's trio.

On August 1 and 2, 1969 Brown was again recorded live at Shelly's Manne-Hole, this time with an ensemble of Milt Jackson on vibes, Teddy Edwards on tenor sax, Monty Alexander on piano, and Dick Berk on drums. The result was the Milt Jackson Quartet Featuring Ray Brown, *That's the Way It Is* (Impulse! AS-9189). The show begins with Brown playing the melody on a boogie-woogie-style version of "Frankie and Johnny" before giving way to Edwards, Jackson, and Alexander. After their solos, Brown returns to the theme, and the crowd responds with light laughter. Another highlight is a Ray Brown original called "Blues in the Basement," which begins with an unaccompanied Ray Brown introduction in which he plays some perfectly in-tune chorded figures and a bluesy melody. Once again, the audience responds favorably. Brown's most extended feature is his solo arrangement on the ballad "Tenderly," a tune he continued to use as a solo vehicle, and his many interpretations of which demonstrate his prowess as a jazz improviser. *That's The Way It Is* shows a musician who can still impress without studio trickery or lavish arrangements.

During this period, Ray Brown was also appeared with vocalists who were either known as jazz vocalists or incorporated jazz elements into their repertoire. Brown's first known date of 1966 was a big-band studio project for the smooth-voiced singer Johnny Hartman for the album *Unforgettable Songs* (ABC-Paramount ABCS-547).[137] The session dates to only a few days after his Los Angeles arrival, between February 15 and 18. Brown can be heard playing on the tracks "Biding My Time," "Down in the Depths," "The More I See You," and "What Do I Owe Her." Drummer Stan Levy is on here too, his old bandmate from his days with Charlie Parker and Dizzy Gillespie.

In May of 1966, Brown recorded with a Hollywood nightclub singer named Ruth Olay for her album *Soul in the Night* (ABC Records ABCS-573). The ensemble also includes guitarists Herb Ellis and Al Hendrickson, with Victor Feldman on piano and vibraphone. The absence of drums brings Ray Brown to the forefront. *Soul in the Night* gives us a gifted singer with a great ensemble on highlights such as "I Loves You Porgy," "Willow Weep for Me," and "I'm Getting Sentimental Over You."

One of the singers Brown worked most frequently with was Della Reese, an American jazz and gospel singer, actor, and ordained minister, whose career spanned seven decades. Her voice and overall spirit are superb, and she deserves to be mentioned in any list of great blues and jazz singers. Brown can be heard performing live with her on *Della Reese Live* (ABC Records ABCS 569), captured on May 17, 1966, with an ensemble of Herb Ellis, Shelly Manne, organ master Bill Doggett, pianist Gerald Wiggins, and drummer Bobby Bryant. This is one of the finest live vocal albums of the 1960s. Brown also recorded with Reese on certain tracks on *Della on Strings of Blue* (1967; ABC Records ABCS-612) and *I Got to Be Me . . . This Trip Out* (1968; ABC Records ABCS-636)

One of the more notable releases of the year was the heavily arranged album Leontyne Price and André Previn, *Right as the Rain* (RCA Victor LSC-2983). Leontyne Price is an American soprano opera singer and the first African American soprano to achieve international fame. Price has appeared at nearly every major opera house. On this album, she sings versions of standards in an operatic style.

Between May 26 and 30, 1969 Ray Brown recorded with Ella Fitzgerald on her album *Things Ain't What They Used to Be (And You Better Believe It)* (Reprise Records RS-6432), produced by Norman Granz. The album includes an all-star cast of Tommy Flanagan, Joe Sample, Louie Bellson, Victor Feldman, Bobby Hutcherson, Herb Ellis, J.J. Johnson, Harry Edison, Harold Land, and many others. The recording provides Fitzgerald with an updated soulful late '60s/early '70s sound courtesy of arranger Gerald Wilson. Brown's presence is instantly felt on the opening track, "Sunny," where he plays some funky electric bass lines. He also plays some serious electric grooves on "I Heard It Through the Grapevine" and "Manteca."

By the time of this recording, Fitzgerald's voice had begun to deepen, and she no longer had the cutesy vocal quality of her younger years. Despite the changes in her range and timbre, she was still an incredibly gifted singer. The work was an apparent effort to update Fitzgerald's sound, but she still sounds most at home singing standard material like "Days of Wine and Roses," "Tuxedo Junction," and "Black Coffee."

Outside his bass playing role, Ray Brown now found further recognition as a businessman in the jazz sphere. From September 16–18, 1966, he served as director of the Monterey Jazz Festival, an event featuring various jazz, blues, and folk acts. Ray most likely attended all performances and may have appeared on stage. Day one of the festival included performances by Count Basie's Orchestra, Randy Weston, the Dave Brubeck Quartet, and Vi Redd. The Saturday September 17 performance included Big Mama Thornton, Bole Sete, Jefferson Airplane, Muddy Waters, the Cannonball Adderley Quintet, and the Paul Butterfield Blues Band. The festival concluded on Sunday with performances by Carmen McRae, Don Ellis's Orchestra, Duke Ellington's Orchestra, and John Handy.

In 1967 Ray Brown was again hired as festival director in a year marking its tenth anniversary. Headliners included Dizzy Gillespie, the Modern Jazz Quartet, Carmen McRae, Ornette Coleman, and Earl Hines. Also included were the Clara Ward Singers, Richie Havens, T-Bone Walker, B.B. King, and Big Brother and the Holding Company with Janis Joplin.

Moving into the 1970s, Ray Brown had fully re-established himself as an individual entity, now quite free from the shadow of Oscar Peterson.

21 Sessions 1970–1974

In the 1970s straight-ahead jazz became even more unfashionable, with electric rock and funk rhythms further permeating the genre. And film and television work was becoming less lucrative for Los Angeles-based jazz musicians. Many musicians of Ray Brown's generation took on more commercial work or relocated to Europe to make a living playing jazz. But Ray was fortunate to be still regarded as a first-call studio bassist with enough opportunities to keep working in the early 1970s. We can continue to categorize Brown's recordings of this period into instrumental jazz, supporting vocalists, and commercial studio work. All the same, as far as actual jazz was concerned, even Ray's recording output severely declined during the earlier part of the decade: from 1970 to 1972 he appeared in only a few instrumental jazz sessions, primarily for smaller independent labels.

One such project was the 1971 Joe Pass album *Better Days* (Gwyn LP-1001). Guitarist Joe Pass began working professionally as a teen but much of his early career was disrupted by heroin addiction, leading to several imprisonments and a two-and-a-half-year stay at a rehab facility. Pass re-emerged in the 1960s as one of the most brilliant and virtuosic jazz guitarists and he and Brown would work together frequently until his death in 1994. Ray Brown split the *Better Days* session with Gwyn label owner and electric bass master Carol Kaye, who also co-produced the record. Brown provides some solid acoustic funk lines on tunes like "Free Sample," "Balloons," "It's Too Late," "Head Start," and "After School." Pass and Brown sound incredible together throughout this highly underrated release, and the bassist's ability to play funk on an upright bass is deserving of praise.

Ray Brown returned to recording and performing with Herb Ellis during this period, with Joe Pass on some of these projects. Such efforts were encouraged by Carl Jefferson, an automobile dealer in Concord, California, and a jazz enthusiast. In 1969 Jefferson founded the annual Concord Jazz Festival before launching his Concord label to support jazz guitarists who were no longer in the mainstream. The list initially included Herb Ellis, Charlie Byrd, and Barney Kessel but was later expanded to include veteran jazz musicians on other instruments, such as Stan Getz, Benny Carter, and Dave Brubeck. Jefferson rarely interfered with the musicians during sessions, and his hands-off approach endeared him to his talent.

On July 29, 1973 Ray Brown performed with Ellis, Pass, and drummer Jake Hanna at the Concord Jazz Festival. The concert was recorded, resulting in the celebrated album Herb Ellis and Joe Pass, *Seven Come Eleven* (Concord Jazz CJ-2). This stands as a superior live jazz guitar recording, because Ellis and Pass are incredible technicians and equally matched. The opening number, "In a Mellow Tone," straight away introduces us to their great interplay and virtuosity. Ray Brown takes a solo, and the audience responds enthusiastically. The second tune, "Seven Come Eleven," is pure magic, with the band playing at a rapid tempo. On the hard-swinging final number, "Concord Blues," Ray Brown again takes a lengthy solo, improvising with a walking bass line before shifting to eighth-note bop runs, fragmented bluesy statements, and double-stop figures. The audience again rewards him with fervent applause. The group's performance was a highlight of the festival and most likely of Ray Brown's year.

The same group also recorded the album *Jazz/Concord* (CJS-1), which, albeit less exciting absent a live audience, is more subtle and clearly shows how ideally suited and musically like-minded Ellis, Pass, Hanna, and Brown were. If there was any question about how Brown felt about his association with Concord and the jazz festival, look no further than the title of his song, "Happiness Is the Concord Jazz Festival," an uptempo swing piece based on the standard "Sweet Georgia Brown." Brown's only solo on the album comes on the soulful final track "Bad News Blues," exemplifying his ability to connect as an improviser over a typical blues format with phrasing and note choices perfectly capturing the spirit of the form.

Ellis and Brown returned to the Concord Jazz Festival in 1974, along with Harry Edison, Jake Hanna, Plas Johnson (saxophone), and George Duke (piano). This performance resulted in the live album *After You've Gone* (Concord Jazz CJ-6). The group is particularly spirited on a funky rendition of "After You've Gone." On the Herb Ellis original "Mitch's Lament," Brown impresses the audience with a solo that includes higher-register statements and clever motifs. Ellis jokes that they will offer some original material to "earn additional money from ASCAP royalties."

Ellis also presents "Detour Ahead," a standard he wrote while with the Soft Winds trio, which was made famous by Woody Herman in 1949. Again, Ellis delivers the quip that its inclusion is "to get more ASCAP money." Brown shows us his sense of humor by joking, "I'll be selling ice cream on the break," before playing a beautiful introduction to set up Ellis who takes the lead. What follows is a back-and-forth display of solo statements between Brown and Ellis. Following the duo performance, the entire group rejoins for a jam-style blues credited to Ray Brown called "Fatty McSlatty." Brown knew how the business worked, so frequently wrote simple blues tunes like this one to get writing credits and therefore royalties. The set concluded with an uptempo rendition of "Flintstones II."

That year, the same group recorded the studio album *Herb Ellis and Ray Brown, Soft Shoe* (Concord Jazz CJ-3), taking its title from an original Ray Brown ballad. The record is not remarkable and does little to shine any new light on the musicians. The most interesting tracks are "The Flintstones Theme" and "Easter Parade," which each begin with a Brown–Ellis duo.

By this time there weren't many jazz legends or personal heroes that Ray Brown hadn't yet recorded alongside. But there were two significant gaps in his discography, Miles Davis, with whom Ray Brown would never record, and Duke Ellington, Brown's favorite bandleader as a child. It was on January 8, 1973 that Ray Brown fulfilled his childhood dream and played on the album *Duke's Big 4* (Pablo 2310 703). The session came about through the encouragement of Norman Granz, who launched his new label, Pablo Records, in 1973. Named after Picasso, whose artwork Granz collected, the label was set up to support artists whom Granz managed as well as legendary jazz musicians who had passed their commercial prime and no longer automatically attracted interest from major labels. Joining Ellington and Brown on the album were Joe Pass and Louie Bellson. Playing with Ellington on some of his most beloved compositions, such as "Cottontail," "Prelude to a Kiss," and "Just Squeeze Me," must have been a thrill for Ray Brown, who gets several opportunities to solo on the record. He is most impressive on "Love You Madly," where he plays the opening intro and takes a full solo chorus, showing off sliding figures, double-time licks, and a series of pull-offs. *Duke's Big 4* is among Duke Ellington's most exemplary later small-group efforts.

Around this time, Norman Granz approached Ray Brown about teaming up with Ellington to re-record the duo material of Duke Ellington and Jimmy Blanton from the early 1940s. Of course, Brown agreed. The celebrated collaboration between Ellington and Brown, entitled *This One's for Blanton* (Pablo 2310 721), was recorded on December 5, 1973. In the liner notes, Brown talks about the session:

> It is not often that I get a chance to express my thoughts or feelings about a record I've played on. However, after thirty years of recording, this is the first time that I absolutely insisted that I have my say . . . First and foremost, the two reasons I began to play bass were Duke Ellington and Jimmy Blanton . . . I can remember clearly, as a young boy, standing outside a neighborhood bar, listening to "Things Ain't What They Used to Be," and always waiting to the end to hear the last two bass notes. I was playing piano at the time, but I was continually fascinated by bass. It seemed to be the heartbeat of the orchestra, especially on Duke Ellington records . . . When I began playing bass and started practicing with the records, I found myself continually playing Duke's records because you could hear the bass clearly.
>
> It is so funny that nowadays, if you read a review of a performance or a recording and the bass plays fast and high or plays some good solos, he will get special merit, but if he lays down some good time, with a good

sound and good intonation, he may not even be mentioned. You know, when they want to see if somebody is dead, they listen for the pulse (heartbeat). Maybe that's what a lot of people think happened to some music . . . In the fall of 1972, Norman Granz called me and said, I want you to go to Las Vegas in a couple of weeks and do a duo album with Duke of all the things Blanton and Duke did together. First, I panicked, and then the desire began to return. It had been over thirty-five years since I stood outside those bars listening to that sound.

This One's for Blanton allows us to hear an exceptional musical dialogue, beginning with the Ellington classic "Do Nothin' Till You Hear from Me." It follows with a version of "Pitter Panther Patter," one of Blanton's most impressive features. While the arrangement and feel of the opening tracks are similar to the original recordings, Brown puts his unique stamp on them with signature fills and countermelodies. On "Things Ain't What They Used to Be," the bassist handles the head of the tune and then plays double-stop figures behind Ellington's solo before switching to a walking bass line. Brown follows Ellington's solo with a restatement of the melody.

The next track is "Sophisticated Lady," one of Ellington's most romantic ballads, and which the bassist opens with an unaccompanied solo interpretation. Ellington then joins in before Brown drops out, allowing Ellington his moment of expression until he once again cedes to Ray to play unaccompanied before bringing the composition to rest. "See See Rider" is a traditional piece not associated with Blanton, throughout which – as with others on this recording – Ellington favors harmonic clusters over fast pianistic runs, creating a loose and airy feel.

The distinctive material is saved for the close: an unrehearsed jam session, separated into four movements and organized under the title "Fragmented Suite for Piano and Bass." Here we are treated to some of Brown and Ellington's most unconventional playing. During these exceptional moments of interplay, Brown favors ostinatos and walking bass lines, and sometimes breaks from his traditional role as the two engage in loose conversational interplay. Ray Brown has often cited *This One's for Blanton* as his favorite, and recording two albums with Ellington during the year may have given Ray Brown a new creative push.

On May 24, 1974, not long after the release of *This One's for Blanton*, Duke Ellington passed away. Joe Pass paid tribute by recording *Portraits of Ellington* (Pablo 2310 716) with the help of Ray Brown and Bobby Durham. Here we have three phenomenal musicians playing Ellington's most inspirational material, with Pass playing solo guitar on three of the nine tracks, "Sophisticated Lady," "I Got It Bad (And That Ain't Good)," and "Solitude." Ray Brown is most heavily featured on "Satin Doll," "In a Mellow Tone," "Don't Get Around Much Anymore," and "Do Nothin' Till You Hear from Me." The most ambitious track is the trio's uptempo rendition of "Caravan." The speed is so incredibly fast that even Pass seems to stumble; however, he plays enough impressive and cohesive lines to make up for it. There are many Ellington tribute albums, and *Portraits of Jazz* ranks among the finest.

If recording with Ellington twice during 1973 was not thrilling enough, Ray Brown also recorded with his other boyhood idol, Count Basie, when Granz assembled an all-star group of Eddie "Lockjaw" Davis, Zoot Sims, J.J. Johnson, Harry Edison, Irving Ashby, Louie Bellson, and Ray Brown. The result was the album Count Basie and Joe Turner, *The Bosses* (Pablo 2310 709). Blues shouter Big Joe Turner is one of the most significant and famous blues vocalists, who, unlike many early jump-blues creators, enjoyed crossover success and stardom in the early 1950s. Turner's collaboration with Pete Johnson on the song "Roll 'Em Pete" in 1938 is often regarded as the "first rock and roll song." Hearing him perform the song thirty-plus years later with this ensemble is undoubtedly a highlight.

It is possible that *The Bosses* was recorded on or near December 10, 1973, since that date is given for the recording of *Basie Jam* (Pablo 2310 718), an album using the same musicians minus Joe Turner. *Basie Jam* features five simplistic blues-based numbers credited to Basie. On June 3, 1974 Brown recorded again with Joe Turner with an ensemble that included Roy Eldridge, trombonist Al Grey, drummer Earl Palmer, saxophonist Lee Allen, organist/pianist Jimmy Robbins, and guitarist Thomas Gadson. Despite being a solid blues recording, *Life Ain't Easy* (Pablo 2310-883) remained unreleased until 1983.

On May 22, 1974 Ray Brown was back recording with Basie on a trio session with Louie Bellson, resulting in the Count Basie Trio, *For the First Time* (Pablo 2310 712). Basie's improvisational style on the album is one of sparse statements with long rest periods, affording his music a great deal of breadth, with plenty of space for Brown and Bellson to be heard clearly. Brown plays some nuanced short solos throughout, but he primarily provides solid walking bass lines characteristic of the "Basie sound." He is particularly impressive in his feature "Blues in the Church." In the intro and an outro of this gospel-flavored blues, he plays a series of bluesy licks with hybrid swing and bop phrases. He is again featured as a soloist on "Royal Garden Blues." *For the First Time* has a superb vibe and ranks among Basie's most impressive later-period small-group recordings.

In the early 1970s, Ray Brown reunited with Oscar Peterson for several projects, including a July 1971 trio recording with Louis Hayes at Hans Georg Brunner-Schwer's German recording studio. The result was the album Oscar Peterson Trio, Ray Brown, Milt Jackson and Louis Hayes, *Reunion Blues* (BASF MPS 21-20908-5). Although the musicians attempted to update their sound by opening with a hard-swing version of the Rolling Stones' hit "Satisfaction," the group played mainly in the traditional swing/bebop style that had made them stars. The album's most special quality is that it is not special at all: it is simply a showcase of four like-minded musicians playing quality music. Brown's playing on "Reunion Blues" is a highlight: a funk bass line played against a shuffling backbeat before shifting into a more traditional walking swing feel. His solo includes many of his signature blues-based licks and phrasing. Also notable is Brown's interpretation of the melody on "When I Fall in Love," including a cadenza that demonstrates his mastery. It is apparent that Peterson has consciously incorporated more modern phrasing and interpretations; however, these subtle stylistic transitions do not dilute his overall approach and personality as a piano virtuoso.

Ray Brown finished 1972 by recording again with Oscar Peterson on December 27 and 29. The recordings would be find their way onto a retrospective Oscar Peterson double album from 1974, *The History of an Artist* (Pablo 2625 702), which showcased some of his most popular groups. The record starts with two tracks, "R.B. Blues" and a lengthy interpretation of "I Wished on the Moon," featuring only Peterson and Brown. On "R.B. Blues," Brown provides a fast signature walk and an impressive solo that surpasses the technicality of his earlier duo recordings with Peterson from 1949 to 1951. The next two tracks, "You Can Depend on Me" and "This Is Where It's At," are by the first working trio of 1952, with Irving Ashby and Ray Brown.

Ashby's replacement in the original trio, Barney Kessel, performs with Peterson and Brown on "Okie Blues." Herb Ellis arrives on "I Want to Be Happy" and "Texas Blues" – Oscar Peterson's first "classic" trio. Ray is prominently featured as a soloist on all tracks, which was uncharacteristic of his earlier recordings with Peterson. Record two is of Peterson's post-Ray Brown trios with bassists Sam Jones and George Mraz and drummers Louis Hayes and Bobby Durham. The exclusion of Ed Thigpen from the album is curious.

On December 2, 1974 Norman Granz set up one of his famous "pairing" sessions when he recorded Oscar Peterson and Count Basie for the album *"Satch" and "Josh"* (Pablo 2310 722). The name pays tribute to Satchel Paige and Josh Gibson, the great stars of "Negro League Baseball." Granz hired Freddie Green, Louie Bellson, and Ray Brown for the meeting of these two great pianists. Brown is given a special shout-out on the improvised blues "R.B.," a tune in which only the bassist accompanies Peterson and Basie.

One of the most impressive efforts of 1974 for Brown was a trio recording called *The Giants* (Pablo 2310 796) credited to Oscar Peterson, Joe Pass, and Ray Brown. The album was recorded on December 7, 1974, but was held back from release until 1977. Putting these three musicians together was an inspired move, with an underlying energy underpinning a propulsion of the swing tempo that connects perfectly. One of the finest tracks is "Jobim," with its conversational countermelodies, and the trio's rapidly paced interpretation of "Caravan" is virtuosic. Ray Brown is most prominently featured on the gospel-flavored "Blues for Dennis," with Peterson on the organ, and also solos on "Who Cares" and "I'm Getting Sentimental Over You."

Continuing the theme of playing with past associates, on September 19, 1974 Ray Brown returned to the studio to support his most significant mentor, Dizzy Gillespie. This session would be preserved on the album *Dizzy*

Gillespie's Big 4 (Pablo 310 719), one of Brown's finest sideman projects of the 1970s. Also featured on the recording were Joe Pass and Mickey Roker, and this pianoless context creates an attractive, open dynamic for Gillespie. Dizzy, like Ray, was comfortable bending but not fully committing to fashions in jazz and popular music. However, in the 1970s and beyond, both seemed comfortable incorporating and expanding on funk, blues, and Latin elements, fused with straight-ahead swing and bebop. Furthermore, neither Gillespie nor Brown allowed their skills to diminish and continued to work hard to keep up their "chops."

The album starts with a super-funky Latin Gillespie original called "Frelimo,"[138] introduced by a soulful Ray Brown bass line. Gillespie is masterful on his muted trumpet solo, maintaining a perfect balance between long and short melodic phrases. Roker plays an impressive drum solo while Gillespie pounds out quarter-note rhythms on a percussion instrument. The second track, a spacious ballad called "Hurry Home," features Gillespie, Brown, and Pass. The final track on Side A of the original LP is an Irving Berlin composition called "Russian Lullaby," which begins with Gillespie and Brown playing out-of-tempo statements before the piece moves from a quasi-Latin groove to an uptempo bebop exploration.

Side B begins with "Be Bop (Dizzy's Fingers)," which is played at an unbelievably fast tempo, at which even the most gifted performers would struggle to play cohesive statements. Still, Gillespie and Pass welcome the challenge and masterfully attack the rapidly moving chord changes. Brown and Roker are equally impressive in laying down the groove. The next tune is Gillespie's "Birks Works," a minor blues in which Brown plays part of the melody with Pass. Brown is given a solo and displays some tasteful bluesy statements before the theme is reintroduced. Next is the beautiful "September Song," played with some "cool jazz" interplay and subtlety. The album concludes with Fats Waller's "Jitterbug Waltz," in which, at one point, the band breaks from the jazz waltz rhythm and smoothly shifts into a fast four.

While Brown is not featured as a primary soloist on *Dizzy Gillespie's Big 4*, his hookup with Roker is pure perfection, and all four masters seem to be in the same creative headspace required of a jazz classic. The album delivers a perfect balance of variety, repertoire, and 1970s grit to create a masterwork. *Dizzy Gillespie's Big 4* should be in any jazz fan's collection.

Although widely disregarded, another notable album Brown played on is Don Ellis's *Haiku* (MPS MC-25341), a through-composed concept album with a string orchestra alongside a rhythm section of Milcho Leviev on piano, John Guerin on drums, and Tommy Tedesco on guitar. Recorded in June of 1973, each of the ten original tracks is based on a Japanese haiku. Ellis was a brilliant trumpeter and composer celebrated for his early use of mixing various meter changes into the jazz format. The music on *Haiku* is more symphonic and modernistic than most recordings that included Ray Brown.

Another notable jazz recording from this era was *Red Rodney Plays Superbop with Sam Noto* (Muse MR-5046), recorded on March 26, 1974. This marked Brown's return to playing an entire album of bebop. Red Rodney came to fame as a member of Charlie Parker's group from 1949 to 1951, following which he led groups in Philadelphia, although heroin addiction greatly affected his career. Sam Noto was not a well-known name when it came to small-group jazz and was mainly known for his past work with Stan Kenton and the Count Basie Orchestras throughout the 1950s and '60s. Pianist Dolo Coker and drummer Shelly Manne join Brown in the rhythm section. Album highlights include "Superbop," "Fire," "Green Dolphin Street," and "Hilton." A small-label bop-style album had little chance of being commercially viable during this era, but *Superbop* offers another example of how Ray Brown and Shelly Manne could create absolute magic together and how, when played right, bop music could still sound fresh in the 1970s.

Other notable instrumental jazz releases of the period include the live record *A Night on the Coast* by the Shelly Manne All-Stars (Moon Records MLP 008-1), recorded some time during 1969 or 1970 at Shelly's Manne-Hole, with Brown joined by saxophonist Bob Cooper and pianist Hampton Hawes. Brown is included on three tracks on the album and is awe-inspiring during the intro, melody, and lengthy solo on "Blues in the Basement" with his right-handed chording techniques, blues licks, string slides, and bebop phrasing. Brown's performance seems to silence the chatty audience, as there is a noticeable intensification in the crowd's attention as the tune builds. The bassist also provides a solo on "Milestones," and finds a way to improvise over the extremely rapid tempo by altering the harmonic rhythm without losing the tempo. The recordings on *A Night on the Coast* are rough in sound quality but impressive in musicality.

Another is a 1973 live set that produced the album Harry "Sweets" Edison, *Seven Eleven* (51 West Records Q-16076). Joining Edison and Brown were saxophonist Jerome Richardson, pianist Gerald Wiggins, and drummer Larry Bunker. The performance took place in Los Angeles, but the venue and date are not listed. Highlights from the show include "Black Orpheus" and "Seven Come Eleven." To go by the sound of the applause, the event was likely held at a small jazz club rather than a festival or theater.

There was a live recording with tenor saxophonist Teddy Edwards. Edwards first gained attention on the West Coast scene, known for its tenor saxophone battles, and ranked among the best along with Dexter Gordon and Wayne Marsh. Edwards recorded steadily as a leader from 1947 till 1962 but after that only released two more records, in 1966 and 1967. After a seven-year recording gap as leader, Edwards was finally offered another date: a March 25, 1974 session which yielded the album *Feelin's* (Muse Records MR-5045), with Conte Candoli on trumpet, Dolo Coker on piano, Frank Butler on drums, Jerry Steinholz on percussion, and Ray Brown on bass. The record consists of four Edwards originals played in a late-1960s hard-bop style, along with the slow ballad "Georgia on My Mind." Also included is the Ray Brown original, "Ritta Ditta Blues," with a tightly syncopated head arrangement followed by a typical twelve-bar blues solo section. Brown plays arco on the melody and takes an extended solo. *Feelin's* is a strong effort, with each tune and solo offering enough variety to make for a successful jazz album.

As well as supporting jazz instrumentalists, Ray Brown continued working as bassist for jazz- and blues-based vocalists. The vocal records generally offer fewer displays of Brown's technical ability; however, his professionalism, overall spirit, and musicality are evident. On February 19, 1970 he recorded two tracks for jump-blues singer Jimmy Witherspoon on his album *Handbags and Gladrags* (ABC Records ABCS-717). On "Spoon's Beep Beep Blues," Brown plays upright bass, and his hookup with session master Earl Palmer on the drums is noteworthy. On the funky blues "Elmira," Brown plays electric bass.

On May 30, 1971, Brown participated in a performance and live recording for Ketty Lester at the Second A.M.E. Church in Los Angeles. Lester was a singer who scored her only major hit with a version of "Love Letters" in 1962. She became more well known as an actor than a musician while working on television shows like *Little House on the Prairie, Days of Our Lives,* and films like *Uptight, Julia,* and *Blacula.* This gospel date was released as *Ketty Lester in Concert* (Sheffield S-15).

Two more notable 1972 projects were the albums Joe Williams, *With Love* (Temponic TB-29561) and Carmen McRae, *Carmen* (Temponic TB-29562). Both records featured compositions by Bob Friedman and large-ensemble arrangements by Benny Carter. Williams and McRae were incredibly gifted vocalists who, at this point, were less commercially relevant than in the 1960s. Ray Brown is not heavily featured on either record.

In 1974 (possibly 1973), Brown recorded again with McRae with an ensemble that included Joe Pass on guitar, Larry Bunker on vibes and percussion, Frank Severino on drums, and Dick Shreve on piano. The recording yielded the album *It Takes a Whole Lot of Human Feeling* (Groove Merchant GM-522). Brown plays his Fender electric bass on the album's title track and then returns to upright for the remainder of the album. He is most impressive as a soloist on the standards "Nice Work If You Can Get It" and "All the Things You Are." Carmen McRae's ability is revealed at its best on the beautiful ballad "Inside a Silent Tear."

One of the most impactful jazz vocal records made during this time was an all-star recording session on January 8, 1974 organized by Norman Granz to showcase Ella Fitzgerald, called *Fine and Mellow* (Pablo 2310 829). The session was a throwback to the famed 1950 JATP jams and included stars like Harry Edison, Clark Terry, Zoot Sims, Eddie "Lockjaw" Davis, Joe Pass, Tommy Flanagan, Louie Bellson, and Ray Brown. Although she was well past her commercial prime at the time of the recording, and her voice has changed somewhat from her younger years, Fitzgerald is impressive, showing off her range, breath control, vibrato, and scat vocalizations. Ray Brown is best represented in the group's funky interpretation of "I'm Just a Lucky So and So," and in moments during the songs "I'm in the Mood for Love" and "The Man I Love," where only the bass accompanies the vocals. Surprisingly, the album was held back from release until 1979 because the following year it netted a Grammy for "Best Vocal Jazz Album."

Brown also had a small part to play in the large studio ensemble album Sarah Vaughan, *Orchestrated, Arranged and Conducted by Michel Legrand* (Mainstream Records MSL-1006). The album also includes bassists Chuck Berghofer and Bob Magnusson. Like Fitzgerald, Vaughan's voice had deepened from her younger years, forcing the vocalist to revamp her repertoire and keys.

During this period, Brown also recorded with Japanese singers; by 1972, he had become more involved with the Japanese jazz scene. Having first traveled to Japan in 1953 with JATP, Brown visited the country frequently and considered Japan his second home. He was treated well by Japanese fans and was encouraged by audiences' respect and knowledge. A consummate businessman, Brown recognized the opportunity in this foreign market. He would now regularly record in Japan with native artists, as he had done years before with Toshiko Akiyoshi.

On April 20–21, 1972 Ray Brown supported Japanese jazz vocalist Yoshiko Goto for her album *Yoshiko Meets Ray Brown: I'm Glad There Is You* (Denon CD-7039). The recording includes pianists Jimmy Rowles and Mike Wofford, guitarist Joe Pass and drummers John Guerin and Paul Humphries. In addition to playing bass, Brown was active in this project and is listed as an arranger and musical director. The album primarily included standards played in a straight-ahead format. Brown demonstrates his ability to offer subtleties to small-group arrangements, and Goto proves to be a gifted vocalist. Highlights include "Day by Day," "Wave," and "Aquarius." *Yoshiko Meets Ray Brown* was only ever issued in Japan, and few American jazz fans are even aware of this fine recording.

On August 28 and 29, 1974 Ray Brown recorded with another Japanese vocalist, Kimiko Kasai, resulting in *Thanks Dear* (CBS/Sony 25AP 734). Oliver Nelson supervised the album, and the ensemble included Joe Sample and Shelly Manne. Today, Kasai is rarely mentioned by jazz historians but between 1968 and 1990 she recorded over twenty albums as a leader. *Thanks Dear is* a solid record of jazz standards, and although a Japanese accent can often be detected, Kasai sounds authentic when singing the songs from the Great American Songbook. Pianist Joe Sample, who became famous for playing electric jazz fusion with his band the Jazz Crusaders, is particularly impressive playing in a more mainstream format. As expected, Brown and Manne are perfectly matched.

During the 1970s and beyond, Ray Brown maintained a deep connection with Quincy Jones, whose career Brown was managing. On March 25 and 26, 1970, Brown was included on Jones's album *Gula Matari* (A&M Records

SP-3030). The record is only four tracks long and includes many guest musicians such as Freddie Hubbard, Herbie Hancock, Hubert Laws, Milt Jackson, and Valerie Simpson. Brown plays electric bass on a heavily arranged soulful version of "Bridge Over Troubled Water," sung by Valerie Simpson, and on the fusion-based number "Hummin'," which also includes bassist Major Holley, who adds vocalizations. Ray Brown returns to the familiar upright bass on the jazz standard "Walkin'." He is not present for the lengthy title track on which Ron Carter and Richard Davis share the bass duties. *Gula Matari* offers various levels of fusion experimentalism but is still rooted in jazz traditions.

Brown would again work with Quincy Jones on an October 1971 studio date for the album *Smackwater Jack* (A&M Records SP-3037). Once again, Jones assembled dozens of studio musicians and soloists. The bass chair was shared by electric bassists including Chuck Rainey, Bob Cranshaw, and Carol Kaye, but Ray Brown is the only bassist in the "double bass" category. Brown can be heard most prominently playing impressive acoustic funk grooves, double-stop figures, and walking lines on "Ironside." He is also well represented on Jones's lengthy remake of Marvin Gaye's classic protest song "What's Going On?" where he retains a similar feel to bassist James Jamerson's original electric bass line, before shifting to a walking bass. The song of most interest with regard to Ray Brown is his original composition "Brown's Ballad," a slow poppy number featuring Toots Thielemans on harmonica, Bob James on piano, and Jim Hall on guitar.

Other Quincy Jones projects that included Ray Brown are the 1972 film soundtracks for *Dollar$* (Reprise 9362-47879-2) and *The Hot Rock* (Prophesy Records SD-6055). Since he is one of several bassists listed on both albums, it is not always clear when we are listening to him. But his playing is evident and impressive on tracks like "Candy Man," "Kitty with the Bent Frames," and "Brook's 50¢ Tour" from *Dollars$* and on "Listen to the Melody," "Main Title," "Seldom Seen Sam," and "Dixie Tag" from *The Hot Rock*.

Throughout the early 1970s, Brown remained attached to Henry Mancini's projects, in 1971 participating in the recording of *Mancini Concert* by Henry Mancini and His Concert Orchestra (RCA Victor LSP-4542). There are smooth arrangements, including medleys of Simon and Garfunkel hits, Mancini originals, swing big-band chart-toppers, and themes from the show *Jesus Christ Superstar* and the rock opera *Tommy*. Ray Brown is not heavily featured on the recording and can be most prominently heard walking the bass on "Big Band Montage."

Brown also worked with Mancini on projects aiming to promote the recordings and compositions of film composer and organist Artie Kane. He is credited on the albums *Henry Mancini Presents ... Artie Kane Plays Organ* (1972; RCA Victor LSP-4595) and *Henry Mancini Presents ... Artie Kane Playing the Swinging Screen Scene* (1972; RCA Victor LSP-4693). Both works sound dated and unremarkable.

Ray Brown was, in addition, still being called on to support projects that many would not necessarily associate with him. One unique session was in 1971 for the Paul Beaver and Bernie Krause album *Gandharva* (Warner Bros. WS-1909). Beaver and Krause began collaborating in 1966 on electronic music and were particularly influential in introducing the sound of the Moog synthesizer into film music. *Gandharva* is notable for its early heavy use of synthesizers and its incorporation of jazz, blues, rock, and gospel. Part of the album was recorded live on February 10–11, 1971, at San Francisco's Grace Cathedral.

This ambitious project was meant to showcase the possibilities of quadraphonic sound. Quadrophonic sound is similar to 4.0 surround sound, in that it requires a system of four speakers placed in four corners of a room, with independent channels going to each speaker. Although it was a colossal commercial failure, thousands of recordings like *Gandharva* were made to demonstrate its possibilities. *Gandharva* is heavily synthesized, wildly experimental, and most likely not something that would interest Brown as a listener. Also on the album are guitarists Mike Bloomfield and Howard Roberts, as well as reed specialist Bud Shank. One of the more notable pieces is the Gerry Mulligan original "By Your Grace" in which Mulligan's baritone sax part is treated to a heavy reverb effect against spacey organs and synth layers. Ray Brown is best represented on the gospel number "Walkin' by the River" and on the hypnotic "Short Film for David."

The bassist also lent his services to trumpeter and producer Jack Daugherty for his album *The Class of Nineteen Hundred and Seventy One* (1971; A&M Records SP-3038), a super-session with a massive cast of musicians. Another lesser-known recording was Marc Benno's *Ambush* (1972; A&M Records SP-4364). Benno was a singer and guitarist who achieved notoriety as a member of the group Asylum Choir in the late 1960s with Leon Russell. As a session musician, Benno worked with the Doors, Eric Clapton, and Stevie Ray Vaughan, among others. Brown is featured on the folky track "Either Way It Happens." Another unusual project for Ray was the Richard Roundtree album *The Man from Shaft* (MGM Records SE-4836). Roundtree was perceived as the "first black action hero" for portraying John Shaft in the eponymous 1971 film.

Some other rock-related projects included the Priscilla album *Gypsy Queen* (1970; Sussex SXBS-7002). "Priscilla" was Priscilla June Coolridge and the one-time wife of renowned multi-instrumentalist Booker T. Jones. Following the breakup of her marriage to Jones in 1979, Coolridge then married famed television journalist Ed Bradley, a marriage that also ended in divorce; tragically, her third husband shot and killed her in their home in 2014 before also killing himself. *Gypsy Queen* is a 1970s art rock album, an extreme departure for Ray Brown. It is unclear what tracks he played on as he is one of three bassists listed. Unable to produce a hit, Priscilla had only a slight impact.

In 1972, Brown was also listed as having recorded with folk-rock artist Craig Doerge on his self-titled album (Columbia KC-32179). Although his solo career never afforded him celebrity status, Doerge was a well-known session keyboardist in the early 1970s, and his work with artists like Crosby Stills & Nash, James Taylor, Jackson Browne, and others is significant. *Craig Doerge* is a strong album that failed to produce a hit single.

The most notable 1972 guest appearance Ray Brown was on the jazzy rock song "Razor Boy" by legendary rock band Steely Dan on their certified gold record *Countdown to Ecstasy* (ABC Records ABCX-779). Steely Dan have been widely celebrated for bringing jazz harmonies into rock music. Another impressive guest album appearance from that years was on saxophonist Tom Scott's album *Great Scott* (A&M Records SP-4330), on which Brown plays electric bass on the fusion track "Liberation."

Other overlooked sessions include a folk-rock song called "No One's Going to Change You," written and recorded by singer-songwriter Cheryl Ernst for the album *Always Beginning* (1973: Bell Records, BELL 1126). Brown also performed on the Bob Friedman double album *Twenty-Five Years: To My Genie with Love, Bob* (1973; Temponic Records RGF-4004). He would also record a fast folky swing track for folk singer Maria Muldaur called "Walking One and Only" for her self-titled album (Reprise Records MS-2148). The album produced the hit "Midnight at the Oasis," which reached number three on the *Billboard* charts. The following year he recorded again with Muldaur on the album *Waitress in a Donut Shop* (Reprise Records MS-2194). Other albums from this period include self-titled albums by Dory Previn (1974; Warner Bros. BS-2811) and Caston & Majors (1974; Motown M6-814S1).

22 The L.A. Four
1974–1983

One of Brown's more essential relationships in the 1970s was with Brazilian guitar master Laurindo Almeida – one of the first musicians to mix samba music with jazz. He played with the famous Stan Kenton Orchestra in the late 1940s, and by the mid-1950s was working in Hollywood studio orchestras and leading small bands. He became a star when his 1962 album *Viva Bossa Nova* (Capitol Records ST-1759) made the pop charts. Brown and Almeida had worked together on several studio projects, and the two masters formed a bond during the 1970 recordings of their first album together, *Bach Ground Blues & Green* (Century City Records CCR 80102). The liner notes accurately describe the album as a "rare and pure album with classical overtones; a Brazillian influence and a blues flavor." They also mention that "among devotees of jazz, the name of Ray Brown stands alone as possibly the finest bass player in the world. For eleven years running, he has been awarded the first place in both the *Playboy* and *Downbeat* polls."

Bach Ground Blues & Green begins with an experimental Ray Brown composition with a '70s funk vibe called "Brazilian Greens." The piece is uncharacteristic of anything Brown had written to this point, and it sounds as if it was more a jam than an actual written composition. Brown is heard as a soloist on "Make the Man Love Me," played against only Almeida's nylon string guitar. The blend of double bass and classical guitar makes for a brilliant tonal palette, and Brown's playing on the track is one of his more impressive ballad solo interpretations. Brown also introduces another original called "Just a Bossa, Not a Symphony," which can be best described as a funky bossa nova and on which he again is featured as a soloist. It is fresh and exciting to hear him playing in this context. The final track of Side A is another impressive collaboration called "Conversa Molé."

The first four tracks of Side B – "Preludio II," "Preludio I," "Fughetta IV," and "Fughetta II" – are Almeida's interpretations of J.S. Bach, marking Brown's first departure into classical music recording. Hearing Brown accompany and solo in a classical context is testament to his versatility. The record concludes with another Brown creation called "Mo' Greens," which is essentially a reprise of "Brazilian Greens." While *Bach Ground Blues & Green* had little impact and is known only to hardcore fans of Brown and Almeida, it is an undoubtedly worthwhile listen that supports the argument that Ray Brown was willing to move beyond his traditional jazz roots.

Nearly eleven years later, in 1981, Brown and Almeida recorded a second duo album, *Moonlight Serenade* (Jeton 100 3315). Any project with a classically trained musician such as Almeida, not much given to improvisation, had to be carefully written and arranged. The opening track is "Mondscheinsonate," a blend of Bach's "Moonlight Sonata" and Thelonious Monk's "Round Midnight." Brown's bowed melody on the "Round Midnight" segment is his most impressive arco playing to date. On the notable second track, "Samba de Angry," Brown presents the theme and plays some expressive material that blends samba and blues licks. Another noteworthy Ray Brown showcase and arrangement follows on the standard "But Not for Me," on which he returns to arco for the final statement. Side A closes with a clever reworking of Bach's "Air on a G-String."

Side B continues the world musical journey with the Spanish classic "Malagueña," which again puts the bassist in the spotlight as a soloist. The two then offer arrangements on the standards "Blue Skies" and "Make the Man Love You," both of which include solid Ray Brown solos. Following the standards is a reworking of "Inquietação" by Ari Barroso. The album ends with George Gershwin's "My Man Is Gone" from his monumental folk opera *Porgy and Bess*. Brown hauntingly plays the song's melody on the track while shifting between standard and thumb positions.

Moonlight Serenade demonstrates Ray Brown's gifts as a melodic player, accompanist, and arranger. It is one of the most comprehensive documents of his technical ability and musical sensibilities. Few other bassists from the jazz world could create an album like *Moonlight Serenade,* a study of which is an absolute must for any Ray Brown devotee.

Since moving to Los Angeles in 1965, Ray Brown had not attached himself to any working group, instead remaining a hired gun dividing his time between jazz activities and commercial studio work. Perhaps he missed the development and unity a steady unit can achieve, because in 1974 he joined and helped lead the group the L.A. Four. This revamped group initially included Laurindo Almeida, drummer Chuck Flores, and alto saxophonist and flutist Bud Shank. Flores was replaced early on by Shelly Manne, and each member of the L.A. Four had already enjoyed a degree of fame as bandleaders and sidemen and had been frequent visitors to recording studios by the 1960s.

On July 27, 1974 the L.A. Four was successfully introduced at the Concord Summer Festival to an audience of 6,000. For the next eight years, it would exist as a part-time working unit, and create music that ranks among Ray Brown's most outstanding achievements. With their eclectic mix of bossa nova, swing, classical, blues, and funk, the L.A. Four was among the most unique and accomplished jazz-related acts of the mid-1970s and early '80s. They could be described as a fusion group based on traditional folk, classical, and jazz elements. Unwilling to entirely abandon their solo efforts and session work, the group was set up to create annual recordings, usually followed by a short tour. Bud Shank spoke about the history of the group, the Los Angeles studio scene, and Ray Brown:

> As the jazz business started to wind down in the late '50s and early '60s, I started doing more and more [studio] things. If you want to get into the real technical part of it, in the '50s, all the movie studios had staff orchestras, and all the jazz musicians were banned from them. And it wasn't until 1959, when Hank Mancini started doing "Peter Gunn," then jazz musicians were suddenly taken out of their box and permitted to do something with that. We all crept in after the door was opened, and I credit Hank Mancini as the guy who opened the door. Then there was more and more studio work because the jazz business was going out the window. Still, at the same time, more and more composers, like Michel Legrand, Dave Grusin, Johnny Mandel, and Quincy Jones, were starting to do more and more movies, and they were our guys, or we were their guys, or whatever. So we went with them.[139]
>
> Laurindo and I made some records in the early '50s, known as the Laurindo Almeida Quartet with Bud Shank. They were somewhat successful. Laurindo, in the 1960s, was also doing studio work just like Ray and I and everybody else. In the early '70s, maybe in '73, Laurindo and Ray worked as a duo in a club on the Sunset Strip. It might have been the Crescendo. Laurindo got a call from a guy in Santa Barbara who said, "Would you want to try to recreate the recordings which you did in the early '50s?" Those recordings had a significant resurrection during the early '60s when the bossa nova thing started happening when Stan Getz and Charlie Byrd did their thing. But this guy asked, "Would you be willing to recreate that?" So Laurindo called me, and we said, "Yeah." [I asked] who should be playing bass. He said, "Well, I've been working with Ray. It would be good to have Ray play bass." Who should play drums? Well, Chuck Flores was still around, and he was the drummer who played with Laurindo and me on the last records we made in the late '50s. So we played the concert and used the same old material that we had used twenty years before, but it was interesting, and again we had still been buried in the studios. There was no inkling that we would ever get out of that. And so Ray and I said, "Well, why not? Let's give it a shot and see what we can make out of it."
>
> By coincidence, we went to Mexico City and took Chuck with us. Chuck Flores, well, I hate to put it this way, but he has always been very dominated by his wife. So Chuck shows up with his wife, his mother-in-law, and two kids to go to Mexico City to play a concert, which we did and put up with. When we came back . . . we went to Shelly's Manne-Hole. We stood before the club and saw a billboard listing "The Laurindo Almeida Quartet featuring Ray Brown, Shelly Manne, and Bud Shank." I said, "Who in the hell will get that on any billboard?" And so we had always had before and still were plagued with the problem that Laurindo Almeida thought it was the "Laurindo Almeida Quartet." So I said, "What if we call it the L.A. Four?" "Laurindo will think it means the "Laurindo Almeida Quartet,"

and the rest of the world will think it means the "Los Angeles Four." We got away with that, and that's how the whole thing started. And so Shelly said, "Wait a minute, I want to come to stay with this band." The club thing started going down the drain. By this time, he was out of the original Manne-Hole, and this was a new club on Wilshire that didn't really last very long.

Then we got on a booking in Australia. This was 1975, I guess. Maybe '74. We decided to get serious about this thing because jazz music was still not back. We were still in the throes of what had happened in the '60s and the influences of rock and roll . . . So Ray and I said, "This looks like a good way to put a group together to feel our way back. To see if anything is going to happen." That's why it happened. That's why we stuck with it. Ray started booking it. He was working with Quincy [Jones] as his manager by this time, and he spent time booking the L.A. Four. Ray made all the bookings, and I took care of all the money. Then Shelly left, Jeff Hamilton came in, and Jeff took care of calling the sets, and Laurindo didn't do anything because he was a delightful guy but a mess [*laughs*].

At one point, we had one trip to Europe that lasted six weeks, and I don't think we had but a couple of days off. We went from the top to the bottom to the side of Europe. Up and down and whatever, it was a good tour, and when we all came back, we divided everything up. It was a co-op group, and we were incorporated by this time. We divided everything four ways, and we each had $25,000 coming, which wasn't bad for six weeks, especially in the early '80s.[140]

One of the finest aspects of the L.A. Four was the group's use of intricate arrangements. While Brown, Shank, and Manne were comfortable with improvisation, Almeida relied on written music. Specific arrangements were necessary to incorporate Almeida into the group. By now, Ray Brown was familiar with classical music and technique, and Shank was equally comfortable performing in just about any musical style. Both Manne and later Jeff Hamilton could also use percussive colorations that broke from pure swing. The unit borrowed from all its creative resources in working out arrangements, and no one member was featured as the primary soloist. Everybody got a taste of the solo spotlight and rarely has a jazz unit been divided so equally in terms of solo space. The group broke from the jazz jam tradition and incorporated classical forms, easily moving in and out of rhythmic modulations, key changes, and dynamics.

Bud Shank discusses how the arrangements were conceived:

> They were collaborative, but Laurindo would bring a lot of stuff in because Laurindo had to do his thing. So he would bring things in, and then we would tear them apart and make sense of them. Ray had a lot to do with the arrangements. I did, and so did Jeff. We all did, but still, Laurindo had to write his parts out, and none of us knew how to write guitar parts. Those are very complex, especially when dealing with a classical guitar player. He was a classical guitarist who happened to be born in Brazil, and

he couldn't get that Brazilian thing out of him. So he knew the essence of swing from a samba standpoint but not from a swing standpoint. He was not an improviser. He did literally write his solos out on those records, and then he always played the same solo every time.[141]

The L.A. Four's 1974 Concord performance was recorded and released as *The L.A. Four Scores!* (Concord Jazz CJ-8). Each track shows an incredible amount of variation and experimentation. The opening number is a Bud Shank tune called "Sundancers," which offers a mixture of Latin funk and some strong interplay between Brown and Manne, Shank showing his mastery as a flute improviser. Shank plays the alto saxophone for track 2, "Carioca Hills," an Almeida original played with a traditional Brazilian feel that shifts to an uptempo swing. The third piece is "Allemande and the Fox," adapted from part of a suite written by the German Baroque lutist Silvius Weiss and offering a unique blend of samba and classical music. Side A concludes with "Berimbau Carioca," with Shelly Manne on the berimbau, a traditional Brazilian instrument that originated in Africa.

The album's second side opens with Almeida's composition "Cielo," played in 3/4 time using syncopated bass figures. Chopin's "Prelude, Opus 28" follows, mixed with Antonio Jobim's "How Insensitive," on which Brown bows the melody, his arco playing now demonstrating a subtle vibrato. Brown then shifts to a funky bass line, yielding the theme to Almeida. His impressive bass solo begins with a flurry of bop-style eighth-note rhythmic phrases against the bossa rhythms. Towards the middle of the improvisation, he plays less rhythmically and more melodically before shifting back to a more dynamic rhythm. By manipulating rhythmic density, his solo creates interest by describing a rhythmic arc. Almeida impresses with his solo vehicle "Old Time Rag," before the show and album conclude with a lengthy version of Luis Bonfá's classic "Manhã de Carnaval," which begins with just Brown and Shank. Midway through the piece, Brown's unaccompanied solo references the melody. The performance concludes to loud applause. Both the concert and album introduced the L.A. Four to the wider public. During the year, as Shank recalled, the group would tour in Australia, and much of their touring activity was on the international stage, where jazz was met with more appreciation than in the States.

In 1976, the L.A. Four released their first studio album, *The LA4* (Concord CJ-18). On the liner notes, Ray Brown is quoted as saying:

> I love this group because it's doing jazz, classical, bossa nova, a lot of different things. We don't have to cater to anything. It's not a straight up and down jazz group. We write all our own music, and it's not something you can just sit down and jam with. It's a diversion from what we normally do, but even though it's different, the group seems to be shaping up to an original personality anyway.

The L.A. Four. Left to right: Ray Brown, Laurindo Almeida, Bud Shank, and Shelly Manne. Ray Brown Papers, Archives Center, National Museum of American History, Smithsonian Institution

The album begins with an inspired rendition of the Antonio Carlos Jobin classic "Dindi." Brown's solo references the main melody and develops melodic phrases. Shelly Manne is particularly impressive in his ability to navigate the time and feel changes smoothly. The second track, a Shank original called "Rainbows," primarily features Almeida and Shank. The third, "Rondo Espressivo," is an interpretation of the music of J.S. Bach. The band again demonstrate their connectivity and superiority when presenting advanced small-group arrangement characterizations such as melodic theme shifts and time feel manipulations. In addition to soloing on the piece, Brown plays bass chords, a technique not often used by double bass players. Side A concludes with an extended version of Gillespie's "Manteca," which begins with an almost free jazz musical conversation between Brown and Manne. The bassist then presents the melody against the brushwork of Manne while also incorporating perfectly in-tune double stops. He concludes the section with a solo cadenza. After a pause, he returns with a fast variation on the famous bass ostinato, and the group returns as they move between Afro-Cuban statements, swing, bebop, and funk.

Side two of *The LA 4* begins with "St. Thomas," on which each member has the spotlight; Brown's solo is played with only the backing of Shelly Manne, allowing him to be heard with clarity. The album concludes with *Concierto de Aranjuez*, written in 1939 by Joaquin Rodrigo. It was Rodrigo's signature work and helped him to earn a reputation as one of the most celebrated Spanish composers of the twentieth century. Clocking in at over thirteen minutes, the performance is one of the most ambitious projects Ray Brown had been a part of.[142] The group begins slowly, foregrounding Shank and Almeida. Through an unexpected dynamic lift, the music intensifies before settling again. The musicians give way to more spacious melodic trading between the saxophone and guitar. It's not until around eleven minutes into the piece that a solid time feel is established before returning to the more free interpretations. Overall, *The LA 4* is an artistic triumph by four brilliant musicians dedicated to making music of the highest quality.

By 1977, it seemed fairly clear that the L.A. Four's records would not make a significant commercial impact in the U.S., but the group had a large enough following to survive, despite their lower profile. For the most part, electric fusion jazz and crossover continued to dominate the American jazz market, and much of the L.A. Four's activity was overseas, where acoustic jazz was better appreciated. In 1977, Len Lyons interviewed Ray Brown and Shelly Manne about the group for *DownBeat* magazine. Brown talks about the band and his frustration with the current U.S. music scene; his opinions about the jazz media and crossover music are strongly voiced:

> "Concord is a straight up and down jazz label which means no electronics or crossover music. I find the media people are largely unaware of it." Brown says this with obvious resentment. For him, it implies that "you people in the media should do some soul searching. Why don't people know about Concord Jazz? Why is non-commercial jazz being neglected in the press?"
>
> **Lyons:** As veterans, what do you think of some newer styles that are getting a lot of attention in the press? Crossover, for example.
>
> **Brown:** You yourself said it's been getting a lot of attention in the press, and I think that's one of the reasons for the crossover. We'll probably never get into it. We'd have no reason to since we've all existed well without it.
>
> **Manne:** I told kids at my last clinic that they have to listen to what's been played before by listening to records. Everything that's happening now comes from what was happening years ago. I asked, "How many kids know Sonny Rollins?" In a 100 kids, not one raised his hand. How many kids know Roy Eldridge? Not one hand. If you mention Chick Corea or Joe Zawinul, then they know who you're talking about because we're getting into crossover.
>
> **Brown:** And I imagine you guys in the music press have had something to do with that. You ought to do a little soul-searching. Why don't kids know who Sonny Rollins is?

Lyons: What is your assessment of the avant-garde acoustic style of playing? It seems closer to what all of you are involved in.

Brown: Musicians didn't give it that name [avant-garde]. They don't label music. They just play it .

Possibly because of a general lack of interest on the part of American consumers, the L.A. Four released their following two records on the Japanese label East Wind. The first of these was *Going Home* (East Wind EW-10004), recorded September 29 and 30, 1977. The first track, "Going Home," was a jazz remake of a theme from Antonín Dvořák's *Symphony 9, Movement #2* ("The New World Symphony"). Ray Brown plays several arco statements and a pizzicato solo played against light accompaniment. A Latin-flavored reinterpretation of the jazz standard "Softly As in a Morning Sunrise" is followed by a version of the English folk classic "Greensleeves," in which the group blends classical chamber stylings with straight-ahead jazz. Brown's soloing against Manne's brushwork offers a well-placed interlude.

Side B begins with the Ellington classic "Things Ain't What They Used to Be," played in typical swing fashion, and while it offers a fine solo segment from Shank and Brown, there is nothing unique in the arrangement which is surprising for an L.A. Four vehicle. The next track is "Recipe of Love," an original samba written by Almeida, which includes an expressive bass solo. The third track, "Romance de Amour," is an Almeida solo arrangement of a traditional guitar melody played in the Spanish classical style. The album concludes with a version of the John Lewis classic "Django." Brown introduces the piece with an opening statement on the bass's lower register before he and Almeida perform the melody as a duo. The bassist takes the first solo over Manne's medium-swing brushwork – a solid improvisation that captures the spirit of Brown's use of bop, blues, and swing phrasing. Throughout the piece, the group works through a variety of time feels, ending with a classical chamber-sounding presentation in which Brown plays arco.

On October 15 and 16, 1976[143] the L.A. Four recorded their second Japanese release, *Pavane pour une Infante Défunte* (EastWind EW-10003),[144] the title track by the great French impressionist composer Maurice Ravel. The album begins with an intricate Laurindo Almeida arrangement of Ravel's masterpiece which includes various time feels and is a vehicle for each member's abilities. In Ray Brown's extended solo he first plays lines against just Shelly Manne's brushwork before being left to solo unaccompanied. "Pavane pour une Infante Défunte" is the album's centerpiece and shows the the L.A. Four's brilliance and imagination. Side A continues with standard "Autumn Leaves" and a Bud Shank original samba called "C'est What," which includes Ray Brown playing some double-stop arco statements before settling into a Latin groove. He also plays a well-crafted solo against only Manne's drum grooves, a reminder of his ability to pace his solos to produce cohesive statements.

Side B begins with Antonio Carlos Jobim's classic "Corcovado," which begins with only Almeida and Brown and also features a bass solo benefiting from Brown's ability to connect themes and scale-like runs. Jobim's "Wave" is played in a pretty standard format whereas the following track is an impressive Laurindo Almeida solo called "Reveil." The final track, "Samba de Orfeu," begins slowly, with Brown presenting the melody against only guitar accompaniment. Ray Brown and Bud Shank subsequently trade eight-bar statements. *Pavane pour une Infante Défunte*, like all L.A. Four releases, has imagination, character, and virtuosity.

After working with the L.A. Four for four years, drummer Shelly Manne left the band in 1977. Replacing Manne, who was comfortable interpreting the multiple styles that the L.A. Four drew on, would be difficult, especially since the musical bond between Brown and Manne was so strong. A contemporary of Manne would likely be torn between a role that required periods of intense rehearsal and the short-term demands of lucrative work. The group therefore looked to the talents of Indiana native Jeff Hamilton, who was only twenty-four years old when he joined. But by this time he had already worked in Monty Alexander's trio and with Woody Herman's orchestra. He was already showing a unique technical ability and was remarkable on brushes. For the next fifteen years, Hamilton would be the drummer most connected with Ray Brown as he also served as a member of Ray Brown's trio.

In an interview with Ted Panken, Jeff Hamilton reflects on first meeting Ray Brown and his early years as a member of the L.A. Four:[145]

> I met Ray in 1976 at the Lighthouse in Los Angeles. He was booking Milt Jackson and had booked Milt with the Monty Alexander Trio and came into the club to see how we were doing. That's the first time I met him. I asked him that night if I could meet with him and ask him some advice on what I should do with my career. I was all of twenty-two years old. He said, "Sure, we can meet – if you buy lunch." So that was the beginning of our long friendship. Based on what he heard that night, he kept me in mind and hired me for the L.A. Four when Shelly Manne left.
>
> When I came in, he looked more to me as "you need to be an equal with me," I think he kind of classified me in his generation. There is thirty years between us. And I've always kind of been old for my age anyway, and I think he picked up on that . . . The first night that I played with him, I thought, "Well, this is a lot more intense than I thought it was going to be from listening to the records." When I was able to adjust to that and make that happen, then I thought, "Okay, now I can play with Ray Brown."
>
> I couldn't believe what I was hearing from night to night. First of all, his stamina from night to night was something that I had never witnessed before. I have played with musicians who wanted to be great every night and were trying to do it and had that in mind. But I've never seen anybody like Ray, be able to get on the bandstand and play like it might be his last night. I don't know where that came from, but it was so intense . . . I keep going back to that word because that's Ray Brown. In every walk of his

life, he was very intense. And the need to get up there and really stretch out and try to push us was, I think maybe instilled by the days with Dizzy, and playing with Bird, and having that need to play some new music and try to push the arrangement into something else.

Jeff Hamilton's first release with the band was one of their finest: *Just Friends* (Concord Jazz CJD-1001). It begins with Laurindo Almeida's "Nouveau Bach," an adaptation of Bach's "Prelude in Cm." The lengthy arrangement incorporates spacious rhythmic themes, creating an open palette for Bud Shank and Ray Brown to improvise. Brown focuses his solo in the higher register, showing his ability to play in the thumb position. The following piece is is another Almeida original, "Carinhoso," which begins with a musical conversation between Almeida and Brown before a light Latin groove takes over. The final track of Side A is "Just Friends," with its numerous time feels and solos, including an unaccompanied bass solo. On "Just Friends," we get to hear Jeff Hamilton's brilliance as a brush player and soloist.

Side B begins with a Ray Brown arrangement titled "Love Medley," which mixes two standards, "Love for Sale" and "Love Walks In," and has some of Ray Brown's funkiest bass playing to date. The album concludes with the Chick Corea masterpiece "Spain," and the ensemble proves to be the perfect group to master the complicated composition. With *Just Friends* the L.A. Four again proved why they were one of the unique jazz units of the 1970s and early '80s.

In 1978 the L.A. Four also recorded the lesser-known album *Watch What Happens* (Concord Jazz CJ-63), on which the opening title track is a highlight, with Bud Shank spotlighted and a Ray Brown solo played with very clear phrasing in which the bassist creates clear melodic phrases over technical runs. Another notable track for Brown is "Mona Lisa," a slow ballad on which he presents the lyrical theme. He also delivers fast double-timed bebop licks in his solo on "Nuages."

In the summer of 1979 (likely July), the L.A. Four performed at the Montreux Jazz Festival, which resulted in their *Live at Montreux* album (Concord Jazz CJ-100). Carl Jefferson introduces the band before they go into a lengthy version of Cole Porter's "I Love You," followed by a Latin piece called "Hammertones," written by Jeff Hamilton. Concluding Side A is an uptempo version of "Just in Time," featuring an inspired Ray Brown solo. Side B begins with the Laurindo Almeida original "Return of Captain Gallo," reminding us of Almeida's love for classical and Brazilian music. The group concludes the set with a fourteen-minute-long Ellington medley titled "Duke's Mélange." Ray Brown is featured on each track, and the audience respond favorably to his improvisation. Brown was continuously improving, developing his combination of technique, creativity, tradition, melodic quotes, and a rich tone on the bass. And he retained an ability to connect with audiences, as evidenced by the fervent applause after each of his solos. As with all L.A. Four records and performances, the group's material was tightly arranged, with impeccably played tempo and feel changes.

The group was at it again in 1980 with another outstanding album: *Zaca* (Concord Jazz CJ-130). Once more, there were elements of European classical music, swing, Latin forms, and blues. On Side A, Brown is most heavily featured on "O Barquinho (Little Boat)," where he trades eight-bar statements with Hamilton. Side B begins with Johnny Mandel's "Close Enough for Love," with Brown playing arco statements in the chamber-like introduction. A highlight is the group's arrangement of Gabriel Fauré's "Pavanne Op. 50" – rarely has a jazz unit interpreted French impressionistic composition with such grace and creativity. *Zaca* has to be one of the group's finest studio efforts.

April 1981 saw the L.A. Four recording their next album, *Montage* (Concord Jazz CJ-156). It begins with Brown's bluesy bass introduction on "Madame Butterball," on which he continues to be featured during impressive stop-time solo breaks. From the outset, it is evident that Brown is intended to be a co-equal soloist on the record. The next track, "Syrinx," is an impressionistic chamber work composed by the French master Claude Debussy and arranged by Bud Shank. The group reinforce their ability to adapt impressionistic concert works in a way that sounds neither formulaic nor sterile, but breathing new life into masterworks. Track 3, "Samba for Ray," is a Laurindo Almeida creation with Ray Brown as the principal melodic voice – and the bassist does not disappoint. The first side ends with a samba version of the standard "Teach Me Tonight."

Side B kicks off with Brown's tune "Rado's Got the Blues," with its ostinato bass line, rhythm kicks, and a unison melody played by Almeida and Shank. The name "Rado" may be a play on the first names "Ray" and "Laurindo." The next track is a nuanced take on Richard Rodgers' "My Romance," on which Brown trades solo statements with Jeff Hamilton. The following track, "Bachianas Brasileiras #5," is based on a composition by Villa-Lobos and combines Baroque chamber style with Brazilian music. The album's final cut is an arrangement of the Johnny Hodges composition "Squatty Roo," a combination of funk and swing.

The L.A. Four's final release was 1983's *Executive Suite* (Concord Jazz CJ 215) – yet another impressive vehicle with a blend of standards, like "My Funny Valentine" and "Chega de Saudade (No More Blues)," originals like "Blues Wellington" (Hamilton) and "Amazonia" (Almeida), and classically based works like "Entr'Acte" (Ibert) and "Simple Invention" (Bach).

Shank discusses the breakup of the L.A. Four:

> We lasted until 1983 with a totally impossible group. There was no way this should work: three jazz guys and one classical guitarist. No way. On paper, this was not ever going to work. And we made it work, Jeff and Ray and I. Laurindo just did Laurindo, and we just worked our way around it. It was very successful. We all made a lot of money, considering the times. When we got to around '83 or '84 or somewhere around there, Laurindo was getting worse and worse to handle . . . That was the end of that.

23 Sideman Sessions
1975–1979

Ray Brown remained incredibly active throughout the mid to late 1970s. When not working with the L.A. Four, he continued to record with past associates, younger jazz musicians, and on projects that were less connected to jazz. He was involved in such a wide variety of projects during this period that this chapter by necessity will focus just on the more notable releases.

Ray Brown had a busy time supporting vocalists. On May 19, 1975 he recorded with Ella Fitzgerald and Oscar Peterson, with Side A of the original *Ella and Oscar* LP (Pablo 2310 759) including duo performances between Fitzgerald and Peterson. Brown was added to fill the sound on four tracks, "Midnight Sun," "I Hear Music," "Street of Dreams," and "April in Paris." It had become clear by this point that Fitzgerald's voice had changed considerably and that to continue as a recording artist she must now rely on material that had both a lesser range and a lower key. On April 25, 1978 Brown, Peterson, Joe Pass, and Louie Bellson accompanied Sarah Vaughan in the studio, leading to her Pablo Records release *How Long Has This Been Going On?* (Pablo 2310 821). Vaughan's voice had also dropped considerably from her younger years but she could still deliver a standard masterfully and *How Long Has This Been Going On?* was nominated for a Grammy award. "Body and Soul" is a duo performance between Vaughan and Ray Brown.

Ernestine Anderson was a vocalist who found fame in the early 1950s but did not achieve the same level of prominence as some of jazz's better-known female singers. After spending much of the late 1950s and '60s performing in Europe, in the mid-1970s she returned to the U.S. whereupon Ray Brown became her manager. He first presented her at the 1976 Concord Jazz Festival and then helped her to secure a recording contract with the label. On 1977's *Hello Like Before* (Concord Jazz CJ-31) she is backed by Brown, Hank Jones, and drummer Jimmie Smith, It's a solid vehicle for the singer, with her rich, soulful voice lending itself perfectly to the variety of material, which includes R&B numbers, swing tunes, ballads, blues, and Latin-based tunes. Brown is well represented here as an accompanist but not as a soloist. Anderson delivers a vocal interpretation of Ray Brown's "Soft Shoe," in which the lyrics speak of a crush on someone she has not yet met or spoken to, although she fantasizes about dancing with her crush: "come on and do the old soft shoe with me."[146]

Ray Brown worked with many iconic singers throughout his career, few more celebrated than Aretha Franklin, the "Queen of Soul," with whom he played on the 1977 album *Sweet Passion* (Atlantic SD-19102). The record was considered a commercial failure but did include the single "Break It to Me Gently," which briefly topped the R&B charts. Brown plays electric bass on three tracks, "What I Did for Love," "Meadows of Springtime," and "Mumbles/I've Got the Music in Me," which includes Franklin singing scat vocals.

Ray joined Milt Jackson in the studio in 1978 for the album *Soul Believer: Milt Jackson Sings and Plays* (Pablo 2310 832), with Jackson coming forward as a soul-type singer. Brown was both bassist and producer for the album which also included Cedar Walton, Billy Higgins, Frank Severino, and Plas Johnson, all frequent collaborators with Brown at the time. The stand-out track is a vocal interpretation of Brown's original "Parking Lot Blues." Jackson emerges as a competent singer; in fact, he sang regularly as a youth and revealed he was a "gospel singer from seven to sixteen" in an interview with Alyn Shipton.[147] A similar release was Roy Eldridge's 1975 *Happy Time* (Pablo 2310 746). Eldridge's decision to sing on the record as well live during this period may have had something to do with the challenges of playing difficult trumpet parts during the course of an entire concert or album. On "All of Me" Brown begins the tune by playing unaccompanied blues licks before Eldridge joins on muted trumpet.

Brown also recorded with vocalist Nancy King on her 1978 album with Steve Wolfe, *First Date* (Inner City Records IC-1049). Although *First Date* reached number 1 on the *Billboard* jazz charts, saxophonist Steve Wolfe is relatively unknown today and reportedly suffered from heroin addiction. Nancy King continued working as a jazz vocalist well past the 1970s. She would later appear on Ray Brown Trio recordings but never achieved celebrity status.

There were also vocal albums with less of a jazz connection. One such was Ted Gärdestad's *Blue Virgin Isles* (Polar PMC-284). Gärdestad was a Swedish singer-songwriter who began as a child actor and this was his English-language debut. The album was a commercial failure, and in 1981 Gärdestad left the music scene at the age of twenty-five to become a devotee of a controversial Eastern cult. Gärdestad suffered from several psychiatric problems and died in 1997 aged forty-one.

Brown also appeared on well-known Los Angeles singer, songwriter, and guitarist Stephen Bishop's 1978 album *Bish* (ABC Records AA-1082). *Bish* was the follow-up to his successful 1976 debut release, *Careless* (ABC Records 9022-954) and both albums went gold. The biggest single from *Bish*, "Everyone Needs Love," reached number 34 on the *Billboard* charts. A lesser-known vocal album was Steve and Eydie's 1976 *Our Love Is Here to Stay (The Gershwin Years)* (Stage Records 711). Steve Lawrence and Eydie Gormé were a famous husband-and-wife act that came to national fame in the 1950s.

While backing vocalists was an essential part of Ray Brown's career, his most celebrated work was always instrumental jazz. On June 3, 1975, he was part of an all-star session that included Roy Eldridge, Dizzy Gillespie, Oscar Peterson, and Mickey Roker, resulting in the Pablo album *Jazz Maturity . . . Where It's Coming From* (Pablo 2310 816). There are several exciting dynamics at play within the session. For starters, Brown was with the two most important bandleaders of his own career, Gillespie and Peterson. Additionally, Gillespie was paired with Roy Eldridge, his most significant personal musical hero. Finally, the session featured five musicians who had long reached "maturity" but were now in the throes of a 1975 music scene that seemed to have little interest in mainstream jazz.

A comparison between Eldridge and Gillespie is inevitable, and instructive. While Eldridge proves that he could still play with some of the mastery of his younger years, Gillespie is in fact playing some of his best material in the 1970s. He displays the bebop technicality that made him a star but also facility for new exploratory solo material that was not derivative of his former days. Peterson had also become slightly more experimental and relied less on rapid note runs and signature licks and phrases. Each of the six tracks allows for multiple solo choruses by Eldridge, Gillespie, and Peterson. Ray Brown is mainly relegated to an accompanist role and solos only on "When It's Sleepy Time Down South." His solo is swing-based and relatively conservative in terms of technical exploration.

Another session with Gillespie was on February 3, 1977, and featured Count Basie and Mickey Roker. Count Basie and Dizzy Gillespie, *The Gifted Ones* (Pablo 2310 833) has an overall group sound and connectivity, making it one of the best late-'70s straight-ahead jazz albums. Basie's subtle approach against Brown's driving bass lines and Roker's solid grooves is a perfect combination, giving Gillespie room for his blend of bop, swing, blues, Latin, and funk. Basie's spacious solos offer melodic contrast to Gillespie's note-heavy offerings. Making the album even more interesting, all bar one (the standard "St. James Infirmary") of the six numbers are originals credited to Gillespie or Basie/Gillespie. Ray Brown soloes on "Constantinople," "St. James Infirmary," and "Follow the Leader." None of his solos are overly flashy, and his phrases are well connected and capture the mood.

On three sessions – July 26 and 28 and August 16, 1975 – Ray Brown was assisting trumpeter Art Farmer with his album *On the Road* (Contemporary Records S7636). Farmer was one of the finer jazz trumpeters to emerge in the 1950s, and his playing was characterized by a distinctive tone and lyrical approach. This recording includes alto saxophonist Art Pepper, pianist Hampton Hawes, and either Shelly Manne or Steve Ellington on drums. Most impressive is Pepper, arguably one of the finest alto soloists after Charlie Parker. Unfortunately, Pepper struggled mightily with heroin addiction, leading to several career interruptions. *On the Road* has a "searching" quality in which the musicians are open to exploration. The result is an impressive

Ray Brown with Count Basie, Montreux Jazz Festival, July 18, 1977.
ZUMA Press, Inc. / Alamy Stock Photo

six-track album that should be included on a list of best jazz releases of the year. Ray Brown soloes on "Namely You," "What Am I Here For?" and "I Can't Get Started," but more important in this setting is his ability to lay down a foundation to let Farmer, Pepper, and Hawes explore.

On August 14, 1976 a one-day session for Hampton Hawes resulted in *Hampton Hawes at the Piano* (Contemporary Records S7637). Unfortunately, Hawes passed away less than a year after this recording, suffering a brain hemorrhage at the age of only forty-eight. Brown and Shelly Manne connect perfectly with Hawes and it is a shame that this record, and indeed Hawes, did not attract more attention. Brown is impressive as a soloist on "Soul Sign Eight" and "When I Grow Too Old to Dream."

One of the artists Ray Brown was most connected to during this period was the soul-jazz tenor saxophonist Plas Johnson. In 1976, his release *The Blues* (Concord Jazz CJ-15) included Brown, Herb Ellis, Jake Hanna, Mike Melvoin, and percussionist Bobbye Hall. It's a solid effort, and the repertoire is well suited to Johnson's style. Added excitement comes when Melvoin plays the Fender Rhodes on "Our Day Will Come" and "Bucket o' Blues." It being a Concord release, at least one Ray Brown original would be expected, and in this case it was "Parking Lot Blues" again. This understanding was likely an agreement he had with label owner Carl Jefferson to augment his income from royalties. Ray Brown is best represented on "Time after Time," beginning and ending the tune in a duo performance with Johnson. Surprisingly, there are no Brown solos on the *Blues* record. He appeared again on Plas Johnson's second release of the year, *Positively* (Concord Jazz CJ-24) – recorded on May 7–8, 1976 – as did the other musicians on *The Blues*, albeit with drummer Jimmie Smith replacing Jake Hanna on four tracks. An exceptional track is "Let's Get It All Together," a pop-jazz vehicle written by Melvoin. The final track, "Dirty Leg Blues," is Ray Brown's contribution, well written and expertly performed as a soul-jazz number. Except for some duo statements between Johnson and Brown on "Careless Love," the bassist is again unused as a soloist.

The jazz album that garnered the most interest during this period was Bill Evans' *Quintessence* (Fantasy F-9529), recorded between May 27 and 30, 1976. Pianist Bill Evans was a style innovator who came to fame in the late 1950s as a member of Miles Davis's sextet (1958) and through his work with his trio beginning in 1956. Writers and critics viewed Evans' more subdued style as a reaction to bop players like Bud Powell and Oscar Peterson. With his trios, Evans developed a specific vision in which the bassist and drummer would not always be required to play straight swing time. Instead, his musicians were encouraged to engage in a conversational approach that required reactionary collective improvisation. With his albums *Portraits in Jazz* (Riverside RLP 315), *Explorations* (Riverside RLP 12-351), and *Sunday at the Village Vanguard* (Riverside RLP 376), which included bass master Scott LaFaro and drummer Paul Motian, Bill Evans changed the shape of jazz. We have already discussed LaFaro in Chapters 13 and 17. The tragedy of LaFaro's untimely death, along with the death of Bill Evans' girlfriend and his ongoing heroin addiction, blighted the pianist's life and career, which had many ups and downs. But Evans retained his skills and creativity as a pianist until his death at only fifty-one in 1980.

As with Oscar Peterson, Bill Evans was known for trios with virtuosic bassists. Following LaFaro's demise, Evans' trio included technicians like Chuck Israels, Gary Peacock, Eddie Gomez, and Marc Johnson. Adopting Evans' unique approach could be challenging for a bassist such as Ray Brown, who was more comfortable providing foundational swing bass lines. The Evans "conversational" style requires a connection and a level of mutual comfort between musicians that can often only be achieved hours of practice. With regard to the album in question, it should be noted that Evans is often most brilliant in duo and trio contexts. While there are some strong moments on *Quintessence,* it is apparent that the supporting cast of Ray Brown, Harold Land, Kenny Burrell, and Philly Joe Jones was not comfortable with this looser way of playing, leading to a slight disconnect at times. Ray Brown, in particular, overplays, and cannot seem to help himself from trying to suggest time playing and often resorts to a walking bass line. Brown and the ensemble are most impressive on the more straight-ahead tracks, "Bass Face" and "Nobody Else But Me" (the latter a CD bonus track.) Unfortunately, it is in these more straightforward performances that Evans seems less comfortable, and the brilliance of his concept and approach is lost. Ray Brown and Bill Evans would not record together again after this session.

In 1976, Ray Brown recorded two more well-regarded studio albums with the piano master Phineas Newborn Jr.: *Back Home* (Contemporary Records C-7648), recorded September 17–18, and *Look Out: Phineas is Back!* (Pablo 2310 801), recorded December 7–8, 1976. As reported in Chapter 20, due to mental-health and physiological issues, Newborn's output had slowed considerably since 1969, leaving a five-year gap in his recording activities. In the trio with Newborn and Brown was drummer Elvin Jones, the same unit that had recorded *Please Send Me Someone to Love* in 1969. For the second of the 1976 sessions, Jones was replaced by Jimmie Smith. Both recordings display Newborn's remarkable ability to blend creativity and technicality. Highlights from the albums include "Salt Peanuts," "You Are the Sunshine of My Life," and Ray Brown's original "Abbers Song." These would be Brown's final recordings with Newborn.

Another "comeback" release worthy of more attention was Tal Farlow's 1977 *A Sign of the Times* (Concord Jazz CJ-26). The title was a play on the fact that since 1958 Farlow had got married, moved to the New Jersey shore, and begun a career as a sign painter, henceforth recording infrequently. *A Sign of the Times* marked his return to more consistent activities as a performer and recording artist. These drummerless recordings with Brown and Hank Jones offer a degree of experimentation and modernism, mainly via Farlow reaching for new ideas and reharmonizations. At times, it seems that Farlow's fingers cannot keep up with his brain, and his playing is less clean and consistent than in the past. While he might not be at his finest technically, he is still remarkable at times. His quest to put himself in musical predicaments during improvisations creates an active experience for Jones and Brown, who seem eager to grasp Farlow's desire to create and explore. The group is most impressive on "In Your Own Sweet Way," with tight rhythmic hits on the melody and trading solo statements by the trio. Ray Brown's original slow "Bayside Blues" is worth noting and he impresses as a soloist on "You Are Too Beautiful," with unaccompanied statements, rapid scale-like lines, sliding figures, and pull-offs.

Another guitarist-led album was 1978's *The Real Howard Roberts* (Concord Jazz CJ-53), with painist Ross Tompkins and drummer Jimmie Smith. Although he had recorded several jazz records before 1978, Roberts was a guitar wizard mainly known for his Los Angeles studio work as a member of the "Wrecking Crew." On *The Real Howard Roberts*, he was allowed to play without limitations and in the jazz style he most enjoyed. As he often did on Concord releases, Brown provided one original piece and once again it was "Parking Lot Blues," with Brown and Roberts playing the head in unison. His decision to offer the song again was likely due to the fact that it was easily adaptable, and of course he appreciated the royalty income. Brown's solos on

"Dolphin Dance," "Gone with the Wind," and "Angel Eyes" blend creativity with technicality. For jazz guitar fans *The Real Howard Roberts* is a gem.

One of the more unusual recordings was the 1979 Tiny Moore and Jethro Burns album *Back to Back* (Kaleidoscope Records F-9), a bluegrass/jazz album giving Brown a further chance to demonstrate his versatility and include another genre in his discography. It was made on January 6 and 7, with Brown, Shelly Manne, and guitarist Eldon Shamblin backing the two mandolin masters. David Grisman, another mandolin virtuoso, produced the album, and also performed on "Moonlight Waltz" and "Tiny's Rag."

Billie "Tiny" Moore came to fame playing both electric mandolin and fiddle in the Western swing band Bob Wills and the Texas Playboys in 1940. Willis's brand of Western swing included a unique mixture of Appalachian fiddle, swing, country, Hawaiian music, pop crooning, and polka. The Texas Playboys were fashionable in the 1940s, and the group regularly charted higher than many of the famous swing big bands of the day. Although highly active in the mid-1930s, Kenneth "Jethro" Burns was widely disregarded until the 1970s, when bluegrass began to enjoy a revival. Burns was known for his ability to incorporate more advanced jazz chord voicings and phrasing into traditional bluegrass music. His playing and style led to the more exploratory "New Grass Revival" movement. On *Back to Back*, the mandolinists present a repertoire of jazz and bluegrass classics and two Moore originals. Ray Brown's job is to provide a solid bass foundation to match the brushwork of Shelly Manne. He gets one solo, on "Diane," and the album is a superb and welcome departure from the mainstream jazz projects that dominated Brown's recording schedule.

As explained at the beginning of this chapter, a detailed evaluation of all Brown's jazz-based studio appearances during this period is beyond the scope of the chapter; however, it's worth reeling off the following in a list in order to appreciate the breadth of Brown's activities. Not being discussed at greater length is not necessarily a judgment of their artistic merit.

- Herb Ellis and Freddie Green, *Rhythm Willie* (1975; Concord Jazz CJ-10)
- Milt Jackson and Strings, *Feelings* (1976; Pablo 2310 774)
- Quincy Jones, *I Heard That!!* (1976; A&M Records SP-3705)[148]
- Hank Jones, *Just for Fun* (1977; Galaxy GXY-5105)[149]
- Paul Smith, *Heavy Jazz* (1977; Outstanding Records 009)
- Paul Smith, *Heavy Jazz – Vol. 2* (1977; Outstanding Records 011)
- Ross Tompkins, *Lost in the Stars* (1977; Concord Jazz CJ-46)
- Richie Kamuca, *Drop Me off in Harlem* (1977; Concord Jazz CJ-39)
- Bill Berry and His Ellington All-Stars, *For Duke* (1978; M & K RealTime Records RT-101)
- Snooky Young and Marshal Royal, *Snooky and Marshal's Album* (1978; Concord Jazz CJ-55)[150]

- Snooky Young, *Horn of Plenty* (1979; Concord Jazz CJ-91)
- Remo Palmieri, *Remo Palmieri* (1979; Concord Jazz CJ-76)
- Richie Kamuca, *Richie Kamuca's Charlie* (1979; Concord Jazz CJ-96)
- Billy Preston and Syreeta, *Music from the Motion Picture "Fast Break"* (1979; Motown M7-915R1)[151]

Ray Brown was also captured on live recordings during this period, most frequently at the Concord and Montreux Jazz Festivals. In July 1975, he accompanied veteran soprano saxophonists Bob Wilber and Ken Davern at the Concord Summer Jazz Festival. In the 1970s, Wilber and Davern had formed the Soprano Summit group, as co-leaders playing clarinets and various saxophones. The festival performance was recorded and released as *Soprano Summit in Concert* (Concord Jazz CJ-29), a highlight being "The Grapes Are Ready," in which Wilber, Davern, guitarist Marty Grosz, and Brown all solo.

One of the finest live recordings from 1976 has to be Tal Farlow, Hank Jones, Red Norvo, Ray Brown, and Jake Hanna, *On Stage* (Concord Jazz CJ-143) from the August Concord Jazz Festival. The album, released in 1981, was the first time Ray Brown was captured playing with vibraphonist Red Norvo, a significant star from the 1930s through the mid-'50s. Norvo remained active in jazz until failing health forced him to retire in the mid-1980s. In his trio with Farlow, Red Norvo introduced the world to Charles Mingus, who served as his bassist from 1950 to 1951. This live set includes only jazz standards, and Brown does not solo.

On March 22 and 23, 1976, Ray Brown returned to Japan to perform with Milt Jackson, which led to the release of the double live album *Milt Jackson Live at the Kosei Nenkin* (Pablo Live 2620 103). Joining Jackson and Brown on long-form versions of popular standards are tenor saxophonist Teddy Edwards, pianist Cedar Walton, and drummer Billy Higgins. Ray Brown highlights include "St. Thomas," "The Prophet Speaks," "Stolen Moments," and Walton's original "Bolivia." The audience is incredibly responsive, and the musicianship is remarkable. From May 3, 1976, Brown can also be heard performing with the same group during a Tokyo performance on a German release under Brown and Jackson's names: *Fuji Mama* (1990; West Wind 2054).

During much of July 1977, the annual Montreux Jazz Festival was under way, and some of the biggest names in jazz, blues, and rock made their way to Switzerland to perform. From July 13–17, Ray Brown and many of Granz's artists took the stage and were both captured on film and recorded for Granz's Pablo label. On July 13, Ray Brown and Milt Jackson presented their "All-Star Jam," leading to the album *Montreux '77: Milt Jackson/Ray Brown Jam* (Pablo Live 2308 205), a nearly hour-long performance featuring Eddie "Lockjaw" Davis, Clark Terry, Monty Alexander, and Jimmie Smith. Brown solos on almost every track, and on this and other performances during the week he seemed determined to show that he could still play with a technical prowess that few could match. Brown's determination may have had something to do with the fact that Danish bass virtuoso Niels-Henning Ørsted Pedersen (NHØP) appeared frequently, joining guest artists in spots that Ray Brown would have customarily been invited to. Brown's best moments are on "Slippery" and "A Beautiful Friendship."

The next day Brown participated in *Montreux '77: Dizzy Gillespie Jam* (Pablo Live 2308 211), which featured Jackson, Alexander, Smith, and trumpeter Jon Faddis. The jam provides some fireworks with Brown soloing on the lengthy "Girl of My Dreams." In the evening he was part of *Montreux '77: Count Basie Jam* (Pablo Live 2308 209), with Roy Eldridge, Benny Carter, Zoot Sims, Al Grey, Vic Dickenson, and Jimmie Smith. While all-star jams can sometimes seem contrived and miss the mark, this one is remarkable, mainly because each musician's voice is unique, allowing for the right level of variety to hold an audience's interest. In addition, the crowd's engagement is such that their energy can be felt through the recording. One highlight is "Trio Blues," a Ray Brown showcase, as he plays with only Basie and Smith. As he takes his solo, you can hear the banter of the other musicians on stage, offering encouragement and conversing about the performance. The applause that ensued is staggering, and in the background you can hear one of the musicians saying, "We can't follow that."

If there was a time for Brown to feel any pressure during the festival, it would have been during a July 15 set that paired him against NHØP, the current bassist in Oscar Peterson's trio. The performance was captured and released on video and on the album *Montreux '77: Oscar Peterson and the Bassists* (Pablo Live 2308 213). Pairing two bassists together as soloists was rarely done, especially two as gifted as Brown and Ørsted Pedersen. Their set begins with an uptempo rendition of "There Is No Greater Love." Niels plays rapid lines for his solo, displaying his unique right-hand three-finger technique. Oscar Peterson solos for a second time, giving way to Brown for his solo. While Brown is impressive, Ørsted Pedersen may have bested him here. From the outset, the latter's expression is all business, while Brown seems more relaxed and appears to be enjoying the contest.

Before the second piece, "You Look Good to Me," Brown and Pedersen engage in some light banter, and now both bassists appear to be smiling. Brown begins this piece with Oscar Peterson, and after providing accompaniment plays a characteristic solo using many of his signature licks. Now Ørsted Pedersen accompanies Oscar Peterson and plays a solo, demonstrating his remarkable comfort and mastery of the upper range of the bass. By this point, it has become clear that, brilliant though he is, Ray Brown cannot match NHØP's technicality. That is in no way to denigrate Brown's skills, who, even by 1977 standards, was still one of the most technically gifted bassists on the scene. The set continues with "People" (neither bassist solo), "Reunion Blues," a set highlight, and "Teach Me Tonight." The album concludes with an uptempo version of "Sweet Georgia Brown." *Oscar Peterson and the Bassists* and the accompanying video should be in the collections of all fans of jazz bass. Tragically, Niels Henning Ørsted Pedersen died in 2005 from heart failure aged only fifty-eight. He will long be remembered as one of the all-time most gifted jazz bassists.

On the same day, Ray Brown performed with Eddie "Lockjaw" Davis, Oscar Peterson, and drummer Jimmie Smith in a well-received jam-style set. Brown can be heard soloing on "I Wished on the Moon," "The Breeze and I," and "Telegraph." These tracks were released on *Montreux '77: Eddie "Lockjaw" Davis 4* (Pablo Live 2308 214). Another live release from 1977 was Joe Venuti's and George Barnes' *Live at the Concord Jazz Summer Festival* (Concord Jazz CJ-30), an album that would be one of Venuti's and Barnes' last. At the time of the release, Venuti, the "father of jazz violin," was seventy-three and would pass away the following year. Guitarist George Barnes died on September 5, 1977, aged only fifty-six, from a heart attack. Joining Brown in the ensemble playing popular jazz standards were drummer Jake Hanna and pianist Ross Tompkins. The performance is impressive throughout with the musicians seeming well connected, and both Venuti and Barnes deserve praise. Brown solos several times and is featured explicitly on "Things Ain't What They Used to Be." Also captured from the evening was a performance by Ray Brown in an ensemble with Tompkins, Venuti, Hanna, and Scott Hamilton on tenor sax. This can be heard on Ross Tompkins, Joe Venuti, Ray Brown, Scott Hamilton, and Jake Hanna, *Live at Concord '77* (Concord Jazz CJ-51).

In July 1979 Ray Brown was back at the Montreux Jazz Festival to perform with L.A. Four. He was also captured performing on an inspired set for Herb Ellis that resulted in *Herb Ellis at Montreux: Summer 1979* (Concord Jazz CJ-116). The album is split between two separate bands. Joining Brown and Ellis on their set are Tompkins and Hanna. Brown is featured on "Love Walked In," "Georgia on My Mind," and "Secret Love," all on Side A. Side B has Ellis playing with bassist Michael Moore and drummer Jeff Hamilton. In August 1979, Brown appeared again at the Concord Jazz Festival and was recorded playing a set with Marshal Royal, Jake Hanna, and guitarist Cal Collins, available on Ross Tompkins and the Concord All-Stars, *Festival Time* (Concord Jazz CJ-117).

24 *Brown's Bag*: Albums Listing Ray Brown as a Leader 1975–1979

By 1975, Ray Brown was showing a greater interest in leadership and as the later years of the decade saw him appear several times as a leader or co-leader, eventually leading to the formation of his famed Ray Brown Trio. Although, by now, the inclusion of Ray's name on the cover of an album added value from a marketing point of view, there is a more consequential reason for delving into these more deeply, as they were more prominent vehicles for his individualism.

On August 25, 1975 he joined his old friends Milt Jackson and Joe Pass to record *The Big 3* (Pablo 2310 757). It opens with "The Pink Panther," and a groovy Ray Brown bass intro. Brown takes the final solo, which begins with a quote of "Bye Bye Blackbird," followed by some bebop statements and a quote from Parker's "Moose the Mooche." The trio follows with a set of jazz standards: "Moonglow," "You Stepped Out of a Dream," and "Wave," with the only original piece being "Blues for Sammy," credited to Milt Jackson and published by Brown's company Ray Brown Music. The songs on *The Big 3* are primarily played in the formulaic fashion of melody followed by solos, offering little in terms of unique arrangements; however, the individual talents of this drummerless trio are enough to hold the listener's interest.

Ray Brown took part in another fine trio recording on November 28, 1975, leading to the album Joe Sample, Ray Brown, and Shelly Manne, *The Three* (EastWind EW-10001). From the outset, it is clear that Joe Sample, who was better known for his jazz fusion work with the Jazz Crusaders, has the skills to play mainstream jazz in a style that connects well with Brown and Manne. Highlights include a fiery and interactive interpretation of "On Green Dolphin Street," "Manha do Carnaval," and "Round Midnight." *The Three* deserves more attention, and Ray Brown is featured as a soloist on all six tracks.

1976 was a bigger year for Ray Brown-led or co-led projects. One was *Brown's Bag*, under his own name (Concord Jazz CJ-19). The album is split between two bands, the first with Blue Mitchell on trumpet, Richie Kamuca on tenor sax, Art Hillery on piano, and John Guerin on drums, the second with John Collins on guitar, Dave Grusin on keyboards, and Jimmie Smith on drums. *Brown's Bag* begins with a high-flying Ray Brown original blues called "Blues for Eddie Lee," with some fiery double-timed bass solo statements. Track 2 is the Johnny Mandel standard ballad "A Time for Love," in which Brown plays the melody against a background of heavily synthesized pads played by Grusin. After Brown's initial statement, played rubato (out of time), the group shifts to swing with solos first by Grusin, then Brown. The song closes as it begins with a heavy synth bed and Brown's cadenza. This synthesized sound is uncharacteristic of his solo efforts. Next is a super-funky Ray Brown original, "Keep on Pumpin'," played by the first ensemble. The track is a reminder of his ability to play funk grooves on the acoustic bass – a skill that deserves wider recognition.

Side B begins with the classic "Surrey with the Fringe on Top" from the hit Broadway show *Oklahoma!* After a slow bass intro, Ray Brown plays solo statements against a funky groove. "Surrey" was a piece that Brown recorded dozens of times, but this treatment offers a fresh take. Next is "You Are My Sunshine," another Brown favorite, played as a shuffle, with Brown providing the melody against the rhythm section and his own pre-recorded walking line. This use of overdubbing, too, is uncharacteristic of his solo productions. Track 3 of Side B is the gorgeous ballad by Johnny Mercer and Johnny Mandel, "Emily." Grusin introduces the melody, and the music is played against some synth pads. Brown then enters to restate the theme in a rubato fashion. After Grusin, Ray Brown plays an inspired solo. The album concludes with a short jam reprise of "Surrey with the Fringe on Top." While *Brown's Bag* isn't one of his more celebrated works, it is nonetheless fascinating because of its use of synthesizers, which, along with the overdubbing, shows that he was not opposed to assimilating newer concepts and sounds within a jazz context.

A notable 1976 release was Herb Ellis and the Ray Brown Sextet, *Hot Tracks* (Concord Jazz CJ-12). The sextet included Harry "Sweets" Edison, Plas Johnson, Jake Hanna, and pianist Mike Melvoin. Ray Brown provided two original pieces for the session. The first is "Spherikhal," a medium-swing piece that begins with a soulful gospel-flavored piano intro followed by a carefully harmonized melodic statement played only by Edison, Johnson, and Ellis. The tune then settles into a medium-swing groove before returning to the melodic statement. The second is the medium-tempo "Blues for Minnie," a simple and soulful blues played in the hard bop tradition.

The bassist is most impressive on the ballad "But Beautiful," which he begins by interpreting the original melody before shifting smoothly into improvised statements against only Ellis's guitar and the light brushwork of Hanna. Another highlight is a spirited shuffle swing written by Plas Johnson called "Bones." Melvoin adds a cool '70s vibe to the piece by using electric piano. Also of interest is Melvoin's spy-like theme on "So's Your Mother," which includes a two-bar call-and-response melody between Brown and the ensemble. *Hot Tracks* is an album worth exploring as it contains just enough arrangement interest and personality to separate it from the more thrown-together releases of the time.

Another fine recording with Brown as co-leader is *Quadrant, Featuring Joe Pass, Milt Jackson, Ray Brown, and Mickey Roker* (Pablo 2310 837). It was recorded in one day at Los Angeles' Sun West Studios on February 4, 1977. Using vibes and guitar on the record as the primary harmonic instruments works particularly well in creating a sonic environment in which Ray Brown is given ample space to provide well-placed bass lines. Side A begins with Joe Pass's tune "Concorde," followed by "Joe's Tune," which is based on the modal chord changes of Miles Davis's "So What." Both pieces are played rapidly, and Pass and Jackson display their incredible abilities to offer well-connected solo phrases on uptempo material. The tempo slows on the next track, "Lady Be Good," on which Brown provides a bluesy solo, incorporating bop lines and a series of triplet pull-off figures. Unfortunately, his bass distorts several times on this track and elsewhere on the album. The final cut of Side A is "Ray's Tune," an original funky sixteen-bar blues written by the bassist which sees him drawing on '70s funk and soul. Side B is somewhat less remarkable and includes Carl Perkins' tune "Grooveyard," Gershwin's "The Man I Love," and Milt Jackson's "Blues for the Stone." Ray Brown is featured as a primary soloist on the latter two.

In 1980, the Quadrant group released a second album: *All Too Soon: Quadrant Toasts Duke Ellington* (Pablo Today 2312 117), featuring nine tunes associated with Ellington. The album's interest comes from the talents of Pass and Jackson as soloists. The ensemble mainly presents Ellington's best-known themes with clarity, taking few risks with regard to arrangements or experimentation. *All Too Soon* is nothing more noteworthy than a throwback to 1940s jazz, albeit played by outstanding musicians. Brown is most heavily featured on "Rocks in My Bed," "Main Stem," "Sophisticated Lady," and "In a Sentimental Mood." A highlight is "Caravan," which includes a funky bass line played during the intro and A section.

Some time during 1978, the Louie Bellson, Ray Brown, and Paul Smith album *Intensive Care* (Discwasher Recordings DR-001) was issued as a "limited edition." These seven tracks of Broadway-based jazz standards are an absolute masterclass in swing-based jazz. Paul Smith's technical ability, enhanced by theatrical showmanship, matches and even surpasses the skills of some historically celebrated jazz pianists. Bellson, with simply flawless fast swing and bop time feels, proves that his skills are not diminished, and of course Ray Brown holds it all down with solid bass lines creating a forward-moving propulsion of the beat. The record begins with an uptempo version of "The Lady Is a Tramp," in which Ray moves in and out of two feel and walking bass lines. His hookup with Bellson is evident from the outset. The second cut is the Jerome Kern classic "Yesterdays," which begins with an incredible Paul Smith display of technicality somewhat reminiscent of Oscar Peterson. The dynamic lightens, and Brown's improvisation begins with a quotation from the melody before a display of less rhythmically active phrases. Following the energy of the opening track, the group settles into the ballad "Everything Happens to Me," before the medium-tempo "On a Clear Day," which includes a bass solo. To begin Side B, the trio launches into a short version of "Surrey with a Fringe on Top," followed by the more medium-paced "My Heart Stood Still" from the songwriting team of Rodgers and Hart. It is on this track that Brown is most impressive as a soloist. His statements include precise phrasing, well-placed melodic developments, select moments of double-time phrasing, triplet pull-offs, and even a quote from "Ol' Man River." The piece concludes with Brown playing a three-octave scale-like figure. The group returns to playing at a breakneck speed with their interpretation of "Chicago" before finishing with the standard "Lover," played at medium swing before a fast interlude ends the record with a bang.

One of the stronger 1977 releases was the album *Jones, Brown, Smith* (Concord Jazz CJ-32). The trio of Hank Jones, Ray Brown, and Jimmie Smith made for a well-suited musical relationship, and of course Jones and Brown had a musical history that dated back nearly thirty years. A unique element of this album is hearing Jones play the Fender Rhodes keyboard on several tracks. Highlights included the Ellington classic "Rockin' in Rhythm," with a signature-sounding Ray Brown solo. Also of interest is the bluesy presentation of the novelty classic "Your Feet's Too Big" and a funk/swing version of "Bags Groove." While *Jones, Brown, Smith* is not considered a masterwork, it contains enough repertoire variation and improvisational skill to be of interest.

In 1978, Ray Brown found another worthy musical companion in pianist Jimmy Rowles when they recorded two duo albums. Rowles was best known for his work accompanying singers such as Ella Fitzgerald, Billie Holiday, and Peggy Lee. On *As Good As It Gets* (Concord Jazz CJ-66) Rowles's less note-heavy style allows Brown's voice to be heard clearly throughout. Brown presents the melody on "Honey," and "Who Cares" and shares solo duties. If you are looking for a Ray Brown recording to relax with, *As Good As It Gets* may be your best choice, as the tempos never get too fast and the solos are never too exploratory or jarring. On their second duo album, 1980's *Tasty!* (Concord Jazz CJ-122), the pair once again demonstrate a solid musical connection that is conversational, subtle, and sophisticated. Highlights include "A Sleepin' Bee," "Nancy (With the Laughing Face'), and "My Ideal."

During this period, Brown also released two Japanese albums listing him as co-leader. On the 1978 record by Ray Brown and Ichiro Masuda, *The Most Special Joint* (JVC/Victor SGS-6), are Masuda, a Japanese jazz vibraphonist who was not well known in America, and Cedar Walton and Billy Higgins. On 1979's Tsuyoshi Yamamoto with Ray Brown, *Smoke a Moto's Blues* (Yupiteru Records YJ25-7028), along with Yamamoto on the piano is drummer Donald Bailey and Japanese saxophonist Kounosuke Saijo. The album is all standards except for the Ray Brown composition "Smoke a Moto's Blues," which begins as a bass vehicle in which Brown offers a solo call-and-response by playing single-note lines answered by double stops.

From June 22–24, 1977 Ray Brown set out to record one of the first of many Ray Brown Trio albums that would soon describe his future pattern as a performer and recording artist. Brown hired two jazz heavyweights, Cedar Walton and Elvin Jones, for this recording and the result was *Something for Lester* (Contemporary Records S7641), a tribute to Lester Koenig. Koenig was a fascinating man who had studied as a lawyer and worked as a screenwriter and record producer. In 1951, Koening founded Contemporary Records, the source of numerous opportunities for jazz musicians like Ray Brown. On November 20, 1977, Koening died aged fifty-nine from a heart attack, representing the loss of another of Ray Brown's friends and associates.

Something for Lester begins with the Latin-flavored Cedar Walton vehicle "Ojos de Rio." Brown starts by setting up the groove. Elvin Jones, a unique jazz drummer and one of the most gifted, pushes the beat in the busy polyrhythmic style he developed while working with John Coltrane from 1960 to 1966. The next track is a slow bluesy Ray Brown original called "Slippery." Brown presents the tune's melody and takes a solo, offering a series of slides, double stops, and well-connected blues statements. The third track is another Walton original, "Something in Common," on which Jones, who can undoubtedly be explosive at times, shows us that he can play brushes too. Brown is heavily featured on the track. Side A concludes with the George Gershwin vehicle "Love Walks In."

Side B begins with Ray Brown's presentation of "Georgia on My Mind," a soulful ballad ideally suited to his style. During Walton's solo, it moves from a ballad to a faster swing. The next cut is the Rodgers and Hart ballad "Little Girl Blue," in which Ray Brown presents the melody. The album concludes with the Horace Silver hard bop classic "Sister Sadie," which Ray Brown performed and recorded several times throughout his career, remaining one of his favorite melodies to play. *Something for Lester* is a critical release, not only because it is musically satisfying but because it pointed to the direction in which Brown would present much of his music moving forward. Future Ray Brown Trio albums would contain some of the finest examples of his talents as a bandleader, soloist, and small-group arranger, and each subsequent record would be of considerable interest in evaluating the bassist's later works and development.

25 Milt Jackson, Dizzy Gillespie, Monty Alexander, and Notable Sideman Sessions 1980–1984

By the early to mid-1980s, fusion jazz seemed to have run its creative course. Musicians were returning to acoustic efforts, and excessive pop music influences were watering down fusion's innovations. With the influx of jazz education in high schools and colleges, fans started to look to past musical heroes, and acoustic jazz began to enjoy a resurgence. At the forefront of this renaissance was Ray Brown. Sadly, by the time new fans became aware of the masters, many had already passed; this was especially true of the bass players – by 1980, many of the great bass innovators of the swing and bebop era were gone, leaving Ray Brown the authority and elder statesman of jazz bass.

Certainly, Ray Brown had paid his dues by this time, and was now entirely in control of his own musical and business decisions. He knew his own talents and his worth and demanded fair treatment for himself and his colleagues. Some would argue that Brown was a difficult man in a negotiation. Mike Hennessey asked him if he deserved that reputation, to which Ray replied:

> No, I don't think I do. It is simply that I've gotten to a point in my life where I think: If somebody wants me to come and perform, I've put in enough time, and they ought to think enough of me to pay me decently. If they don't, then I don't come. Today, maybe I can afford not to come – whereas, in days gone by, I would have had to take the gig to stay alive. Musicians in the past were always exploited and ripped off. I can remember times in the early recording days when Dizzy, Bird, and all of us, were just raped. They took our songs and gave us 25 bucks because we didn't know any better. I try to tell the young guys now to protect themselves against that kind of thing.[152]

Many of Ray Brown's early 1980s sideman efforts were not particularly celebrated as he worked primarily with stars of the past, lesser-known talents, and smaller jazz labels. That is not to say that his playing had declined or that the projects were of no value, but it does mean that a good portion of his sideman work from this period has been largely ignored. From here onwards, his more notable material would be as a leader, particularly with the Ray Brown Trio. But, before touring and recording with the trio became his key focus, he began the 1980s playing for others in the studio and in concert, something he would continue to do for the rest of his life. Although many other great technical bass players had emerged in the 1970s, Ray Brown was still considered the hardest-swinging bassist in the business and one of the instrument's most outstanding technicians.

Brown remained connected to Milt Jackson, producing and performing on Milt's 1980 *Bags' Bag* (Pablo 2310 842). This was gathered from three studio sessions: December 12, 1977, January 20, 1978, and January 21, 1980, the latter resulting in two duo tracks between Jackson and Brown, "Slow Boat to China" and "I Cover the Waterfront." All the other cuts feature a combination of Cedar Walton on electric piano, Jerome Richardson on soprano saxophone, and Billy Higgins on drums.[153] The music ranges from soulful blues to vocal numbers, sambas, and standards. Brown offers his original "Blues for Roberta," a medium-tempo soul-style blues featuring a simple bass ostinato. He is most impressive during his solo phrasing on "Blues for Tomi-Oka," and on the unaccompanied intro, contrapuntal bass lines, and expressive solo on "I Cover the Waterfront." Thanks to the material as well as the tonal qualities derived from the unique instrumentation, *Bags' Bag* ranks as one of Milt Jackson's finest solo albums.

Brown played on and produced another Milt Jackson release from 1980: *Big Mouth* (Pablo 2310 867). He was included on three tracks, "The Look of Love," "I'm Getting Sentimental Over You," and "I Owes Ya." The remainder were handled by the Mexican-American bass legend Abe Laboriel. With a large cast of sidemen, *Big Mouth* is one of Jackson's stronger efforts. Brown also recorded with Jackson on two other records that year: *Night Mist* (Pablo D2312124) and *Ain't But a Few of Us Left* (Pablo 2310 8730). *Night Mist* had Harry "Sweets" Edison on trumpet Eddie "Cleanhead" Vinson on alto sax, Eddie "Lockjaw" Davis on tenor sax, Art Hillery on piano, and Larance Marable on drums, and is a fine blend of blues played by some of the best stylists in the business. Ray Brown provides the simplistic uptempo original blues "Double B." *Ain't But a Few of Us Left* is a quartet session with Oscar Peterson and drummer Grady Tate, with highlights from Brown being his funky bass line on "Body and Soul," and his groove-based intro on "What Am I Here For." The appearance of Oscar Peterson is of interest.

On April 23 and 24, 1982 Ray Brown performed at Ronnie Scott's jazz club in London with Milt Jackson, Monty Alexander, and Mickey Roker, performances that would be released on Milt Jackson's *A London Bridge* (Pablo 2310 932) and *Mostly Duke* (Pablo PACD-2310-944-2). On the former, the ensemble performs the Ray Brown originals "F.S.R." ("for Sonny Rollins") and

"Captain Bill." Some material was also recorded on April 28, which found its way onto the album *Milt Jackson in London: Memories of Thelonious Sphere Monk* (Pablo Live 2308 235).

One of the choice releases of 1983 was Milt Jackson, J.J. Johnson, and Ray Brown's *Jackson, Johnson, Brown, and Company* (Pablo 2310 897), recorded between May 25 and 26, 1983 and with Ray Brown again given a producing credit. While it offers little experimentation, it is always a treat to hear great masters at work. In 1984 Brown teamed up again with Jackson on his annual trip to Japan, resulting in a live video and recording titled the Milt Jackson Quartet, *Used to Be Jackson Vol 1.* (TDK Records T28P-1006), recorded between April 8 and 9, 1984, with Cedar Walton and Mickey Roker. The video offers one of the most exemplary visual representations of Brown during this era. He is particularly impressive on his bowed interpretation of "Body and Soul," which leads in to "Work Song." We see his virtuosity in a solo rendition of "Manhã de Carnaval" on which he performs solo runs and double-stopped techniques. Following the tour, the same group went into a New York studio in July to record the album Milt Jackson, Ray Brown, Cedar Walton, and Mickey Roker, *It Don't Mean a Thing if You Can't Tap Your Foot to It* (Pablo 2310 909), with two Brown originals, "Used to Be Jackson," and "Ain't That Nothin'." Coming off the tour, the group sounds well connected and unified.

The bassist recorded again with Milt Jackson on November 30 and December 1, 1983 for the Milt Jackson Quartet album *Soul Route* (Pablo 2310 900), with pianist Gene Harris and drummer Mickey Roker. As with many Milt Jackson releases from this period, Brown was in the producer's chair. *Soul Route* marks the first time Brown would record with Harris, one of his most significant mid-1980s and early 1990s contributors and a working member of the Ray Brown Trio.

In the late 1950s, Gene Harris had gained popularity as the pianist in the group the Three Sounds, a trio in which Harris proved he could play dazzling, blues-influenced solos flavored with swing, bebop, soul, and gospel. When the Three Sounds disbanded in the early 1970s, Harris settled in Idaho, playing local gigs. In 1983, Ray Brown was instrumental in helping to reintroduce Gene Harris to the jazz public when he recommended him to Concord Records. The hookup between Brown and Harris on *Soul Route* is instantly recognizable.

Another past associate Brown continued to work and record with was Dizzy Gillespie. On March 10, 1980, Ray Brown recorded with Gillespie, Freddie Hubbard, and Clark Terry with a rhythm section that included Oscar Peterson, Joe Pass, and Bobby Durham for the record *The Trumpet Summit Meets the Oscar Peterson Big 4* (Pablo Today 2312-114). The album consists of four songs in which the three trumpet legends engage in a musical battle. While all are brilliant, the youngest, Freddie Hubbard, arguably edges ahead, but of course the real winner is the listener. The same session later produced the 1981 release Clark Terry, Freddie Hubbard, Dizzy Gillespie, plus Oscar

Peterson, *The Alternate Blues* (Pablo Today 2312 136), comprising alternate takes and out-takes. The original LP had a warning label reading, "The Surgeon General has determined that if you don't love the blues, this album is dangerous to your health."

The following day, Brown was with Clark Terry again, recording his Clark Terry Five album *Memories of Duke* (Pablo Today 2312 118) with guitarist Joe Pass, pianist Jack Wilson, and drummer Frank Severino. On this record, Clark Terry shows why he should considered one of the most outstanding jazz trumpeters, and Joe Pass is nothing short of miraculous. One of the most notable tracks is an uptempo Latin interpretation of "Sophisticated Lady."

On February 26, 1981, Brown performed again with Dizzy Gillespie, the outcome being Dizzy Gillespie, *Live at Concerts by the Sea* (single-sided laserdisc; Pioneer LDC MJ126-15CS). Ray Brown's presence is somewhat curious because the band included electric bassist Michael Howell. The two bassists sometimes trade off to ensure they are not playing over each other. The group is impressive, particularly on the Gillespie classics "Be-Bop" and "Birk's Works." Gillespie's incredible ability never diminishes and equally impressive is saxophonist Paquito D'Rivera. Brown is well represented throughout, and a video of the performance is in circulation.

Another of Ray Brown's significant connections during this period was pianist Monty Alexander. When forming a group to perform at the 1979 Concord Jazz Festival, Ray hired Alexander and Jeff Hamilton, which led to the first official Ray Brown Trio release, the Ray Brown Trio with Special Guest Ernestine Anderson, *Live at the Concord Jazz Festival 1979* (Concord Jazz CJ-102). In their first set, the trio kicks off the performance with an uptempo version of "Blue Bossa," followed by a gorgeous arrangement of "Bossa Nova do Marilla." Brown is then featured on "Manhã de Carnaval," an expressive intro preceding a creative interpretation of the melody. He breaks from each phrase of the written melody to present virtuoso solo fills, then sets up the band with a standard bossa nova bass line. He concludes with a fiery solo cadenza. This track is one of Brown's finest recorded displays of mastery from the period. The set concludes with the classic W.C. Handy composition "St. Louis Blues": Brown interprets the melody before setting up a funky bass line that slides into a traditional walk.

Having warmed up the large audience, they announced Ernestine Anderson to enthusiastic applause. With spirited performances of standards "Fly Me to the Moon," "Georgia on My Mind," "Here's That Rainy Day," "Please Send Me Someone to Love," and "Honeysuckle Rose," Anderson and the trio cause an uproar, their performance a highlight of the festival. The group's connectivity with Anderson is remarkable, considering they only had about an hour to rehearse together.[154] In 1980, Alexander and Brown then went on to work together on releases such as Marshal Royal's *Royal Blue* (Concord Jazz CJ-125), Ernestine Anderson's *Never Make Your Move Too Soon* (Concord Jazz CJ-147), and Alexander's *Facets* (Concord Jazz CJ-108).

Brown and Alexander also joined forces to record the German album *Ray Brown, Monty Alexander, Johnny Griffin, and Martin Drew, Summerwind* (Jeton 100.3312), a lesser-known recording beginning with an inspired unaccompanied solo by Brown on his original composition "Blues for Groundhog." He also impresses with another unaccompanied solo on Ellington's "Rocks in My Bed," and continues to use his bass as a solo vehicle on his original, "Put Your Little Foot Right Out." When not soloing on the piece, Brown is engaged in a duo performance with Griffin, who is outstanding. Other Brown features include "Delaney's Dilemma" and "Thanks for the Memories." In 2000, a second album from the session was released as *Summerwind II* (Jeton JET 60-016), with Brown the improviser much in evidence, to splendid effect on tracks like "Fungii Mama," "Orfeo Negro (Black Orpheus)," "Papa's Got a Brand New Bag," and "Please Send Me Someone to Love."

Another 1981 Alexander–Brown record was the Japanese release *Shelly Manne, Monty Alexander, and Ray Brown, Fingering* (Atlas Record LA27-1013). Like foreign labels sometimes did, the liner notes specify what kind of microphones were used in the recording: on this session, the engineers blended Ray Brown's sound using a Sony ECM 50 microphone, a Barcus Berry pickup, and a Polytone pickup. Throughout his career, Brown often used and endorsed Polytone products. A highlight from the record is an extended version of the classic "Easy Does It," including a Ray Brown solo with slides, pull-offs, and upper-structure statements.

Also in 1981 came *Monty Alexander, Ray Brown, and Herb Ellis, Trio* (Concord Jazz CJ-136). Using Oscar Peterson's two most celebrated sidemen in a trio format was a bold choice and would undoubtedly lead to comparisons between Alexander and Peterson. Monty Alexander fares well, as his technicality and borrowings from Peterson's style are evident. However, Alexander's playing would be at its most exciting and acquire its uniqueness in later contexts when he incorporated more of his Jamaican heritage and spirit. On this album, Ray Brown is most impressive as a soloist on his original, "Blues for Junior." His solo playing over simple blues changes continues to hit the mark. *Trio* is a well-presented throwback album highlighting the gifts of three fantastic musicians, but the work is not daring or original.

The trio was also captured live on the album *Overseas Special* (Concord Jazz CJ-253), recorded at a March 1982 performance at the Satin Doll Club in Tokyo. The playing is satisfying, and includes the Ray Brown original "F.S.R.," but one of the strongest numbers was the group's hard-swinging reworking of the American folk classic "C. C. Rider." This group, with Alexander and Ellis, later adopted the name "Triple Treat." While less remarkable than his work with the Poll Winners and the L.A. Four, Triple Treat was a notable Ray Brown side project. In an interview, Monty Alexander discussed his connection to Ray Brown and the group's formation:

I met him in New York. He was playing at Basin Street East with Oscar Peterson, and I had already come to New York, and I think it was about '64 or '65. I played at a little club where the bassist Bob Cranshaw played with me. He would often speak about Ray in glowing personal terms. I remember that was my introduction when I went backstage. I said, "I play, and Bob Cranshaw is with me, and he is always speaking of you and [he told me] to refer to him if I ever met you." He looked at me with extra acceptance, which was the beginning of his knowing me. That was my first meeting. I did not experience him as a bandleader because ninety-five percent of the time, we played in this combination we had called Triple Treat, and he designated that his role would be a three-in-one thing. It was like [he would say], "All right, what do you guys think?" I saw him in an equal partner [role], but behind it was a man with a powerful personality.

The first time I worked around him was in '68 or '69 when we were at Shelly's Manne Hole in LA with Milt Jackson. He and Bags [Jackson] had this brotherly relationship; they were very close friends. Of course, he knew they were perfect for each other when they made music together. He [Ray] would call the shots pretty much at that time, and I think he spent so many years helping everybody to sound their best that he wanted to be a bandleader. To call the shots. He wanted to have his own team. His own piano player, his own drummer, and he did that after that Hollywood studio thing. Up until then, he was the greatest studio guy and was the top called bass player.

After that time in LA, when he started to go out on the road, I recognized him moving into the bandleader thing, and he became wonderful at that. Many musicians were almost intimidated by his larger-than-life strength because he liked to yell certain sounds when he was playing. If the drummer did not understand that it was Ray's way of expressing his enthusiasm, the guy would get scared. He would look up and Ray and say, "What the hell? What is the matter with this guy?" But he [Ray] was just saying, "Geronimo!" you know, like when a guy jumps out of a plane with a parachute [*laughs*].

Regarding Triple Treat, Ray recommended the project to Carl Jefferson [Concord Records]. He told Carl Jefferson to give me a shot. I made a few records, and things were rolling nicely. I had met Herb and Ray together when they were doing *The Joey Bishop Show* before *The Merv Griffin Show*, I got to know them, and we would do sessions. Merv Griffin once heard me jamming in the corner; he said, "Yeah, man, we got to get you in the show today." Sure enough, that afternoon, I ended up being featured on *The Merv Griffin Show*, and this thing happened with me, Herb, and Ray. We played a couple of tunes, and the fire started to burn, and there was laughter and happiness. We accompanied Merv on a song, and I felt this kinship. He liked my attitude at the piano, and I thought, "Wait a minute, we are all Concord-connected people." I had this feeling that if I could pull them together as they've been together all through the years, and if I was the piano player in there with them, it would take on a unique kind of a thing. I knew people would say, "Hey, here is this guy trying to do this Oscar Peterson thing again," but I was so in love with the Nat King Cole Trio that I felt no conflict in that area [being compared to the Peterson trio] because I heard those quieter subtle things. Sure enough, I suggested let's record, and they said, "Yeah, let's do that." We made a record, and it was beautiful. The fun and the spirit and everything, and that was the first record. Not long after, the idea came to go out and play some gigs. So that was it. It was just an effortless thing that happened. Nobody said, "We're gonna be a group." One thing just rolled into another, and we had a lot of fun and we made quite a few records. That was Triple Treat.

Many years had gone by [since the Oscar Peterson Trio], and [then there was] all of this Hollywood jive [*laughs*]. They both ended up doing a kind of work you would never imagine. Such great artistry to be serving in *The Red Skelton Show* or all these shows. Wonderful people that they were, but it's almost like they needed to be restimulated to crank out this music. I was a serious road warrior by that time with my combos, and I guess maybe this was the kind of a group where we had the fire to burn. We played certain numbers that were like hard-swinging things. However, the subtleties were also available because that was something that meant a lot to me. It was easy-going. Certainly, the thing that Oscar Peterson had was this incredible ethic and hard work. [Oscar's concept was more like], Let's get this thing to be every time you play to be the greatest moment we've ever had. It is like [Mike] Tyson in the first round, and here I come with this sometimes almost stupid way of looking at life. We were light-hearted, but we were hard-swinging. You know we would burn them up. No doubt.

I had this little toy electric keyboard, and they were so used to rehearsing [in a formal way]. They were like, let's find a piano, room, and studio, especially if there was a piano player. I would just bring this little electric keyboard, put it on the bed in somebody's room, and learn the songs in the hotel room. That is how we would do it, and those things came together. Once in a while, something unusual would happen like I would bring something with a Jamaican influence to it, and there was some variety in the repertoire because Ray loved variety. He would love to play something classical and something with a different flavor.

He enjoyed my love of blues music. I love the spirit of Charles Brown and Ray Charles. I remember Herb was just in heaven to play that kind of music because he'd talk about his roots and growing up in Texas on the farm. We'd just have a ball, and people would love it so much.[155]

Triple Treat released three albums: *Triple Treat* (1982; Concord Jazz CJ-193), *Triple Treat II* (1988; Concord Jazz CJ-338), and *Triple Treat III* (1989; Concord Jazz 3), the last two including John Frigo as special guest.

Ray Brown was involved in several other strong efforts during this period. One of the finest was a March 1980 trio recording for Swiss jazz pianist Marc Hemmeler called *Walking in L.A.* (Musica Records MUS-3037), with Shelly Manne on drums. A highlight is an uptempo interpretation of Brown's most famous composition, "Gravy Waltz." Hemmeler is impressive throughout, and Brown is featured as a soloist on "My Romance," "Walking in L.A.," and "Do You Know What It Means." He displays his funky side on the final number,

"I'm an Old Cowhand." Most noteworthy is the fantastic hookup between Manne and Brown.

On March 17–18, 1981 Brown recorded another impressive piano trio album with Hemmeler in Paris called *Easy Does It* (Musica Records MUS-3043), which included Swiss-born drummer Daniel Humair[156] and a guest appearance by violin legend Stéphane Grappelli on "Stéphane's Song." *Easy Does It* is a solid album incorporating elements of swing, chamber jazz, samba, ballads, and funk. It is evidence of an interest in acoustic jazz in Europe that long outlasted its American commercial impact. Brown is featured consistently throughout the album, highlights on which include "Samba de Angry," "La Vie en Rose," and "Con Alma."

Another notable piano trio album was made on August 6 and 7, 1980 for Bulgarian piano master Milcho Leviev with drummer Peter Erskine, who was most known for his work with the jazz fusion band Weather Report. Throughout *What's New* (Atlas Record LA27-1005), Leviev displays remarkable technical ability, and his use of reharmonization, phrase lengths, modernistic approaches, and dynamic awareness is fully in evidence. Erskine has a unique approach to interpreting rhythm, incorporating grooves and feels that provide an underlying sense of expressiveness without being overwhelming. Brown falls perfectly into the mix, and he is often foregrounded, with solo statements, broken bass figures, funk grooves, and bluesy statements. Particular praise goes to his playing on "Medley," a pair of Irving Berlin ballads, which allow us to hear him playing "How Deep Is the Ocean" with the bow.

One of the more unusual projects of 1981 was the album *Shades of Dring* (Cambria C-1016) by Madeleine Dring, a noted English classical composer who worked primarily from the 1930s through the 1960s. Her music is known for its use of jazz harmonies, her influences coming from such composers as Francis Poulenc, George Gershwin, and Aaron Copland. The record features arrangements by jazz saxophonist Lennie Niehaus, and the musicians include Bud Shank, Shelly Manne, flutist Bill Perkins, and pianist Leigh Kaplan. The material has a distinctive third-stream quality, fusing jazz and classical – another fine example of Ray Brown's versatility.

The most commercially successful release of this period was 1983's Linda Ronstadt and the Nelson Riddle Orchestra, *What's New* (Asylum Records 96-0260-1). Rondstadt was an influential folk and country-rock star, most popular in the 1970s and early '80s, so this standards album was a significant change of direction, but the public responded favorably. *What's New* spent a remarkable eighty-one weeks on the *Billboard* charts, reaching as high as number 3 behind only Michael Jackson's *Thriller* and Lionel Richie's *Can't Slow Down*. Ronstadt won a Grammy for "Best Pop Vocal Performance" and the album sold three million copies! Ray Brown played on seven of the nine tracks, making *What's New* probably the highest-selling album with his name on it.

Some time in April and May of 1984, Ray Brown had a part to play in Frank Sinatra's fifty-seventh and final studio album, *L.A. Is My Lady* (Qwest Records 1-25145). The album was produced by Quincy Jones and included a huge cast of musicians and production assistants. The sessions were filmed and released on video as *Frank Sinatra: Portrait of an Album* with cameos from Dean Martin, Michael Jackson, Eddie Van Halen, and many others. A deep dive into all of Ray Brown's recorded efforts from the early 1980s would be outside the scope of this work, but a brief list of other releases follows:

1980
- Charles Owens New York Art Ensemble, *Plays the "Music of Harry Warren," Volume 1* (Discovery Records DS-811)
- *Don Glaser* (Horn Records HR-4001)
- J.J. Johnson, *Concepts in Blue* (Pablo Today 2312 123)
- Jack Sheldon, *Singular* (Beez BEEZ2)
- Eddie Barefield, *Introducing* (Discomate DSP-8101)

1981
- Jimmy Smith, *The Cat Strikes Again* (Wersi SLP-128)
- Cal Collins and Herb Ellis, *Interplay* (Concord Jazz CJ-137)
- *The Soundtrack Music from Burt Reynolds Sharky's Machine* (Warner Bros. BSK 3653)

1982
- The Claude Williamson Trio, *Tribute to Bud* (Eastworld EWJ-90009)
- Cleo Laine and Dudley Moore, *Smilin' Through* (Finnese Records FW 38091)

1983
- Johnny O'Neal, *Coming Out* (Concord Jazz CJ-228)
- Darji, *The Genes of Jazz* (Joy Of Sounds Records 45033)
- The Spike Robinson Quartet and the Charles Owens Sextet, *Music of Harry Warren* (Discovery Records DSCD-937)
- The Jack Sheldon Quartet, *Stand By For* (Concord Jazz CJ-229)
- Judy Roberts with Jeff Hamilton and Ray Brown, *Trio* (Pausa Records PR7147)

1984
- Jay Arrigo and Friends, *Sounds Like Fun* (AVI Records AVI 8624)
- Joe Williams, *Nothin' but the Blues* (Delos DMS 4001)
- J.J. Johnson and Al Grey, *Things Are Getting Better All the Time* (Pablo 2312 141)

26 The Ray Brown Trio with Gene Harris and Further Leadership
1980–1991

Although he would continue to work as a sideman – on select projects – as the 1980s progressed, Ray Brown was clearly keen on having a working band and taking a more active role as a leader. With his trio, Brown would be free to play the jazz he enjoyed most: a blend of swing, bebop, blues, and funk. He could showcase the bass as a solo instrument and oversee well-designed and tightly played small-group arrangements. His first "classic" trio was with Gene Harris and Jeff Hamilton, but before that line-up was established there were a few other trio recordings with Ray as leader.

As mentioned in the previous chapter, the first official full-length Ray Brown Trio record appeared in 1979 (*Live at the Concord Jazz Festival 1979* with Ernestine Anderson). The next trio record to bears his name as leader was 1983's *A Ray Brown 3* (Concord Jazz CJ-213) credited to Ray Brown, Monty Alexander, and Sam Most. Although not among Brown's more celebrated trio efforts, it is nonetheless of interest because of the instrumentation of only piano, bass, and flute; flutists are under-represented in jazz. Sam Most came onto the scene in the early 1950s; he is rarely discussed, although jazz critic Chris Sheridan has called him "the first bop flutist."[157]

Two other Ray Brown Trio records were made for Japanese audiences; not being released in the U.S., they fell under the radar. On *Echoes from West* (1981; Atlas Record LA27-1008) pianist Roger Kellaway and Louie Bellson team up with Ray, and on *Bye Bye Blackbird* (1984; Paddle Wheel K28P 6303) it's Cedar Walton and Mickey Roker, with guest appearances from vibraphonist Ichiro Masuda and vocalist Emi Nakajima.

Although he already had some eponymous albums under his belt, in 1985 something changed: a shift in energy regarding his leadership ambitions. He was now looking to form a working trio to record and tour; with the L.A. Four now defunct, he had more time to do so. The jazz community's interest in Ray Brown albums bloomed with the 1985 release of the Ray Brown Trio's *Soular Energy* (Concord Jazz CJ-268). Unlike the trio releases that preceded it, *Soular Energy* was released on an American label; additionally, Gene Harris was now on piano. Brown chose Gerryck King to play drums for this record, and Red Holloway (saxophone) and Emily Remler (guitar) guested on the original blues "Mistreated but Undefeated Blues." Highlights from the record are "Sweet Georgia Brown," "Take the A Train," and "Exactly Like You."

Brown returned to a formula of standards with carefully crafted small-group arrangements, with prearranged introductions, outros, interludes, time feel changes and occasional key shifts, and pre-planned song form structures. This style of arranging was a carry-over from his time with the Oscar Peterson Trio, the Poll Winners, and the L.A. Four. The main difference now was a greater focus on the bass.

In May 1985, we heard Brown as a leader again on *Don't Forget the Blues* (Concord Jazz CJ-293) by the Ray Brown All Stars. The ensemble here is guitarist Ron Eschete, pianist Gene Harris, trombonist Al Grey, and drummer Grady Tate. This record begins with "Blues'd Out," a slick blues-based jam credited to Brown, and concludes with the title track, another original. Although a fine instrumental blues album, *Don't Forget the Blues* is unremarkable compared to other Ray Brown releases of this era.

On the heels of this record Gene Harris joined the Ray Brown Trio. Meanwhile, on November 19 and December 19, 1985, at the Blue Note in New York, Harris led an ensemble that included tenor master Stanley Turrentine, Ray Brown, and Mickey Roker, and the resulting album was *The Gene Harris Trio Plus One* (Concord Jazz CJ-303), produced by Ray Brown. It is one of the period's best and hardest-swinging live jazz releases. There are two simple Ray Brown originals: "Gene's Lament," a jam-style shuffle blues, and the more groove-based "Uptown Sop." The final number is an unexpected jazz interpretation of the Civil War classic "Battle Hymn of the Republic." The spirit of these four fantastic musicians is apparent in the recording, and the audience reaction speaks to a well-received performance. Clearly, with regard to Gene Harris's comeback, Ray Brown's managerial efforts were successful.

Likely recorded during the Blue Note performances was another first-rate live presentation, *The Red Hot Ray Brown Trio* (Concord Jazz CJ-315). Once again, Brown, Harris, and Roker connect perfectly on an album that ranks among Brown's finest 1980s offerings. Unlike Harris's evening with Turrentine, in this trio setting Ray Brown's bass gets more airtime as a solo vehicle, highlights being "Meditation," "Lady Be Good," "How Can You Do a Thing Like This to Me?" and "Love Me Tender." His most impressive moment of the evening has to be his original bass feature, "Captain Bill," on which he displays his mastery of pull-off figures, slides, and double-stops, all with his characteristic solid time sense enhanced by bluesy feel and phrasing. Even with the influx of younger talented bassists in the 1980s, few could impress in the way Ray Brown still did. The album, released in 1987, is one of Brown's strongest small-group releases.

In 1988, Jeff Hamilton joined Ray Brown's trio to create the first "classic" line-up along with Harris. There was a connectivity and musical sensibility that perfectly suited Ray's small-group arrangements. In December that year the new line-up recorded some excellent live albums, beginning with a taped concert from the Fujitsu Jazz Festival in Japan, available on *Bam Bam Bam* (Concord Jazz CJ-375).[158] This swing-fest opens with a new interpretation of the Brown original "F.S.R." and closes with Brown's "Bam Bam Bam," played as an uptempo swing number with a tightly performed head arrangement. Further highlights include Ray Brown's presentation of the melody on "Put Your Little Foot Right Out," his funky bass breaks on "Rio," and his gorgeous arco interpretation of "If I Loved You." Brown also generously features Gene Harris on a soulful version of "Summertime." Hamilton also impresses on his lengthy solo on "A Night in Tunisia." Overall, the performances are simply masterful.

Another inspired live release was recorded in July 1988 at a club that Ray Brown partially owned called The Loa in Santa Monica. *Summer Wind: The Ray Brown Trio Live at The Loa* (Concord Jazz CCD-4426) is another spirited example of how well-connected and -rehearsed musicians can create magic on stage. The first of two original Brown numbers is "Real Blues," which begins with an unaccompanied bass solo and melody that includes double-stop figures; the second is his tribute to Art Blakey, "Buhaina Buhaina." It is brilliant in its entirety, with standouts being a funky version of "It Don't Mean a Thing If It Ain't Got That Swing" and Brown's melodic statement on "Mona Lisa."

In 1989, the Ray Brown Trio backed Red Holloway and Harry "Sweets" Edison on *The 20th Concord Festival All Stars* (Concord Jazz CJ-366). The annual Concord Festival was always a highlight for Ray, and on this twentieth anniversary event he unveils a new original, "Blues for Sam Nassi." Another 1989 release for the rhythm section was with the skilled Japanese vibraphonist Takashi Ohi on his album *Mr. Blue* (Denon CY-3322). Brown plays several impressive solos on the album including on his original "Bam Bam," as well as on "It's Time We Talk" and "Love for Sale. *Mr. Blue* is a solid albeit hard-to-find album.

On May 22, 1990, the group recorded *Moore Makes 4*, credited to the Ray Brown Trio with Ralph Moore (Concord CCD-4477). Moore is an English-born tenor saxophonist who gained attention in the 1980s as a member of Horace Silver's band. Despite being a confident player, he never achieved the level of recognition of some other tenor saxophonists who emerged at that time, such as David Sanborn, Michael Brecker, Bob Mintzer, or Joshua Redman. The addition of Moore was reminiscent of the times when the Oscar Peterson Trio was used to back other soloists. The most notable tracks are Brown's funky original, "Ralph's Boogie," and an incredibly uptempo version of Dizzy Gillespie's "The Champ."

The classic line-up continued to display its finesse on the 1991 Japanese release *Georgia on My Mind* (Lob Inc. LFA-1063), highlights from two live sessions from the Good Day Club in Tokyo on May 23, 1989 and February

2, 1991. Brown, Harris, and Hamilton sound magnificent throughout this collection of standards arranged by Brown, top picks being "Sweet Georgia Brown," "You Are My Sunshine," and "My Romance." A second release from these performances was issued in Japan in 1992 on the album *Black Orpheus* (Paddle Wheel KICJ-109).

On August 4, 1991, the Ray Brown Trio recorded *3 Dimensional* (Concord Jazz CCD-4520) in San Francisco – a masterclass of small-group interplay, with arrangements carefully crafted to display the unit in its finest light. Brown brings two new original numbers: "Gumbo Hump," which incorporates a funky second-line groove and an overall celebratory feeling, and a quick mood change with his arco intro on "Classical in G," which then moves into a soulful medium swing before concluding in more classical style to mirror the intro. As a soloist, Ray Brown is best represented on "You Are My Sunshine," and "Take Me Out to the Ball Game." Brown is particularly impressive in his unaccompanied performance of "Sophisticated Lady." *3 Dimensional* was the final release of this "classic" line-up, with Gene Harris departing to pursue solo ambitions.

Brown and Harris recorded together on other small-group and big-band projects during these years. Among these is 1989's *Listen Here!* by the Gene Harris Quartet (Concord Jazz CJ-385), which is essentially the Ray Brown Trio plus guitarist Ron Eschette, and on which Brown delivers some funky lines on the title track. Another is the 1990 album *At Last*, credited to the Gene Harris/Scott Hamilton Quintet with Ray Brown, Herb Ellis, and Harold Jones (Concord Jazz CCD-4434). Harris and Hamilton's soulful, bluesy approach gives the recording a joyful lift, and Herb Ellis displays his northern Texas blues roots. Picks from this album are "At Last," "Blues for Gene," and a Ray Brown original based on "Killer Joe" called "Sittin' in the Sandtrap," a title that references the bassist's love of and occasional frustration with golf.

Also of interest is hearing Brown return to big-band playing, which he does with the Gene Harris All Star Big Band on the 1988 album *Tribute to Count Basie* (Concord Jazz CCD-4337). Brown splits the album with bassist James Leary, playing only on "Captain Bill," "Night Mist Blues," "Blue and Sentimental," and "Riled Up." Although he doesn't play on the track, Ray Brown's composition "Rejection Blues" closes the record.

In a sponsorship deal with the Philip Morris Tobacco Company, Harris renamed his band the Philip Morris Superband, and Brown is included in each of that group's three releases: *Live at Town Hall, N.Y.C.* (1989; Concord Jazz CJ-397); *World Tour 1990* (1990; Concord Jazz CCD-4443); and B.B. King's *Live at the Apollo* with Gene Harris and the Philip Morris Superband (1991; GRP GRD-9637). One track of particular note is the big-band arrangement of Brown's composition "Buhaina Buhaina" on the *World Tour 1990* album. The B.B. King release won a Grammy in the "Best Traditional Blues Recording" category, adding to the list of Grammy-winning albums to which Ray Brown contributed.

Brown also released an album in 1990 without Harris called *Evergreen 4403* and credited to Ray Brown and His West Coast All-Star Giants (GML GML-20181).[159] This Japanese album features Jeff Clayton on saxophone and flute, Pete Christlieb on tenor saxophone, Conte Candoli on trumpet, Cedar Walton on piano, Billy Higgins on drums, and Ichiro Masuda on vibes. Ray Brown offers several originals including "Couch Potato Blues," "Drum Feature," "Brown Ballad," "Lined with a Groove," and "F.S.R." He is most prominently featured as a soloist on "Time after Time," and "Lined with a Groove."

27 Sideman Sessions 1985–1989

By 1985, Ray Brown was mostly focused on presenting his trio. However, he still accepted select sideman engagements throughout the mid and late 1980s. One of these was the 1985 Concord album by Mary Fettig: *In Good Company* (Concord Jazz CJ-273). Female jazz instrumentalists, particularly saxophonists, have been generally under-represented throughout jazz's rich history. While Mary Fettig never achieved widespread acclaim, the San Francisco native saxophonist was the first female member of Stan Kenton's Orchestra and worked with dozens of other artists ranging from Woody Herman to Lady Gaga. *Good Company*, which was her only release for the Concord label, also features pianist Marian McPartland, guitarist Peter Sprague, and drummer Jeff Hamilton. Unfortunately, the album attracted little attention.

A more commercially successful project from 1985 was the Manhattan Transfer album *Vocalese* (Atlantic A1-81266), the group's biggest seller, receiving twelve Grammy nominations and winning three. Brown played bass on two tracks, "Rambo" and "Blee Blop Blues."

Brown continued to work with Ernestine Anderson, as well as managing her career. In 1985, she released her blues-based album *When the Sun Goes Down* (Concord Jazz CJ-263), one of her finest releases, on which joining Brown are saxophonist Red Holloway, pianist Gene Harris, and drummer Gerryck King. An album highlight is a funky vocal version of Joe Zawinul's "Mercy, Mercy, Mercy." This was followed in 1987 by *Be Mine Tonight* (Concord Jazz CJ-319), featuring a cast of Ray Brown, Benny Carter on saxophone, Ron Eschete on guitar, Jimmie Smith on drums, and Marshall Otwell on piano, on a repertoire of mostly standards.

In 1985 Brown rejoined his good friend Monty Alexander on *Full Steam Ahead* (Concord CCD-4287) with drummer Frank Gant. On the record we are treated to a new version of Brown's composition and former old Gillespie showcase "Ray's Idea." Surprisingly, Brown does not play the head but does take a short yet impressive solo. His bass tone sounds less natural and more processed than on past recordings, a growing trend in late 1980s jazz recordings. Another highlight is "Once I Loved," which shifts between funk bass, bossa nova, and samba. Ray is most prominently featured as a soloist on "Happy Talk," where he plays intervallic leaps, slides, and bop-style phrasing.

In August that same year, Ray Brown recorded with trumpeter Jon Faddis on his album *Legacy* (Concord Jazz CJ-291). Faddis is a trumpeter of considerable talent whose playing style at this point owed much to his mentor Dizzy Gillespie. This Concord release, which pays tribute to the great trumpeters in jazz, has a fine line-up: Harold Land on saxophone, Kenny Barron on piano, and Mel Lewis on drums. Brown fans will hear solos on "West End Blues," "A Night in Tunisia," and "A Child Is Born." *Legacy* is a well-balanced traditional jazz album and one of Faddis's finest releases.

Ray was back in Japan in October for a series of concerts and recordings. A show was captured on October 15, 1985 and released in Japan as *Great Jazz Quartet Live in Japan* – Hank Jones, Ray Brown, Sam Most, Alan Dawson (All Art K32Y 6109). The next day, the same line-up recorded with Japanese flutist Tamami Koyake for her album *Hot Flutes* (Paddle Wheel K32Y 6102). Although not a particularly innovative or daring album, it's a strong document of Koyake's ability and should be interesting to jazz flute enthusiasts, with Koyake and Most playing flute together on several tracks. Ray Brown's only solo is on "Woogie Boogie." The quartet also appears on part of another Japanese record, their contribution being recorded on October 16, 1985 at the P.S.C. Studio in Tokyo. This time, the group was accompanying the singer Junko Miné for what became Side A of her album *Love Me Tender* (All Art K28P 6443). She reconvened with Ray Brown's trio in October the following year at King Records in Tokyo, Brown's fellow musicians on that date being Gene Harris and Mickey Roker.

For studio output, 1986 was Ray Brown's least productive year. His only notable release during the year as a jazz sideman was recorded on February 3–4, his last date with Phineas Newborn Jr. – a trio session that included drummer Marvin "Smitty" Smith. Despite the tracks being shelved until the 1990 release *C Jam Blues* (Paddlewheel 220R-50511), Newborn is remarkable throughout, with inventive melodic runs and harmonic choices. Brown and Smith have a great hookup, too. Smith was one of the more prolific and impressive jazz drummers of the 1980s and '90s, also for much of his career being the resident drummer on *The Tonight Show with Jay Leno*. By 1986, Newborn's physical and mental health problems had left him financially strapped and separated from the jazz community, and he passed away in 1989. Phineas Newborn Jr. was among the most skilled jazz pianists, and *C Jam Blues* would be one of his final releases.

Brown's most notable guest appearance in 1986 was Elvis Costello's *King of America* (Columbia FC-40173), on two tracks: "Eisenhower Blues" and "Poisoned Rose." While Brown's playing is somewhat masked on the former he is more prominent on "Poisoned Rose," as he begins the track alone with just Costello on vocals. Brown clearly remained a highly respected session musician who would sometimes "cross over" to play with big names in the pop/rock field.

The next year was a slightly busier one in the studio. One of the finer sessions was *Breakin' Out* by the George Shearing Trio with Ray Brown and Marvin "Smitty" Smith (Concord Jazz CJ-335). The blind, British-born pianist was known for his over-the-bar phrasing and block chording, which became known as the "Shearing Sound." In 1949 Shearing formed a quintet which found fame with a recording of Harry Warren and Al Dubin's standard "September in the Rain" whch sold nearly a million copies. Through the 1950s and beyond, he offered a lighter, more classically influenced style which served as an alternative to the frantic sounds of bebop.

But the finest sideman project of 1987 must be *Magical Trio 1* (EmArcy Digital 832 859-1), recorded on June 26 at New York's Power Station Studios, the magic provided by Brown and Art Blakey under the leadership of James Williams. Williams was a soulful, imaginative, and highly underrated pianist who recorded primarily from the late 1970s through to the 1990s but best known for his time in Art Blakey's Jazz Messengers and the ten albums he recorded with the group. To hear the two Pittsburgh natives Ray Brown and Art Blakey playing in a trio format is to witness an incredible dynamic. On this album, Brown brings his medium-swing tribute to Blakey, "Buhaina, Buhaina," a title that references Blakey's Muslim name Abdullah Ibn Buhaina, which he adopted in the 1940s. Other notable moments are Brown and Williams duetting on the standard "The Night We Called It a Day," and Brown's solo intro on "Mean What You Say." The album's final track, "J's Jam Song," is a funky freeform-style jam and a perfect closer.

The follow-up, *Magical Trio 2* (EmArcy Digital 834 368-1), recorded in November 1987, saw Art Blakey replaced by Elvin Jones, a drummer of comparable skill and imagination. Brown's highlights are a fantastic bowed melody on "Too Late Now" and inspired solos on "Portrait for Elvin" and "You Are Too Beautiful." While *Magical Trio 2* is undoubtedly a strong effort, it doesn't quite match the cohesiveness of the Blakey recordings.

In 1988, Ray Brown began a significant association with Telarc Records. The first recording was the all-star project Cincinnati Pops Big Band Orchestra, *Big Band Hit Parade* (Telarc Digital CS-30177). Erich Kunzel conducted an assemblage that included Dave Brubeck, Cab Calloway, Eddie Daniels, Buddy Morrow, Gerry Mulligan, Doc Severson, and Ed Shaughnessy, performing classic big-band standards. While the arrangements are somewhat over the top, it was a chance for Ray Brown to work with a tremendous cast and return to his big-band roots.

Previously, Ray Brown had strong connections with a number of major record labels, including Verve, Contemporary, Pablo, and Concord, but from this point on most of his releases would be on Telarc. Telarc International Corporation was founded in 1977 by audiophiles and classically trained musicians Jack Renner and Robert Woods, and was based in Cleveland, Ohio. Using the highest-quality digital equipment, it began by recording Midwestern symphonies but diversified into jazz, blues, and country. Brown's new association with Telarc meant he could rely on his music being issued on CD having been recorded with outstanding clarity and detail.

In 1988, Brown reconnected with pianist Jimmy Rowles in a session that included the latter's daughter, trumpeter Stacy Rowles, Harry "Sweets" Edison, and drummer Donald Bailey. *Sometimes I'm Happy, Sometimes I'm Blue* (Orange Blue OB 003LP) was released on a French label and not widely available in the U.S.

As the decade was drawing to a close, Ray Brown was still performing and recording. On March 29, 1989, a trio session with André Previn and Joe Pass resulted in *André Previn After Hours* (Telarc Digital CD-83302). Recorded just days before he resigned as principal conductor of the Los Angeles Philharmonic, Previn proved once again that he could play exemplary jazz piano while Joe Pass had clearly retained his guitar virtuosity. Brown's various projects with Previn over the years represent some of his most remarkable yet overlooked recordings.

Recorded in November and December of 1989 was the debut record by James Morrison, a twenty-seven-year-old Australian trumpeter and multi-instrumentalist phenomenon. On *Snappy Doo* (WEA 9031-71211-2) he overdubs himself playing trombone, trumpet, piano, euphonium, and saxophone, creating a big band-sound. Also joining the virtuoso were Herb Ellis and Jeff Hamilton. Bassist John Clayton arranged the material; as one of Brown's protégés, we are not surprised to see him give Ray a number of opportunities to shine. Ray's finest solo is on the opening track, "You Are My Sunshine," with signature phrasing and a quote from "Ol' Man River." Ray Brown provides the uptempo title track, a slick swing with stop-time figures and a written bass part that at times mimics the trumpet. *Snappy Doo* was one of the most exciting new jazz releases of the early 1990s.

Brown was occasionally called on for more commercial studio work. One lesser-known such recording is "What's Shakin' on the Hill" by British singer-songwriter Nick Lowe. It appeared on 1990's release *Party of One* (Reprise Records 9 26132-4) and was recorded between 1988 and 1989 near Brown's residence in Sherman Oaks, which may explain why he accepted the session.

28 Sessions 1990–1994

The 1990s ushered in a new direction in popular music. No longer satisfied with gimmickry and saturated studio trickery, audiences and musicians were in search of something more honest and pure. Ray Brown entered the decade as a man about to turn sixty-five. He had been on the scene for nearly forty-five years and had little to prove, yet he still had a great deal of music to offer. By 1990, he was considered an elder statesman of jazz and one of the few remaining figures who could claim links with legends such as Louis Armstrong, Duke Ellington, and Charlie Parker. In his final years, Brown would continue to work with his trio, record with other remaining jazz legends, manage several artists, offer instructional materials, and conduct clinics. Although much of his focus remained on his trio and recordings as a leader, Brown continued to do what he always did: serve as an accompanist for some of the most notable names in music, with most of whom he had previously worked. Additionally, a vast amount of his past recordings were now being reissued.

During this period, Oscar Peterson set up reunion shows for the first "classic trio," which was dismantled in 1958. Peterson, Ellis, and Brown performed for two weeks in Tokyo, followed by two weeks at the Blue Note in New York. Enhancing the trio was drummer Bobby Durham. Performances from March 16 and 17, 1990 resulted in four album releases: *The Legendary Oscar Peterson Trio Live at the Blue Note* (Telarc CD-83304), *Saturday Night at the Blue Note* (Telarc CD-83306), *Last Call at the Blue Note* (Telarc CD-83314), and *Encore at the Blue Note* (Telarc CD-83356). Highlights are versions of "Sweet Georgia Brown," "Let There Be Love," "Kelly's Blues," "You Look Good to Me," "Yours Is My Heart Alone," and "Wheatland." We hear Oscar Peterson communicate how impactful this reunion was for him, calling the tour "four of the most gratifying weeks of his life." Special praise is reserved for Ray, whom he calls "the genius," in an address discussing his history with the bassist, which precedes the track "Blues Etude."

Brown continued his association with André Previn, participating, on March 9 and 19, 1990 in the recording of André Previn, Mundell Lowe, and Ray Brown, *Uptown* (Telarc Jazz CD-83303) – another fine example of Previn's talents as a jazz artist. Highlights include "A Sleepin' Bee," which begins with a sliding bass intro figure, and "Five O'Clock Whistle," on which the bass presents part of the melody. The same group recorded again on August 24, 1991 at La Jolla Music Society's SummerFest in California, resulting in *Old Friends* (Telarc Jazz CD-83309). In 1993 André Previn released *What Headphones?* (Angel Records CDC 0777 7 54917 2 2) with a rhythm section of Ray Brown, Mundell Lowe, and Grady Tate. Also featured were French horn player Richard Todd, cornetist Warren Vaché, and trombonist Jim Pugh. The album includes vocal tracks provided by the Antioch Baptist Choir as heard on the spirited gospel "You Are the World to Me." While Ray is not heavily featured on *What Headphones?* it is an extraordinarily well-arranged and -conceived album. It should be regarded as one of Previn's stronger jazz efforts.

In May 1991, Ray Brown cut fifteen jazz standards with Previn and Mundell Lowe for singer Kiri Te Kanawa, the noted New Zealand-born opera singer, for the album *Kiri Sidetracks (The Jazz Album)* (Phillips Digital Classics 434 092-2). A documentary film called *Kiri and André Together on Broadway: The Making of Sidetracks* was also filmed, throughout which you can witness Ray Brown making numerous suggestions to help serve the arrangements. He is also interviewed about the project. This glimpse of him working in the studio offers an insight into his process as a musician, arranger, and producer.

A month previously, Brown had recorded for the first time with pianist Ellis Marsalis, a skilled musician and the patriarch of one of the most famous families in jazz. He was mainly known in New Orleans but found wider opportunities when his sons Branford and Wynton became famous in the 1980s. Their brothers, trombonist Delfeayo and drummer Jason have also enjoyed successful careers in jazz. Brown's session with Ellis Marsalis resulted in the release *Heart of Gold* (Columbia CK 47509), on which they are joined by Billy Higgins. Highlights for the bassist include renditions of "Sweet Georgia Brown," "I Can't Give You Anything but Love," and "Surrey with the Fringe on Top." The most notable track to feature Brown is "El-Ray Blues," an original blues.

A session of note was a 1993 hybrid symphonic-style album: Lalo Schifrin, *Jazz Meets the Symphony* (Atlantic Jazz 782506-2), which saw Ray Brown and Grady Tate recording with the London Philharmonic. Even for a man of Ray Brown's age and experience, it must have been an incredible thrill to perform with such a prestigious group of concert musicians. He is featured as a soloist on "Don't Get Around Much Anymore," from the medley "Echoes of Duke." as well as the song "Bach to Blues." He also impresses with his original "Blues in the Basement."[160] Some time in 1994, Schifrin released a follow-up, *More Jazz Meets the Symphony* (EastWest 4509-95589-2), on which he added James Morrison, Jon Faddis, and Paquito D'Rivera to Brown and Tate for his new installment of classically infused jazz arrangements. Ray Brown is heavily featured on "Sketches of Miles" and is given moments to shine as a soloist on other tracks.

When it came to recording, 1994 was an active year for Ray Brown. One such project was Itzhak Perlman and Oscar Peterson, *Side by Side* (Telarc CD-83341). Perlman is a virtuosic Israeli American violinist (and conductor) who found internationally fame in the early 1960s. When this recording was made, Peterson's ability was limited: a stroke in 1993 rendered him predominantly a one-handed pianist. Ray Brown is not heavily featured but adds the perfect support. Joining the rhythm section are Herb Ellis and Grady Tate. In an interview conducted by Alyn Shipton in New York on June 1, 1994, drummer Grady Tate recalled the session:

> When I got the call from Telarc, I was thrilled to hear I'd be working with Oscar, Ray, and Herb. That's enough to astound one, but when I heard that Itzhak Perlman was going to do it, I was just fascinated because I've been a fan of his for so long. He's an amazing musician, but on the date, I found out he is an equally amazing human being. He's a joy to be around, keeps you laughing, and is not uptight about anything. He's so accomplished on the instrument that it is almost a throwaway!
>
> Of course, it seemed like Oscar, Ray, and Herb had worked together collectively for something like 150 years! Their understanding of one another is telepathic, but then all of the good jazz musicians are telepathic. We're playing to and for each other, and if we're not playing, we're listening. We're all of the same mind. We know the library, we know the literature, and that's 75% of the battle – knowing the material. Itzhak said it was very reassuring for him, too, that we largely played standards because that meant he knew the material too!
>
> When it came to fine details of the arrangements – things like most of us dropping out to leave just Herb and Itzhak duetting – Oscar made most of those decisions. But overall, I saw Ray as the "overseer," making the choices of repertoire and some of the decisions about the arrangements. On the date, which took place in the Astoria Complex in Queens, we all had some input, but on each number, it was either Ray or Oscar who made the final decision as to what would happen. One thing I remember Ray suggested was the way he and Itzhak did little pizzicato patterns together. That was cute! I liked that.

On May 18 and 19, 1994 Ray Brown recorded a session led by Benny Carter called *Elegy in Blue* (MusicMasters Jazz 01612-65115-2) with an ensemble that included Harry Edison, Cedar Walton, Mundell Lowe, and Jeff Hamilton. The album pays tribute to influential artists that had passed on, and in most cases the song performed was either written by or associated with the dedicated artist. For example, Carter and the band pay tribute to Duke Ellington with "Prelude to a Kiss," Thelonious Monk with "Blue Monk," and Django Reinhardt with "Nuages."

On August 29 and 30, 1994 the bassist hooked up with Clark Terry to play on his album *Remember the Time* (Mons Records 874 762). This German release was made to celebrate Terry's seventy-fifth birthday and from the outset it is clear that Terrry's skills have not diminished with age. Terry lived to be ninety-four and recorded in eight decades. Highlights include Brown playing duo statements with Terry on the tracks "The Story of Love," "Definitely

So," and "Gwen." Also featured on the album are Italian-born pianist Dado Moroni, drummer Jeff Hamilton, British trombonist Mark Nightingale, and Swiss alto saxophonist George Robert. Ray Brown is offered several solos throughout the album.

Some time in 1994, Ray Brown recorded Herb Ellis, Ray Brown and Serge Ermoll, *The Jazz Masters* (AIM AIM 1039 CD), an album of standards.[161] Ermoll was a talented Russian/Australian jazz pianist who regularly worked on the international scene with artists such as Phil Woods, Joe Henderson, and Sonny Stitt. The album includes Australian musicians Barry Duggan on sax and flute and drummer Stewie Speers and is another fine example of Ray Brown's impact internationally. Highlights include "Doxy" and "Au Privave." Another star-studded recording was made on April 6, 1994. When Verve Records threw a party at Carnegie Hall to celebrate its fiftieth anniversary, with an ensuing recording titled *The Carnegie Hall Salutes the Jazz Masters* (Verve 314 523 150-2), Ray Brown was included on the opening track "Tea for Two," along with saxophonist Joe Henderson, trombonist J.J. Johnson, pianist Herbie Hancock, guitarist Kenny Burrell, drummer Kenny Washington, and singer Venessa Williams.

While most of his session work involved older, more established jazz stars, less familiar jazz artists included *The Doug MacDonald Quartet* (1990; Cexton Records CR 5678), Lucy Reed, *Basic Reeding* (1992; Audiophile ACD-273),[162] La Velle, *Straight Singin': Tribute to Nat King Cole* (1991; OMD CD 1528), Marion Williams, *Strong Again* (1991; Spirit Feel Records SF 1013), Bobby Enriquez, *The Wildman Returns* (1993; Evidence ECD 22059-2), *Søren Lee Quartet* (1993; Bellaphon CDLR 45013), Mark Nightingale, *What I Wanted to Say* (1994; Mons Records 874 763), Till Brönner and Gregoire Peters, *Generations of Jazz* (1994; Minor Music MM 80 10 37), Joe Chindamo, *The First Take with Ray Brown* (1994; Muzak, Inc. MZCS-1236), and Judy Argo, *True Love Ways* (1994; Sterling Records S1008-2).

Ray Brown also remained active as a manager. One of his most recent discoveries at this time was Canadian pianist and singer Diana Krall, whom he saw performing in a restaurant in Nanaimo, British Columbia. After convincing Krall to move to Los Angeles, he introduced her to bassist John Clayton and mentored her on her debut 1993 album *Stepping Out* (GRP GRD-9825). Krall would go on to sell over fifteen million albums and marry iconic rocker Elvis Costello.

29 Green and Brown: The Ray Brown Trio 1991–2002

On December 22 and 23, 1991, Ray Brown was recording, producing, and arranging James Morrison's latest, *Two the Max* (EastWest 9031-77125-2), which featured Morrison playing a mixture of standards and originals, including Ray Brown's "Ain't That Nothin'." Joining Brown on the album were Jeff Hamilton and a young piano virtuoso named Benny Green. Not only is this album an exemplary representation of Morrison's and Brown's talents but it was the first time Ray Brown recorded with Green, who would come to replace Gene Harris in his trio.

In the late 1980s, Benny Green was one of the newest talents destined to keep the tradition of mainstream jazz alive. The young pianist was to find a mentor in Ray Brown, and his eventual position as a trio member could only elevate his status as a young lion on the jazz scene. At the time of the Morrison recording, Green was still in his twenties and yet had already worked in groups led by Betty Carter and Art Blakey and had made a few albums as a leader. Like Art Tatum and Oscar Peterson, Green has the kind of virtuosity that only surfaces once every other decade, with his playing revealing from the outset a remarkable technicality and a link to the jazz tradition. His improvisations showed an absorption and stylistic connectivity to nearly every notable player that came before, including Oscar Peterson. Over time, Green developed an individualistic approach and a remarkable ability to propel a band to new creative heights. Here, the pianist talks about meeting Ray Brown:

> The first time I got up the courage to introduce myself to Ray, I had already been listening to him for years and was attending his performances. It was, I guess, 1983 when we first met. I was working with the late vocalist Betty Carter at a festival in Edmonton, Alberta, Canada. At the festival, Ray co-led a quartet with Milt Jackson, Cedar Walton, and Mickey Roker. So after our performance with Betty that evening, I went to another venue where the quartet with Ray played and listened. The music was so beautiful. The group played a beautiful version of Erroll Garner's "Misty" that night. The notes Ray was playing were so beautiful as a separate entity. As a bass line, it had so much integrity to it, but the way those notes supported

the melody, it was just golden. So I meekly approached Ray after the show. I introduced myself after the show and said, "I was a pianist, and I was playing with Betty Carter," and asked him if it would be alright to ask him a musical question? He said, "Alright." I asked, "When you were playing 'Misty,' what were the changes you were playing in the fifth and sixth bar of the bridge? Ray leaned down, got right up in my face . . . he said, "The right changes, kid." [*laughs*] I was so intimidated. I said, "Okay, thank you," and I sort of backed away.

The next few years, I was frightened to speak to Ray again, but I would still hear him whenever I could [like] when he would come to the Blue Note in New York with his trio with Gene Harris and Jeff Hamilton. So, a few years after that, Christian McBride and I were playing a duo engagement at a restaurant in New York called The Knickerbocker. Ray was in town with his trio at the same time, and our manager at the time, Mary Ann Topper, was Ray's old friend. She had told him about Christian and myself and was encouraging Ray to give us a listen. So, after he finished his last set, she dragged him down to our show, and he walked in, and Christian and I were just beginning our final set of the evening. Ray sat at a table right in front of the piano, which was quite intimidating. He watched Christian and me very intently. We finished our performance, and I came over to greet Ray and thank him for coming. Ray had tears in his eyes, saying, "Hearing you two young fellows reminded me of Oscar and me when we were young." That was a tremendous affirmation for Christian and I. Christian and Ray immediately hit it off. Just a couple of months after that, Christian and I were playing with a group in Japan that opened up for Ray's trio at a concert. When we finished our performance, Ray met me backstage and asked if I would be available to record. Needless to say, I didn't hesitate. I said, "I would love that." "Definitely, I'm available." He asked me for my information and said, "I'll get in touch with you." Sure enough, he called me a few weeks later to arrange for me to fly out to Los Angeles and participate in a recording session. So that recording session was my first opportunity actually to play with Ray.

The first thing I noticed from playing with Ray, which I hadn't noticed just from listening, was how much he would always take chances, and every time he would land right on his feet. I hadn't noticed that while I was listening to the records. I was always aware of that wide beat, beautiful tone, and perfect intonation. That time feel he has is so personal; you could always make him out just from the rhythmic pulse alone. Once I started playing with him during that recording session, I saw that he would play these beautiful fills and runs and always land right on [beat] one, almost as if he had planned the whole thing out, but he was really challenging himself all the time. It was remarkable to see that he could exude such mastery and still always be challenging himself.

We recorded for a couple of days in Los Angeles, and at the end of the record date, Ray asked me another question. He said Gene Harris was playing piano in his trio then and would be unavailable for about the first week-and-a-half of an Australian tour. Ray asked if I would be interested in playing those gigs until Gene could rejoin the trio. I told him I would really love that. So, Ray said, "Well, here is what you should do. Go get a few of our CDs, learn maybe about ten of the tunes, the ones that you are most comfortable with, and that will sort of form our core repertoire for tunes that we will play while you're with us."

So little did Ray know I already had all of his records, and I had a couple of months to prepare. So for the next couple of months, I just practiced those arrangements. All of the trio arrangements, maybe about forty, that I had on CD, which he was playing with his current trio. We finally got together in Australia, and Ray asked me at the first rehearsal, "What tunes could I play?" I told him, "We can play anything from your book, Ray." Ray said, "Really?" and I said, "Yeah." I wanted to be a member of Ray's trio someday, and I figured it would be better to show him that than to tell him that by knowing the music.

So, we rehearsed tune after tune, and I knew all of the arrangements, and Ray played it cool. Later Jeff Hamilton told me that during a break that we took in rehearsal, I stepped out of the room, and Ray turned to Jeff and said, "I can't believe that that kid learned all of those arrangements." I wanted him to know how much it would mean to me to play with him. I finished that portion of the tour before Gene returned to the group, and Ray told me he would be in touch with me. Just a few weeks after that, Ray called me. They were winding down their tour, and he told me Gene would be leaving the group pretty soon, and Ray asked if I would like to join the band. I told him, "There is nothing that I want more in the world."

I played my first gig as a member of the trio in the spring of 1992 at the Dakota Bar and Grill in St. Paul, Minnesota. The bulk of the repertoire that Ray was playing at the time were arrangements that Ray had specifically tailored for Gene Harris, and there were certain things that Gene did that really only he could do. Ray told me after our first night, "We are going to make a transition now. These are things that I wrote for Gene, but in the next few weeks, I'm going to be listening to how you play and seeing what you do. Then I'm going to start writing some new arrangements centered around your personality." Which is just what he did, and he continued to do that after I left the group. He just considered the characteristics of who he had in the band in his writing. He did that very much with Jeff Hamilton on the drums. Jeff is one of the foremost big-band drummers in the world, and Ray would write a lot of shouts and material in a big-band genre because Jeff could really fill out the group. Make it feel full and feel like it was more than just a trio. That was very exciting for us.[163]

The first recorded evidence of the new trio comes from an April 1–2, 1993 recording called *Bassface* (Telarc Jazz CD-83340), recorded live at Kuumbwa Jazz Center in Santa Cruz, California. The album is an absolute gem, showcasing Brown's new direction with Benny Green as his pianist, with arrangements perfectly catering to Green's virtuosic style. Additionally, Ray Brown is in top form as a bassist. He introduces two new original numbers: "CRS – Craft," a toe-tapping throwback medium swing that includes a lengthy bass solo, and the heavily arranged and perfectly executed "Phineas Can Be," during which Green is brilliant in copying and expanding on Phineas Newborn's style.

In April 1993, Ray Brown and his trio recorded the James Morrison album *This Is Christmas* (Warners Music 4509938632) in Berlin with the RIAS Orchestra. Morrison's versatility impresses again, as we hear him playing trumpet, trombone, alto horn, flugelhorn, tenor saxophone, piccolo marimba, and organ. Ray Brown is listed as the album's executive producer, with John Clayton the arranger and conductor.

On April 22–23, 1994 Ray Brown's trio with Benny Green and Jeff Hamilton recorded the hard-swinging *Don't Get Sassy* (Telarc Jazz CD-83368). The liner notes list the album as being recorded at Signet Sound Studio in West Hollywood, and although there is no mention, a small audience is in attendance. Brown's two originals are "When You Go," which begins with an unaccompanied piano intro played as a ballad Brown's ostinato bass line moves it into a quasi-Latin-style time feel, and "Brown's New Blues," an impressive bass feature. The latter begins with an accompanied bass intro in which he plays blues licks, slides, rapid eight-note runs, and a call-and-response pattern, after which the music settles into a slow blues.

Most tracks last over five minutes and contain plenty of improvised material supported by tight arrangements. The uptempo "Tanga" consists of a funky interlude and a display of Jeff Hamilton's celebrated brush playing before he shifts to rapid time with sticks. Brown plays part of the melody of "Con Alma" with the bow – a tune with several time-feel shifts and an inspired solo by Benny Green.

A lesser-known trio release from 1995 is *It's a Wonderful World* (Mons Records MR 874-765) by Allan Harris, a gifted jazz vocalist from Harlem. The German release features the trio with guitarist Mark Whitfield, trumpeter Claudio Roditi, and French hornist Tom Varner. Fans of jazz vocals are advised to check out *It's A Wonderful World*, a fine recording of jazz standards. That year, Green and Brown also recorded with saxophonist Lisa Pollard for her record *I See Your Face Before Me* (Concord Jazz CCD-44681), along with Grady Tate and Red Holloway. Pollard, known as the "Sax Lady," never enjoyed much recognition outside of the San Francisco area.

By 1995, long-time Brown associate Jeff Hamilton had left the trio to pursue other opportunities. As a replacement, Brown hired drummer Gregory Hutchinson, who, like Benny Green, had previously worked in Betty Carter's band and had a style that was well rooted in the jazz tradition. Green talks about the transition from Hamilton to Hutchinson:

> Well, Jeff adored Ray, and he knew him musically and personally as well as anyone. He had spent so many years with him. It was not just a reflection of the time spent, but probably the bridge between the two was love and respect. Jeff had been like my big brother on the road. He was really looking out for me and explaining a lot of things to me at the time I joined

the group. He was just so supportive and encouraging to me. So it was really a family kind of environment from the beginning, and it was sort of emotional for Jeff to leave.

I had already known Greg for some years. He's from New York. He was quite young but talented and full of creative ideas and fire. Ray talked with me when he realized Jeff would be leaving about possible drummers to join the trio. I appreciated that after I had joined the group Ray was interested in continuing that sort of direction like Art Blakey and Betty Carter had done in not just hiring peers who would be eager to play with him but taking some young players and nurturing their talents and giving them some on-the-job training. I feel really grateful to have come up when those kinds of situations were still accessible.

Greg was very much about wanting to learn from the older musicians, so it seemed like he would be the perfect candidate. So, Ray set aside a short week for Greg and myself to fly to Los Angeles for concentrated daily rehearsals and to break Greg into all of the existing arrangements before beginning to write new arrangements incorporating Greg's personality. So Greg mainly had been playing in small groups at that time. He had just left Roy Hargrove's group to join Ray. He had worked with Betty Carter, as I had prior to that, and probably a few other people I am surely leaving out.

He was making that transition just as I had to try to step into Gene Harris's shoes, which is rather an impossibility. Greg first had to step into the feeling and dynamics that Jeff had been supplying Ray and I for years. That was a big transition for Greg to make. On the surface, it was a different kind of ensemble-oriented drumming. Still, once you get past that surface, of course, it's really all music, and Greg was quite eager to sink his teeth into the whole situation, which is perfect for Ray – like I had experienced with Art Blakey.

As an older figure, Ray thrived off of younger musicians. If not embodying a lot of experience, at least it would bring some fire to the table, and Greg sounded and felt great from the beginning. Even though I was already a fan of his drumming and he and I were already friends, I was quite impressed by the rehearsals and Greg's focus. Just how much he watched Ray, physically watched him walking [the bass], watched his hands on the fingerboard, and watched him change positions. From day one, he was looking to connect his cymbal beat with the pulse of Ray's bass. He continued to make that a focus throughout the whole time he was with the group. While we were so sad to see Jeff go, it was wonderful to see Greg completely put his heart into the music, and we were able to continue and have a great time with this next edition of the trio.[164]

Ray Brown often discussed why he hired younger musicians for his trio:

The young musicians of today, guys in their early-mid twenties, are now good musicians; they play better than we did in my time. Guys at 23–24 are playing as well as guys in their early 30s when I was young. I like working with young musicians because if you want to play fast for half of the night they can do it, they don't get tired. If I had three guys in my band my age, I don't know what would happen in the second set [*laughs*].[165]

The group's first album with Hutchinson was *Seven Steps to Heaven* (Telarc Jazz CD-83384), recorded May 22–23, 1995. In addition to Green and Hutchinson, the recording featured Swedish guitarist Ulf Wakenius as a guest. It begins with the Ray Brown original "Two RBs," a soulful swing with stop-time breaks. Brown also included his "Dejection Blues," on which he takes a lengthy solo. By this time, Brown was using the faster bebop phrasing more sparingly, and his improvisations were now beginning to show even greater sophistication in terms of pacing and phrasing. For the remaining material, Brown chose standards, one of the most impressive being the title track. It is evident from the outset that Hutchinson was a strong fit and that Wakenius is an incredibly gifted guitarist.

On July 28, Ray Brown was showcased at the 27th Concord Jazz Festival, which saw light of day on the compilation *Fujitsu-Concord 27th Jazz Festival* with Karrin Allyson, the Scott Hamilton Quintet, and the Concord Jazz Festival All-Stars (Concord Jazz CCD-7004). Ray Brown was one of those All-Stars, an ensemble that included Louie Bellson, Benny Green, Gregory Hutchinson, guitarist Howard Alden, trumpeter Randy Sandke, and saxophonists Chris Potter and Rickey Woodard.

In 1995 Ray Brown helped introduce the young jazz vocalist and bassist Kristin Korb to the greater jazz community by playing on her debut album, *Introducing Kristin Korb with the Ray Brown Trio* (Telarc Jazz CD-83386). Recorded August 1–2, it was enhanced by Plas Johnson on saxophone, Conte Candoli on trumpet, and Oscar Castro-Neves on guitar. Although a gifted bassist – for some time, Brown was her bass instructor – Korb is featured only as a vocalist on the record. One of the album's highlights is a collaboration between Brown and Korb called "Funky Tune for Ray." Once again, Brown displays his ability to play funk lines and solos on the double bass, one of his greatest strengths. Since 2011, Korb has lived in Copenhagen, Denmark, and is still heavily active as a performer.

On September 10–11 the trio recorded the Oscar Peterson and Benny Green album *Oscar and Benny* (Telarc Jazz CD-83406). Hearing Brown work with one of his oldest friends and collaborators and at the same time with one of his finest "discoveries" must have been a special moment. Brown is not heavily featured on the album as a soloist but adds the perfect swing feel and rhythmic drive to allow the pianists to impress.

On October 17–18, 1996 the Ray Brown Trio recorded a live album at Scullers Jazz Club in Boston. Many attendees[166] were Berklee students looking to hear one of the greatest living masters of jazz bass. The album *Live at Scullers* (Telarc Jazz CD-83405) is a solid release and reveals the development of Hutchinson within the trio. The current line-up was now more connected and more exploratory than it had been, a unity that could only be achieved through time and trust. Although the band was playing tunes that were decades old, and to mainly younger audiences, the music sounded relevant and fresh, creating a party atmosphere that can be felt throughout the record. *Live at Scullers* would be the final full-length release by this line-up.

At the end of 1996, Benny Green left the Ray Brown Trio. While he was grateful for his time with the group, Green had always aspired to present his music as a leader. Although he had found some time to pursue this ambition with the Ray Brown Trio, its schedule limited his band-leading opportunities. The split was amicable; on occasion, Green and Brown would reunite in the recording studio and on stage. Benny Green has described his four years with the Ray Brown Trio as "magical."[167]

With Green's departure, Brown hired Geoff Keezer, another young Art Blakey alumnus. Keezer had a modernistic approach to improvisation and a highly creative musical voice incorporating a vast harmonic knowledge. Keezer remembers the time he spent with the legendary bassist:

> I first met Ray when he heard me play in Philadelphia. It was an outdoor concert, and Christian McBride, Ray, and Milt Hinton were on the bill. I didn't play with Ray at that point, but he heard me play, and several months later, on my birthday, he called me up when he was making that record *Some of My Best Friends Are . . . The Piano Players*[168] entirely out of the blue and asked me if I would be on the record. I just said, "Wow, what a great birthday present."
>
> [I was] twenty-four, and it was 1994. The assignment was basically to come to the studio that evening, and I did. We played two songs. One of which made the record. Then after that, before I officially joined his group, he had called me a couple of times to sub for Benny Green, once in Europe and once in Japan. I told him over dinner one night, "If Benny ever leaves, I would really like to do this gig." Several months later, he called me and said, "Benny had given his notice. Do you still want the gig? "I said, "Yeah, let me check my calendar," and I made some artificial flipping noises as if I was flipping through the pages of a calendar; of course, there was nothing on my calendar, and I said, "Yeah, I think that will work." [*laughs*]. So, I played with him from 1997 till February of 2000. It was a fantastic experience.
>
> He would go to Hawaii every January and write arrangements. Nine or ten new arrangements, and when he returned, we would rehearse for a week and then go out for the rest of the year and play all the new music. I only remember rehearsing with him about three or four times. Occasionally if he wrote something new, he would bring it into a soundcheck. We didn't rehearse much, and when I joined his band I knew most of his book already because I made it my responsibility to learn all the music beforehand . . . So we didn't need to do much rehearsing, and a lot of the things in the arrangements that you hear, for example, if you listen to that *Live at Starbucks* record that we did, a lot of those things evolved live. In other words, we played an original arrangement, but after months of playing it, the arrangement evolved into something different. There is no way to explain it other than, night after night, things started to shift and change, and after several months you have something entirely different from what you started with.

> The funny thing about Ray in the studio was that, while he was always well prepared for the live shows, he seemed to make up his records as he went along. We'd get into the studio, and he would basically make up arrangements on the spot, which is kind of the opposite of what most people do. Most people sit down and write all kinds of music and prepare and go in to record. When they play live, they are a little bit freer. But with Ray, he seemed to enjoy being more spontaneous in the studio. So pretty much everything that we recorded was made up on the spot.
>
> He was pretty lenient, and I certainly took full advantage of it. I tried to push as far as I could [*laughs*], not only in terms of what I played but also what I wore on stage. I was really feeling quite rebellious. At one point, I had my hair dyed five different colors. I didn't want to be anything like any of the other pianists he had, but I know that Ray liked to hear the blues and loved it when I played simple, straight-ahead, and funky. But even though he loved that way of playing the most, he never really said, "I want you to play like this." I always felt like I had a tremendous amount of room to be myself. And for that, I am very grateful because there are very few bands where you can have that much freedom.[169]

Geoff Keezer played on three Ray Brown Trio records. The first was Ray Brown Trio with Ulf Wakenius, *Summertime* (Telarc Jazz CD-83430), recorded in August 1997. Keezer's virtuosity, creativity, and fire are immediately evident on the opener, "West Coast Blues," and are fully displayed in his solo on "It's Only a Paper Moon." Wakenius's playing is impressive throughout, and the guitarist is particularly soulful on "Summertime." Brown is most heavily featured on "It's Only a Paper Moon," where he plays the intro, melody, solos, and the cadenza. Other memorable moments displaying his talents as a bassist include his solo on "Topsy," his bowed introduction on "My One and Only Love," his ultra-funky bass line, and his solo on "Reunion Blues" and "Honeysuckle Rose."

The second Geoff Keezer record is Ray Brown Trio, *Live at Starbucks* (Telarc CD-83502), recorded at the Jackson Street store in Seattle, Washington, September 22–23, 1999. The coffee chain has long supported jazz and in the 1990s often played jazz records and sold CDs in many of their locations. By this point, a young drummer named Karriem Riggins had replaced Greg Hutchinson in the group. Before joining the trio, Riggins worked with trumpet sensation Roy Hargrove. In addition to his work as a jazz drummer, Riggins has since done celebrated production work with some of the biggest names in hip-hop.

Live at Starbucks has three Ray Brown originals, including the opener "Up There," a medium swing with tight rhythm kicks, first released in 1961 on Teddy Edwards and Howard McGhee, *Together Again!* (Contemporary Records M3588). Another Ray Brown vehicle is "Brown Bossa," a clever, perfectly played uptempo bossa nova. Brown's final offering is an improvised bass feature titled "Starbucks Blues." Another highlight is the bassist's interpretation of Duke Ellington's "Mainstream," played against the clapping beat of the audience, where he impresses with bluesy statements, upper-register playing, and familiar solo phrases that never fail. A notable moment is when Brown bows the melody of "Caravan." Brown's soloing is pure perfection on "When I Fall in Love," and the group sounds incredibly well connected on "Lament." *Live at Starbucks* contains some of Ray Brown's most inspired playing of his final years.

A final trio recording with Keezer and Riggins was issued posthumously in 2003 on the collection *Walk On: The Final Ray Brown Trio Recording* (Telarc Jazz 2CD-83515). Disc one of this double album includes recordings from January 10–14, 2000, beginning with Ray playing a gorgeous solo arrangement of "America the Beautiful" before a spirited hybrid Latin/swing feel from the band. On "Stella by Starlight" Brown begins with a solo introduction before providing a series of perfectly played countermelodies against the central theme. Following Keezer's masterful solo, Brown also impresses with his improvisation, which offers precise phrasing, solid intonation, and a round, rich tone. His playing remains solid as he introduced the uptempo melody of "Lined with a Groove." Equally brilliant is the bass solo on "Honeysuckle Rose." One of the funkiest numbers is "You Are My Sunshine," in which Brown plays a serious groove along with the melody and a solo.

Walk On is a masterwork and a fitting final release from Ray Brown's trio. One of the album's features is Brown's original three-part "Suite." "Movement I" begins with a rubato bass statement before shifting to a medium swing which eventually settles back to a ballad feel. The second movement starts with a unique bass-line pattern offering wider intervallic spreads which serve as a centralized theme before Keezer improvises over a more medium/uptempo swing feel. Riggins then shines during some solo breaks. Brown follows with a well-formulated solo before a return to the centralized theme. "Movement III" begins with Keezer playing an intro in a minor key, thus creating a sense of wondering and suspense. After playing rubato, the pianist sets up a jazz waltz as he plays solo runs and chorded statements. The suite then ends as it began, with Ray Brown offering a solo cadenza.

Also included is the Ray Brown composition "Hello Girls," in which the bassist demonstrates his development as a classical performer before the music shifts into a light funk groove, a pattern that is then repeated. *Walk On* displays Brown's continued desire, even in his final years, to explore, create, and challenge. The second disc offers previously unreleased material from concerts and studio dates, including tracks from November 21, 1994, a performance at Scullers Jazz Club from October 17–18, 1996, and a Blue Note performance from December 15–17, 2000.

In 2000, Geoff Keezer left Ray Brown's group and was replaced by Larry Fuller, a gifted pianist who had previously worked with Ernestine Anderson and Jeff Hamilton. There are no commercial recordings with the Fuller and Riggins version of the trio. The final member to join the trio was drummer George Fludas, who replaced Riggins in 2001.

30 *Some of My Best Friends* and Final Sideman Sessions
1994–2002

While working with his trio, Ray Brown began a popular series of recordings known as *Some of My Best Friends Are . . .* , in which he would feature several musicians playing the same instrument on a single album. The first installment was *Some of My Best Friends Are . . . The Piano Players* (Telarc Jazz CD-83373), recorded November 18 and 21, 1994. Brown hired Lewis Nash, one of the most gifted and in-demand drummers on the scene, to support the pianists. Throughout the recording series, Brown selected both his contemporaries and younger musicians. The first three tracks feature Ahmad Jamal, a brilliant and inventive pianist who played with a more laid-back style than many of his peers. As with Brown, Jamal grew up in Pittsburgh. He found fame in 1958 with the record *Ahmad Jamal Trio at the Pershing* (Argo LP 628).

The next to be featured was Benny Green, the exciting pianist in Ray Brown's current trio and, as discussed in the previous chapter, one of the most gifted voices in jazz to emerge in the early '90s. Green provides an original called "Ray of Light," and his more rapid-fire approach contrasts with Jamal's more subdued style, adding variety and interest. Following Green is Italian piano master Dado Moroni, who had worked with Ray Brown on the 1988 releases *Two Bass Hits* (European Music Productions EP 881) and Mark Nightingale's *What I Wanted to Say* (Mons Records 874 763). Moroni presents a version of the John Coltrane classic "Giant Steps," in which Brown bows the melody before the time feel moves between ragtime and bop.

The next pianist featured was Geoff Keezer, a rising star who would eventually replace Benny Green in Brown's trio. Keezer is featured on only one track, "Close Your Eyes." Including Keezer on such an album was a stamp of approval for the young pianist and helped announce his arrival to the wider jazz community.

Naturally, Brown included Oscar Peterson in the collection. The veteran pianist plays the final two tracks: "St. Tropez" (a Peterson original) and "How Come You Do Me?" Although Peterson was no longer in the best physical condition, his playing still has a fantastic sense of swing; Ray Brown solos on both tracks.

In 1996 came the follow-up, *Some Of My Best Friends Are . . . The Sax Players* (Telarc CD-83388). By this time, Greg Hutchinson had joined the trio on drums. In addition to the music, the original CD release included short interviews between Brown and each participating saxophonist, during which Brown asked about their early influences. The album begins with tenorist Joe Lovano playing "How High the Moon." By the time of the recording, Lovano was in his mid-forties; having worked in the big bands of Woody Herman and Mel Lewis, he had gained a reputation from his recordings with Lonnie Smith, Paul Motian, and John Scofield. As displayed on the opening track and his version of "Easy Living," Lovano has a robust tone and a creative improvisational style that never sounds derivative or contrived.

Lester Young, Charlie Parker, Coleman Hawkins, and Ben Webster had all passed long before these recordings. However, one early legend still standing at this point was Benny Carter, who, like Ray Brown, had a decades-long career. He plays on the second track, "Love Walked In," and on "Fly Me to the Moon." His gorgeous tone and lyricism are on full display, and, unlike many musicians of his generation, Carter's playing never faltered. Particular attention should be paid to Brown's solo on "Love Walked In."

For both the third track, "Polka Dots and Moonbeams," and for "Just You, Just Me," Brown introduces one of the most discussed and celebrated saxophonists on the scene at the time: Joshua Redman, son of the well-known saxophonist Dewey Redman. At the time of this release, Redman was only in his mid-twenties, yet he was being recorded regularly as a leader and hailed as the new star of jazz. His popular releases, *Wish* (1993; Warner Bros. 9 45365-2), and *MoodSwing* (1994; Warner Bros. 9 45643-2), earned Grammy nominations and *DownBeat* poll awards. Although Redman often favored original works, his take on the two standards further links him to the great jazz tradition and to the playing styles of the masters who came before him.

Next is the English-born saxophonist Ralph Moore with whom Ray Brown had already worked on the 1990 release *Moore Makes 4*. Moore impresses with an uptempo version of Charlie Parker's "Crazeology." Having demonstrated his bebop chops and overall technicality, Moore returned to perform "(When It's) Sleepy Time Down South," a 1931 composition made famous by Louis Armstrong.

Following Moore is the soulful big-toned tenor saxophonist from Pittsburgh, Stanley Turrentine, who recorded dozens of well-received albums for Blue Note Records throughout the 1960s. Ray Brown also played on his final record, the 1999 release *Do You Have Any Sugar?* (Concord Vista CCD 4862-2). Here, Turrentine performs "Port of Rico" and closes the album with "God Bless the Child." Both tracks manage to capture the spirit of this legend.[170]

The last to be featured was Jesse Davis, a New Orleans alto saxophonist who gained some notoriety in the 1990s for his bebop phrasing and recordings as a Concord Records artist; he was a member of Illinois Jacquet's big band at the time. Davis offers his take on Charlie Parker's "Moose the Mooche" and the standard "These Foolish Things." Although he attracted a lot of notice in the '90s, he has not maintained the same level of fame as Lovano and Redman. In sum, this a solid concept album.

Ray Brown's next installment was 1998's *Some of My Best Friends Are . . . Singers* (Telarc CD-83341). As we have seen, throughout his career he worked with some of the finest singers, including Ella Fitzgerald, Billie Holiday, Sarah Vaughan, Louis Armstrong, and Frank Sinatra. Accompanying the chosen singers on this album is his current trio by this time: Geoff Keezer and Gregory Hutchinson. One of the featured vocalists is Dee Dee Bridgewater, who appeared, recorded, and traveled with Brown several times during his later career and numbered among his favorite singers. Bridgewater talks about recording and touring with the bassist:

> I participated in two of his album projects. One of them was *Some of My Best Friends Are . . . Singers*. For that album, we did "More Than You Know" and "Cherokee" [with guest Ralph Moore]. He [Brown] was really kind of from the old school. He didn't want to write down any kinds of arrangements and spend any time doing that. So, we just went into the studio on the day that we were recording and talked through the two songs and how we were going to do them. We went into the studio and basically did them in one or two takes. Then he really was the catalyst for me getting off my butt to do my *Dear Ella* [Verve 314 537 896-2] album. Because I was a bit overwhelmed by this project, I procrastinated in booking studios and stuff. And I actually got on my knees and prayed on New Year's Eve going into '97 and asked God to give me a sign that was clear; otherwise, I was going to cancel the date.
>
> I was awakened by a call from Ray Brown on January 1st of '97 saying, "Are we doing this album? You better do this album. So, when are we going in the studio?" So, he was really the man that got my ball rolling, so to speak. In the studio, Ray was . . . he's wonderful in the studio. He was very democratic and open to suggestions. He told jokes in between takes and was pretty easy-going. He was very precise about what he wanted. He was very kind in making changes that he would like to have made by musicians.[171]

Another featured vocalist on the album was Diana Krall, whose career Ray Brown had begun managing and with whom he recorded on her 1995 release *Only Trust Your Heart* (GRP GRP-9810-2). Krall opens the album with "I Thought About You" and later presents "Little Boy," on which she scats.

Singing "Poor Butterfly and "No Greater Love" (with guest guitarist Russell Malone) was Etta Jones. Born in 1928, Jones began recording in 1944 and found commercial success in 1960 with her album *Don't Go to Strangers* (Prestige PRLP 7186). While she could never match that album's success, Jones recorded and performed consistently till her death in 2001.

Also included is Marlena Shaw. Born in 1942, Shaw began recording soul, R&B, and jazz in the late 1960s; she achieved some prominence recording albums for Blue Note and Columbia in the 1970s. From 1980, her output became somewhat sporadic, and her career was in decline. However, Ray Brown knew talent, and occasionally worked again with Shaw after this recording, on which she sings "At Long Last Love" and "Imagination."

The fourth female vocalist is Nancy King, a masterful singer from Oregon with a fine ability to scat. King performs "But Beautiful" and the album closer "The Perfect Blues" (both with guest saxophonist Antonio Hart).

The only male vocalist is Kevin Mahogany. Born in 1958, Mahogany's vocal quality was similar to that of Johnny Hartman and Billy Eckstine. He first began recording in the 1990s and soon came to be seen as one of the finest male voices in jazz. Things began to slow somewhat for Mahogany in the 2000s, and sadly he passed away in 2017 aged only fifty-nine. Here, Mahogany impresses with his versions of "Skylark" and "The Party's Over."

Brown continued with the concept, presenting the same singers on the album *Christmas Songs with the Ray Brown Trio* (Telarc CD-83437) but adding Venessa Rubin, a jazz singer who had had crossover success in the 1990s. Many jazz artists have produced holiday albums, but this represents Ray's only holiday-related work as a leader. In typical Ray Brown fashion, it is also one of the hardest-swinging and finest representations of holiday music played in a jazz context.

Brown's next *Best Friends* album was the 2000 release *Some of My Best Friends Are … Trumpet Players* (Telarc CD-83495). The trumpeters are backed by Brown's trio of Geoff Keezer and Karriem Riggins. Opening the album, performing "Our Delight," is Roy Hargrove, a young trumpeter new to Brown's orbit. By 1990 Hargrove was impressing as a leader and sideman, quickly establishing himself as one of the most celebrated jazz trumpeters. Sadly, he died in 2018 aged forty-nine after suffering from kidney disease. Hargrove also played on the track "Stairway to the Stars." Next is a soulful rendition of "Bag's Groove," played by Jon Faddis. As we saw in Chapter 27, Brown first recorded with the trumpet master in 1985 on his record *Legacy*. For his second track, Faddis offers his own composition "Original Jones," which includes some high notes at the top of his range.

Track 3 sees James Morrison playing at times alone with Ray Brown on "I Thought About You." Brown had a fondness for the Australian multi-instrumentalist and was pivotal in helping to introduce him to U.S. artists when he played on his major-label debut *Snappy Doo* (see Chapter 27). Morrison also showed his writing skills with the ballad "When You Go." Next up is Terence Blanchard, a brilliant trumpeter and composer, who offers an uptempo swing version of "I'm Getting Sentimental Over You" and the closing track "Goodbye." Blanchard, who is from New Orleans, had been on the scene for some time and first came to notoriety as a member of Lionel Hampton's Orchestra and then Art Blakey's Jazz Messengers in 1982.

Another New Orleans native is Nicholas Payton, a young lion (at the time) who impresses with his version of "Violets for Your Furs" and "The Kicker." Payton remains one of the most inspirational trumpeters on the scene. The last to enter the mix is Clark Terry, by far the most senior member of the ensemble. Terry and Brown had recorded together frequently, beginning in 1964. Terry presents two originals, "Itty Bitty Blues" and "Clark's Tune (Legacy)." The master remains impressive.

The final installment from this series was released in 2002 as *Some of My Best Friends Are... Guitarists* (Telarc CD-83499) and was also made with the backing of Keezer and Riggins. As we have seen in these pages, Ray Brown had a long association with some of the greatest jazz guitar masters, including Barney Kessel, Joe Pass, Wes Montgomery, and Tal Farlow (none of which were alive, or in the case of Kessel, capable of performing), so once again Brown recorded with whatever "old friends" were still around, along with newer friends. The album begins with John Pizzarelli playing "Just Squeeze Me" and later "Tangerine." Pizzarelli is the son of the late legendary swing guitarist Bucky Pizzarelli and has had a storied career as a singer, guitarist, and entertainer. "Just Squeeze Me" offers some fine solo interplay between Brown and Pizzarelli. Next up is Herb Ellis, one of Brown's closest friends and the guitarist with whom he recorded the most. Their nearly fifty-year musical connection is instantly felt on the tracks "I Want to Be Happy" and "Blues for Junior."

During Brown's final years, Russell Malone was his first call when it came to guitarists. While many younger jazz guitarists at this point had a more "washed out" or "processed" tone, Malone's sound and approach were more directly connected to the players of the past. The guitarist is heard on "Heartstrings" and "Little Darlin'," the latter including some impressive four-bar solo trading statements between Malone and Brown. Swedish guitarist Ulf Wakenius had been a guest on previous Ray Brown Trio recordings and was at this point the regular guitarist with Oscar Peterson. His performances on "Blues for Ray" and "My Funny Valentine" show why he is worthy of attention.

Brown had worked with Kenny Burrell several times before this recording, including the 1964 album with Milt Jackson *Much in Common* (see Chapter 18). Burrell is as tasteful as ever on "Fly Me to the Moon" and "Soulful Spirit." Bruce Forman is heard on the tracks "The Song Is You" and "Blues for Wes." Before this recording, Forman had little connection with Brown. He was releasing solo albums as early as 1981, and was most connected with saxophonist Richie Cole, although he also recorded with Johnny Griffin, Bobby Hutcherson, and Tom Harrell.

In addition to his work with his trio, Ray Brown continued to lend support as a sideman on full albums and selected tracks. And 1995 was an incredibly active year for him. To begin with, on January 15–16, Oscar Peterson was recording his album *The More I See You* (Telarc Jazz CD-83370), his first after a stroke in 1993. One wouldn't necessarily think a mainstream jazz album featuring older stars such as Oscar Peterson, Benny Carter, Clark Terry, and Ray Brown would be particularly interesting. Nonetheless, the album has a sense of swing and a maturity to create a solid connection for listeners. Adding to the interest is the inclusion of drummer Lewis Nash and Canadian guitarist Lorne Lofsky. Highlights are "In a Mellow Tone" and "When My Dreamboat Comes Home."

One of the standout 1995 releases was *André Previn and Friends Play Show Boat* (Deutsche Grammophon 447 639-2), on which the pianist rejoins colleagues from the albums *After Hours* and *Old Friends*: guitarist Mundell Lowe and Ray Brown. Grady Tate joins them on drums to play the music of Jerome Kern's 1927 hit musical. The concept continues Previn's work begun in the 1950s with Shelly Manne on *My Fair Lady* and continued with his jazz interpretations of *West Side Story* and *Camelot*. *Show Boat*'s tightly organized small-group arrangements make this one of Previn's best jazz efforts. In addition to the *Show Boat* material, Previn offers three new compositions.

On June 24, 1995, Ray was performing with André Previn and Mundell Lowe in Austria. The concert was recorded and released on *André Previn, Jazz at the Musikverein* (Verve 314 537 704-2). Brown is most impressive on "Captain Bill," a bass feature. Although Brown's work with Previn has been overshadowed by his recordings with other pianists such as Oscar Peterson, Bud Powell, and Phineas Newborn Jr., the records he made with Previn are among his finest. Previn's ability to blend traditionalism and modernism, along with his deep knowledge of concert music and his sense of swing, should combine to elevate Previn as one of the finest names in jazz piano playing. Rarely has an individual shown such a remarkable ability to shift seamlessly from classical to jazz.

In early February 1995, Ray Brown recorded for the first time with legendary New Orleans singer, songwriter, and pianist Dr. John on the big-band release *Afterglow* (Blue Thumb Records GRB 70002). This was the third jazz effort for Dr. John and producer Tommy LiPuma. While Brown is listed as appearing on the album, bassist John Clayton handled some of the playing and did excellent arrangements. Also appearing in the ensemble are Jeff Hamilton and percussionist Larry Bunker. *Afterglow* is a solid effort revealing one of the most distinctive voices in popular music in a different light.

Also in 1995 was the album *Double R B: Ray Bryant Meets Ray Brown +1* (EmArcy PHCE-57). The "+1" is drummer Lewis Nash. The trio sounds well connected throughout, and Brown gets ample space to solo. He also provides two original offerings, "Two RB's" and "Just Sweet Enough," which include a series of tightly performed stop-time figures and breaks. The trio of Bryant, Brown, and Nash was an active side project, and the group toured Europe and Japan. An album highlight is their rendition of "Smack Dab in the Middle," a hard-bop vehicle that features Bryant and Brown. Brown explores some arco playing on "Come Sunday" and "First Song."

On March 7–8, 1995, Ray Brown recorded with saxophonist Frank Morgan on the album *Love, Lost & Found* (Telarc CD-83374) with Cedar Walton and Billy Higgins. Morgan was a gifted alto saxophonist who played in the swing and bebop tradition, although his heroin habit led to several incarcerations. Following his final release from imprisonment in 1986, Morgan returned to the jazz scene. Much of the *Love, Lost & Found* material is ballads. Brown is most prominently featured on "All the Things You Are" (a duo for Foster and Brown), "What Is This Thing Called Love," and "I Can't Get Started with You."

That year, Brown participated in a third installment of Lalo Schifrin's *Jazz Meets the Symphony* and was included on the album *Firebird: Jazz Meets the Symphony No. 3* (Four Winds FW 2004) with the London Symphony Orchestra. For this collection, Schifrin looked to the music of Fats Waller, Charlie Parker, George Gershwin, Igor Stravinsky, Wolfgang Amadeus Mozart, and others to present another strong release of symphonic jazz. Ray Brown is most heavily featured on "It's You Or No One." Other notable guest performers include Paquito D'Rivera, James Morrison, Jon Faddis, and Grady Tate. In 1998 Brown was also included in a fourth installment of the series, *Metamorphosis: Jazz Meets the Symphony #4* (Aleph Records 004). The recording is particularly impressive and includes Jeff Hamilton, James Morrison, and violinist/guitarist Markus Wienstroer. It includes reworkings of compositions and tracks associated with Gil Evans, Thelonious Monk, Bix Beiderbecke, and opera composer Giacomo Puccini. Ray also appeared on George Duke's *Illusions* (Warner Brothers 9 45755-2), playing on the closing track, "So I'll Pretend," featuring vocalist Dianne Reeves.

In 1996, Ray Brown hooked up with Brooklyn-born vocalist and actor Ranee Lee for the recording of her album *You Must Believe in Swing* (Justin Time JUST 88-2). Lee had come to prominence after her starring role as Billie Holiday in the musical *Lady Day* and later for her original musical *Dark Divas*, which paid tribute to the great female jazz vocalists of the past. The record's most notable aspect was the appearance of drummer Ed Thigpen: it had been years since the celebrated team of Brown and Thigpen had worked together. Lee is well represented on this standards album, and Ray Brown is most prominent on "Nice and Easy," "Angel Eyes," "Yesterdays," and "Fine and Mellow." Thigpen and Brown would work together again the following year on the Shelly Berg album *The Will: A Tribute to Oscar Peterson* (CARS Productions CARS CP0030). Berg is a Cleveland-born classical and jazz pianist who began recording in the early 1990s. He is currently the Musical Dean at Frost School at the University of Miami.

On October 1, 1996 a live concert event at the Town Hall in celebration of Oscar Peterson's seventieth birthday was recorded as *A Tribute to Oscar Peterson: Live at the Town Hall* (Telarc Jazz CD-83401). Performing standards with the legend were many of his past and current associates: Herb Ellis, Milt Jackson, Clark Terry, Stanley Turrentine, Shirley Horn, Niels-Henning Ørsted Pedersen, Benny Green, Roy Hargrove, Lewis Nash, and the Manhattan

Transfer. The concert was a fitting tribute to a man who meant so much to jazz music.

Ray Brown and Jeff Hamilton teamed up again in 1997 for a trio album with Oliver Jones: *Have Fingers, Will Travel* (Justin Time JUST 102-2). Jones is a pianist from Montreal who is mainly known in Canada and the UK. Brown recorded again with James Williams that year for the Magical Trio release *Awesome!* (DIW DIW-623), which had Elvin Jones on drums. Ray also played on four tracks for the Manhattan Transfer album *Swing* (Atlantic 83012-2) in 1997. In 1999, with Jeff Hamilton and Herb Ellis, he recorded for saxophonist Harry Allen for his release *When I Grow Too Old to Dream* (BMG BVCJ-34007). Allen has been recording since 1989.

As the new millennium dawned, Brown was still working, in a limited way, on releases for others. He can be heard on the 2000 Holly Hofmann Quintet album *Live at Birdland* (Azica AJD-72214). Hofmann is a gifted jazz flutist who has been on the scene since the 1980s. Also included in the performance are pianist Bill Cunliffe and drummer Victor Lewis. In 2001, Brown was heard on pianist Ray Kennedy's release *I'm Beginning to See the Light* (Victoria Company VC4336), which had three members of the Pizzarelli family on it: Bucky, John, and bassist Martin.

31 SuperBass
1991–2000

Bass players are often most appreciative of those Ray Brown recordings in which he performs with other bassists or on which the instrument is presented in an uncharacteristic way. Brown was constantly challenging himself and was highly supportive of other bassists. He was one of the key figures behind the emancipation of the bass from its accompanist role and one of the most notable names to use the instrument as a solo vehicle. As discussed in Chapter 23, Brown's first bass duo recording came in 1977 with the live record *Montreux '77: Oscar Peterson and the Bassists*, where he went head to head with Niels-Henning Ørsted Pedersen. He subsequently recorded in collaborative situations with other bass players but in more limited contexts, never again in such a way as in 1977.

One remarkable project was the 1985 Arni Egilsson album *Basses Loaded* (Bay Cities BCD 2002).[172] The Icelandic classical bass virtuoso, in an ensemble with Brown, pianist Pete Jolly, and drummer Jimmie Smith, bows melodies and solos over standard material as Ray Brown lays down a solid foundation. Brown is prominently featured, and the contrast between Egilsson's arco statements and Brown's pizzicato playing is of great interest. On "Blues for Ray," Brown gets to shine with his double-stop figures played against a medium-swing tempo. Following Pete Jolly's fine piano solo, Egilsson's blues solo with bow goes into a trading of solo statements with Brown, who plays some tasteful phrases.

"Body and Soul" begins with a Brown solo. He then interprets the first half of the melody in his signature style, which is reminiscent of Jimmy Blanton and Duke Ellington's 1941 version. Egilsson then takes over for the second half of the melody, and again note the contrast of his arco playing against Brown's pizzicato. Following the piano solo, Ray's improvisation blends bebop phrasing with more subtle swing-based material. Egilsson returns with a solo that references the main melody and plays some perfectly articulated solo statements. While all the tracks are remarkable, "Astin" is particularly inspiring and built around Egilsson's gorgeous opening minor statement which shifts into a pop-funk time feel. Brown is equally impressive with his solo. *Basses Loaded* is a masterpiece for any fan of arco bass; and it opened the door to Ray for similar presentations.

Brown then hooked up with French jazz bass master Pierre Boussaguet to record the 1988 release *Two Bass Hits* (European Music Productions EP 881) along with Dado Maroni. Boussaguet had worked with Monty Alexander as well as other jazz musicians visiting Europe. An inspired track is "Pitter-Panther Patter," a reworking of Jimmy Blanton's great recording. There is a reworking of one of Brown's most often-played originals, "F.S.R.," and he also provides the original "Blues for Sugar Daddy Queen." One of the more impressive cuts (but not released until the CD version) is an uptempo reworking of the classic "Sweet Georgia Brown" called "Sweet Raymond Brown." From 1988–1993 Brown and Boussaguet toured Europe with material featuring the bassists playing melodies and two-part harmonies.

A second, more carefully arranged and more exploratory sequel is called *Ray Brown's Two Bass Hits Featuring Pierre Boussaguet and Jacky Terrasson* (Capri Records 74034-2), which was released in 1991. It is another masterclass exploring the possibilities of the bass as a solo instrument. Highlights are the original tracks "Something for the Bass Boss," "Trictatism," and a clever reworking of "America the Beautiful." Also of note are two carefully arranged and orchestrated medleys, "Ellington Medley" and "Bossa Nova Medley."

In 1991, Brown was filmed at a concert called *Bass All-Stars, with Edgar Meyer and Victor Wooten*. Meyer is one of the most innovative and impressive voices of modern acoustic bass, and Wooten a technical master of electric bass. The concert sees the three playing in various solo, duo, and trio settings. At one point, all three bassists work a routine in which they all play on one bass in a remarkable display of mastery and comedy. The video is now available on YouTube and is required viewing for fans of bass improvisation.

Another bassist Ray Brown showed interested in was John Clayton, a talented musician from Los Angeles whom Brown began instructing at sixteen. Thanks to his support, Clayton recorded with many of Brown's associates, including Milt Jackson, Monty Alexander, Jeff Hamilton, and Count Basie, starting in the late 1970s. With his Clayton Brothers band and other extensive projects, John Clayton has been one of the most impactful bassists of the last four decades. In 1990, Ray Brown released the first of a series of recordings with Clayton called *SuperBass* (Capri Records 74018-2).[173] Clayton is also a highly gifted composer/arranger and his precise arrangements are a perfect vehicle for two basses playing together, often in harmony, as well as providing meticulous background lines and specific form details. The pair reveal the bass as a melodic force, playing counter-lines, upper-register figures, and arco melodies. All the reeds (which are often overdubbed) are played by his brother, Jeff Clayton, with Jeff Hamilton on drums and Freddie Green on guitar.

Each track, whether a jazz standard or a Brown or Clayton original, is a carefully crafted inspiration in terms of bass technicality. The first, by Brown, is "One Armed Bandit," a clever medium swing played in a big-band style, with Brown on the main melody along with harmonies, and bass lines provided by John Clayton. The arrangement includes carefully placed solo stop-time figures and compelling call-and-response passages. Brown's second original is "Goodbye Freddie Green," a tribute to the guitarist who passed away before the release: a medium swing and a fitting tribute to one of history's most celebrated rhythm guitarists; it is rhythm-based and hard-swinging.

We first hear Clayton's strength as a writer on "Swing Jig," which begins as a chamber-style showcase with the bassists playing counterpunctual statements. After a drum break, the time feel shifts to medium swing. Clayton's second original is "Hues," which reveals his classical roots and technical skills as a composer. If two basses together might seem complicated, then surely recording ten basses must be an impossibility? But Brown and Clayton do exactly that and pull it off on the tune "Happy Days Are Here Again."

Making the *SuperBass* album is just one of many fond memories John Clayton has of Ray Brown. The two remained close friends throughout Brown's life, and many see Clayton, who remains an essential and creative force in jazz music, as Brown's protégé. Clayton retells how he met his most important teacher and how the first *SuperBass* album developed:

> I was 16 years old, having fun with the bass and playing in school ensembles. A student friend of mine told me that I HAD to check out this record he had found at the public library – THE TRIO, by Oscar Peterson. It had Ray Brown on bass and Ed Thigpen on drums. He played "Billy Boy" for me, and my eyes got the widest they have ever been. I had never heard the bass played like that before. Not long before that, I had just started taking private classical bass lessons. I asked my teacher if he had ever heard of Ray Brown. Not only had he heard of him, he KNEW him! He read a letter to me from Ray Brown, which told of an evening extension course that he was going to teach at UCLA called WORKSHOP IN JAZZ BASS. That was my last classical lesson with that teacher (later, Ray insisted that I continue the classical studies). I saved $65 and enrolled in the course. Who could have guessed that that would be the beginning of one of the most important and influential relationships I would ever have in life?
>
> Ray always insisted that one learn the bass from the bottom to the top. All scales, major, minor, diminished, and whole tone. Arpeggios: major and minor triads, dominant 7ths, minor 7ths, major 7ths, minor-major 7ths, diminished, augmented, and more. Tone! "Your sound is the first thing the listener hears," he used to say. When amplified, he was always searching for an amplified sound that didn't change HIS sound. Even though he was a partner in the Polytone company, he would never let that get in the way of his search for the best and most natural-sounding model pickup he could find.
>
> He stressed the importance of a driving bass line, something that would excite the band and soloist. Good intonation. Got some problem intervals? Some notes that always seem to be out of tune? Isolate them and fix them. Period. We're all human; we all have those challenges. But it is of crucial importance that we fix the problems so that the music doesn't suffer. He was strict about that. Swinging, melodic bass lines. He used to

say that "90% of what you do as a bass player is play bass lines. If you can't do that, you might as well go home. Ella, Frank Sinatra, Joe Williams, Quincy Jones, and everyone else don't hire me to play solos all night! They hire me to play some good time and good bass lines. That's going to be your bread and butter. Good, steady time (rhythm, pulse). Melodic, lyrical solos. Study with someone. Don't try to figure it all out yourself."

He "told me off" on several occasions when I was younger, but I always knew it was out of love. He was always coaching, advising, and trying to help set people that were lost on the right path. He gave countless lessons in his hotel rooms around the world.

The first time Ray and I did a SuperBass project, it was to be for Concord Records. As he did for Telarc Records in later years, Ray was an unofficial consultant to the label, advising them regarding which artists to consider, helping to arrange the music, and produce the recording while saving the label lots of money. Concord Records, however, did not think that a SuperBass record would sell. After being pleased with the first four tunes that we recorded, Ray pushed to finish the recording – and we did. That recording, which eventually came out on Capri Records, featured Ray and I overdubbing bass parts to create bass ensembles – at one point, we had as many as ten basses going at the same time. My brother, Jeff, overdubbed woodwinds and saxophones, Freddie Green played guitar, and Jeff Hamilton played drums. That was the first SuperBass.[174]

In his later career, Ray Brown would continue to find opportunities to feature the bass and perform with other bass players. In the *SuperBass* liner notes he writes, "This is not my last attempt at showing off the bass violin in a variety of settings, and you can be assured that the next *SuperBass* album will be twice as good as this one."

In 1993, Brown pushed his limits again when he premiered his symphonic jazz composition "Afterthoughts" with the American Jazz Philharmonic, released as simply *American Jazz Philharmonic* (GRP GRD-9730). "Afterthoughts" is a feature for solo bass and orchestra separated into three movements. During the first movement, Brown plays in the middle to the upper register of the bass against a light orchestral backdrop. He begins the second movement soloing against sparse piano chords before presenting a funky blues theme which the orchestra mimics. The piece's final movement is similar to the first, bringing the composition together. "Afterthoughts" must be considered among Ray Brown's finest achievements.

A quite different bass project was Carol Kaye's 1995's ultra-funk album *Picking Up on the E-String* (Groove Attack Productions GAP 00131), the session bassist's first release as a leader. Brown gets writing credits on three originals: "Bass Catch," "Greenapple Quickstep," and "Moke and Poke Stomp." Kaye's bass lines are the feature of an album that includes an extensive cast of guest artists, such as Joe Sample, Howard Roberts, Joe Pass, and J.J. Johnson.

Although many young bassists impressed Ray Brown, none seemed to do so more than Christian McBride. Brown took particular interest in McBride's career, and the two formed a tight bond. Even at a young age, McBride had carved his place in history as one of jazz's most outstanding bass technicians. Brown first recorded a track ("Splanky") with McBride and bass legend Milt Hinton on Christian McBride's solo debut *Gettin' to It* (Verve 523 989-2). McBride dazzles with the first solo, Milt Hinton follows, and Ray Brown offers the final improvisation.

On the back of this encounter, Brown restructured his SuperBass group, bringing McBride in. The new line-up did several concerts resulting in two wonderful full-length live albums: *SuperBass: Recorded Live at Scullers* (1997; Telarc Jazz CD-83393) and *SuperBass 2* (2001; Telarc Jazz CD-83483). These collaborations represent some of the most imaginative and remarkable examples of bass exploration. Many of the arrangements are Brown's, and feature arco melodies, three-part harmonies, upper-register statements, percussive attacks, funky vamps, and even vocal-shout choruses. Christian McBride recollects:

> I first performed with Ray in 1992 in Pittsburgh at a place called the Manchester Craftman's Guild. I was so proud to be a part of that concert. Benny Green had just become his permanent pianist a few months before, so he was living his dream, and Ray asking me to be a part of what was to be known as "SuperBass" put my smile at an unbelievable width. It was a very memorable engagement. It was somewhat of a Ray Brown extravaganza. He played with his trio, with SuperBass, and solo.
>
> Ray and John Clayton had already been doing two bass concerts under the SuperBass moniker for at least a few years prior to me joining. They even made one record. When Ray had a big concert in Pittsburgh in 1992, he asked me to play with him and John. He seemed to like it so much; he kept it going with me on board.
>
> Collectively, we would decide who played melody on what song, who would play rhythm, who would walk, etc. One thing I remember Ray telling John and I in Seattle back in 2000 was, "Although they have my name as the leader of the group since I'm the old m___f___, I want you both to know that this group belongs to all of us." So, he viewed it as truly a collective effort. Although, John and I always knew that ultimately, it was Ray's group. We loved listening to everything he played.
>
> I don't think I would be wrong if I said that Ray was like my second father. After a certain period, we had many talks about non-musical issues. Things dealing with life, money, career, and of course, girls! I've saved many voice messages from Ray through the years. I'm sure he's had many close relationships with protégés of his, but inherently I know it was different with us. He once called up and told me about a new song he'd been writing called "Taco with a Pork Chop." Needless to say, I started laughing hysterically (as did he!). He said to me, "I'm not sure how much Clayton [John] will dig this, "cause he ain't as crazy as me and you!" Somehow, being "crazy as him" meant the world to me.[175]

Typically, the SuperBass arrangements were such that one bassist was playing the melody in the upper register while another played a guide tone or countermelody and the third walked time or played roots. On October 17–18, 1996 the Ray Brown Trio recorded their first live SuperBass album at Scullers Jazz Club in Boston:[176] a wonderful document of the possibilities of the bass as a solo vehicle.

The album opens with the short "SuperBass Theme," with only the three bassists playing together in perfect harmony, announcing an evening of bass mastery. Track 2 is a slow version of "Blue Monk." After the carefully arranged melody, each bassist plays superb solos, McBride's a perfect blend of taste and technicality that is remarkable given his youth. The album's third track, "Bye, Bye Blackbird," pairs only Brown and McBride, with the two bassists splitting the melody. McBride is outstanding on the first solo; Brown counters, and, although impressive, the student overshadows the mentor. The next cut, "Lullaby of the Leaves," is a feature for John Clayton, whose arco playing has a gorgeous vibrato.

After a version of "Who Cares?" performed by Ray Brown's trio with Benny Green and Gregory Hutchinson, in which Green dazzles the audience, the three bassists return with a clever arrangement of "Mack the Knife." Brown takes the first solo, followed by Clayton and then McBride, who closes the song by interpreting the final melody. The three bassists then play a perfectly crafted arrangement of "Centerpiece," on which McBride eclipses the others again on his solo by displaying his arco chops. After a long slow blues by Brown and his trio called "Sculler Blues," the three bassists excite the crowd with McBride's original "Brown's Funk," backed by drummer Gregory Hutchinson. The album concludes with a return to the "SuperBass Theme." Few could have conceived the bass being presented in such a way as it was in this performance; this author was in attendance, and I feel privileged to have witnessed such a magical evening.

The *SuperBass 2* album was recorded live at the Blue Note in New York between December 15 and 17, 2000. In order to separate the bassists, the Telarc engineers put Ray Brown in the center of the mix, John Clayton on the left and Christian McBride on the right. The album begins with the "SuperBass Theme" before moving into a medium version of "Get Happy." Following the arranged head, solos are taken by Brown, Clayton, and McBride. While all three bassists are impressive, McBride is the most dazzling. Following a prearranged interlude, the main melody is presented before a harmonized outro. Next comes the group's take on Thelonious Monk's "Mysterioso," which has an ominous feel. The bassist plays the theme pizzicato before Clayton and McBride switch to bowing. Clayton impresses with a bluesy and well-conceived first solo; McBride counters with a remarkable arco solo that retains a bluesy quality throughout. Brown encourages both soloists with on-stage commentary before playing the final solo.

The group then gets funky with their version of "Papa Was a Rolling Stone," on which McBride and Clayton trade arco statements against Brown's fundamental line. The group sings the chorus along with the audience. Ray Brown plays a slapped bass solo, a technique he rarely used. Clayton and McBride return to arco statements played with perfect technique and intonation. The two masters conclude the piece playing high up on the neck and fading out. This version of "Papa Was a Rolling Stone" is one of the most enjoyable and impressive displays of bass technicality caught on record. As the piece concludes, the audience applauds in an uproar.

The next offering is three selections from George Gershwin's *Porgy and Bess*: "Summertime," featuring Christian McBride, "I Loves You Porgy," featuring John Clayton, and "It Ain't Necessarily So," featuring Ray Brown. At this point, Ray Brown tells the audience he is going to "show off the kids." First up is a duo performance between McBride and Brown on "Birk's Works." After a jaw-dropping solo introduction by McBride, the duo presents the melody and Brown and McBride solo. Clayton is featured next on a superb bowed interpretation of "My Funny Valentine." The three bassists come together again for Clayton's original "Three by Four," with a pizzicato solo by Brown followed by arco improvisations by McBride and Clayton. Next up is Brown's clever Latin-feel original "Taco with a Pork Chop," which has George Fludas and Larry Fuller playing percussion. Brown and the ensemble sing the chorus "Taco with a pork chop" as a call-and-response with the audience. The fun and spirited atmosphere it creates is a testament to Brown's humor and effervescent spirit. The album concludes with the "SuperBass Theme." Had Brown lived longer, it is highly likely he would have continued along this route, showcasing the possibilities of the bass in projects of this nature.

32 Coda: Remembering Ray Brown

In his final years, Ray Brown continued to work, travel, and perform at an remarkable pace, and retirement never seemed to be an option. When asked how he kept it up, Brown told interviewer Ray Comiskey:

> First, you have to get up in the morning. That'll get you started. Second, you have to love what you do. And I like to travel; if I had to stay in one place, it'd run me crazy. I tried to settle once, and it didn't work.[177]

As he advanced in age, Brown remained healthy and full of life and spirit. However, in January 2002 he was slowed down somewhat when he entered the hospital for knee surgery. Dee Dee Bridgewater recalled:

> I knew he had this knee surgery. I was not particularly in favor of him doing this because my stepfather had a severe knee problem and had been told to try and hold out as long as he could before doing anything. And I know that he started back to work too soon after the surgery. I don't know. You know he loved being on the road. If he were home for a month, Cecilia would say, "He'd start acting crazy." He lived for the music ... He had surgery in January, and he was supposed to stay home for a minimum of two months, and then in February, he was back out there on the road.[178]

In March 2002, Brown recorded his final album: *Ray Brown, Monty Alexander, Russell Malone* (Telarc Jazz CD-83562). There is no indication on this record of any deteriotarion in his bass-playing ability. That October, he celebrated his career and his many musical associations by launching a tour for his seventy-fifth birthday. This featured his trio with invited musicians to join him in the performances.

On July 2, 2002 Ray Brown was scheduled to perform at the Jazz Kitchen in Indianapolis, as he had done the previous night. That morning, he played golf and settled down for a nap before his gig. He never awoke. Everybody was in a state of great shock on hearing the news: nobody had been aware of any serious physical problems – not even his wife Cecilia:

> It was not like that for him to go that way. I wasn't with him at the time. I couldn't see anything that would bring him to that point. If he had

anything troubling him or anything, he never spoke about it. I'm a little bit unaware of how it all came about. I think it probably ended up with a heart attack, really, because otherwise, there was nothing physical that I was aware of. He had knee surgery, but that wasn't the cause. He seemed to have been recuperating from that.[179]

Benny Green also ruminated on Ray's death:

> I didn't see any indication of illness. Russell Malone and I played a private party in Minnesota with Ray maybe three weeks before Ray passed. In hindsight, I realized after Ray left us, he must have known because, after this engagement, Ray sat with me. Everyone had left the venue. He sat with me for a couple of hours, and we talked about music. I know Ray hadn't had much sleep. He had a long travel day to get to the performance and he had told me as much. We hadn't seen each other in a while. He was really concerned, and I think he knew and maybe wasn't talking to anyone about it. I think he must have had some sort of sense that he was getting ready to leave.
>
> He talked to me about music and the piano and great pianists, and there was just a feeling; there was a way that he was looking me in the eye that, in hindsight, I realized that he must have known that it might have been our final conversation. I am so thankful [for that night]. We said "Goodnight" after a long talk, I gave Ray a hug and a kiss on the cheek, and I thanked him for charging my battery. That's how we parted ways.
>
> No one saw it coming, and that was just the saddest day. It didn't seem real to us because Ray was so strong and vital and at the very top of his game. I realize that when I was trying to make peace with Ray's passing on that, it was sort of a beautiful and peaceful rite of passage that we never saw Ray frail. You never heard him in any other way than sheer mastery. He lived right up until the end, as he wanted. He played a performance, had a good night's sleep, played a round of golf, went back to his hotel room and got into his bed, and went out gracefully like that. So, there was a kind of perfection in it other than none of us were ready to leave him.
>
> It seemed like a final stage in his gift to the world for him to pass on [that way] . . . We were fortunate to have him with us . . . to realize what a powerful and beautiful thing we have all been blessed with just to have felt him, his music, and his laughter. For the younger musicians like myself who were privileged enough to be around Ray, we had to realize that we must try to move on now. [We have to] keep whatever it is that he's instilled in us and whatever it is that we witnessed him representing in his life . . . [we have] to try to keep that alive.[180]

In a career that spanned six decades, Ray Brown accomplished nearly everything possible in music. It is estimated that he has appeared on well over two thousand recordings, making him one of the most recorded musicians ever. His music and personality touched thousands. Many paid tribute to Ray Brown after his death in the form of concerts and awards.

Raymond Mathews Brown
October 13, 1926 — July 2, 2002

Loving father. Devoted and cherished mentor. He lives on through his music and through the memory of all those whose lives he has touched with generosity.

Ray Brown Papers, Archives Center, National Museum of American History, Smithsonian Institution

Throughout his storied career, Ray Brown has frequently topped nearly every popular jazz poll and received numerous accolades and rewards, including a Grammy award for his composition "Gravy Waltz." In the December 2003 issue of *DownBeat*, Ray Brown became the 100th member of the Jazz Hall of Fame, becoming only the third bassist to receive the award. Whether it be on an Oscar Peterson trio album, a Frank Sinatra special, a late-night television show, or a film score, it is nearly impossible to have never heard the dark rich tones of Ray Brown's bass. In such a rapidly changing world, that is simply astonishing.

When I began this project and asked people to comment about Ray Brown, most everybody gave me their full cooperation. In most of my interviews, I asked a few stock questions. I would ask "How did you meet Ray?" "What was your relationship with him?" "How do you feel Ray should be remembered?" In most cases, all my questions were answered and people spoke freely about Ray and told wonderful stories. Without their help, this biography would not have been possible. I cannot thank them enough for their efforts.

To conclude, there follows a section of interview excerpts painting a picture of how Ray Brown is remembered and cherished.

Monty Alexander

Pianist who worked with Brown in Triple Treat and various other groups.

Well, he was just wonderful to be around because he was just big fun. He would just be so full of humor and never took himself seriously in front of people. You know, he would talk about life and sports. He was just lovely to be around, but you knew that this guy who was light-hearted was this king when he picked up that instrument. To me, there was no one that was even a close second to him. The way he played his music, I was just taken with the spirit of the man. He was constantly being good at himself . . . This robust live-life-to-the-fullest [attitude]. If he played golf, he would go out there and try to kick your ass. It was like almost a family relationship in that I felt a great closeness with him, but at times, he would get serious about certain things – he could go off in a different direction. He was very much like a relative. Like an uncle. In fact, he looked a lot like my mother's brother, so I had this feeling in me like there was this kinship. This is one of the most unforgettable people in our lives. The people that passed by him are going to know that they had a moment . . . I don't look at him in terms of musical prowess only, it's the spirit of the guy, and my life was definitely greater for having met him and being invited into, I call it, the "royal chamber" because he ran with the giants. It was a real joy to know him.

Dee Dee Bridgewater

Vocalist who worked with Brown on several recordings and tours.

He was a mentor in that he provided me with a lot of counsel on how to handle my business and my financial affairs and booking dates. He wanted me to return to the singer he knew when I started in the business, which was being able to sing anything at a moment's notice, in any key, without arrangements, or to fit into an arrangement that's been done. In that way . . . He was just a hoot. I miss him dearly.

Cecilia Brown

Ray Brown's wife.

I'm not too good at this time in putting my feelings into words, but I know that people that he touched also touched him. They have stories and everything you know that they were able to share with him – memories that they will always keep. We haven't lost him because we have his music . . . which is a lot! Then we have the memories, and we've had very nice times. The people that I've talked to now they have certain memories and then things that we have all done together. We always talk about and laugh about it because we have had some good times. Those types of things we will always cherish, and it is so wonderful to talk to people because they will come up with, "Yes, there was one time that Ray told me this . . .". Or "I've asked him about such and such a thing, and he gave me good advice."

Whit Browne

Noted bassist and bass professor at Berklee College of Music.

I met him in 1978 for the first time, and I was like the kid in the candy store. Matter of fact, he was playing with L.A. Four, and they were playing up at this club in Beverly, Massachusetts, called Sandy's. I had a gig in the afternoon or early evening that got out kind of early, so I went up to the club afterward . . . Then the big thrill, which was a thrill for me and a big thrill for my wife [was] when I went up to introduce myself to Ray. As soon as I mentioned my name, he said, "Oh, yeah, I've heard about you" and he started mentioning some people that had told him about me and everything. That was like, wow, what a thrill that was, you know. I'm thinking that's nice that he said that. That made me feel so good. You know he didn't have to say anything. He could have just said, "Oh yeah, fine, cool." I love him. I don't know what else I could say other than that . . . I can't say enough wonderful things about the guy because he's been such a major influence on me.

Ron Carter

Legendary bassist.

Ray Brown was a wonderful player. A person I never got to know very well because he was working with Oscar Peterson all of the time. As I got busy, my schedule always conflicted with seeing the group play and establishing a relationship with him. Clearly, he was a very important voice in the history of jazz bass and a person we should all tip our hats to as a person who showed us what the bass could do. He was an inventive player with a great sound. I would imagine a great bandleader. He was a link to Bird and Diz for bass players – a really nice man.

Stanley Clarke
Legendary bassist.

Spiritually, Ray Brown was very influential to me because he was extremely up-toned. He was very positive and one of the first guys I felt had the most amazing sound that came out of his bass. I used to love to go and see him play, and I loved to hang out with him. He was always talking about sound. He wasn't talking about technical things like what you play on a Cm chord or how to play in the key of G♭; all that stuff is secondary. It's actually really the third most important element. First, you have what comes from your heart, then you have your sound, and then you have a technique which is the tools that carry you to what you wish to play. You do have to have some kind of technique, but whether it's a lot or a little if you have a great sound, that's what matters. Ray was very inspiring to me in that way.

John Clayton
Bassist, composer, and former student of Brown's. Member of SuperBass.

Ray was strong. He voiced his feelings about things freely. He loved laughing. And he had a special, falsetto laugh that no one can imitate! I recently realized that I cannot remember a single conversation with him that didn't include a laugh. That's pretty remarkable. He wanted to have fun. Jokes abounded. He loved nice clothes . . . He was always concerned about helping young artists, especially Black artists. But he truly didn't care about your skin color, especially if you were seriously interested in jazz. He always spoke of a jazz "family" of musicians and listeners. Still, he had concerns about there not being enough young African American artists to play this music. He loved good food, good music of any sort, gambling, bass organizations, and supporting youth – oh – and golfing. There were times that he could golf and not even miss the bass – or so it seemed. He was gentle. He was loving. Ray will be remembered as a pivotal bassist in jazz history. His musical concept, his sound concept, and his approach to the instrument were all beacons that bass players use to guide them.

John Goldsby
Bassist and writer.

Throughout the '90s, Ray was often a guest with us in the WDR Big Band [Westdeutscher Rundfunk, Cologne Germany Radio Big Band]. I got to work beside Ray on several occasions and watch and listen to him up close . . . Ray has influenced me over the years – I guess all bass players from the 1950s on! . . . I think the things that made Ray great were his natural talents for the bass, but also his personal drive to be the best and his years on the road playing night after night with the best in the business. He remains an inspiration not only for his bass playing but as a musician who was always striving to present the music in a good light . . . to cultivate the audience and the younger musicians, and to show them that the music he played was music that they could groove to and love. He was like a salesman who sold you something you really wanted even if you didn't know that what you really wanted [and] was the world's most swinging bass player.

Benny Green

Pianist with the Ray Brown Trio.

I think Ray should be remembered as a proud and graceful warrior who played the music with love, pride, and dignity. [As somebody] who fought throughout his life for the respect of his music all over the world. He seemed to devote every breath of life to play with vitality, enthusiasm, respect for the audience, and beauty. He never compromised these values and his integrity. I see that as Ray's homage to what had come before and what was given to him.

Burkhard Hopper

Brown's European manager, 1988–2002.

This friendship started off as a business relationship but became closer over the years. Especially in the early years of our relationship. I used to travel a lot with the musicians, and while I was driving, Ray used to take the front-row seat and talk with me about music, politics, sports, and private stuff. Those rides lasted six to seven hours, which is a lot of time to get to know each other. Due to my young age, he became a mentor and got other artists interested in my company . . . Ray loved the road. He had friends in every city we went to. They would all come down to the show and afterward go to dinner or just come backstage to say hello. I remember those nights when we were leaving the place at 2 am, and he was rolling his bass in his flight case down the street while I was already on all fours crawling behind him. He was so full of energy . . . [He should be remembered] as one of the best musicians on his instrument that the world has ever seen – an innovator for music and a person that would fill your heart with a smile.

Hank Jones

Legendary pianist who worked with Ray early on with JATP and Ella Fitzgerald.

Music was a full-time thing with him. It was a complete 24/7 occupation with Ray. I think that automatically made him involved. Involved him in all of those activities that concerned music. He had a lot of things going for him, and it was always a pleasure to work with him. He always had a definite idea, and he was always right. For instance, on a recording date ... on a date that was disorganized, that wasn't particularly well prepared. You know, on somebody else's date, he would bring instant order to the date because of his organizational ability. That is what I remember about him besides his musicianship and his friendship. Ray and I were lifelong friends ever since about 1944. Ray was a great loss.

Geoffrey Keezer
Pianist with the Ray Brown Trio.

In a few words, I would say he was funny and quite positive and never bitter. Never like some of those older musicians, who sometimes carry a lot of baggage and bitterness. He was always quite fun to be around and had a seemingly unlimited energy reserve. He would get up at six in the morning, play golf, and then come back and spend hours on the phone making phone calls because he managed himself. He didn't farm out his business. Then he would nap, get up, play the show, and do this day after day. And the young guys were just sort of dragging our tails [*laughs*] trying to keep up with him. I think that was a quality that maybe existed in that older generation. I really feel fortunate that I had a chance to tell him the last time that I saw him in LA how much I really appreciated playing with his band and how I felt that it was really the best thing that ever happened to my piano playing, as far as acoustic jazz playing. It was really an incredible experience all around, and he was a very good bandleader all around. He was quite generous and treated us very much like equals and was like a friend.

Christian McBride
Bassist, bandleader, and member of SuperBass.

Ray was fun yet forceful, simplistic, but very informative. He was very much a "life's not that deep" kind of person. It seemed as if Ray believed if you know what you're supposed to do in life, then do it! It's not that hard. He was very intelligent. [Ray should be remembered] as a man who always brought a smile to people's faces – not only through music but through the joy of everyday life. He loved to laugh, tell stories, and keep us young players grounded through humorous but deep education. He was able to get a point well across without taking the condescending approach as most musicians his age do.

Mary Ann McSweeney
Bassist, bandleader, and teacher. Former student of Ray Brown.

I was a student at California State University, Northridge, and my teacher Dr. David Young brought him to the school to do a masterclass, and they asked me to play. Ray Brown was one of the first bass players I saw live as a kid. So, I was really excited. So I went to the class, and I played for him . . . [Ray] had been talking to my classical teacher about getting bowing lessons. They had been switching off a bit, so my classical teacher said, "Would you like to take lessons with Ray?" I said, "Absolutely, but I don't think I can afford it." He said, "Well, just give him a call and talk to him about it." So, I called Ray, "He said, yeah, come up for lessons." So I went to Sherman Oaks, where he was living, and I went to his house, and he had me play for him, and then he played. I asked him a bunch of questions like, "How do you play all of these tunes in any key at any time?" At the time, he was around sixty-two years old. He said, "Well, I'm sixty-two, and it has taken me a long time to do this." He said, "If you don't practice and you come back here in a couple of weeks, I will charge you sixty bucks for your next lesson. If you practice, it's thirty." So I had to pay thirty. It was almost a two-hour lesson. I had no money at the time. I could barely afford the thirty dollars, and I was probably borrowing money at the time, and I practiced. It lit a fire under me to practice and prepare for him. Probably over a year's time, I went to him maybe eight to ten times tops because he was really busy.

He was just really, really kind to me. He was the reason why I started the bass. I don't know if I was ever able to tell him that, but over the years, I would go to his concerts, or I would see him here or there playing. I would always go backstage, and he would hug me and ask how I was doing . . . He was always really encouraging to me. He never treated me any differently because I'm a female or anything like that. He was always like, "Hey, how are you doing?" He'd give me a hug. "What's up?" "What are you doing these days?" He was very, very cool. I miss him today.

James Moody

Legendary saxophonist. Worked with Brown in Dizzy Gillespie's Orchestra.

I met him when I joined Dizzy's band. In 1946 at the Spotlite Club in New York on 52nd Street . . . Well, he was always kind of businesslike. I remember one thing that stood out: he always kept a hundred-dollar bill in his wallet in 1946. That's pretty good, isn't it? Not bad in 1946. I remember that about Ray. Oh, I know how he is going to be remembered. As a great bass player, a great innovator, and as a truthful nice guy. And, like, just straightforward. Business, business, business all the time . . . I wish him all the best all the time, wherever he is. Ray was okay.

Oscar Peterson

Legendary pianist and bandleader. Brown's closest musical companion.

I think he was fun-loving, very happy-go-lucky. Just a wonderful person to be around. He was always very effervescent . . . We were like brothers. Well, he should be remembered . . . The way I remember Ray is as a very happy young man. He will always be young in my memory because that is how I remember him. He's a year younger than I am. When I think of Ray, I still think of him as being twenty-five and thirty. I can't see him any other way because his music is still young and will always be young. And as I say, that particular album by Milt [Jackson] called *Ain't But a Few of Us Left*. I have it on my car player, and whenever I come home from somewhere, they go in the house, and I sit, and I always play that first track. It draws me very close to Ray because I think this is Ray at his best. I think it's the best thing he ever recorded. If someone were to say, "Paint me a portrait of Ray Brown," I would put that particular tune on.

Rufus Reid

Legendary bassist and educator.

He was kind of like a Pied Piper: he had a very infectious personality. He was very bubbly and a personable person . . . He should be remembered as like Louis Armstrong and John Coltrane or people who, when you say their names, you have their image and a place on your mantel – where you put your heroes. Ray Brown played so many styles and so many important gigs. Up until he died, he was probably the last one who played with so many [innovative musicians]; I mean probably more than anybody, which was so amazing. So, I mean, he needs to be remembered for being able to have that ability.

He set the bar for us to strive for clarity, excellence, and consistency. Without doubt, he will always be a part of the fabric of bass players. I believe that all young musicians should study his work. Ray, with his entire persona, took the bass to another level. His influence was as powerful, and his legacy as monumental, as Coltrane's, Louis Armstrong's, or Art Tatum's. He undoubtedly belongs among those greats, and if you put his name next to theirs, I don't think anyone would dispute it.

Bud Shank

Saxophonist, flutist, and co-founder of the L.A. Four.

He's probably one of the most intelligent guys I've ever known. Not from book learning but just from natural [ability]. It came there naturally, somehow from experience, from desire. I had never met anybody who could work with numbers how he could. He was a walking adding machine. Now he did not have a college degree. He could handle numbers like nobody I have ever seen, and I come from a family of mathematicians who all ended up being attorneys. So I've been around people like that but nobody like him. It was positively amazing . . . He was a very open and loving person. As you know, the black-and-white thing has had its problems. Up and down and whatever, but he had the idea, especially during L.A. Four. We were like brothers because he chose to have it that way, and I chose to have it that way. We got along beautifully, and again he was a very intelligent person, and he didn't let it show until it came down to a business proposition, and then he let it show big time . . . [He will be remembered] as a great man, a great person.

Ed Thigpen

Drummer and bandleader. Member of the Oscar Peterson Trio, 1958–1965.

He was like a big brother to me. He was always very open. He played bass like no one [else]. His solos were incredible. I just lived to play with him. His time was impeccable. Everything he did was impeccable. He dressed impeccably. He had perfect manners. He was a gentleman. Ray was a good person. You know he could be an orchestra unto himself. So his contributions, he led the pack. He had people he came up behind, like Blanton, Oscar Pettiford, and "The Judge" Milt Hinton. But he never failed to acknowledge all of the great ones before him or his other contemporaries.

He always studied. Always practiced every day. So, he was a student as well as a teacher. He was a great role model in that sense . . . He took care of a lot of people. As I said before, he was a kind person. He was a good person. He was a man's man. He was number one. We always stayed in contact. I'd call him up when he'd come on the road over here [Copenhagen]. You know I've been over here for thirty years, but we'd still stay in contact whenever possible. [He should be remembered] as a beautiful human being, a beautiful spirit. Kindness and greatness.

Phil Woods

Legendary alto saxophonist, clarinetist, and leader who worked and recorded with Ray on several occasions.

Well, let me put it this way. In 1987 I had a terrible fire. I lost everything, and my wife was in the hospital. I lost all my clothes. It was December of '87, and I had a New Year's Eve gig, and it was with Ray Brown, Joe Williams, Milt Jackson, and a whole bunch of cats at a place in Baltimore. It called for a tuxedo, and I said, "Oh shit, I can't be buying a tuxedo." To make a long story short, I was getting all kinds of calls, and people were commiserating [saying], "Sorry about your loss." And all that stuff. About ten days after I had this fire, I got this huge . . . I mean a huge package as big as half a refrigerator box from Ray Brown. It had a tuxedo in it. It had a tux shirt. It had the hippest shirts in the world. They all had golf clubs on them. Man, he was there. He was the shit. I mean, it was all good stuff. It wasn't cast-off clothing. I mean, he had a heart as big as his tone. I never forgot that. As I said, he lived in California, and we didn't exactly do cocktails and dinner that often because of distance, but man, if he heard one of the guys was in trouble, he was there man. That's the kind of guy Ray Brown was. He was a sweetheart. He was always in my corner, and I did a lot of gigs with him. I did his seventy-fifth-birthday tours in Europe with him. Keeping up with him wasn't easy. He'd get up at five in the morning and just boogie. You know, we'd be all hanging from traveling the day before, and he had more energy than any ten people. He was a dear sweet friend, and I miss him terribly. He's the premier bassist of his generation.

Select Bibliography

Barris, Alex, and Albert Annabeth. 2002. *Oscar Peterson: A Musical Biography.* New York: Harper Collins.
Berendt, Joachim-Ernst. 2009. *The Jazz Book: From Ragtime to the 21st Century.* Chicago: Lawrence Hill Books.
Berliner, Paul. 1994. *Thinking in Jazz: The Infinite Art of Improvisation.* Chicago: Chicago University Press.
Brown, Ray. 1999. *Bass Method: Essential Scales, Patterns, and Exercises.* Milwaukee: Hal Leonard.
Cook, Richard. 2004. *Blue Note Records: The Biography.* Boston: Justin Charles & Company.
Cook, Richard, and Brian Morton. 2008. *The Penguin Guide to Jazz.* London: Penguin Books.
DeVeux, Scott, and Gary Giddins. 2015. *Jazz.* New York: W.W. Norton.
———. 1999. *The Birth of Bebop: A Social and Musical History.* Berkeley: University of California Press.
Ellington, Edward Kennedy. 2002. *Duke Ellington: Music is My Mistress.* New York: HarperCollins.
Giddins, Gary. 2000. *Visions of Jazz: The First Century.* Oxford, Oxford University Press.
Gillespie, Dizzy. 2009. *To Be or Not to Bop.* Michigan: University of Michigan Press.
Gio, Ted. 2021. *A History of Jazz.* Oxford, Oxford University Press.
Gitler, Ira. 1987. *Swing to BeBop: An Oral History of the Transitions in Jazz in the 1940s.* New York: Oxford University Press.
Goldsby, John. 2002. *The Jazz Bass Book: Technique and Tradition.* London, Backbeat.
Gottlieb, Robert. 1999. *A Gathering of Autobiography, Reportage, and Criticism From 1919 to Now.* New York: Vintage.
Groves, Alan, and Alyn Shipton. 2001. *The Glass Enclosure: The Life of Bud Powell.* London: Bloomsbury Academic.
Hasse, John Edward. 1995. *The Life and Genius of Duke Ellington.* Boston: Da Capo Press.
Havers, Richard. 2013. *Verve: The Sound of America.* New York: Thames & Hudson.
Hershorn, Tadd. 2011. *Norman Granz: The Man Who Used Jazz for Justice.* Berkeley: University of California Press.
Holiday, Billie, and William Dufty. 2006. *Lady Sings the Blues.* New York: Crown.
Jones, Quincy. 2001. *Q: The Autobiography of Quincy Jones.* New York: Doubleday.
Lees, Gene. 1988. *Oscar Peterson: The Will to Swing.* Toronto: Key Porter Books.
Meeker, Davis. 1982. *Jazz in the Movies: A Guide to Jazz Musicians.* Boston: Da Capo Press.
Nicholson, Stuart. 2014. *Ella Fitzgerald: A Biography of the First Lady of Jazz.* London: Routledge.
Owens, Thomas. 1996. *BeBop: The Music and Its Players.* New York: Oxford University Press.
Peterson, Oscar. 2002. *A Jazz Odyssey: The Life Of Oscar Peterson.* London: Continuum.
Porter, Lewis. 2005. *Lester Young: Jazz Perspectives.* Michigan: University of Michigan Press.
———. 1997. *Jazz: A Century of Change.* New York: Schirmer.
Porter, Lewis, and Michael Ullman. 1999. *Jazz: From Its Origins to the Present.* London: Pearson.

Priestley, Brian. 2007. *Chasin' the Bird: The Life and Legacy of Charlie Parker*. New York: Oxford University Press.
Rybicki, Mathew. 2015. *Ray Brown: Legendary Bassist*. Milwaukee: Hal Leonard.
Sculler, Gunther. 1986. *Early Jazz: Its Roots and Musical Development*. New York: Oxford University Press.
———. 1989. *The Swing Era*. New York: Oxford University, Press.
Shapiro, Nat, and Nat Hentoff. 1996. *Hear Me Talkin' to Ya: The Story of Jazz as Told by the Men Who Made It*. Mineola, NY: Dover Books.
Shipton, Alyn. 1999. *Groovin' High: The Life of Dizzy Gillespie*. New York: Oxford University Press.
———. 2007. *A New History in Jazz*. London: Continuum.
———. 2022. *On Jazz: A Personal Journey*. Cambridge, UK: Cambridge University Press.
Sweet, Jay. 2021. *A History of American Music 1750–1950: An Origin Story*. Dubuque, IA: Kendall Hunt.
Sywed, John. 2016. *Billie Holiday: The Musician and the Myth*. London: Penguin.
Taylor, Arthur. 1993. *Notes and Tones: Musician-to-Musician Interviews*. Boston, MA: Da Capo Press.
Teachout, Terry. 2014. *Duke: The Life of Duke Ellington*. New York: Avery.
Vail, Ken. 2000. *Bird's Diary: The Life of Charlie Parker 1945–1955*. Cambridge, UK: Vail Publishing.
———. 2000. *Dizzy Gillespie: The BeBop Years*. Cambridge, UK: Vail Publishing.
Ward, Geoffrey, and Ken Burns. 2000. *Jazz: A History of America's Music*. New York: Knopf Publishing.

Notes

Chapter 1
1. Cecilia Brown, interview with the author, May 9, 2003.
2. Ervin Dyer, "Revisiting the Great Migration." *The Post-Gazette*, February 25, 2001.
3. Alwyn and Laurie Lewis, "Ray Brown Interview." *Cadence*, September 1993, 13–20.
4. Ted Panken, WKCR radio interview with Ray Brown, 1996.
5. *Cadence*.
6. Jesse Hamlin, "Ray Brown Passing It Down." *The San Francisco Chronicle*, August 6, 1995, 30.
7. *Cadence*.
8. Monk Rowe, interview with Ray Brown, April 16, 2000. https://jazzarchive.hamilton.edu and https://youtu.be/wOJ8zPi4tBc?si=PGxit8dNl04Gydi3
9. *Cadence*.
10. "About Schenley: Schenley High School." http://schenleyhs.pghboe.net/about.htm
11. Antonio Garcia, "Ray Brown: Making Every Chorus Count." *Jazz Educators Journal*, March 2001, 33–36.
12. *Cadence*.
13. *Jazz Educators Journal*.
14. Ray Comiskey, "Bass Instincts." *The Irish Times*, July 2, 1999, 14.
15. Walt Harper, interview with the author, 2000.
16. Cecile Brooks, interview with the author, 2000.
17. Ted Panken, WKCR radio interview with Ray Brown, 1996. https://tedpanken.wordpress.com/2011/10/13/a-1996-wkcr-interview-with-ray-brown-born-85-years-ago-today-and-some-interviews-about-him-for-a-downbeat-obituary-in-2002
18. *Cadence*.

Chapter 2
19. *Cadence*.
20. Hank Jones, interview with the author, April 3, 2003.
21. Jack Tracey, "Rhythm and Rosin." *DownBeat*, January 29, 1976, 12–13.
22. *Cadence*.
23. Tracey, "Rhythm and Rosin."
24. Panken, WKCR radio interview.
25. Ray Brown's interview within the Dizzy Gillespie documentary, *To Bop Or Not To Be*, which aired on the Arts & Entertainment (A&E) Network.

Chapter 3
26. *Cadence*.
27. Monk Rowe interview.
28. Ray Brown's timeline of these gigs may be incorrect.

29 Alyn Shipton, *On Jazz: A Personal Journey*. Cambridge, UK: Cambridge University Press, 2022, 153.
30 John Chilton, *The Song of the Hawk: The Life and Recordings of Coleman Hawkins*. Ann Arbor, University of Michigan Press, 1990, 222–23.
31 *Soundstage: Dizzy Gillespie's Bebop Reunion* (dir. Bill Heitz; PBS TV show, 1976).

Chapter 4
32 Dizzy Gillespie and Al Foster, *To Be or Not To Bop*. New York: Doubleday Books, 1979.
33 Alyn Shipton, *Groovin' High: The Life of Dizzy Gillespie*. New York: Oxford University Press, 1999, 179.
34 "Stitt Article," SonnyStitt.com. https://www.sonnystitt.com/biography/stitt-article
35 Brown told Alyn Shipton in his book *Groovin' High* that he approached Gillespie after a month. In the Gillespie A&E documentary, Brown says he asked Dizzy the question after six months.
36 Dizzy Gillespie A&E documentary.
37 Shipton, *Groovin' High*, 185.
38 "Moody Speaks" b/w "Smokey Hollow Jump" by the Be Bop Boys (Savoy Records 902); "Boppin the Blues" by the Be Bop Boys (b/w "Serenade to a Square" by Sonny Stitt and His Be Bop Boys) (Savoy Records 940); and "For Hecklers Only" by Ray Brown's All Stars (B side of "Ice Freezes Red" by Fat's Navarro Quintette) (Savoy Records 976).
39 *Soundstage: Dizzy Gillespie's Bebop Reunion.*

Chapter 5
40 Brown's increased use of chromaticism was undoubtedly influenced by the bebop music he was playing.
41 Shipton, *Groovin' High*, 201.
42 *Groovin' High*, 193.
43 Dizzy Gillespie A&E documentary.

Chapter 6
44 Don Heckman, "The Complete Singer Remembered." *Los Angeles Times*, June 26, 1997.
45 This assessment may be a bit of an oversimplification. Fitzgerald likely had more awareness of bebop by 1945 than Brown suggests, but simply chose not to incorporate bop into her repertoire.
46 Heckman, *Los Angeles Times.*
47 Stewart Nicholson, *Ella Fitzgerald: A Biography of the First Lady.* Boston, MA: Da Capo Press, 1995.
48 "Joe's Roadhouse." KPFT Pacifica broadcast, December 8, 2007.
49 Email correspondence with Ray Brown Jr., August 26, 2022.
50 *Cadence*, 16.
51 Tadd Hershorn, *Norman Granz: The Man Who Used Jazz for Justice.* Berkeley: University of California Press, 2011.
52 Shipton, *Groovin' High*, 262.
53 Hank Jones, interview with the author, April 2, 2003.
54 Antonio Garcia, "Ray Brown: Making Every Chorus Count." *Jazz Educators Journal*, March 2001.

55 Phil Shaap, interview with Ray Brown for WCKR, September 20, 1989.
56 Garcia, *Jazz Educators Journal*, 36.

Chapter 8
57 Oscar Peterson, interview with the author, January 30, 2002.
58 Gene Lees, *Oscar Peterson: The Will to Swing*. New York: Cooper Square Press, 1988, 69.
59 Oscar Peterson, interview with the author, January 30, 2002.
60 Stuart Nicholson, *Ella Fitzgerald: A Biography of the First Lady of Jazz*. New York: Da Capo Press/C. Scribner's Sons, 1994.
61 Lees, *Oscar Peterson: The Will to Swing*, 69.

Chapter 9
62 Oscar Peterson and Richard Palmer, *Jazz Odyssey: My Life in Jazz*. Ann Arbor: University of Michigan Press, 2002, 18.
63 Peterson and Palmer, *Jazz Odyssey*, 107–108.
64 These and other early Peterson recordings can best be heard on *The Complete Clef/Mercury Studio Recordings of the Oscar Peterson Trio (1951–1953)* (Mosaic Records MD7-241).
65 Oscar Peterson, interview with the author, January 30, 2002.
66 Peterson and Palmer, *Jazz Odyssey*, 86.
67 *The Complete Clef/Mercury Studio Recordings*.
68 J.C. Heard replaced Alvin Stoller.
69 Hershorn, *Norman Granz*, 274–80.
70 *The Complete Clef/Mercury Studio Recordings*.
71 Due to the amount of material, two volumes were released: *Norman Granz Jam Session #1* (Mercury MGC-601) and *Norman Granz Jam Session #2* (Mercury MGC-602)
72 The original releases were titled *Lester Young with the Oscar Peterson Trio #1* (Norgran MGN-5), *Lester Young with the Oscar Peterson Trio #2* (Norgran MHN-6), and *The President* (Norgan MGN-1005).
73 Tracks released on the compilation Benny Carter, *Cosmopolite* (Clef MG-C141). Recorded in Los Angeles.
74 *The Roy Eldridge Quintet* (Clef MGC-150). Recorded in New York.

Chapter 9
75 Peterson and Palmer, *Jazz Odyssey*, 80.
76 *Ella Fitzgerald: Something to Live For*, 1999, dir. Charlotte Zwerin.
77 Heckman, *Los Angeles Times*.
78 Oscar Peterson, interview with the author, January 30, 2002.
79 Heckman, *Los Angeles Times*.
80 This recording and other JATP performances were issued on *Norman Granz' Jazz at the Philharmonic Vol. 16* (Clef MG VOL. 16).
81 "Easy Going Bounce" and "Indiana" were initially released as two sides on Norgan Records 113. Along with "Johnny's Blues" they both later appeared on the Johnny Hodges and His Orchestra album *The Blues* (Norgran MGN-1061).
82 Shipton, *Groovin' High*, 26.

Chapter 10
83 Count Basie and His Orchestra, "Bluebeard Blues" b/w "Golden Bullet" (Columbia 38888).
84 Scott Yanow on Allmusic.com. https://www.allmusic.com/album/plays-count-basie-mw0000107116.
85 According to *Both Sides Now Publications* (https://www.bsnpubs.com/new/clef.pdf), this was unissued on Clef and transferred to Verve (MGV 8024), the first pressings of which had "Clef Series" on the label.
86 Matthew Rybicki, *Ray Brown: Legendary Jazz Bassists.* Milwaukee: Hal Leonard, 2015, 14, 46–53.
87 Oscar Peterson and Gerald Wiggins, *Sessions, Live* (Calliope CAL 3001).
88 Oscar Peterson and Leroy Vinnegar, *Sessions, Live* (Calliope CAL 3007).
89 Oscar Peterson, interview with the author, January 30, 2002.
90 Jack Tracy, "Ray Brown: Rhythm + Rosin = Royalty." *DownBeat*, January 29, 1976.

Chapter 11
91 Richard Havers, *Verve: The Sound of America*. London: Thames & Hudson, 2013, 122.
92 Shipton, *Groovin' High*, 260.
93 Hershorn, *Norman Granz*, 326.
94 Oscar Peterson, interview with the author, January 30, 2002.
95 Hershorn, *Norman Granz*, 388–91.
96 Hershorn, *Norman Granz*, 400–401. Further details of the incident are included in Shipton, *Groovin' High*, 265–66.
97 Scott Yanow on Allmusic.com. https://www.allmusic.com/album/the-modern-jazz-quartet-and-oscar-peterson-trio-at-the-opera-mw0000894106

Chapter 12
98 Cecilia Brown, interview with the author, May 9, 2003.
99 Released soon after as two single LPs: *Volume 1* (Verve MG V-4017) and *Volume 2* (Verve MG V-4018).
100 Havers, *Verve*, 50.
101 The 45 rpm "Somebody" b/w "Stay With It" came out at the time; those and fourteen others can be heard on the 1999 compilaiton *Smooth Operator* (Verve 314 547 514-2).

Chapter 13
102 Walking bass lines had been heard before Page but rarely with the same energy and precision.
103 The recording took place the same day as the session for the album *Krupa and Rich* (Clef MGC-684).
104 Neither track was included on the original album but appeared as bonus tracks on later reissues.
105 Many of the Benny Carter recordings were reissued in 1994 on Benny Carter, *Cosmopolite: The Oscar Peterson Verve Sessions* (Verve 521 673-2).
106 Benny Carter, Charlie Parker, Johnny Hodges, and Willie Smith, *Alto Sax* (1955; Norgran MGN-1035); it's also on the *Cosmopolite* compilation.
107 The recording was made the same day as a session that included Benny Carter, Dizzy Gillespie, and Bill Harris, plus the Peterson trio along with Buddy Rich.
108 Skip Martin may have arranged three tracks on the album.
109 FrenchFilms.org, "Les Tricheurs." http://www.frenchfilms.org/review/les-tricheurs-1958.html

Chapter 15
110 Reprinted on the Blue Sounds website. https://www.freshsoundrecords.com/barney-kessel-albums/5105-the-poll-winners-the-poll-winners-ride-again.html

Chapter 16
111 Peterson and Palmer, *Jazz Odyssey*, 80.
112 Ed Thigpen, interview with the author, February, 21, 2003.
113 They had actually been together nine years at that point.
114 Reviews excerpted in Martin Williams, *Where's the Melody? A Listener's Introduction To Jazz*. New York: Pantheon Books, 1969, 177.
115 See Richard Severo, "Oscar Peterson, 82, Jazz Piano's Virtuoso Dies," *New York Times*, December 25, 2007. https://www.nytimes.com/2007/12/25/arts/25peterson.html
116 Also quoted in Williams, *Where's the Melody?*
117 Ed Thigpen, interview with the author, February, 21, 2003.
118 Oscar Peterson, interview with the author January 30, 2002.
119 That year (1959) Sidney Poitier starred in the film version of *Porgy and Bess*, with a score created and conducted by musical director André Previn and with a soundtrack that was received both an Academy Award and an Oscar. The same year saw the release of the album Diahann Carroll and the André Previn Trio, *Porgy and Bess* (United Artists UAS 5021).
120 Oscar Peterson, interview with the author, January 30, 2002.
121 Ed Thigpen, interview with the author, February, 21, 2003.
122 Years later (1998) Jackson, Peterson, and Brown performed as the Very Tall Band.

Chapter 17
123 Ed Thigpen, interview with the author, February, 21, 2003.
124 Leonard Feather, "The New Life of Ray Brown." *DownBeat*, November 4, 1965.
125 Oscar Peterson, interview with the author, January 30, 2002.

Chapter 18
126 For more on Mance's connection to Gillespie, see Shipton, *Groovin' High*, p. 10.
127 Joshua Weiner, "Jimmy Giuffre 3: The Easy Way." All About Jazz, October 14, 2003. https://www.allaboutjazz.com/the-easy-way-jimmy-giuffre-verve-music-group-review-by-joshua-weiner
128 Katz can be seen and heard playing Bach's Cello Suite #1 in the film *Jazz on a Summer's Day*.
129 Liner notes to the *Jazz Cello* album.

Chapter 19
130 Feather, *DownBeat*.
131 David Meeker, *Jazz in the Movies: A Guide to Jazz Musicians*. New Rochelle, NY: Arlington House Publications, 1977.
132 Jesse Hassenger, "In 'The Party', Peter Sellers' Brownface Is the Elephant in the Room." Pop Matters, October 27, 2014. https://www.popmatters.com/187041-the-party-2495602023.html
133 "There Was a Time" appears only on the 2004 reissue (Verve B0002928-01).
134 Charles Lloyd, "Apex," from *Of Course, Of Course* (Columbia CL-2412), with Lloyd (composer, tenor saxophone), Ron Carter (bass), and Tony Williams (drums).

135 Bob James, "Explosions" from *Explosions* (ESP Disk 1009), with James (piano composer), Barre Phillips (bass), and Robert Pozar (percussion, prepared tapes).
136 Len Lyons, *The Great Jazz Pianists: Speaking of Their Lives and Music*. New York: W. Morrow, 1983.
137 In 1995, Impulse! released a CD version entitled *Unforgettable* (Impulse! IMP 11522), which also included Side B of *I Love Everybody* (1967), Hartman's other LP with ABC.
138 "Frelimo" seems to be listed as "Tanga" (or "Tenga") on early releases.

Chapter 22
139 By the mid-1950s several jazz musicians including Shank were working on films. For example, Johnny Mandel was using jazz musicians in film before Mancini. A good example is the film *I Want to Live* from 1958 which included Gerry Mulligan's Jazz Combo with Bud Shank playing alto sax and flute.
140 Bud Shank, interview with the author, May 12, 2003.
141 Ibid.
142 It is interesting to note that Miles Davis also recorded a version of the tune for his collaboration with Gil Evans on the album *Sketches of Spain* (1960; Columbia CL-1480), but that version was made with a much larger ensemble. Among several jazz interpretations of the piece, there are chamber jazz versions by the MJQ and by Jim Hall.
143 Although recorded before *Going Home*, it was released after.
144 Known in English as *Pavane for a Dead Princess*.
145 Ted Penkan interview with Jeff Hamilton for the 2002 *DownBeat* obituary.

Chapter 23
146 A "soft shoe" is a type of slow tap dance that was popularized on the vaudeville stage.
147 Shipton, *On Jazz*.
148 This includes Ray Brown's composition "Brown Soft Shoe," played as a light funk with a serious '70s vibe.
149 This includes Ray Brown's original "A Very Hip Rock Song," with an exceptional bass solo.
150 This includes Ray Brown's original "Cederay," based on the chord changes to "I Got Rhythm."
151 The soundtrack featured keyboardist/vocal star Billy Preston and Motown recording artist Syreeta Wright, who was once married to Stevie Wonder. Brown played on an instrumental version of "With You, I'm Born Again." The vocal version of the song was an international hit. The instrumental version shows Billy Preston's skills as a pianist and links Ray Brown to yet another major musical force.

Chapter 25
152 Mike Hennesey, "First Bass." *Jazz Journal International*, July 1982.
153 Guitarists John Collins, Vaughn Andre, and drummer Frank Severino all appear on one track.
154 According to the original liner notes.
155 Monty Alexander, interview with the author, March 24, 2003.
156 Although Humair was born in Switzerland, he spent much of his career in Paris.

Chapter 26
157 *The New Grove Dictionary of Jazz*. Oxford: Oxford University Press, 2nd edn, 2002.

158 *The Red Hot Ray Brown Trio* and *Bam Bam Bam* were later issued together as the double CD *Live from New York to Tokyo* (Concord Jazz CCD2-2174-2).
159 The album was later released as *I'm Walking* (GML GML-XRCD-30331).

Chapter 28

160 Later recorded in 1993 as "Afterthoughs (Part II)" on the album *American Jazz Philharmonic* (GRP GRD-9730).
161 Later reissued on streaming services as *Ray Brown with My Friends Herb Ellis and Serge Ermoll*.
162 The album includes a unique version of "Gravy Waltz" combined with the lyrics of an old standard called "Umbrella Man."

Chapter 29

163 Benny Green, interview with the author, December 23, 2003.
164 Ibid.
165 Willard Jenkins, "Ray Brown: Father Time." *JazzTimes*. https://jazztimes.com/archives/ray-brown-father-time
166 Which included this author in their number.
167 Benny Green, interview with the author, December 23, 2003.
168 Ray Brown's *Some of My Best Friends . . .* series is covered in the next chapter.
169 Geoff Keezer, interview with the author, April 10, 2003.

Chapter 30

170 Alyn Shipton, who wrote the album liner notes to the album, recalls that "Stanley had a terrible morning. As they arrived at the Power Station, his wife was mugged on the sidewalk outside, and her purse was stolen. We all had to rally round to give her support and calm things down. Meanwhile, Stanley had just signed a deal to promote Keilwerth Saxophones. So he had his new tenor with him. But as he launched into 'Port of Rico,' probably because of the unfortunate incident outside, he wasn't able to settle, and he couldn't get the sound he wanted. So he came out of the studio into the control room, called Manny's and asked them to send up a Selmer Mark VI. Everyone took a break, and then his long-time favourite saxophone was delivered. The incredible swing of 'Port of Rico' and that sumptuous version of 'God Bless the Child' are the result."
171 Dee Dee Bridgewater, interview with the author, 2003.

Chapter 31

172 First released under the title *Fascinating Voyage* (Arneaeus Music, Inc. AE 201).
173 The date of these recordings is somewhat unclear. Session logs list the recording date as September 4 through 9 of 1988; however, Freddie Green, who plays on the record, passed away on March 1, 1987, so any tracks with Green had to have been recorded before that date.
174 John Clayton, email correspondence, January 11, 2004. I have retained his original punctuation and capitalization.
175 Christian McBride, email correspondence, 2003.
176 It was during that same evening that the Ray Brown Trio recorded *Live at Scullers* (see Chapter 29).

Chapter 32
177 Ray Comiskey, "Bass Instinct." *The Irish Times*, July 2, 1999.
178 Dee Dee Bridgewater, interview with the author, 2003.
179 Cecilia Brown, interview with the author, May 9, 2003.
180 Benny Green, interview with the author, December 23, 2003.

Index

Numbers in *italics* refer to images.

A

Aarons, Al 177
Abney, Don 93, 95, 96, 173
Adderley, Julian "Cannonball" 132, 148, 158, 161, 162. *See also* Cannonball Adderley Quintet
Adderley, Nat 148, 161
Akiyoshi, Toshiko 78, 191
Alan Copeland Singers 170
Aldcroft, Randy 177
Alden, Howard 248
Alexander, Monty 126, 168, 179, 213, 214, 222–227, 230, 235, 261, 267, 270. *See also* Monty Alexander Trio; Triple Treat
Allen, Harry 259
Allen, Lee 186
Allen, Steve 150, 165
Allyson, Karrin 248
Almeida, Laurindo 134, 195–205, *200*. *See also* Laurindo Almeida Quartet with Bud Shank
Alvis, Hayes 6
American Jazz Philharmonic 263
Anderson, Ernestine 206, 224, 235
Andrews Sisters 150
Andy Kirk Orchestra 17
Antioch Baptist Choir 240
Archey, Jimmy 36
Argo, Judy 242
Arlen, Harold 82
Armstrong, Louis 3, 4, 41, 50, 61, 66, 95, 96, 102, 103, 111, 113
Arrigo, Jay 229
Art Blakey's Jazz Messengers 132, 237
Ashby, Irving 67, 81, 186, 187
Astaire, Fred 71, 104
Asylum Choir 193
Atkins, Chet 150
Atomics of Modern Music 35
Audino, John 177

Ayers, Roy 173

B

Babasin, Harry 160
Bailey, Donald 219, 238
Bailey, Pearl 122
Bain, Bob 166, 167
Balliett, Whitney 140
Ball, Ronnie 138
Barbour, Dave. *See* Dave Barbour Orchestra
Barefield, Eddie 229
Barker, Danny 36
Barlow, Varney 173
Barnes, George 215
Barnet, Charlie 11, 15
Barone, Gary 174
Barron, Kenny 236
Basie, Count 3, 4, 10, 38, 47, 54, 69, 70, 84, 109, 163, 186, 187, 208, *209*, 214, 261. *See also* Count Basie Orchestra; Count Basie Octet; Count Basie Trio
Bauer, Billy 36, 58, 65
Beaver, Paul 193
Bellson, Henry 121
Bellson, Louie 15, 81, 90, 91, 93, 99, 102, 103, 110, 112–114, 116, 117, 135, 180, 184, 186, 187, 190, 206, 218, 230, 248
Bennett, Max 100, 171
Benno, Marc 193
Benny Carter Orchestra 41
Benny Goodman Orchestra 9, 76, 115, 117, 120
Benny Goodman Quartet 115
Benny Goodman Trio 76
Berg, Billy 20, 21
Berghofer, Chuck 166, 191
Berg, Shelly 258
Berk, Dick 179
Berry, Bill. *See* Bill Berry and His Ellington All-Stars
Berry, Chu 111

Berry, Emmett 76
Best, Clinton "Skeeter" 96
Best, Denzil 19, 22
Betts, Harry 160
Betts, Keter 159, 160
Big Brother and the Holding Company 181
Bill Berry and His Ellington All-Stars 212
Bill Evans Trio 149, 178
Billy Eckstine Orchestra 11, 28, 38
Bishop, Joey 165
Bishop, Stephen 207
Blakey, Art 2, 8, 237, 247, 249. *See also* Art Blakey's Jazz Messengers
Blanchard, Terence 255
Blanton, Jimmy 6, 7, 8, 14, 15, 17, 38, 110, 113, 118, 129, 184, 185
Blesh, Rudi 36
Bloomfield, Mike 193
Blumberg, Dave 177
Bob Florence Big Band 170
Bob Wills and the Texas Playboys 212
Bond, Jimmy 166
Boone, Pat 165
Boussaguet, Pierre 261
Bradley, Ed 193
Bregman, Buddy. *See* Buddy Bregman Orchestra
Bridgewater, Dee Dee 254, 267, 271
Brisbois, Bud 174, 176
Brönner, Till 242
Brooks Sr., Cecile 9, 10, 11
Brown, Alice (granddaughter) 42
Brown, Bam 21, 101
Brown Buddies, the 11
Brown, Cecilia (wife) 1, 128, 267, 268, 271
Brown, Clifford 97, 123
Brown, Clifton (father) 1, 2, 3
Brown, Clifton Jr. (brother) 1
Browne, Whit 271
Brown, James 170
Brown, John 32
Brown Jr., Ray (son) 42, 43, 102
Brown, Lawrence 76, 159
Brown, Leroy 11
Brown, Margaret (mother) 1
Brown, Marguerite (sister) 1, 3
Brown, Ralph 12
Brown, Tiny "Bam" 89
Brubeck, Dave 79, 90, 132, 182, 237. *See also* Dave Brubeck Quartet
Brunner-Schwer, Hans Georg 152, 153, 154, 186
Bryant, Bobby 179, 180

Bryant, Clora 22
Bryant, Ray 257
Buddy Bregman Orchestra 119
Budimir, Dennis 174
Budwig, Monty 138
Bunker, Larry 166, 167, 174, 175, 189, 190, 257
Burns, Dave 31
Burns, Kenneth "Jethro" 212
Burns, Ralph 65, 117
Burrell, Kenny 93, 157, 163, 210, 242, 256
Butler, Frank 159, 189
Byas, Don 18, 21, 27, 28
Byers, Bill 174
Byrd, Charlie 182, 197

C

Cab Calloway Orchestra 15
Callender, Red 89, 166
Calloway, Cab 19, 32, 39, 237. *See also* Cab Calloway Orchestra
Campbell, Glen 167
Candoli, Conte 174, 189, 234, 248
Candoli, Pete 127, 167
Cannonball Adderley Quintet 180
Capp, Frank 174
Carman, Charles 17
Carroll, Diahann 284
Carter, Benny 19, 69, 70, 71, 77, 90, 111, 113, 136, 165, 173, 182, 190, 214, 235, 241, 253, 257. *See also* Benny Carter Orchestra
Carter, Betty 243, 244, 246, 247
Carter, Freddie 33
Carter, Lou 126
Carter, Ron 161, 192, 271
Castle, Lee 104
Caston & Majors 194
Castro-Neves, Oscar 248
Cave, Jack 160
Cecil, Malcolm 100
Chambers, Paul 144
Charles Owens. *See also* Charles Owens Sextet; New York Art Ensemble
Charles Owens Sextet 229
Charles, Ray 167
Chick Webb Orchestra 41
Chico Marx Orchestra 125
Childers, Buddy 177
Chindamo, Joe 242
Christian, Charlie 3
Christlieb, Pete 179, 234

INDEX **289**

Cincinnati Pops Big Band Orchestra 237
Clara Ward Singers 181
Clarke, Arthur 76
Clarke, Kenny 28, 30–32, 35, 65
Clarke, Stanley 272
Clark, Petula 170
Clark Terry Five 224
Claude Williamson Trio 229
Clayton Brothers 261
Clayton, Jeff 166, 234, 263
Clayton, John 238, 246, 257, 261–266, 272
Cleveland, Jimmy 161, 164, 176
Cobb, Jimmy 144
Cohn, Al 117, 161
Coker, Dolo 189
Coleman Jr., Bill 42
Coleman, Ornette 133, 180
Cole, Nat King 155. *See also* Nat King Cole Trio
Collette, Buddy 165, 173
Collins, Cal 215, 229
Collins, John 60, 217
Collins, Johnny 52
Collins, Joyce 159
Coltrane, John 52, 53, 132, 144, 220
Concord Jazz Festival All-Stars 248
Connor, Cecilia 101
Cooper, Bob 160, 174, 189
Copeland, Alan 170. *See also* Alan Copeland Singers
Corea, Chick 201
Cosby, Bill 168
Costello, Elvis 236, 242
Count Basie Octet 84
Count Basie Orchestra 70, 108, 109, 114, 133, 163, 180, 189
Count Basie Trio 186
Craig, Danny 100
Crane, Mickey 49
Cranshaw, Bob 192, 226
Crawford, Jimmy 70
Criss, Sonny 22, 49
Cunliffe, Bill 259

D

Dandridge, Dorothy 104, 105
Daniels, Billy 19
Daniels, Eddie 237
Darji 229
Daugherty, Jack 193
Dave Barbour Orchestra 66
Dave Brubeck Quartet 180
Davern, Ken 213
Davidson, Wild Bill 36
Davis, Eddie "Lockjaw" 17, 70, 120, 186, 190, 213, 215, 222
Davis, Jesse 253
Davis, Jim 149
Davis Jr., Sammy 163, 164
Davis, Miles 65, 132, 184, 210, 285. *See also* Miles Davis Quintet
Davis, Richard 192
Davis, Wild Bill 162, 163
Davis, William 16
Dawson, Alan 236
De Arango, Bill 27, 28
Dearie, Blossom 122, 136, 157
DeFranco, Buddy 90–94, 115, 116, 140
Dickenson, Vic 214
Dizzy Gillespie Orchestra/Big Band 21–24, 29, 31–34, 37, 40, 42, 51, 65, 149, 275
Dodds, Baby 36
Dodo Marmarosa Trio 23
Doerge, Craig 194
Doggett, Bill 66, 180
Don Ellis Orchestra 180
Dorham, Kenny 31
Dorsey, Jimmy 126
Douglass, Bill 42
Doug MacDonald Quartet 242
Drakes, Jesse 44
Drayton, Charlie 89
Drew, Martin 225
Dring, Madeleine 228
D'Rivera, Paquito 240, 258
Dr. John 257
Duggan, Barry 242
Duke Ellington Orchestra 15, 73, 110, 159, 180
Duke, George 183, 258
Dulong, Jack 127
Durham, Bobby 185, 187, 223, 239

E

Eager, Allen 44
Eckstine, Billy 2, 18, 30. *See also* Billy Eckstine Orchestra
Edison, Harry "Sweets" 58, 64, 96, 103, 109, 110, 112, 114, 127, 128, 170, 176, 177, 179, 180, 183, 186, 189, 190, 217, 222, 232, 238, 241. *See also* Harry Edison Sextet
Edwards, Teddy 22, 173, 176, 177, 179, 189, 213

Egilsson, Arni 260
Eldridge, Roy 2, 43, 50, 65, 70, 71, 73, 75, 77, 79, 90–93, 95–98, 100, 111, 113, 114, 117, 119, 123, 125, 138, 148, 150, 158, 162, 186, 201, 207, 208, 214. *See also* Roy Eldridge and His Orchestra
Ellington, Duke 4, 6, 7, 17, 47, 54, 76, 90, 110, 136, 184–186, 218. *See also* Duke Ellington Orchestra
Ellington, Steve 208
Elliot, Bruce 36
Elliott, Don 167
Ellis, Don 188. *See also* Don Ellis Orchestra
Ellis, Herb 73, 74, 76–82, 84, 85, 87, 88, 91, 93, 94, 96, 100, 101, 104, 113, 114, 116, 118, 119, 122, 123, 125–129, 135, 137, 138, 155, 162, 163, 170, 174, 179, 180, 182, 183, 184, 187, 209, 212, 215, 217, 225–227, 229, 233, 238, 239, 241, 242, 256, 258, 259. *See also* Triple Treat
Enriquez, Bobby 242
Ermoll, Serge 242
Ernst, Cheryl 194
Erskine, Peter 228
Eschete, Ron 231, 235
Esposito, Nick. *See* Nick Esposito Sextet
Evans, Bill 132, 149, 210, 211. *See also* Bill Evans Trio
Evans, Gil 285
Evert, Fred. *See* Fred Evert Big Band

F

Faddis, Jon 214, 236, 240, 255, 258
Fagerquist, Don 160
Farlow, Tal 121, 211, 213
Farmer, Art 208, 209
Faulise, Paul 161
Felder, Wilton 176, 177
Feldman, Victor 158, 170, 174, 177, 179, 180
Feliciano, José 169
Fettig, Mary 235
Fields, Dorothy 82
Fitzgerald, Ella 12, 34, 38–44, 46–50, *48*, 56–58, 60–62, 64–66, 72, 74, 75, 77, 78, 90–96, *98*, 98–103, 138, 146, 155, 162, 180, 190, 191, 206, 281
Fitzgerald, Frances 42
Flanagan, Tommy 161, 179, 180, 190
Fletcher Henderson Orchestra 111
Flip Phillips and His Orchestra 49
Flip Phillips and Howard McGhee Boptet 38
Florence, Bob 174. *See also* Bob Florence Big Band
Flores, Chuck 42, 196, 197
Flory, Meredith 160
Fludas, George 251
Fontana, Carl 179
Fonville, Benny 89
Foster, Henry 10
Foster, Pops 36
Franklin, Aretha 207
Fred Evert Big Band 11
Freeman, Russ 138
Friedman, Bob 194
Frigo, John 125, 126, 227. *See also* Triple Treat
Fuller, Larry 251
Fuller, Walter "Gil" 28, 30

G

Gadson, Thomas 186
Gaillard, Slim 21, 39, 101
Gale, Eric 168, 169
Gammage, Gene 135, 136
Gannons, Jimmy 138
Gant, Frank 235
Garcia, Russell 116, 143, 160. *See also* Russell Garcia Orchestra
Gärdestad, Ted 207
Garner, Erroll 89, 91, 132
Garrison, Arvin 24
Gaylor, Hal 56
Geller, Herb 127
Gene Harris All Star Big Band 233. *See also* Philip Morris Superband
Gene Harris Quartet 233
Gene Harris/Scott Hamilton Quintet 233
Gene Krupa and Buddy Rich Nonet 117
Gene Krupa Sextet 120, 121
George Shearing Trio 237
Gertrude Long and Her Nighthawks 3
Getz, Stan 78, 79, 90, 96, 98–100, 111, 112, 119, 125, 138, 146, 182, 197. *See also* Stan Getz Quartet
Gibbs, Terry 42, 112
Gibeling, Howard. *See* Howard Gibeling Orchestra
Gibson, Harry the Hipster 21, 39
Gibson, Josh 187
Gillespie, Dizzy 15, 19–21, 23–33, 35, 36, 39, 40, 42–44, 46, 47, 49, 52, 64, 75, 78,

INDEX **291**

79, 90–97, 100, 102, 113, 114, 117, 119, 157, 180, 187, 188, 208, 214, 223, 224, 281. *See also* Dizzy Gillespie Orchestra/Big Band
Giuffre, Jimmy 118, 127, 158. *See also* Jimmy Giuffre 3
Glaser, Don 229
Gold, Don 129
Goldsby, John 272
Gomez, Eddie 210
Goodman, Benny 3, 4, 64. *See also* Benny Goodman Orchestra; Benny Goodman Quartet; Benny Goodman Trio
Gordon, Dexter 89
Gordon, Joe 138
Gordon, Richie 138
Gormé, Eydie 207
Goto, Yoshiko 191
Gozzo, Conrad 127
Gramercy Five 121
Grantz, Irving 90
Granz, Norman 37, 38, 43, 44–47, 49–51, 54–58, 60, 61, 64, 66, 69, 71, 75, 78, 80, 81, 84, 86, 89–102, 104, 106, 107, 109, 112, 114, 115, 117, 118, 135, 138, 139, 144, 146, 149, 180, 184, 185, 187, 190
Grappelli, Stéphane 97, 118, 228
Gray, Wardell 22
Green, Bennie 68
Green, Benny (pianist) 243–249, 252, 258, 264, 268, 273
Green, Benny (writer) 142
Green, Freddie 52, 68, 70, 109, 116, 163, 187, 212, 261, 263
Green, Urbie 164
Greer, Sonny 110
Grey, Al 186, 214, 229, 231
Griffin, Johnny 225
Griffith, Merv 165
Grisman, David 212
Grosz, Marty 213
Grusin, Dave 197, 217
Guerin, John 188, 191, 216
Guy, Fred 110

H

Hagood, Kenny "Pancho" 32, 33, 101
Haig, Al 20, 23–25, 27, 28, 125
Hall, Bobbye 209
Hall, Edmond 36
Hall, Jim 158, 192, 285
Hamilton, Chico 121, 160

Hamilton, Jeff 198, 203–205, 215, 224, 229, 230, 232, 233, 235, 238, 241–247, 257–259, 261, 263
Hamilton, Scott 215, 233. *See also* Gene Harris/Scott Hamilton Quintet; Scott Hamilton Quintet
Hammond, John 176
Hampton, Lionel 55, 75, 90, 91, 115, 116. *See also* Lionel Hampton Orchestra
Hancock, Herbie 192, 242
Handy, George 24
Handy, John 180
Hanna, Jake 183, 209, 213, 215, 217
Hardaway, Bob 174
Hargrove, Roy 247, 250, 255, 258
Harmon, Charles 16
Harnott, Billy 89
Harper, Herbie 127
Harper, Toni 104
Harper, Walter 8, 9, 10, 11, 13
Harris, Allan 246
Harris, Benny 18
Harris, Bill 38, 58, 76, 77, 90, 91, 93, 113, 117, 120
Harris, Gene 223, 230–233, 235, 236, 243–245. *See also* Gene Harris All Star Big Band; Gene Harris Quartet; Gene Harris/Scott Hamilton Quintet; Philip Morris Superband
Harris, Joe 8, 16, 32, 33
Harrison, Max 140
Harry Edison Sextet 114
Hartman, Johnny 179
Haskell, Jimmy. *See* Jimmy Haskell's French Horns
Havens, Richie 181
Hawes, Hampton 189, 208, 209
Hawkins, Coleman 18, 19, 22, 28, 50, 54, 61, 62, 97, 98, 100, 108, 111, 119, 158
Hayes, Louis 155, 156, 158, 159, 186, 187
Haynes, Roy 44
Heard, J.C. 27, 28, 38, 68–71, 73, 76, 77, 78, 98, 135
Heath, Albert "Tootie" 163
Heath, Jimmy 52, 164
Heath, Percy 35, 65, 99, 160
Hemmeler, Marc 227, 228
Henderson, Bill 150
Henderson, Fletcher 111. *See* Fletcher Henderson Orchestra
Henderson, Joe 242
Hendrickson, Al 179
Henry, Georgiana 94

Hepstations Orchestra 27, 34
Herman, Woody 15, 104. *See also* Woody Herman and His Orchestra
Higgins, Billy 207, 213, 219, 222, 234, 240, 258
Hillery, Art 216, 222
Hill, Teddy. *See* Teddy Hill Band
Hines, Earl 2, 180
Hinsley, Jimmy 12, 13, 14. *See also* Jimmy Hinsley Sextet
Hinton, Milt 15, 166, 249, 264
Hodges, Johnny 69, 75, 76, 146, 159. *See also* Johnny Hodges and His Orchestra
Hofmann, Holly 259. *See also* Holly Hofmann Quintet
Holiday, Billie 18, 55, 68, 70, 91, 101, 103
Holland, Dave 160
Holland, Milt 166, 169
Holley, Major 57, 192
Holloway, Red 231, 232, 235, 246
Holly Hofmann Quintet 259
Holman, Bill 127
Holmes, Johnny. *See* Johnny Holmes Orchestra
Hood, Bill 160, 173
Hopper, Burkhard 273
Horn, Jim 169, 176, 177
Horn, Paul 160
Horn, Shirley 258
Howard Gibeling Orchestra 103
Howell, Michael 224
Hubbard, Freddie 168, 192, 223
Humair, Daniel 228
Humes, Helen 33, 101
Humphries, Lex 157
Humphries, Paul 177, 191
Hutcherson, Bobby 180
Hutchinson, Gregory 246, 247, 248, 253, 254

I

Ink Spots, the 12
Israels, Chuck 210

J

Jack Sheldon Quartet 229
Jackson, Chubby 89
Jackson, Milt 20, 22–25, 27, 28, 30, 32, 35, 37, 38, 52, 65, 101, 147, 163, 164, 176, 177, 179, 186, 192, 203, 207, 212–214, 216, 218, 222, 223, 226, 243, 258, 261, 276, 277. *See also* Milt Jackson Quartet
Jacquet, Illinois 38, 70, 75, 94–96, 98, 117, 123
Jamal, Ahmad 2, 8, 11, 252
James, Bob 168, 173, 192
Jasper, Bobby 157
Jazz Crusaders 216
Jazz Messengers. *See* Art Blakey's Jazz Messengers
Jefferson Airplane 180
Jefferson, Carl 182, 209, 226
Jefferson, Fred 44
Jeffries, Norm 126
Jimmy Giuffre 3 158
Jimmy Haskell's French Horns 171
Jimmy Hinsley Sextet 13
Joe Lippman Orchestra 68
Johnny Hodges and His Orchestra 159
Johnny Holmes Orchestra 54
Johnson, Budd 158, 161
Johnson, Gus 43, 70, 100, 119, 162
Johnson, J.J. 16, 98, 99, 168, 180, 186, 223, 229, 242, 263
Johnson, John T. 177
Johnson, Marc 210
Johnson, Osie 123, 128, 161
Johnson, Plas 167, 183, 207, 209, 210, 217, 248
Johnson, Walter 111
Jolly, Pete 260
Jones, Booker T. 193
Jones, Dill 100
Jones, Elvin 175, 211, 220, 237, 259. *See also* Magical Trio
Jones, Etta 254
Jones, Fritz. *See* Jamal, Ahmad
Jones, Hank 13, 14, 19, 31, 38, 44, *45*, 47, 49, 50, 57, 58, 70, 76, 121, 122, 161, 163, 164, 206, 211–213, 219, 236, 273
Jones, Jimmy 123, 158
Jones, Jo 38, 49, 65, 73, 96–99, 109, 118, 121–123, 158
Jones, Oliver 259
Jones, Philly Joe 210
Jones, Quincy 134, 150, 164, 166–168, 191, 192, 197, 198, 212, 229
Jones, Sam 156, 160, 161, 187
Joplin, Janis 181
Jordan, Louis 60, 61. *See also* Louis Jordan's Tympany Five

INDEX **293**

K

Kamuca, Richie 212, 213, 216
Kane, Artie 175, 192
Kaplan, Leigh 228
Kasai, Kimiko 191
Katz, Fred 160
Kay, Connie 99, 135
Kaye, Carol 167, 175, 182, 192, 263
Keezer, Geoff 249, 250–252, 254–256, 274
Kellaway, Roger 230
Kelly, Ted 44
Kelly, Wynton 144
Kennedy, Ray 259
Kenton, Stan 64, 91, 104, 189. *See also* Stan Kenton Orchestra
Kessel, Barney 66–71, 73, 78, 80, *98*, 114, 117, 129, 130, 131, 134, 170, 173, 182, 187. *See also* Poll Winners
King, B.B. 181, 233
King, Gerryck 231, 235
King, Nancy 207, 255
Kirby, John 111
Kirk, Andy 18, 42. *See also* Andy Kirk Orchestra
Kirk, Roland 167, 168
Koenig, Lester 123, 220
Konitz, Lee 65
Korb, Kristin 248
Koyake, Tamami 236
Krall, Diana 242, 254
Krause, Bernie 193
Krazy Katz, the 10
Krupa, Gene 76, 77, 91, 96, *98*, 104, 117, 138. *See also* Gene Krupa and Buddy Rich Nonet; Gene Krupa Sextet
Kunzel, Erich 237

L

Laboriel, Abe 222
LaFaro, Scott 113, 149, 210
L.A. Four 134, 196–205, *200*, 215, 271, 276
Laine, Cleo 229
Land, Harold 177, 179, 180, 210, 236
LaPorta, John 36
Lateef, Yusef 161
Laurindo Almeida Quartet with Bud Shank 197
La Velle 242
Lawrence, Steve 207
Laws, Hubert 168, 192
Leary, James 233
Lee, Ranee 258

Lee, Søren. *See* Søren Lee Quartet
Legrand, Michel 174, 177, 178, 197
Leighton, Bernie 60
Leonhart, Jay 145
Lester, Ketty 190
Levey, Stan 20, 23–25, 110, 125, 135, 179
Leviev, Milcho 188, 228
Levy, Lou 100, 112, 125
Lewis, John 31, 35, 65, 86, 90, 133, 145
Lewis, Mel 127, 236
Lewis, Ramsey 150
Lewis, Victor 259
Linn, Ray 127
Lionel Hampton Orchestra 10, 38, 69
Lippman, Joe. *See* Joe Lippman Orchestra
LiPuma, Tommy 257
Liston, Melba 161
Little Charlie 10
Lloyd, Charles 172
Lofsky, Lorne 257
London Philharmonic 240
London Symphony Orchestra 162, 258
Long, Gertrude. *See* Gertrude Long and her Nighthawks
Longo, Mike 145
Los Angeles Philharmonic 162
Louie Bellson and His Orchestra 122, 170
Louis Jordan's Tympany Five 60, 162
Lovano, Joe 253
Lovett, Leroy 76
Lowe, John 174, 176
Lowe, Mundell 122, 173, 239, 240, 241, 257
Lowe, Nick 238
Lunceford, Jimmie 3, 4, 47, 54

M

MacDonald, Doug. *See* Doug MacDonald Quartet
Machito 50, 51, 64, 90
Magical Trio 259
Magnusson, Bob 191
Mahogany, Kevin 255
Malone, Russell 254, 256, 267, 268
Mance, Junior 157
Mancini, Henry 2, 165–167, 192, 197
Mandel, Johnny 197, 285
Manhattan Transfer 235, 258, 259
Manne, Shelly 49, 112, 124, 129–131, 133, 134, 162, 163, 167, 174, 175, 177, 178, 180, 189, 191, 196, 198–203, *200*, 208, 209, 212, 216, 225, 227, 228. *See*

also Poll Winners; Shelly Manne All-Stars
Marable, Larance 222
Marmarosa, Dodo (Michael) 23, 160. *See also* Dodo Marmarosa Trio
Maroni, Dado 261
Marsalis, Ellis 240
Marx, Chico. *See* Chico Marx Orchestra
Marx, Dick 126
Masuda, Ichiro 219, 234
McBride, Christian 244, 249, 263–266, 274
McGhee, Howard 22, 38, 39, 50. *See also* Flip Phillips and Howard McGhee Boptet
McHugh, Jimmy 82
McKay, Billy 103
McKibbon, Al 19, 45, 89
McMahon, Bass 11
McPartland, Marian 235
McRae, Carmen 180, 190
McShann, Jay 19, 51
McSweeney, Mary Ann 274
Melvoin, Mike 174, 176, 177, 209, 210, 217
Meyer, Edgar 261
Miles Davis Quintet 144
Miller, Johnny 89
Miller, Mitch 51
Millinder, Lucky 18
Mills, Jackie 23
Milt Jackson Quartet 35, 65, 223
Miné, Junko 236
Mingus, Charles 89, 113, 121, 140, 213
Minor, Honey Boy 11
Mitchell and Ruff 176
Mitchell, Blue 216
Mitchell, Ollie 176
Modern Jazz Quartet (MJQ) 35, 65, 85, 96, 98, 99, 166, 180, 285
Mondragon, Joe 96, 102, 160
Monk, Thelonious 10, 19, 30, 31
Monroe, Clark 27, 28
Montgomery, Wes 158, 159
Monty Alexander Trio 203
Moody, James 30, 32, 35, 38, 42, 148, 275
Moore, Billie "Tiny" 212
Moore, Brew 50
Moore, Dudley 229
Moore, Ralph 232, 253, 254
Morgan, Frank 258
Moroni, Dado 242, 252
Morrison, James 238, 240, 243, 246, 255, 258
Morrow, Buddy 237

Most, Sam 230, 236
Motian, Paul 210
Mraz, George 187
Muldaur, Maria 42, 194
Mulligan, Gerry 90, 112, 125, 193, 237, 285

N

Nash, Dick 167
Nash, Lewis 252, 257, 258
Nash, Ted 167
Nat King Cole Trio 89
Navarro, Fats 16
Nelson, Oliver 164, 170, 174, 175, 191
Nelson Riddle Orchestra 151, 228
Newborn Jr., Phineas 175, 211, 236
Newman, Joe 70, 161
New York Art Ensemble 229
Nick Esposito Sextet 68
Niehaus, Lennie 228
Nightingale, Mark 242
Nilsson, Harry 170
Nimitz, Jack 174
Nimmons and Nine 145
Nimmons, Phil 144, 145. *See also* Nimmons and Nine
Norvo, Red 213. *See also* Red Norvo Trio
Noto, Sam 189

O

O'Brien, Carl "Cubby" 176
O'Day, Anita 104
O'Farrill, Chico 64, 65
Olay, Ruth 179
Oliver, Sy 61. *See also* Sy Oliver Orchestra
O'Neal, Johnny 229
Ørsted-Pedersen, Niels-Henning 156, 214, 215, 258, 260
Oscar Peterson Duo 55, 57, 60, 61, 63, 64
Oscar Peterson Quartet 81, 109, 114, 116
Oscar Peterson Trio 66, 67, 69, 71, 73, 74, 77–88, 90, 91, 93–104, 106–119, 123, 129, 135, 136, 138–140, *139*, 142–144, 146–149, 152, 154, 155, 214, 239, 262, 277
Oslo Philharmonic 162
Otwell, Marshall 235
Owens, Charles 229

P

Page, Walter 109

Paich, Marty 127
Paige, Satchel 187
Palmer, Earl 167, 177, 186, 190
Palmieri, Remo 213
Panken, Ted 3, 11
Parker, Charlie 19, 20–26, 36, 49, 50–52, 57, 58, 60–62, 65, 68, 69, 89, 90, 97, 189
Pass, Joe 182–185, 187, 188, 190, 191, 206, 216, 218, 223, 224, 238, 263
Paul Butterfield Blues Band 180
Payne, Sonny 163
Payton, Nicholas 256
Peacock, Gary 210
Pepper, Art 208, 209
Perkins, Bill 173, 174, 228
Perlman, Itzhak 97, 240, 241
Peters, Gregoire 242
Peterson, Oscar 51, 53–57, 60–71, 73–75, 77, 78, 80, 82–88, 95, 96, 98, *98*, 103, 104, 106, 112, 113, 115–117, 119, 128, 129, 133, 135–146, *139*, 148, 150–156, *151*, 175, 186, 187, 206, 208, 214, 215, 222, 223, 226, 227, 239, 240, 241, 248, 252, 256–258, 260, 262, 275. *See also* Oscar Peterson Duo; Oscar Peterson Quartet; Oscar Peterson Trio
Pettiford, Oscar 11, 14, 15, 22, 63, 82, 89, 112, 113, 115, 121, 122, 159
Philip Morris Superband 233
Phillips, Flip 38, 49, 50, 57, 58, 65, 68–70, 75, 77, 91, 93, 95, 96, 98, *98*, 113, 117. *See also* Flip Phillips and His Orchestra; Flip Phillips and Howard McGhee Boptet
Pittsburgh Symphony Orchestra 162
Pizzarelli, Bucky 259
Pizzarelli, John 256, 259
Pizzarelli, Martin 259
Pollard, Lisa 246
Poll Winners (band) 129–134
Poole, John 104
Porter, Roy 22, 23
Potter, Chris 248
Potter, Tommy 60
Powell, Bud 11, 19, 20, 49, 58, 81, 123
Powell, Richie 123
Powell, Seldon 161
Powell, Specs 52
Pozo, Chano 39, 40
Preston, Billy 167, 213, 285
Previn, André 162, 163, 180, 238–240, 257, 284
Previn, Dory 194

Price, Leontyne 180
Priscilla 193
Pruitt, Carl "The Crusher" 7, 9, 11, 12
Pugh, Jim 240
Purdie, Bernard 168

Q

Quadrant (band) 218
Quinichette, Paul 70
Quintette du Hot Club de France 118

R

Rabbath, François 166
Raglin, Junior 15
Rainey, Chuck 168, 169, 192
Ray Brown All Stars 231
Ray Brown Big Band 176
Ray Brown Trio 58, 61, 116, 207, 220, 222, 224, 230–233, 236, 243–248, 249–252, 255–257, 265, 273, 274
Ray Charles Singers 66
Rebennack, Mac. *See* Dr. John
Redd, Vi 180
Redman, Don 111
Redman, Joshua 253
Red Norvo Trio 121
Red Rodney 65, 189
Reed, Lucy 242
Reese, Della 179, 180
Reeves, Dianne 258
Reid, Rufus 276
Reinhardt, Django 97
Remler, Emily 231
Renner, Jack 237
Rhodes, George 164
RIAS Orchestra 246
Richards, Carolyn 101
Richards, Emil 164, 176
Richards, Johnny 23
Richardson, Jerome 128, 129, 161, 164, 168, 189, 222
Richardson, Rodney 89
Rich, Buddy 44, 50, 55, 57, 58, 60, 64, 70, 75, 77, 84, 91, 92, 96, 102–104, 109, 114–117, 135. *See also* Gene Krupa and Buddy Rich Nonet
Richmond, Mike 160
Riddle, Nelson 151, 171. *See also* Nelson Riddle Orchestra
Riggins, Karriem 250, 251, 255, 256
Ritz, Lyle 166, 171

Roach, Max 19, 20, 36, 37, 49, 78
Robbins, Jimmy 186
Robert, George 242
Roberts, Alice 31
Roberts, Howard 175–177, 193, 211, 212, 263
Roberts, Judy 229
Robinson, Fred 176, 177
Robinson, Spike. *See* Spike Robinson Quartet
Roditi, Claudio 246
Rodrigo, Joaquin 201
Roker, Mickey 188, 208, 218, 222, 223, 230, 231, 236, 243
Rollins, Sonny 123–125, 201
Ronstadt, Linda 228
Rosolino, Frank 179
Roundtree, Richard 193
Rowles, Jimmy 127, 159, 160, 166, 167, 191, 219, 238
Rowles, Stacy 238
Royal, Ernie 161, 164
Royal, Marshal 212, 215
Royal Philharmonic 162
Roy Eldridge and His Orchestra 11, 15, 73
Rubin, Venessa 255
Ruff, Willie 176
Russell, Curly 20, 22, 89
Russell Garcia Orchestra 119
Russell, Leon 193
Russell, Snookum 16, 18
Rybicki, Mathew 85

S

Safranski, Eddie 79
Sage Riders 126
Saijo, Kounosuke 219
Sample, Joe 177, 180, 191, 216, 263
Sandke, Randy 248
Schifrin, Lalo 157, 240, 258
Scott, Bobby 167
Scott Hamilton Quintet 248
Scott, Shirley 150
Scott, Tom 194
Sete, Bole 180
Severino, Frank 190, 207, 224
Severson, Doc 237
Shamblin, Eldon 212
Shanahan, Richard 160
Shankar, Ravi 169
Shank, Bud 134, 167, 173–175, 193, 196–205, *200*, 228, 276, 285. *See also* Laurindo Almeida Quartet with Bud Shank
Shaughnessy, Ed 103, 237
Shavers, Charlie 15, 68–70, 76, 77, 90, *98*, 103, 120
Shaw, Artie 121
Shaw, Billy 35
Shaw, Marlena 255
Shearing, George. *See* George Shearing Trio
Sheldon, Jack 229. *See also* Jack Sheldon Quartet
Shelly Manne All-Stars 189
Shepherd, Dave 100
Shipton, Alyn 91, 286
Shreve, Dick 190
Shroyer, Kenny 176
Silver, Horace 132, 133
Simmons, John 89
Simpson, Valerie 168, 192
Sims, Zoot 186, 190, 214
Sinatra, Frank 165, 229
Skelton, Red 165
Smith, Charlie 44, *45*, 66
Smith, Jimmie (drummer) 206, 210, 211, 213, 214, 215, 217, 219, 235, 260
Smith, Jimmy (organist) 175, 176, 229
Smith, Johnny 76
Smith, Marvin "Smitty" 236, 237
Smith, Paul 212, 218
Smith, Stuff 96, 97, 117, 118
Smith, Willie 77, *98*
Smothers Brothers 165
Snookum Russell Orchestra 16
Soft Winds (band) 73, 126
Sonny Stitt Quartet 123
Søren Lee Quartet 242
Spann, Les 158
Speers, Stewie 242
Sperling, Jack 166
Spike Robinson Quartet 229
Sprague, Peter 235
Stan Getz Quartet 144
Stan Kenton Orchestra 195, 235
Steely Dan 194
Steinholz, Jerry 189
Stewart, Slam 15, 16, 58, 89
Stewart, Teddy. *See* Teddy Stewart Orchestra
Stitt, Sonny 28, 31, 96, 97, 100, 123, 138. *See also* Sonny Stitt Quartet
Stoller, Alvin 67, 68, 79, 103, 104, 111, 114, 117, 127, 135, 173
Strayhorn, Billy 2, 6, 110

SuperBass 261, 262–266, 272, 274
Sutton, Ralph 36
Sy Oliver Orchestra 56

T

Tate, Grady 164, 222, 231, 240, 241, 246, 257, 258
Tatum, Art 3, 13, 14, 18, 54, 63, 81, 95, 96
Taylor, Billy 6, 136, 145
Taylor, Creed 146, 147, 149
Teddy Hill Band 28
Teddy Stewart Orchestra 52
Tedesco, Tommy 188
Te Kanawa, Kiri 240
Terrasson, Jacky 261
Terry, Clark 148, 153, 161, 164, 190, 213, 223, 224, 241, 256–258. *See also* Clark Terry Five
Thielemans, Toots 168, 169, 192
Thigpen, Ed 122, 123, 136–139, *139*, 141, 143–145, 147, 149, 150, 154, 155, 157, 159, 176, 179, 187, 258, 262, 277
Thompson, Charles 22
Thompson, Lucky 20, 21, 23, 24
Thornton, Big Mama 180
Three Sounds (band) 223
Timmons, Bobby 133
Todd, Richard 240
Tompkins, Ross 211, 212, 215
Tonight Show Band 153
Topper, Mary Ann 244
Touff, Cy 126
Trent, Alphonse 97
Trent, Tiny 11
Triple Treat (band) 126, 225–227, 270
Tristano, Lennie 36, 37, 91
Tunia, Raymond 77, 92
Turner, Big Joe 186
Turrentine, Stanley 2, 8, 13, 231, 253, 258, 286
Turrentine, Tommy 10, 13, 16
Tympany Five. *See* Louis Jordan's Tympany Five

U

Ulanov, Barry 36

V

Vaché, Warren 240
Valentine, Billy 52
Vallée, Rudy 23
Varner, Tom 246
Vaughan, Sarah 31, 34, 90, 101, 150, 191, 206
Venuti, Joe 215
Very Tall Band 284
Vinson, Eddie "Cleanhead" 222

W

Wakenius, Ulf 248, 250, 256
Walker, T-Bone 181
Waller, Fats 2, 3
Walton, Cedar 207, 213, 219, 220, 222, 223, 230, 234, 241, 243, 258
Warren, Earl 161
Warren, Harry 81, 82
Washington, Dinah 52, 136
Washington, Kenny 242
Wasserman, Eddie 138
Watanabe, Butch 144
Waters, Muddy 180
Watts, Ernie 175, 177
WDR Big Band 272
Webb, Chick 41. *See also* Chick Webb Orchestra
Webster, Ben 6, 69, 73, 75–77, 91, 103, 108, 110, 111, 114, 121, 136, 143, 158, 159
Weiner, Joshua 158
Wein, George 97
Weston, Randy 180
White, Bobby 113
Whitfield, Mark 246
Whitman, Ernie "Bubbles" 22
Wienstroer, Markus 258
Wiggins, Gerald 121, 180, 189
Wilber, Bob 213
Wilkins, Ernie 148, 161
Williams, Buster 173, 174
Williams, Cootie 11, 12, 19, 42
Williams, James 237, 259. *See also* Magical Trio
Williams, Joe 190, 229, 277
Williams, Marion 163, 242
Williams, Martin 140
Williams, Mary Lou 2
Williamson, Claude. *See* Claude Williamson Trio
Williams, Tony 154
Williams, Venessa 242
Wills, Bob. *See* Bob Wills and the Texas Playboys
Wilson, Gerald 180

Wilson, Jack 173, 174, 224
Wilson, Teddy 76, 81, 91, 120, 121
Winding, Kai 44, 49, 125, 168
Witherspoon, Jimmy 190
Wofford, Mike 191
Woldarsky, Joe 63
Wolfe, Steve 207
Woodard, Rickey 248
Wood, Booty 159
Woodman, Britt 161
Woods, Phil 164, 277
Woods, Robert 237
Woody Herman and His Orchestra 38, 112
Wooten, Victor 261
Wrecking Crew, the 165
Wright, Syreeta 213, 285

Y

Yamamoto, Tsuyoshi 219
Yanow, Scott 84
Young, David 274
Young, Lester 11, 16, 17, 24, 44, 50, 57, 70, 77, 90, 98, *98*, 103, 108–110, 133
Young, Ruby 3
Young, Snooky 164, 212, 213

Z

Zawinul, Joe 201
Zito, Jimmy 174

www.ingramcontent.com/pod-product-compliance
Lightning Source LLC
LaVergne TN
LVHW070511250825
819359LV00009B/177